THE AMERICAN POPE

Also by
the author:

The Annenbergs: The Salvaging of a Tainted Dynasty

THE AMERICAN POPE

The Life and Times of
Francis Cardinal Spellman

JOHN COONEY

Times
BOOKS

Published by TIMES BOOKS,
The New York Times Book Co., Inc.
130 Fifth Avenue, New York, N.Y. 10011

Published simultaneously in Canada by
Fitzhenry & Whiteside, Ltd., Toronto

Library of Congress Cataloging in Publication Data

Cooney, John.
   The American pope, Francis Cardinal Spellman,
1889–1967.

   Bibliography: p. 341
   Includes index.
   1. Spellman, Francis, 1889–1967. 2. Catholic Church—
United States—Bishops—Biography. 3. Cardinals—
United States—Biography. I. Title.
BX4705.S74C66   1984   282'.092'4 [B]   84-40096
ISBN 0-8129-1120-2

Designed by Paul Chevannes

Manufactured in the United States of America

84 85 86 87 88 5 4 3 2

For David and Glynis

Acknowledgments

I T IS IMPOSSIBLE TO WRITE A BIOGRAPHY WITHOUT THE HELP OF a great many people. In particular, I am grateful to George Winslow for his research assistance and Jeffrey Tannenbaum for his careful reading of the manuscript and valuable advice. I am further indebted to my literary agent, Dominick Abel, and my editors Jonathan Segal and Ruth Fecych. I also wish to thank the many people who granted me interviews and those, such as John Taylor at the National Archives, who aided me in my archival research. All responsibility for the book, however, is mine alone.

When I began researching this book, I knew little of Cardinal Spellman other than what had appeared in the press and occasional tales about the immense power he had wielded. I became intrigued by his use of power, which, it soon became apparent, existed in many realms not usually associated with a Church figure in the United States. To piece together what he was doing, I interviewed dozens of priests who had worked with the Cardinal and scores of politicians and others. Due to the controversial nature of much of the subject matter, many people would speak only on a background basis. I supplemented the interviews with documents obtained from more than a dozen archives around the nation.

The oral history memoirs from the Columbia Collection are copyright by the Trustees of Columbia University in the City of New York, Spruille Bradon © 1980 and Jonah J. Goldstein © 1984, and are used by permission. Furthermore, I obtained documents from the Federal Bureau of Investigation and the Department of State under the Freedom of Information Act. Unfortunately, the archives of the Archdiocese of New York are closed to researchers. Nevertheless, a copy of one important document found there—Cardinal Spellman's diary—came into my hands thanks to a priest who believes historic records should not simply gather dust.

"Ambition is the ecclesiastical lust . . ."
Reverend Daniel P. Noonan, *The Passion of Fulton Sheen*

Contents

Illustrations follow page 204.

Prologue

NEW YORK WAS BLUSTERY ON WEDNESDAY EVENING, OCTO-
BER 19, 1960. Leaves swirled on Park Avenue and the wind
whipped the flags outside the Waldorf-Astoria as hundreds of
men and women in evening dress scurried in from the night chill and
threaded through the noisy, smoky lobby. Their voices resonated
as they greeted friends and acquaintances. Here were the rich, the
powerful, and the famous, gathering for an extraordinary affair.

The occasion was the fifteenth Alfred E. Smith Memorial Foundation Dinner. Always hosted by Francis Cardinal Spellman, the
archbishop of New York, the annual dinner had become perhaps
the most significant political banquet in the nation. Senators, congressmen, and political bosses all vied for invitations. Ostensibly a
fund-raiser for a Catholic charity, the affair functioned as a glittering
showcase for the Cardinal's ties with businessmen, politicians, and
military leaders. The annual guest list showed who was in or out of
favor with the powerful prelate. Most people whose names had been
removed were troubled. Few willingly risked falling from grace with
Spellman, the most influential religious leader outside the Vatican.

As usual, the dinner was attended by wealthy Republicans and
Pentagon officers whose conservative views reflected the Cardinal's
but mocked the progressive politician after whom the dinner was
named. Among them were the incredibly rich: the press lord Henry
Luce, the industrialist J. Peter Grace, and the financier Bernard
Baruch all sat at the head table, within touching distance of Spellman.

The Cardinal had always had a high regard for military men, and generals and admirals in dress uniform were scattered among the twenty-five hundred guests. They had known Spellman on the battlefields of Europe and Asia or at the Pentagon, where the Cardinal was a familiar figure and even attended military intelligence briefings. They included Army Generals Willis D. Crittenberger and John M. Franklin, and Major General William C. Westmoreland; from the Navy there were Rear Admirals John J. Bergen and Gordon McLintock, among others.

Legions of politicians—both Democrats and Republicans—were everywhere. New York Governor Nelson A. Rockefeller stood in the center of a large pool of well-wishers, booming "hi ya" in all directions. New York City Mayor Robert F. Wagner automatically pressed the flesh of everyone who gravitated his way, while U.S. Attorney General Herbert Brownell buzzed in the background about problems facing the Eisenhower administration. The Democratic warhorse James Farley, whose phenomenal memory rivaled Spellman's, effortlessly recalled the first names of dozens of men and women whom he had met only fleetingly years before.

Former New York Governors W. Averell Harriman, Herbert H. Lehman, and Thomas E. Dewey held court, as did U.S. Senator Jacob K. Javits, the Tammany Hall boss Carmine De Sapio, and the union leader Harry Van Arsdale, Jr. The dazzling array of powerful men included some of the Cardinal's closest confidants, such as John A. Coleman, who wielded great influence at the New York Stock Exchange; and John S. Burke, the president of the B. Altman department store, both of whom were Catholics devoted to their Church.

Judges, ambassadors, and members of the rich Irish society— including the Murrays, the McDonnells, and the Cuddihys—mingled with such guests as Lewis S. Rosenstiel, the ruthless founder of the Schenley liquor company, and Roy M. Cohn, the former special counsel to Senator Joseph R. McCarthy, who also had been close to the Cardinal.

The Cardinal himself edged slowly through the crowd, which parted reflexively whenever he moved. At age seventy-one, his once-brisk walk had been slowed to a shuffle by high blood pressure and heart problems, and he was aided at times by the knot of his own handpicked monsignors and bishops, who executed his commands, carried his word to politicians, and cultivated men and women of prominence. They were priests who had tied their fortunes to those of the Cardinal and who basked in the aura of power that surrounded him. What was startling about Spellman was the sharp contrast between his physical appearance and the length of the shadow he cast over political and economic affairs. A bald, plump man, barely five feet, five inches tall, he was swathed from head to toe in the scarlet robes of his office. A gold pectoral cross, a present from Pope Pius XII, dangled from his neck and sparkled in the light that showered from huge chandeliers. His round face was practically unlined, his canny intelligence visible in sharp eyes that took in everything at a glance.

To many people, Spellman appeared to be a humble little priest who went about God's work in a simple way, with a prayer on his lips. Most of his flock knew little about him other than what they read in newspapers about his moral crusades against motion pictures and Broadway shows, his occasional statements on controversial issues, and his good works. Over the years the Cardinal had raised untold millions of dollars for numerous worthy causes and laid enough cornerstones—for schools, hospitals, and churches—to build a pyramid. At times he might stop on the street to talk to an elderly woman about her problems, visit the sick wife of an acquaintance, or attend the funeral of a friend's relative. What wasn't obvious was that, while very much a part of his office, such activities were often tinged by a political motive.

Adept at flattery and developing personal relationships, Spellman traded in favors, which he actively solicited and usually repaid in full. But the Cardinal could be a terrible enemy as well as a wonderful friend. Beneath his soft demeanor, he was tough, calculating, and iron-willed. He guarded his authority jealously and reveled in exercising power. To the eleven hundred priests of his archdiocese, Spellman was "the Boss," a man who ignored most of them but was a demanding, formidable, and, at times, much-feared figure. A hard worker, he relentlessly drove the priests who ran a bureaucracy that was virtually a state unto itself.

The Cardinal was the friend of many influential conservatives, including Clare Boothe Luce, General Douglas MacArthur, and Speaker of the House John McCormack. "He was a wonderful person," General Albert Wedemeyer would recall.[1] Spellman's social policies and politics, however, had earned him the bitter enmity of countless liberals. The brilliant journalist I. F. Stone referred to him as "a son of a bitch."[2] Supreme Court Justice William O. Douglas was even harsher: "I came to know several Americans who I felt had greatly dishonored our American ideal. One was Cardinal Spellman." (The two others on the jurist's list, J. Edgar Hoover and John Foster Dulles, were close to the Cardinal.)[3]

Spellman's Manhattan chancery was known as "the Powerhouse." Though he was archbishop of New York, his influence within his Church knew few boundaries, and he himself was unique in the annals of U.S. history. What made him stand apart was the amazing power he had acquired over the years in international, national, state, and local politics. This might had enabled him to gain concessions for his Church that many people once believed impossible. His network encompassed officials of the Central Intelligence Agency and the Federal Bureau of Investigation, as well as many presidents, congressmen, governors, and mayors. His contacts circled the globe and included Winston Churchill, Charles de Gaulle, and Francisco Franco. Spellman's role was not that of the policymakers' priest, but rather he was one of them himself—a pivotal figure in Byzantine, clandestine political and military operations that helped shape the history of his nation and others.

Spellman himself was an ardent nationalist who came to view the aims of his Church and those of his country as being the same. A fire-breathing anti-Communist, he saw Marxism as the archenemy of both the Vatican and America, and now, in 1960, he bitterly resented seeing the ardor of Rome's anti-Communism cool while America's still glowed like a hot coal. In time, he would break with the Vatican because the Pope would vainly seek peace in Vietnam, while the United States pursued the war against Communism. The Cardinal himself did all he could to fight what he called the Red Menace. He had wholeheartedly supported the witch-hunts of Joe McCarthy, helped the C.I.A. attack leftist movements around the world, and assisted the F.B.I. at home.

In his pursuit of power Spellman helped pull his Church into the American mainstream, but he also raised new fears and anti-Catholic prejudices. Appearing to head a single-minded political constituency, he used his position to get what he wanted. Politicians accepted Spellman as the political voice of his Church and of the nation's twenty-six million Catholics. But he often applied his immense personal power to pursue his own political aims, even when they opposed those of the Vatican. To both his admirers and his detractors, Spellman was a man of such enormous influence that he was nicknamed "the American Pope."

As the Cardinal moved through the crowded aisles at the Al Smith dinner, he was treated with great deference by all, for entirely individual reasons. There were guests who saw Spellman only as a kindly, soft-spoken man of God and others who knew him as a tough man who didn't liked to be crossed. The latter group gave Spellman greater homage than warranted by the watered-silk robes of his office. Though aging, the Cardinal still made them very wary. Knowing the benignly smiling figure was often vindictive, they could never be sure where he would strike.

The choice of guest speakers at this dinner demonstrated the Cardinal's political adroitness: Richard M. Nixon and John F. Kennedy, who were battling for the presidency. To date, both had been unwilling to share a dais. When the Cardinal asked Nixon to appear at the gathering, the vice president accepted at once, knowing he was guaranteed a strong reception from the largely Republican gathering and could only gain by associating openly with Spellman. Kennedy, though, believed the situation could result in a liability. Striving to minimize his religious affiliation, the Democrat felt he might be harmed if non-Catholic voters thought he was wooing the Cardinal.

More importantly, Spellman was working behind the scenes for Nixon.

Ironically, most members of the Roman Catholic Church hierarchy were opposed to the senator, even though he was the first member of their faith to run for the presidency since Al Smith thirty-two years before. They were aware of his notorious womanizing and his nonchalant attitude toward his religion. Such talk was commonplace in Church centers, nowhere more so than in the New York archdiocese, where the Cardinal habitually traded in scandal and political gossip over his dinner table.

Spellman, like his peers, faulted Kennedy less for his weaknesses than for his political positions. The senator had a spotty record on Catholic issues. From the beginning of his campaign, moreover, Kennedy repeatedly stated that the Church could expect no concessions from him. For the Cardinal, who spent his career blurring the line that was supposed to separate Church and State in America, Kennedy's stance was both a betrayal and a challenge.

Finally, Church officials disliked that Kennedy never went out of his way to curry their favor as did so many politicians, including some Jews and Protestants as well as Catholics. Indeed, some bishops found their encounters with the senator awkward, as their very presence seemed to embarrass him. For his part, Spellman was far more pragmatic than other bishops—he didn't care if he was disliked as long as the feeling wasn't displayed in public. He deeply resented slights by politicians—or anyone else—and he had a long memory. Yet he rarely let emotion interfere with his ambitions. His favoring Nixon was simply a matter of backing the candidate who he believed could do him the most good.

The Cardinal's decision was a calculated gamble, one bound to create problems with the powerful Kennedy clan. Spellman risked the wrath of Joseph P. Kennedy, the candidate's millionaire father, with whom the Cardinal had long-time financial and political interests: Spellman had even introduced Kennedy to the real-estate agent who acquired what became the crown jewel in the Kennedy fortune— the Chicago Merchandising Mart. For decades, Spellman and Joe Kennedy worked together clandestinely for Church causes; they also beat the same anti-Communist drum and became two of Joe McCarthy's prime supporters.

Close social ties, dating from the Cardinal's days as a bishop in Boston, also bound Spellman to the Kennedys. The Cardinal had even officiated at the marriage of three of the Kennedy children. Thus, he dared shatter a relationship that he had nurtured for years. Of far greater importance, he risked antagonizing Jack Kennedy, who might just become President.

Spellman knew that Kennedy hadn't wanted to attend the affair. When Mayor Wagner, at the Cardinal's behest, invited the candidate just after the Democratic national convention, Kennedy was hesitant. The senator's aides debated the pros and cons and finally urged Kennedy to accept. Fearful of offending the Cardinal, they also believed their candidate could score points while speaking.

"How can we get people to realize that he's not supporting me?" Kennedy asked at one point.[4]

"Maybe Spellman will wear his Nixon button," Kenneth O'Donnell, the candidate's friend and aide, suggested wryly.

There were questions of protocol. Kennedy campaign workers argued over whether the senator should kiss the Cardinal's ring. Those in favor contended that the traditional gesture showed respect for the office, not necessarily the man. Those against it found the deference hypocritical in light of Spellman's support of Nixon.[5] When Kennedy arrived at the Waldorf, such concerns were brushed aside. The candidate was in a jubilant mood. The polls indicated he was in the lead, and the day's campaigning had gone extremely well, with noisy crowds mobbing the entourage all along the lengthy campaign route. At times, it had seemed that the sides of the candidate's car would buckle under the press of people straining to touch him. Although Spellman wasn't with him, Kennedy knew that the people who filled the Cardinal's churches were.

The dinner called for formal attire, so Kennedy wore a tuxedo and black tie. He arrived early in order to get the Spellman greeting over, in front of as few eyes as possible. Instead of kneeling and kissing the Cardinal's ring, the candidate shook his hand. If Spellman was fazed by the handshake, he didn't show it. He smiled and gave his strange, double-syllable little laugh—a "heh, heh" that came from deep in his throat. On many occasions, people who heard the sound were made uneasy. They weren't sure whether Spellman was laughing with them or at them.

The meeting was awkward. The Cardinal liked his political maneuvering to be hidden from the public eye, but his anti-Kennedy stance was already widely known. John Crosby had just written a column in the New York *Herald Tribune* in which he twice described Spellman's preference for Nixon. The column, of course, was denounced as "a complete fabrication" by the chancery spokesman, who hastened to assure everyone that the Cardinal was "most discreet," giving no hint to even his most intimate aides of his choice in the presidential contest. In reality, the Cardinal told politicians behind closed doors exactly where he stood.

Spellman acted as though nothing were amiss when Charles H. Silver, a wealthy political operator known as "Spelly's Jew" because he reached the rich Jewish community for the Cardinal, rose as master of ceremonies. Silver, a grade school dropout who had attained his position as president of the New York City Board of Education with Spellman's help, called upon his benefactor to introduce the candidates.

In a calculated show of impartiality, the Cardinal gave an even-handed statement: "Both are completely dedicated to the welfare of our countrymen. Both are endowed with brilliant minds and the ability to face and solve crises. Both are men of good will." With his high-pitched, nasal voice, Spellman was a terrible orator, and he knew it. As usual, he didn't overstay his welcome at the microphone, but returned to his seat, a little figure in red who smiled noncommittally throughout the speeches.

To get as much mileage as possible from the dinner, Kennedy had prepared an extremely witty speech in which he made an allusion to Spellman's political prowess: "Cardinal Spellman is the only man so widely respected in American politics that he could bring together amicably at the same banquet table for the first time in this campaign two political leaders who are increasingly apprehensive about the November election, who have long eyed each other suspiciously and who have disagreed so strongly both publicly and privately—Vice President Nixon and Governor Rockefeller. . . ." Kennedy's remarks sparked roars of laughter. But the Democrat's speech had a carefully conceived serious side as well, in which he compared Al Smith's campaign to his own. When he finished speaking, he was well received. Nixon's talk, likewise skillfully prepared, was delivered with unusual aplomb, but it lacked the wit and luster of Kennedy's. Nonetheless, Nixon's ovation at the end was greater, even though more laughter had gone to the Democrat. The crowd seemed to go for Nixon, just as Kennedy had anticipated.

What continued to perplex Kennedy was the Cardinal's motive in opposing him, a Catholic. He broached the subject with David Powers, his campaign aide, in the back of the limousine as they left the dinner.

"Why is Spellman against me?" he wanted to know.

Powers, a perceptive man who examined all the angles, paused for a moment before replying. "Right now, Spellman is the most powerful Catholic in the country," he said. "When you become President, you will be. He will have to move aside, and he doesn't want to."[6]

Thus, the seeds for the Cardinal's secular disintegration were sown. Moreover, similar seeds had begun to germinate within his Church. Catholics were increasingly disconcerted by the dogmatic, claustrophobic form of Catholicism that Spellman symbolized, none more so than Angelo Roncalli, who had become Pope John XXIII. A gilded age of American Catholicism was drawing to an end and the glittering realm that Spellman had spent a lifetime creating was coming apart. The most powerful Renaissance-style prince of the Roman Catholic Church in America, Spellman was at the end of a remarkable era, one that had a lasting impact on both his Church and his nation.

PART I

THE RISE
TO POWER

CHAPTER ONE

The Making of a Priest

THE ITALIAN SKY WAS SILVERING WITH THE ONSET OF AU-
tumn when Francis Joseph Spellman arrived in Rome in 1911.
After several months touring Europe, the short, thin youth
arrived in the city's crowded, high-vaulted railroad station, weighted
down by suitcases, which he half-dragged behind him until a porter
rushed forward to assist him. Spellman moved on toward a cluster
of men wearing black cassocks. He had just left behind a summer
filled with the kind of undemanding freedom that he would never
know again.

The previous spring he had graduated from Fordham University,
then a tiny college in New York City. Like several of his classmates,
he announced his intention to become a priest. An indication of his
ambition was his choice of seminaries. Unlike others with vocations
in his class who intended to train for the priesthood near their homes,
Spellman was to attend the prestigious North American College in
Rome.

In view of the times, Spellman's desire to be a priest wasn't unusual. Most, if not all, Catholic youths seriously contemplated such
a life at one time or another. For Catholics, religion was also a culture, as much a part of them as breathing, and the world itself was
approached in terms of their Church. Everything from politics to
courtship was cast in terms of Catholicism, and perpetuation of the

faith was as much of a concern as perpetuation of the family. Thus boys, almost from birth, were encouraged to think of the priesthood as a realistic career choice, and a most attractive one. In addition to the mystical lure of living one's life for God, the priest was a figure of power who commanded great respect in the community.

There were also practical considerations. Prejudice against Catholics was strong. The huge influx of immigrants and the rapid growth of the Church in the nineteenth century had led to fear and suspicion on the part of Protestants and a lack of educational and job opportunities for Catholics. Young Catholics joked that their careers were limited to the "Four P's": politics, the police force, prison, and the priesthood. Besides being held in the greatest esteem, the priesthood offered an ambitious man great opportunities.

The spiritual nature of the Church appealed to those who were drawn in that direction, but for those not so inclined the priesthood could still offer a satisfying and rewarding life. Even the vow of chastity required of Catholic priests was viewed within the culture more as a desirable way to avoid temptation than a great hardship. Therefore, some youths entered the seminary hoping to resolve a personal problem. Troubled by desires to commit sins of the flesh, they hoped to dispel the problems that haunted them in the asexual life of the seminarian. In the American Church, sexual sins were among the most serious that a Catholic could commit and some were considered an abomination.

The gray-stone North American College was on Via dell' Umiltà, in one of Rome's oldest and most charming quarters. Here was a jumble of narrow, twisting streets filled with people, churches, shops, cafes, and restaurants. Crisscrossing alleyways spilled into quaint plazas. Such historic landmarks as the Trevi Fountain and the Colosseum were an easy walk.

As a young seminarian, Spellman followed the school's demanding regimen. He was given a small, dank room furnished with a bed, chair, and desk. His garb was an ill-fitting, baglike cassock embroidered with blue piping, a sign of his student status. Seminarians were awakened by 6:30 A.M., and, at night, lights were out by 9:30. The day began with mass and was filled with classes on scripture, theology, morals, French, Latin, and Italian. Students wrote sermons and practiced the rituals of the mass and sacraments. Relying on his prodigious memory, Spellman learned Latin and Italian fluently. It was imperative that students know Italian, the language of many of their teachers and the Church hierarchy as well as the city. Spellman also became proficient in French and later Spanish, speaking all the tongues with a flat Massachusetts accent.

During free periods Spellman could most often be found playing tennis or baseball or walking about. He didn't join the clusters of students avidly arguing philosophical or theological points, and he joked about those who did. "Theologians spend much time talking about the Church, but they could better use the time building a church," he said. He himself always wanted to be a builder.

On occasion, clusters of students, led by a beadle and followed by a prefect, roamed about the city. Like a flock of strange blackbirds, they flew apart and regrouped when they ran into cyclists, vendors, horse-drawn carts, and trucks as they moved along the crowded streets. The seminarians were taken for granted by everyone else. For centuries, the sight of religious figures added to the colorful pattern of Roman life. There were monks in coarse brown tunics, sandals, and rope belts, and Sisters of Charity in their flowing black habits and startling white headpieces that looked like swans. Crowds were always peppered with priests and nuns of all nationalities in their black uniforms. Limousines, their curtains drawn, whisked wealthy cardinals past plazas filled with jugglers, mimes, puppet shows, and organ grinders with their pet monkeys. In Rome, an edge of excitement was always in the air.

Seminarians were not allowed to travel unaccompanied, and Spellman found the rule the most difficult of his new life to abide. Always independent, he longed to be able to move about on his own. Not that he shunned the company of others. He always wanted people around him because he disliked being by himself. What he resented was not being able to follow his instincts, which told him that if he wanted to get ahead in the Church he must know important people. Men of prominence were difficult to approach if one was always amid a party of a dozen or so.

Spellman already knew the kind of men he wanted to meet. His most intriguing discovery in Rome was of a much more sophisticated breed of churchman than he had ever encountered before. A few of them ranked among the professors of the seminary, where their careers were just beginning to bloom. Those in the flush of power were found at the Vatican, the Church's spiritual and political nerve center, where seminarians occasionally had an audience with Pope Pius X. The Church in Rome was a far cry from the Irish-dominated one that Spellman had taken for granted, and so were the priests who governed it. At home priests were usually defensive yet vigorous Irishmen who were locked in a battle of bigotry with Protestants who had long memories about why they were Protestants. In his new surroundings Spellman found priests more aristocratic and the Church itself a very European institution that had known centuries of incredible power. In Rome the men who administered the Church resented that power's dissolution.

Few, if any, of the American seminarians knew much of the history of the institutional Church. Church history in American Catholic education was riddled with lives of the saints, much suffering, persecution, and misunderstanding. The Church as a political entity was rarely, if ever, discussed. But from the vantage point of Rome, where so much of the Holy See's history was written, it was easier to trace the development of the Church and the kinds of men who had become its governors. The history was one of triumphs and disasters, strong and weak personalities, corruption and redemption, and peaks and valleys of political power.

Since Constantine I declared Christianity the State religion of his Roman Empire in the fourth century, the Church had been an important factor in the political and social, as well as spiritual, lives of everyone from emperors to servants. As the political power of Rome later declined, the Pope inherited some of the emperor's position as symbol and defender of civilization. Various popes, such as Julius I, Innocent I, and Gregory I, dealt skillfully and intrepidly with barbarous attacks and the ruthless leaders of emerging States. The papacy's stake in maintaining a strong secular political position, however, didn't emerge until 756, when the Frankish king Pepin the Short gave the Pope vast lands that became the basis for the Papal States. The Pope became a powerful lay ruler, and the intermingling of lay and spiritual powers launched a struggle between Church and State that became the major theme in the West in the Middle Ages. Strong popes tried to establish secular as well as spiritual supremacy over rulers who, in turn, tried to direct the Church.

The secularization of the Church resulted in ecclesiastic offices being bought and sold, vast riches, and blatant worldliness on the part of many members of the clergy. The papacy's worst period of corruption occurred during the tenth century under the rule of such popes as John XII, a nineteen-year-old count whose father had secured the election for him; his papacy was flagrantly immoral and his tempestuous reign was marked by his being deposed and then restored to office before he was finally murdered at age twenty-seven. The papacy was redeemed in the eleventh century by the sweeping reform of the forceful Gregory VII. From that time the relative power of the papacy in quarrels with the Holy Roman Emperor and the kings of England, France, Naples, and Spain depended largely on the skills of individual popes.

Pope Alexander III, for instance, held his own against Holy Roman Emperor Frederick I and English King Henry II. Pope Innocent III, despite the opposition of Emperors Otto IV and Frederick II, became, in the early thirteenth century, the most powerful pope of all time and the virtual arbiter of the West. The power declined thereafter, and a century later, during the so-called Babylonian Captivity, the papal court moved to Avignon, where it was dominated by France. The return to Rome was marked by the Great Schism, which plunged the Church into a confusion of politics and intrigue when there were two, even three, rival popes at a time. The schism ended in 1417 with the Council of Constance, but thereafter the papacy had little influence outside Italy.

Renaissance popes were indistinguishable from other princes in the lavishness and immorality of their courts. The corruption provided the background for the Protestant Reformation, the culmination of dissident movements that decried the worldliness of many of the clergy, the emphasis on money, and oppression. Reform followed, but by the eighteenth century, the papacy was plagued by a problem that reform had left untouched. This was the position of the Church as ruler of the Catholic states in Italy. Catholic princes invariably tried to include the Church within their spheres of influence, even demanding a voice in selecting the clergy. By the eighteenth century, the papacy appeared doomed; its weakness became a spectacle when Pope Clement XIV was forced by secular princes into suppressing the Jesuits, the only group in the Church consistently loyal to the Pope.

Early in the nineteenth century, when Pope Pius VII tried to protect the sanctity of the Holy See, Napoleon ignominiously imprisoned him. After the fall of Napoleon the power of the old absolutist states declined, and the papacy gained somewhat as a result. But papal opposition to the reunification of Italy deepened the suspicions of many Italians about the papacy. Papal armies were called upon one last time to defend a pope, but the gesture was futile.

Thus, forty-one years before Spellman's arrival in the Eternal City, the Church had turned inward. The Pope quite literally locked himself away in the Vatican as a self-exiled "prisoner" after having lost out to the Italian King Victor Emmanuel and, humiliatingly, surrendered his armies and what was left of the Church's once vast principalities. The papacy then embarked in another direction by laying aside secular claims. The Vatican was declared to be the sole seat of spiritual leadership in the world, and the cult of the Pope as a religious personality began. Only in 1870, at the First Vatican Council, did the Church find it necessary to ratify the doctrine of papal infallibility as a way of ensuring the Pope's moral leadership.[1]

Now, in 1911, the memory of the glories of the papacy evoked a yearning within certain members of the clergy for the days when kings humbled themselves before the papal throne. Some churchmen desired to restore the Church's faded power and prestige, but they lacked the opportunity. They too turned inward, dissipating their energies on cabals that could only improve their stature within the Vatican itself. Often they were dedicated to their Church yet were very much men of the world who let little stand in the way of their ambitions. Wealthy bishops and cardinals lived in great villas, had retinues of servants and fabulous art collections, and moved among the rich and powerful. Some were stained with the corruption that had always marked privileged men whose power went virtually unchecked. All were royalty within the Church and expected the homage and tribute traditionally bestowed upon nobility.

While Europeans always took for granted that the Church was very much a human institution and that even men of lofty ecclesiastical office could be sinners, the knowledge was a rude awakening for most American seminarians. The United States had been spared a State Church, so it was difficult for Americans to appreciate the commingling of secular and spiritual influences that had taken place within the Church for centuries. In addition, clergymen in America were cast as being above reproach; the seminarians soon realized that priests and bishops had the same drives as other men, the same ambitions, and the same sins.

Many North American College professors were troubled by the more worldly members of the clergy. They worried about the age-old issue of how far from Christ the institutional Church had drifted, and they debated whether worldliness was a price worth paying for preservation. Some teachers pointed at the Vatican across the murky Tiber waters and exclaimed, "I don't care what *they* do!" Most, though, carefully monitored what transpired there—the Vatican was the seat of power.

What some professors viewed as compromise Spellman saw as practical. Thus, of all the students at the seminary, Spellman, who was openly ambitious, was perhaps the least troubled by the lives of the diplomats, administrators, and politicians who tended to the Church's practical concerns. He began using them as models and mentors to learn the Church's corridors of power. In time, "Spelly," as he was called, became highly skilled at divining the subtle politics of the Vatican. It would be said that, of all the members of the American hierarchy, only Spellman instinctively knew what Rome wanted. Others only guessed.

Though he learned from the sophisticated churchmen in Rome, Spellman wasn't like them in many ways. His manner was much more abrupt and direct than the Italians', who often dealt in innuendo. More importantly, he was an American and as such he wasn't burdened by a crush of history or the lamenting for a bygone era that prevented so many churchmen from acting decisively. Nor was he content to become a materialist who elevated acquisitiveness to the art of a connoisseur, and he came to despise the continental churchmen who did so. He himself had no great interest in a life of splendor. In a very American fashion, he saw greater importance in the power money could bring than the luxuries it could buy. His Americanism was also very evident; unlike the Europeans, he saw the world for its new and exciting challenges that could result in fresh gains for both himself and his Church. As he grew older he came to identify strongly with the United States as it emerged as the most powerful nation. In his very American spirit, he wanted to participate actively in that power and was not content with shoring up an eroding position. Thus, like America itself, Spellman shoved his way onto the world stage and demanded a large sphere of influence.

Little in Spellman's background prepared him to become the twentieth-century Church's most prominent prince. His career illustrated that the Church, though an authoritarian institution where rank and privilege rigidly reigned, was flexible in the process by which men were elevated to its royalty. The Church's leaders, unlike other noblemen, could not leave their titles to heirs. Thus, with very few exceptions, men who came to ecclesiastic power were men who seized power, no matter what their heritage.

Born in the town of Whitman, Massachusetts, on May 4, 1889, Francis Joseph Spellman was the first of five children of William and Ellen Spellman. His grandfather Patrick Spellman had emigrated from Clonmel, Tipperary. Because of his trade as a bootmaker, Patrick had deviated from the well-worn Irish pathway to Boston. Instead, he settled in the small town of Abington, later called Whitman, some twenty miles southeast of Boston in a district where shoe-making was the local industry. Several years later Patrick married Honora Hayes, one of the few Catholic girls in town, who had emigrated from Limerick.

What shaped the personality of the couple's son, William, was primarily the family's hometown. A pleasant village, Whitman was sprinkled with frame houses, large red-brick shoe factories, a one-story post office, a little library housing some fifty-three hundred volumes, a park with a bandstand and a Civil War monument, a volunteer fire company, and a few constables, as they were called, who kept law and order. Whitman was a prosperous, overwhelmingly Yankee-Protestant town. Characteristics often attributed to people from that part of the country were manifested in Patrick and Honora's son, William—ambition, industry, frugality, and taciturnity. About the only Irish trait he retained was a biting wit.

After finishing grammar school William took a job at the Jones & Reed shoe factory that he saw as a mere stepping-stone. He wanted to go into business for himself, and by the time he was twenty-two he had saved enough money to open a small grocery store. Like the town itself, the store prospered, and the grocer was ever vigilant for ways to make a dollar. When a chance arose to buy the entire block on which his store was situated, he grabbed the opportunity. He had to put only $100 down, and thereafter always boasted of his good luck and personal canniness. Gradually the business expanded until it was the largest grocery in town. When he was thirty years old, William squeezed in enough time to marry a girl he had courted for two years. Ellen (Nellie) Conway was the daughter of an ox-cart driver for a Whitman factory. By marrying William, Nellie found herself quite well-off. William bought a large house with a carriage house and stable, on five acres dotted with fruit trees. The property, while not gracious, established the Spellmans as solidly upper-middle-class.

As William's fortunes improved, a larger, more modern store replaced the original. The family grew as well. The firstborn was Francis; then came Martin, Marian, Helene, and John. The father, a diligent Yankee, instilled in his children the value of thrift, and he passed along to his sons his stubbornness, determination, and drive. Francis, of course, rose to power within his Church; Martin and John became doctors.

Outside his store and especially at home, William was a blunt, somewhat harsh man who didn't take guff from anyone. He expected his children to obey him unquestioningly. But wearing an apron and standing behind a counter, William was helpful and courteous. Of all his children, Francis—as a boy, always called Frank—was the most like him. Stubborn, sarcastic, and hardworking, Frank could also be helpful and courteous when he wanted something. His shopkeeper background taught him how to sell himself.

A soft, heavyset woman with a gentle disposition, Nellie was different from her generally aloof husband, who was lean as a whippet all his life. Both parents were small in stature, as were their children. Frank had his mother's round and fleshy face. Nellie was also much closer to the children, especially Frank, who confided in his mother so much that William derided his eldest son at times for being a "mama's boy."

Frank frequently exasperated his father. Once when the youth helped out at the store, his father couldn't stand the way he waited on customers. Frank relentlessly pushed one particular product; he sounded discourteous. "Is that the only thing in the store?" his father finally asked. Then William's Yankee canniness tempered his admonition. "Try selling tea for a change. There's a bigger profit. And another thing . . . don't say 'Is that all?' Ask 'Isn't there something else?' "[2]

At school Frank was an indifferent student. His only extraordinary achievement was a prize in the ninth grade for an essay on the Battle of Gettysburg. There was no Catholic school, so he attended the public Whitman High School, where small classes allowed students a great deal of latitude in extracurricular activities. Spellman both played on and managed the school baseball team. Moreover, he had a hobby that he pursued much more rigorously than his school courses: he took photographs and developed them, a skill that wasn't commonplace and one that later gave him access to prominent people while he prepared to become a churchman. When he graduated in 1907 he was one of the eight students, among the twenty-two in his class, who went to college.

Spellman attended Fordham because it was Catholic and his parents were comfortable knowing they had relatives in New York City who could keep an eye on him. The Jesuit university, founded in 1841, was sixty-six years later a university in name only. When Spellman enrolled, one hundred five students were taught by ten priests and two lay professors.

Spellman's academic career remained unremarkable. He acted in several plays and wrote occasionally for the *Monthly,* a school periodical. What amazed his classmates wasn't his thespian or literary talents but his memory, which he sought constantly to improve. One reason for his diligence was that he was a poor reader, though he rarely forgot what he read. Moreover, he had a knack for remembering people's names and faces, even after many years. Within a few days of his arrival at Fordham, he knew everyone by name. This proved to be another skill that served him well as his world expanded; people, he knew, were pleased when they were singled out.

Though he tried to join the school baseball team, Spellman failed to make the grade. With characteristic pragmatism, he took up tennis, which wasn't so highly competitive.

At the end of his junior year Spellman won the only prize he received at Fordham. The manner in which he later recounted the incident, to the priest whom he made his official biographer, Robert Gannon, illustrated the difficult nature of his relationship with his father. Spellman was awarded the Hughes Medal for Religion, which was highly prized. When he returned to Whitman he immediately went to his parents' bedroom to show them the honor. Instead of greeting him with pride, William glanced at the award noncommittally. His only comment was: "Did you put out the light downstairs?"[3] Such behavior would have made any son feel bad, but Spellman unconsciously absorbed many of his father's mannerisms. He was often brusque and callous himself and when finally archbishop of New York, he often treated his priests coolly, even contemptuously. Also, he adopted his father's attitude toward money: he became thrifty and always cut costs in little ways. As archbishop, for instance, he ordered priests to keep lights out when no one was in a room and to write rather than make long-distance telephone calls.

Thus, William made an impact on his son, but rarely with kindness. Spellman often would attribute to his father, albeit jokingly, a statement that had a nasty edge: "Son, always associate with people smarter than yourself, and that shouldn't be hard to do."[4] Though he joked about the comment, the young Spellman found wisdom beneath the sarcasm. He knew he wasn't brilliant and was smart enough to surround himself with people who would help him. Spellman instinctively realized that there is more power in numbers than in doing anything alone.

Another lesson that Spellman learned from his father was the use of sarcasm. When a priest in his archdiocese overpaid for a service, Spellman would ask, "When do you think *your* time will be worth that much?" The rebuke was similar to one his father gave him when he paid an extra dollar to take a train home while a youth. William remarked: "Don't do that again until your time is worth a dollar an hour—and I don't think it ever will be." When he became a famous prelate Spellman refrained from talking about his father. In response to questions about him he stated merely, "He was a grocer."

It was to his mother that Spellman first disclosed he wanted to become a priest. She was overjoyed. Most Catholic mothers dreamed that one of their sons would enter the priesthood, a direct family link to heaven. The presence of a priest or a nun in a family authenticated all members' goodness in the eyes of others. William didn't share his wife's emotional reaction to the news. He simply asked his son if he was sure that was the life he wanted.

On graduating from Fordham, Spellman sought permission from Boston's autocratic archbishop, William O'Connell, to attend the North American College. O'Connell probably gave little thought to the request; in any case, he granted it. The youth's credentials were in order, and his parents could afford to pay his passage and keep him in spending money. But O'Connell would come to rue the day that he placed Frank Spellman on the road to the priesthood.

That the North American College was situated on Humility Street was somewhat ironic. Neither the reason for the seminary's existence nor the many ambitious men who graduated from there had much to do with humility. In 1855, Pope Pius IX had sought the school's establishment as a way of binding the rapidly growing, very independent, and very distant American Church to Rome. There were too many examples of national Protestant churches in Northern Europe as warnings of what could happen elsewhere. After opening in 1859, the college rapidly gained a reputation as the "West Point of the American clergy," an elite training ground where young Americans who one day might run the U.S. branch of the Church were exposed to the Roman way of Church life. For decades thereafter, nearly all American bishops were graduates of the college.

The years in Rome reinforced Spellman's naturally pragmatic outlook on life. Though seminarians walked the cobblestone streets once bloodied by the feet of early Christian martyrs, they learned that the Church had survived for nearly two thousand years through flexibility, not fanaticism. That understanding was necessary for the cultivation of *Romanita*—the Roman spirit esteemed in high clerical circles and a lyrical euphemism for the harsher sounding "realistic."

Spellman's new world was strange. The inhabitants were men who had renounced marriage, children, and their own families for a single-minded devotion to their Church. There was a rigid ranking system; blind obedience was the primary virtue. Those who stayed became priests and bore the awesome responsibility of being representatives of God. Some were worthy of the challenge, others not. For all of them, the priesthood became their family and loneliness a constant companion. In the seminary a bond of brotherhood and protectiveness was forged, a solid front against the rest of the world. Within the Church's stone walls, however, all was not serenity and the pursuit of God. Like most men, many priests as they grew older forgot the ideals of their youth and even what had propelled them into the life they had chosen. Denied intimate love or companionship—or taken furtively as forbidden fruit—many priests channeled their energies into pursuing personal ambitions. Thus, within the world of the clergy there existed pettiness, personality clashes, and bitter feuds as the more driven among them vied for power. Like other forms of power, ecclesiastic power had its own material and psychological rewards.

The range of characters varied in the seminary, much as in any other college. Besides sharing a desire to be a priest, seminarians often had little in common. There was John Patrick Monaghan, a funny little wisp of a student with a rich Irish brogue who wanted to help the poor. Joe Fitzgerald, a devout youth who took life seriously, wanted one day to be a priest whom people leaned on when life's burdens were heavy. Then there were the three inseparables, McCarthy, Quinn, and Killian, who all spent more time gossiping than studying. Some wanted to be scholars while others set their minds on rising within the Church's administration. Their ranks included the sophisticated and the naive, the political and the holy, the bright and the dull, the calculating and the guileless. No matter what they were like, they knew that this university demanded, above all, loyalty. The Church had to be safeguarded.

In learning to protect the institution, seminarians understood that they must also protect the image of the men who ran the Church. They too were a varied lot. Some prayed a great deal and others prayed little, and still others seemed not to pray at all. Some patterned themselves on the selflessness of St. Francis of Assisi, while more modeled themselves on the cunning of Thomas à Becket. There were some priests who appeared so un-Christian in their behavior that they raised questions about why they had entered a religious life in the first place.

In short, Church administrators were ambitious clergymen who often displayed the same talents and traits found in any other group of successful men in a large institution. They did their jobs, followed orders, occasionally had sparks of initiative, and were political. What made them unique was that they were supposed to be better than other men. When they weren't, their behavior seemed that much worse. Within the Church, priests who weren't involved in the scramble for power criticized, laughed at, and often joked about those who were. But they did this only among themselves. The preoccupation of good as well as bad priests was that they all present a pious front to the world so that the Holy Mother Church would not be criticized. The myth demanded that the public perceive all priests as holy men.

At the outset, Spellman appeared the least likely of his classmates destined for high office. The problem was personality. Spellman was demanding and he offended his immediate superiors. Given permission to leave the seminary to visit someone, he immediately tried to get time away to visit someone else. "When he was allowed to do something, he always pushed for more," a seminary contemporary of Spellman would recall. Spellman was also blatantly ambitious. "He struck everyone as wanting to be a bishop from the day he left Fordham," he said.[5] Spellman lacked tact.

Bishop Francis Kennedy, the sickly rector of the North American College, found Spellman wanting. But the man who liked Spellman least of anyone was the vice rector, Charles A. O'Hern, a strict disciplinarian. This lack of favor with his American superiors was apparent not so much from what was done to the seminarian but what was withheld from him. During Spellman's five years at the school, he was never appointed to student office, nor was he readily allowed to travel alone in priest's garb, although he managed to find ways to do so. What infuriated O'Hern was Spellman's calculated cultivation of American laymen and Italian ecclesiastics who could do him favors and who forced the seminary rectors into bending the rules for him.

Such a person was Cardinal Bisleti, whom Spellman came to know through his brash pursuit of people of influence. When visiting the town of Veroli with a group of students, Spellman learned that the Cardinal had a villa in the area. He boldly suggested to the others that they call upon the prelate so that Spellman could take a picture of Bisleti with the camera Spellman always carried. The suggestion brought comments of disbelief, but the seminarians were beginning to believe they shouldn't underestimate Spellman's canniness. Nonetheless, even the most cynical among them were amazed that Spellman not only approached the Cardinal but soon had him posing for one photograph after another, like a fashion model. The photographer shamelessly flattered his subject all the while. Spellman, however, wasn't satisfied with a minor triumph. He was always thinking three steps ahead. Upon leaving, he asked if he might personally return the finished pictures, even though he had been told that he wasn't allowed to leave the seminary alone. The Cardinal agreed, and, much to O'Hern's dismay, the school had to grant Spellman permission to visit Bisleti. He had circumvented the rules.

While fellow seminarians and the seminary's administrators found such behavior unseemly, Spellman was quite honestly confused when he was criticized. He believed a man was a fool if he didn't make as many important contacts as possible, and he didn't see how the method mattered. Spellman simply considered himself acting cleverly, and the contacts he made he considered his "friends." He himself never hid his ambition, and, as he told anyone willing to listen, "a man needs friends to get ahead in the world."

His circle of friends among the seminarians wasn't large, but they were youths he could rely on for help with his studies and companionship. They included the inseparable gossips, Francis O. McCarthy of Chicago, Edward Quinn of Cincinnati, and Laurence B. Killian of Boston. Years later, long after Spellman had climbed the steep mountain of Church politics, these men remained his closest American friends among the clergy. Yet, while at the seminary and later, he kept photographs of many other classmates as well on his walls, apparently oblivious of the antipathy many of them had toward him.

Yet another student Spellman befriended was Louis F. Kelleher, a Boston youth he had met once during a debate at Fordham who was a year ahead of him. Spellman used Kelleher's insights to give him background about the Italian professors who taught at the Pontifical Atheneum of the Urban College *de Propaganda Fide,* known as "the Propaganda," where students from the North American College studied philosophy and theology. Kelleher gave him thumbnail sketches of each teacher, making special note of such men as Domenico Tardini, a brilliant, irascible Roman who was ever in motion and was supposed to have an outstanding career awaiting him. The professor whom Kelleher dwelled on at greatest length, however, was very different from the blunt, earthy Tardini. This was the lean, intense Francesco Borgongini-Duca, who, though only twenty-seven years old and not even a monsignor, was rumored to be a favorite of men in high Vatican circles.[6]

Spellman stored away the information and used it in his second year, when Borgongini-Duca became one of his teachers. Following his father's admonition to surround himself with people smarter than himself, Spellman began stopping the professor in hallways and along paths between buildings to ask him serious questions. Borgongini-Duca was a brittle, dour man who wore a perpetual frown. Soon, other seminarians noticed Spellman wearing a similar screwed-up, pained look on his own face. Moreover, although he spent so much time taking pictures of notable clergymen that he had to have Kelleher help him cram for exams, Spellman actually studied Borgongini-Duca's course material.

To other Americans' surprise, the reserved Italian responded to

Spellman's persistent attentions. They were seen together constantly, and the relationship bore immediate rewards, helping Spellman to come to the attention of Tardini and other men of influence. More than a decade later, after Spellman had served as a priest in Boston during the most trying period of his life, the bond with Borgongini-Duca gave Spellman a new lease on life.

In his third seminary year, 1914, Spellman fell seriously ill with a kidney ailment complicated by pleurisy. While recuperating, he missed the major Church event to occur during his student days in Rome. Pope Pius X died, and Pope Benedict XV was elected. Spellman was disheartened that he couldn't even glimpse the grandness of the moment, the coming together of the Church's great princes, the beauty of the pageantry. Other than talk of the new Pope, Spellman's friends told him of the rumblings of war. The seminary, in many ways, was like a time capsule where current events didn't intrude on a traditional way of life, but even the teachers spoke of the dire happenings in Europe. Russia was rumored to be mobilizing, then Germany invaded Belgium. It appeared inevitable that Italy would be drawn into the conflict.

Spellman, though, confronted a more immediate problem. Kennedy wanted him to leave the seminary. As Spellman later related the incident, Kennedy believed the seminarian was about to die and told him to go to Boston, attend the local seminary, and, if possible, say a few masses. Spellman's contemporaries, however, circulated reports that the rector just wanted to get rid of him and used the illness as an excuse. Whatever the case, Kennedy told the seminarian he must be off his sickbed by January 1 or else pack his bags. "The doctor told me that I could get better if I stay in the hospital until the warm weather comes," Spellman protested. Kennedy stuck by his ultimatum. The student returned to the seminary on the appointed day. Spellman later said friends devoted themselves to nursing him back to health.[7]

As a result of the friendships he had carefully cultivated, Spellman didn't need Kennedy or O'Hern in his camp. This became obvious when he took the oral examination for receiving a doctoral degree. In an age-old tradition, Spellman had to face three examiners, each of whom measured a student's performance by placing either black or white balls into a wooden box on the table in front of him. Each questioner had three black and three white balls, and at the end of the ordeal, a student had to have at least five white balls in the box or else he failed.

The first test involved scripture, to which Spellman had never paid much attention, and this was soon apparent. The examiner, a Dr. Colombo, obviously struck by Spellman's ignorance, ostentatiously dropped three black balls into the box. Fortunately for Spellman, the next examiner was Tardini, whom Spellman had gotten to know quite well. The subject was sacraments, and Spellman managed to answer Tardini's questions with little difficulty. Tardini dropped three white balls into the box. The final test was on moral theology, and Spellman had reason to be worried. He had expected to be quizzed by Borgongini-Duca. Instead, the examiner was a Dominican, Paban-Segond, who was a last-minute replacement. When the questioning began it seemed obvious that the examiner had spoken to Borgongini-Duca about his little American friend. As Spellman warily watched, three white balls were dropped one at a time into the box.[8]

About the time of his test, Spellman found that a number of his classmates were accelerated a year in their studies by the rector, who apparently feared that the seminary might be forced to shut down because of the war. Spellman was pointedly not given such a reward and was forced to sit on the sidelines while the others were ordained. He didn't complain. Although often quick to anger, he generally—but not always—knew how to remain patient if the stakes were high enough. He wanted to become a priest.

On the morning of May 14, 1916, a year after most of his friends were ordained, Spellman stood among a group of white-robed young men in the center of the cool, high-vaulted Church of the Apollinaire, which had been erected in the eighth century. The stern-faced Giuseppe Ceppetelli, the patriarch of Constantinople, sat before them resplendent in gold-threaded robes. In a centuries-old ritual, an archdeacon called out: "Let those come forward who are to be raised to the order of the priesthood." Spellman prostrated himself before the patriarch, who intoned, "Receive the yoke of the Lord, for his yoke is sweet and his burden is light."

The oil of catechumens was spread in the form of a cross on the new priest's palms. After his hands were wrapped with a white linen cloth, he was allowed to touch the gold paten and the gold- and jewel-encrusted chalice. These contained the bread and wine that, according to his religion, Spellman could now transform into the body and blood of Christ. "Receive the power to offer sacrifice to God," the patriarch's voice rang out, "and to celebrate mass for the living and the dead."

Spellman was twenty-seven years old. His hair was thinning and he had begun to gain the extra weight that would remain a problem for the rest of his life. He had reached the lowest plateau in the Church hierarchy, and he wasn't content. His exposure to Rome had made him certain that he belonged among the power elite within his Church who wore the magnificent robes of royalty, not among those who obeyed the elite's commands. He had chafed under the rule of O'Hern and Kennedy and couldn't see himself in that position again. He was going home to America.

CHAPTER TWO

Boston: Years of Bitterness

THE BOSTON IRISH WERE COMING INTO THEIR OWN. THE Lowells, the Cabots, the Lodges, and the rest of the Beacon Hill crowd still ruled the bustling city's economic life, but the Irish controlled the politics. James Michael Curley, a flamboyant, slippery master politician, had become mayor in 1914, two years before Spellman's arrival. City Hall was riddled with Irishmen who went to mass each morning and spent the rest of each day figuring out ways that the public trough could compensate them for the poverty of their earlier lives.

In Boston churchmen and politicians unhesitatingly recognized their common interests. The huge masses of Irish immigrants looked to the Church to provide food, shelter, jobs, and spiritual nourishment. Priests, in turn, relied on political leaders to help them meet the needs of their flock. In a city where it seemed that everyone except the very rich spoke with a brogue, the power of the Catholic vote was awesome. It was taken for granted in political circles that Boston's archbishop William Cardinal O'Connell had a loud voice in public policy. Thus, young Father Spellman's first assignment was in a city where politics and religion charged the atmosphere like ion particles, and priests and ward heelers were brothers. The cardinal knew every politician in town from the governor to the county clerk, and he seemed to have something to say about every piece of legislation that affected the city or state.

Spellman came to Boston prepared to be impressed by Cardinal O'Connell, a large man with the girth and fleshy big face of a prosperous Irish brewer. He had achieved the level of success that Spellman wanted for himself. A product of Rome, O'Connell was similar in many respects to the churchmen at the Vatican. An ambitious man, he had done what Rome wanted and had been rewarded handsomely. He lived graciously, was treated with great deference by local politicians, and was held in awe by the Catholic laity. His power within the hierarchy of the American Church was such that he was much feared and had a great many enemies. Spellman would become an enemy, a most dangerous one.

The emergence of a figure such as O'Connell in the once Puritan bastion of New England had as much to do with a dramatic change in the American Church during the last century as with O'Connell's drive. Until the nineteenth century, Catholicism in America consisted of a hodgepodge of ethnic groups whose influence was confined to geographic pockets. Catholic Spanish explorers had established the first permanent continental settlement in 1565, and Spanish priests thereafter founded missions in Florida and California. Cecilius Calvert, the second baron of Baltimore, provided himself with a source of income and persecuted fellow English Catholics with a haven when he established Maryland in 1634. French Catholicism made itself felt during attempts to convert Indian tribes, but especially when the United States doubled in size, in 1803, with the Louisiana Purchase. It wasn't until the 1830s, with the onslaught of a major immigration movement that saw some 245,000 Catholics, mostly Irish, enter the country, that the Church largely took on the coloring of the new immigrants. Within a few years the number of Catholics in the country nearly doubled.[1] The priesthood became dominated by the Irish and their culture, with its obsessions with sins of the flesh and rigid moral codes.

In his ancestry only was O'Connell in the tradition of the men who dominated the American Church in the nineteenth century. When scaling the heights of ecclesiastic power, he was the first American churchman whose authority stemmed from mentors in Rome, not the American Church. He was a protégé of the conservative Spanish Cardinal Rafaele Merry del Val, who, in the tradition of continental nobility, entered the Church with the clear intention of holding high office. Merry del Val became Vatican secretary of state. His protégé, O'Connell, held various offices and even served as apostolic delegate, or Vatican representative, to Japan before becoming a cardinal. He was being groomed to replace the aging James Cardinal Gibbons as the unofficial primate, or Church spokesman, in America. Gibbons was far too liberal for the men in Rome.

From its formation in 1789, the American hierarchy had jealously guarded its independence from Rome. During the nineteenth century many American bishops distanced themselves from the Vatican over various issues, including the degree of social and cultural assimilation that they deemed appropriate for their mostly immigrant communities. Wary Roman officials feared the emergence of an independent American Church. Thus, the North American College was opened, an official American primate was never named, and America was kept on short ecclesiastic strings by being considered a missionary territory, a status that wasn't changed until 1908. So worried was the papacy by the liberal positions espoused by American churchmen that a drastic step was taken. In 1899 a papal letter, *Testem Benevolentiae,* actually pointedly condemned "Americanism," which, in ecclesiastic terms, didn't refer to the form of government in the New World but to positions expressed by priests there.

The man who personified Americanism was Edward McGlynn, the first prefect of the American College in Rome, who, upon his return to New York, increasingly adopted ever more liberal stances. As rector of St. Stephen's Church, he refused to build a parish school. McGlynn upset Rome by declaring that the State had the right to educate the young. Next McGlynn embraced the cause of the Knights of Labor, a forerunner of labor unions, which Rome opposed. He also espoused the social theories of Henry George, who, in his book *Progress and Poverty,* advocated that a single tax on land would meet the costs of government and even result in a surplus, which would greatly relieve poverty. McGlynn increasingly made himself unpopular with Romans and with members of the American hierarchy who were getting twitchy about Rome's looking askance at liberals in the American Church. The rector avidly supported George when he ran for mayor of New York in 1886, and he continued speaking out on social policies. Eventually, McGlynn was excommunicated. Finally, in 1889 the Church condemned George himself and his works were placed on the index of books that Catholics were forbidden to read.

When, a decade later, *Testem Benevolentiae* was issued along with deliberate moves to impose conservative bishops on the American Church, the effect was chilling. Activist trends in sociology and theology in the Church in America came to a halt and the flutterings of intellectual curiosity disappeared. The way to advancement was cleared for pragmatic men such as O'Connell and Spellman, to whom religion was something they had little interest in thinking about; their offices were not callings but jobs, albeit special ones.

Thus, as the United States grew in stature, Rome elevated men in the American Church who had been molded in the conservative way of doing things. The first handpicked American was O'Connell. A graduate of the North American College, he had spoken against the liberals within his own country. In 1895 he had returned to the Eternal City as director of the North American College and his mission had been to bring the school in line with conservative Vatican thought. O'Connell had done his job well. By the time Spellman had attended the institution, there was little chance of a seminarian being contaminated by the liberalism of a McGlynn. After he returned to the United States in 1901, O'Connell had continued following the lead of the Vatican. One Roman stand which he avowed was that the Church should have a special status in relation to government. The issue was of grave importance in the United States, especially in regard to education.[2] The Vatican didn't appreciate separation of Church and State in America, and Spellman one day would be the most vocal proponent of destroying the line between the two.

Though favored by Rome, O'Connell was disliked by the American hierarchy. Part of the problem was that he had taken Roman stands opposed to liberal American bishops' positions. O'Connell, for example, had favored the appointment of a papal delegate to America (one had been made in 1893).

Otherwise, O'Connell's problem was personality. Although he was the son of textile-mill workers from the grimy industrial town of Lowell, Massachusetts, O'Connell took on the airs of one to the manor born as he climbed the ecclesiastic ladder. Contemptuous and outspoken, he ruled his archdiocese from an elegant residence that housed an art collection to rival an Italian cardinal's. He imperiously expected his whims to be obeyed by his staff of servants and his legions of priests. Even before becoming a cardinal, O'Connell was disdainful toward people for whom he had little use. A stinging character sketch of him was offered in 1900 when he was named bishop of Portland, Maine, a position he held prior to becoming archbishop of Boston. The author, Ella B. Eddes, a Catholic laywoman, dismissed O'Connell thus: "Monsignor Pomposity is so invariably rude, ill-bred and disobliging . . . I do not suppose he knows any better, being low-born and common, pitch-forked, suddenly, to a position which has turned his head. Like all underbred Paddies I am not, in his eyes, sufficiently rich, or fashionable to be treated with even ordinary courtesy."[3]

In Boston few ordinary Catholics knew the archbishop other than as a figure who blessed them in the cathedral and stood next to the mayor in parades. Just as they appreciated Mayor Curley for his bravado, his wit, and his challenging the blue-blooded establishment, so they admired a cardinal who represented another side of Irish pride. The imposing O'Connell was probably more arrogant than any Brahmin and certainly lived more graciously. The Irish, who had arrived in America sick and so poor that families actually lived jammed in cavelike dirt cellars and were treated like a loathsome, still-emerging life form, reveled in Curley's circus-like politicking and in the pageantry of O'Connell's religion and lifestyle. In Boston the Church and politics were the only arenas in which the barricades of prejudice weren't erected against them.

On the surface it seemed that Spellman and O'Connell should have become natural allies. Both had studied in Rome and acknowledged the Vatican as the Church's ultimate power and decision maker in all matters. Both had patrons in Rome. When Spellman first analyzed the common bonds that he shared with the cardinal, he assumed that Boston held many advantages for him. What he hadn't calculated into his plans was O'Connell's personality. The cardinal instantly disliked Spellman, and their relationship never grew any closer than at the moment Spellman stumbled the first time he assisted O'Connell during mass, and O'Connell hissed loudly, "Fool!"[4]

At first Spellman tried to win over the vain prelate much the way he had won over so many Italian princes of the Church. He flattered him, telling O'Connell how esteemed he was in Rome. But the cardinal refused to let the new man ingratiate himself. With his own close ties to the North American College, O'Connell doubtless had received negative reports about Spellman. Instead of flattery, O'Connell wanted strict obedience not only from Spellman but from all his priests. He dictated their public behavior, forbidding them even to go hatless or to be noted by name in the press. He regulated dress because priests were publicly to maintain irreproachable standards. As for publicity, this was a prerogative he reserved for himself. In time O'Connell treated Spellman far more harshly than other priests. A major factor was Spellman's refusal to kowtow. He spoke back to O'Connell, whereas everyone else backed down.

Spellman's first appointment in Boston was as a chaplain at St. Clement's Home, an institution for elderly women. A short while later he was made a curate at the Church of All Saints in Roxbury, where he was assigned tasks with the Holy Name Society, the first communion and confirmation classes, the Sunday school, and the baseball team. The work was nontaxing, dull, and pleasant, but wasn't exactly designed to make an ambitious priest shine. Easily bored when not challenged, Spellman soon wanted more from life than the simple duties of a young parish priest. Little did he realize that the challenge he would soon face was surviving his cardinal's wrath.

When Spellman took up his parish duties it was readily apparent that he wasn't a spiritual priest. He performed the activities of his office in a matter-of-fact way. Each morning he said mass and read his breviary, the book containing the prayers, hymns, and other religious fare that priests were required to recite daily. He officiated at marriages, baptized children, visited the sick, and buried the dead. But pondering the mysteries of faith or engaging in philosophical discussions didn't interest him. Even as a cardinal, he groggily said mass each day by rote, including the ten o'clock high mass at St. Patrick's Cathedral, and raced through his breviary. "His was the slam-bang approach to religion of a very busy man," one of Spellman's secretaries would recall.[5] As a young priest Spellman's interests were in other realms.

The years he spent in Boston were a trial. Spellman was bursting with ambition but had nowhere to channel his drive. The poor impression he initially made on O'Connell simply worsened. Most priests have little contact with their cardinal, but those who want to get ahead must come to his attention. Spellman's brushes with O'Connell, however, hardly helped his career plans. O'Connell took to calling him "that little popinjay," which made Spellman bristle. When criticized or thwarted, Spellman told people off, no matter who they were. Unwisely he vented his anger in front of the cardinal much as he had before his seminary superiors, but the results in Boston were more severe. O'Connell, a vindictive man, wasn't about to let a subordinate challenge him. Spellman paid the price. In a much later era Spellman probably would have left the priesthood, but in the early part of the twentieth century such a move was just about unthinkable. Both he and his family would have been disgraced. In Catholic eyes a priest who left his calling turned his back on God.

When the United States entered World War I in 1917, Spellman saw the mobilization as his salvation. With the prospect of escaping both O'Connell and the routine of parish work, Spellman petitioned the cardinal to let him become a military chaplain. Spellman's move was a considered one. Besides the advantages to be had in leaving Boston, Spellman liked the idea of a military career, at least for the time being. He admired what little he knew of military life: the regimentation, chain of command, uniforms, and male society made the military similar to the priesthood. What the military offered that the clergy didn't was a chance to prove one's patriotism and bravery. The combative Spellman had a need to enter such an arena, and he was grateful when O'Connell granted the request. The cardinal, however, imposed a condition: he wanted Spellman to enter the Navy, and Spellman at once agreed. He bought a navy chaplain's uniform with $140 given to him by a friend.

The prospective chaplain immediately ran into problems. One major obstacle to enlisting was his poor eyesight. But what finally kept him out of the Navy was his lack of tact. Later, Spellman himself often related this encounter with the naval officer who recruited chaplains:

When the priest entered the officer ignored him. Finally Spellman said, "I've come to be examined."

The recruiter obviously didn't like being disturbed. "You Catholic priests are all too arrogant for your own good," the officer replied. "It's probably because you are used to bulldozing your congregations."

The officer halted his sally. "I see you've got a lot to learn about the Navy," he said. "If I give you a text and an hour to prepare, can you preach a sermon for me?"

Spellman bristled. "I could preach you one on the subject of arrogance right now," he said coldly.[6]

He next applied for a similar post in the Army, and he was interviewed without mishap. The following August, he traveled to nearby Brighton, this time in an army uniform, where he joined a group of newly recruited chaplains who were to receive a blessing from O'Connell before entering training camp. The cardinal majestically offered a flowery farewell, expressing admiration for these men who were about to confront unknown dangers. At the end of his performance O'Connell called Spellman aside to rescind his decision to make Spellman a chaplain. Instead, the cardinal gave him the demeaning task of promoting subscriptions to the diocesan newspaper, the *Pilot*. O'Connell believed that the brash young curate needed a lesson in humility, and the cardinal enjoyed dispensing such instruction. In time, Spellman more than made up for the rebuke.

Spellman told family and friends that he wasn't going into the Army after all. Although it was common knowledge among Boston priests that Spellman was in Cardinal O'Connell's doghouse, few members of the laity knew. One who did was Nellie Spellman, and she wondered what would happen to her son. He still confided in her, and all that he had to tell her about were his problems.

Now that he was living near Whitman, Spellman saw his family regularly. When he first returned home, he had celebrated mass in his former parish, and practically every Catholic for miles around attended. Spellman frequently dined with members of the family, relaxing with them the way he couldn't around the cardinal. He hated the parent-child relationship fostered within religious life. Authority figures treated subordinates like children, not adults. Yet when he himself became a prominent churchman, Spellman enjoyed the role of father, whereas he had resented that of son.

That resentment was never stronger than when Spellman took up his new duties at the *Pilot*. At the cathedral chancery he was placed under the stern eye of the Right Reverend James P. E. O'Connell, who was chancellor of the archdiocese thanks to his uncle's nepotism. Young O'Connell relished being his uncle's hatchetman as well. He was one of the unsqueamish clergy who carried out their superior's more ruthless orders, dealt with troublesome priests, and enforced unpopular policies. Monsignor O'Connell, like his uncle, was a man to be feared. Spellman had few illusions about the precariousness of his situation. One of his first encounters with the monsignor was through a letter of warning: "I trust it will not be wasted advice to suggest to you that it may be well, while you are yet at the beginning of your career, not to allow yourself to get any false conception about your importance, or the importance of your particular work, thus leading you to either the one extreme, temerity, or the other, timorousness. I make this statement because one of your recent letters to me savored of arrogance, a quality which ill befits a subordinate. I passed it over without comment at the time because I attributed the display to your callow inexperience. A change in the attitude which you have so far displayed to my personal knowledge will have wholesome effects for yourself in the future."[7]

Not only were Spellman's plans to advance to the highest echelons of the Church going awry, but he was in the dreadful position of having to watch every step he took. Not even the cardinal, though, realized the steely nature of the man with whom he was toying. Suddenly, Spellman began acting like a model subordinate. He was deferential to both O'Connells and eager to please. Apparently, he began to understand that displaying anger, at the moment at least, could only harm him further. Thus, he tried to discipline himself to let his pragmatism rule his actions. Spellman acted as though the best revenge was to treat the job at the *Pilot,* a chore other priests viewed as deadly, as one of great importance. Privately, he complained about his new assignment, but publicly he acted as though beefing up subscriptions would get him into heaven.

One of Spellman's tactics was to bombard Monsignor R. J. Haberlin, an O'Connell secretary, with information about his own activities. Spellman even informed Haberlin about how he had incorporated suggestions from the *Pilot*'s editor, the Reverend D. J. Toomey, on how to deal with those parishioners whom Toomey called "slackers."[8] Moreover, Spellman worked hard. Tirelessly crisscrossing the archdiocese, he spoke in church after church about the necessity of buying the paper. The *Pilot* had been founded to keep Irish immigrants abreast of political happenings in Ireland and issues that affected them in the United States. O'Connell bought the paper and transformed it into a house organ for his diocese and a platform for self-aggrandizement.

Spellman sold the newspaper as a necessary tool to fight anti-Catholic propaganda. The message that he hammered home was laced with the peculiar purple prose that would color his speeches and testimonials throughout his life. There was also a strange allusion to the Church as a woman that could have been written by a medieval monk fighting sexual temptation within the confines of his cell. In part, the sermon said: "And now, the Church, Our Mother in the supernatural order, asks our protection, asks our cooperation, and we loyal Catholics of _____ parish will not refuse. We will not permit the Bride of Christ to be fettered helplessly while enemies on every side torture her quivering flesh with darts of lies and insult . . . if there is a single household in this parish that will not subscribe to the *Pilot* that household is not doing its duty."

Though his conclusion sounded like a grocer's pitch for something every kitchen needs, the harangues worked. The circulation climbed slowly, and Spellman made sure that Cardinal O'Connell was aware of his success. Spellman was never shy about taking credit. From the first signs of improvement, he sent the cardinal progress reports. On October 8, 1918, for example, he reported that subscriptions had doubled in Whitman, East Cambridge, and Marlboro. He closed his letter with the slavish "Kissing the Sacred Purple, I am Your Eminence's most obedient servant. . . . "[9]

O'Connell remained unimpressed. The two rarely saw each other. But when they did, as often as not, the encounters became confrontations. Spellman still hadn't mastered his temper on all occasions. Once, the cardinal upbraided Spellman because a statement by O'Connell, as reported on the front page of the *Pilot,* contained repeated mistakes. Spellman, who often had to oversee the production of the paper as well as sell it, fumed while the cardinal ranted that the words "Divine Law" were printed over and over again as "Divine Lamp."

When the cardinal finished, Spellman glared at him. "I was working on that edition for more than twelve hours straight," he replied icily. "By then my proof-reading abilities were impaired and, if I have to work like that, I can't say it will ever be any better."

The cardinal stormed away in muted rage. That wouldn't be the end of the matter, as those who witnessed the scene well knew. "You'll get killed one of these days for talking back to him," warned Harry O'Connor, also a young priest at the cathedral. O'Connor was a blunt man, too, but he wasn't as argumentative as Spellman.

About this time a scandal erupted behind the closed doors of the archdiocese that Spellman quite enjoyed, but for which he seemed to suffer in the aftermath. The shameful incident almost destroyed Cardinal O'Connell's career. Somehow Rome had learned that Monsignor O'Connell, the cardinal's nephew, was married. When the secret was discovered, the chancellor and his wife fled Boston, amid rumors that he had absconded with $75,000 in Church funds. The man who was held responsible for such behavior was obviously the cardinal. The one crime Rome could never tolerate was public scandal, and there was the danger that this might happen. A cardinal was supposed to keep his house in order.[10]

Cardinal O'Connell's enemies often spoke against him in Rome as well as America, and the gossip mill at the Vatican traditionally spun nasty tales about him. For example, the cardinal received a letter from Rome dated May 10, 1921, that was written by a friend, Father Charles M. Driscoll. In part, the letter stated: " . . . There was a big battle—and your genuine friend Card. Merry del Val fought your battle—and your unworthy opponents flooded Card. DeLai with vile, dirty, unmanly stuff against you personally. They overreached themselves and disgusted the Cardinal who lined up with Card. Merry for you. . . ."[11]

Pope Benedict summoned Cardinal O'Connell to Rome. According to some reports, O'Connell decided to deny everything. Thus, he confronted the Pope and told him that the tale about his nephew was the creation of enemies who wanted to destroy him. The Pope listened stonily. When O'Connell finished, the Pope, furious, turned to a table by his side and withdrew a copy of the younger O'Connell's marriage license. "He who gives the red hat can take it away," Benedict threatened.

The words were the worst that a cardinal could have heard. Without his office, O'Connell would be nothing. His power would shatter like a Ming vase striking cement. His grand lifestyle would disappear. He would be ridiculed and scorned by the Vatican and American hierarchies. The trapped cardinal, beside himself, flung himself to the floor and begged for mercy. "*I* am the Pope's most obedient son," he wailed, and he wept in his despair.

The elder O'Connell managed to retain his office. His effectiveness as a spokesman for the American Catholic Church, however, was greatly undermined. He never replaced Cardinal Gibbons as the Church's unofficial spokesman in America. In Rome his wishes were treated lightly, and he himself was often humiliated. Nonetheless, the chastening experience had little lasting effect on his character. By the time he returned to Boston, he was as arrogant as ever. He was also intent on learning who had informed the Vatican about his nephew, who had been stripped of his chancery post after his disappearance. Who, the cardinal wondered, had friends in Vatican circles?

Several years later, in 1922, when Benedict died and Pope Pius XI was elected, O'Connell's position didn't improve. The Boston cardinal had been late for the 1914 election and, in 1922, he desperately raced the clock in order to participate in the conclave. To his dismay, he arrived only an hour late; he became furious. O'Connell had intended to vote for his friend Merry del Val, who had been locked in a battle for the papacy with the wily Pietro Cardinal Gasparri. Pius, a compromise between the two powerful Vatican figures, was more Gasparri's man than del Val's. Gasparri had even told the new Pope to pick the name Pius. When he confronted Gasparri, O'Connell accused him of not wanting the American cardinals present so he could manipulate the election. Now, after such criticism of the man who had helped place Pius on the throne, O'Connell hadn't a friend in the new Pope either.[12]

Although Spellman personally didn't get along with O'Connell, he carefully monitored the effect the cardinal had on Boston's political scene. O'Connell considered it his right to have a say in governmental affairs. The exposure to Rome helped shape men such as O'Connell and Spellman. The centuries-old involvement of the Church in secular affairs was taken for granted at the Vatican. But while most American bishops were circumspect about secular issues, and tended to limit their activities to causes that affected Church finances or teachings on morality, O'Connell saw little that he considered to be outside his domain. In this respect he served as a model for Spellman, who quickly learned the kind of political clout a cardinal can wield in America.

That O'Connell became part of the local political establishment wasn't unusual. His parishioners included scores of politicians—John F. ("Honey Fitz") Fitzgerald, James Michael Curley, Frederick W. Mansfeld, and Maurice Tobin, all of whom were mayors of Boston at one time or another. Others were David I. Walsh, the first Catholic governor of Massachusetts and a U.S. senator for twenty-six years; Charles F. Hurley, who along with Curley and Tobin became a governor (Tobin was later President Truman's secretary of labor). The politicians treated O'Connell gingerly because of his moral and political power. O'Connell treated them like men who had better do his bidding.

The cardinal's causes were many and varied. For instance, he crusaded against Prohibition, which didn't make any sense to him, and for State aid to parochial schools, because he didn't see why the Church should have to pay for educating children who would be sitting in public schools if there weren't Catholic schools. His favorite international cause was the self-determination of Ireland. A week before the Armistice ending World War I, he spoke at Madison Square Garden in New York about the fate of poor, unhappy Ireland: "May not an O'Connell one day go back a pilgrim to Lough Derg, the shrine of his ancestors, and there, on the soil hallowed by the footsteps of St. Patrick, kneel, and thank God that at least Erin, long-suffering, unhappy but ever faithful Erin, is herself once more, self-governed, self-ruled, self-sustained? God grant it soon. . . . Is it the Bolsheviki only who are now to be acknowledged as free? Is it because, being Catholic, the Irish people repudiate Bolshevism, that they are now to be repudiated and their just claim forgotten and neglected. . . ."

Spellman himself had little use for the Irish cause. Having grown up in Whitman, a largely Protestant town, he came to think of himself as a Yankee, not an Irishman. In his official biography, he even had all references to himself as an "Irishman" changed to an "American." But he appreciated O'Connell's making his presence felt politically. The cardinal often blatantly supported legislation or worked against it. He had, for instance, campaigned unsuccessfully against passage of a controversial child labor amendment to the Constitution, which the conservative O'Connell saw as a form of socialism. Indirectly, the cardinal supported political candidates for high office by being seen with them, speaking favorably on their behalf, and doing everything but endorsing them from his pulpit. One of O'Connell's favorite political tactics was having his photograph taken with the candidate of his choice. Pictures of the candidate and the cardinal, shown beaming at each other, appeared in the *Pilot* and quite frequently in the city's major newspapers, the *Globe* and the *American*. By watching and listening, Spellman learned a great deal, even though O'Connell never went out of his way to teach the priest the ways of the world. Like O'Connell, Spellman was political by nature.

In the spring of 1924, Spellman was finally relieved of his duties at the *Pilot*. Monsignor Richard J. Haberlin, who had succeeded O'Connell's nephew as chancellor, apparently was impressed by Spellman's diligence and drive, and wanted him as one of his assistants. O'Connell approved the switch, but he added a humiliating touch. Spellman's position was reduced to that of assistant to the chancery, which, in the pecking order, was beneath assistant to the chancellor. When a third assistant was added, the new man was leapfrogged over Spellman when the first assistant's job suddenly opened.

The cardinal, however, wasn't finished with seeing "the fat little liar," as he had taken to calling Spellman, squirm. One afternoon, he summoned Spellman to his office. He said that Spellman was being demoted so far that there would be no doubt of it in anyone's mind. The priest's new assignment was diocesan archivist, a position that hadn't previously existed. He would work in the dirty, dusty basement, out of the cardinal's sight once and for all. The hostility and vindictiveness that O'Connell displayed puzzled his priests. It was almost as though he believed that Spellman was responsible for the ordeal he had suffered in Rome, as though Spellman had informed on the cardinal's nephew to his enemies at the Vatican.

What struck O'Connor and other priests was the icy calmness with which Spellman accepted his fate. He realized he was playing a dangerous game with a powerful opponent. This was no time for a display of anger, which could only further harm him. He didn't rant or do anything that might give O'Connell grounds to force him to leave the priesthood. His anger was cold.

"O'Connell made a mistake putting Spellman in the archives,"

O'Connor would recall. "He came out knowing more about the archdiocese and the cardinal himself than anyone. He came out with things that he could use."[13]

Spellman knew that any opportunities which were to come his way were those he must create himself. But he was limited in the number of places he could turn for help. The friends who could aid him were in Rome. Thus, he sought to ingratiate himself once again with Borgongini-Duca, who, true to predictions, had become a powerful figure in the Vatican state department, where he now assisted the shrewd Cardinal Gasparri. The form of flattery that Spellman selected was to translate into English two books of devotion written by Borgongini-Duca, and he couldn't have done better. His old teacher was grateful. Other churchmen admired his initiative as well. Spellman had chosen, in the eyes of churchmen, an appropriate way to please one of their kind. They liked their religious, rather than secular, deeds to be esteemed. After the first translation appeared, Spellman even received a pleasant note from John Bonzano, the apostolic delegate, or papal representative, in Washington. Spellman's campaign to get out of Boston was working.

When the second volume of devotions was about to appear, Spellman diplomatically asked the cardinal to write the introduction. O'Connell, who loved seeing his name in print, agreed. Spellman next had a copy of Borgongini-Duca's second book specially bound, and he personally presented it to the cardinal. Thus, when Spellman sent him notes asking permission to accompany a pilgrimage to Rome in 1925, which had been deemed a Holy Year, he assumed he had a chance of going. Instead, he was rebuffed once again. O'Connell scrawled "N. A." across the top of Spellman's requests. The initials were the cardinal's shorthand for "No Answer."[14]

Several months later the cardinal reluctantly allowed Spellman to make the trip. His chancellor, Haberlin, who owed Spellman a favor, had interceded on Spellman's behalf. O'Connell, whose nickname among members of the clergy was "Gangplank Bill" because he was always taking cruises, had had Haberlin accompany him on one; during the voyage the chancellor's brother had died and Spellman comforted the family. When Haberlin asked how he could repay him, Spellman asked to be allowed to make the trip to Rome. The trip was extremely important to Spellman, who saw it as an opportunity to escape O'Connell's grasp. He had told his friend Borgongini-Duca about his nine long years of woe under the cardinal. The Italian was naturally sympathetic to the plight of his friend. All too often within the Church, as Borgongini-Duca knew, personality clashes between superiors and subordinates not only stalled promising careers but sometimes dashed them.

So it was that Spellman was among the priests, nuns, and lay pilgrims who boarded a ship bound for Rome. The party was headed by Bishop Joseph Anderson, one of Cardinal O'Connell's auxiliaries and another man who had little use for Spellman. At one point during the crossing, Anderson summoned the pilgrims to one of the ship's lounges and told them that Spellman, who hadn't been warned, would lecture them on the Holy Year. The attempt to put Spellman in an awkward position backfired. The priest started a talk that contained the kinds of flip remarks his superiors so detested. In a mocking voice, he told the gathering that indeed he liked Holy Years, that they didn't come often enough, and that if it weren't for this one he'd be slaving away in the dusty archives instead of sailing the high seas to Rome. The disgruntled Anderson halted his banter. "Stop that nonsense," Anderson said disgustedly. "Give us something solid." Spellman gave a more serious dissertation.[15]

When the Boston group arrived in Rome, Spellman's days as O'Connell's doormat ended. At the railroad station was a reception party led by none other than Borgongini-Duca, who made a great show of welcoming his friend Spellman. Spellman's years of tribulation were ended—he was in friendly Vatican hands. With Borgongini-Duca's help, Spellman planned to leave Boston behind him.

Fortunately for Spellman, he managed to come to the attention of the Pope himself. The Boston pilgrims had an audience with Pius XI, who gave a lengthy address to the gathering. At its conclusion, the Pope asked the party's leader, Bishop Anderson, to translate for him. Either Anderson's Italian wasn't very good or his attention span wasn't very long, for he gave a much-truncated version of the address: "The Holy Father is pleased to see you and he gives you his blessing." The Pope looked askance, and an embarrassed silence followed. Accounts differ as to what happened next. One version has it that after the Bostonians left, a group of New Yorkers trooped in and Spellman remained behind to translate for them. Another contended that, after Anderson's brief translation, Spellman loudly translated, almost verbatim, the whole original message, much to the Pope's pleasure and Anderson's mortification.[16]

In any event, the incident helped ease Borgongini-Duca's attempts to remove his friend from Boston. The influential monsignor managed to attach Spellman to the Vatican state department, making him the first American to be so honored. The move was made without consulting Cardinal O'Connell; rather, he was told of the impending change. Though angered, O'Connell could do nothing to prevent it. His own influence in Rome since the scandal with his nephew, a man the cardinal himself had groomed in Rome, now carried less weight than that of a vendor selling holy pictures in St. Peter's Square. Nonetheless, the cardinal's bitterness was deep, and he blamed his artful subordinate.

CHAPTER THREE

The Vatican Years

WHEN SPELLMAN RETURNED TO ROME IN 1925, HE WAS thirty-six years old. Round and balding, he wore wire-rimmed glasses and an agreeable, somewhat babyish look. He himself appeared bemused by his unprepossessing appearance. The nine long years under Cardinal O'Connell had taught him many lessons, perhaps the most important being that to get what he wanted he must curb his abrasiveness, at least around people of prominence. Thus, Spellman became like the Roman god Janus, who viewed the world through two faces so that he knew what was in front of him and what was behind. Spellman presented two distinct faces to the world. The one he wore most often in public was that of a cherubic, humble man who smiled often, spoke softly, and struck people as being not overly bright. The other face was that of a tough, demanding man who pushed hard, let little stand in his way, and ran roughshod over friend or foe in order to get what he wanted. His polar personalities shifted from guileless to Machiavellian.

There was little doubt that Spellman had great ambitions. Now, he had to make up for all those lost years. Former classmates and men who had been young clerics during his seminary days were moving into positions of responsibility. He was determined not to be left behind. Thus, as in his seminary days, he set about cultivating people of prominence whom he used as stepping-stones to power.

At times his power plays meant betraying the trust of friends. When Spellman entered the world of the Vatican, his American-style drive, pragmatism, shrewdness, and, especially, calculating nature gave him an almost unfair advantage in the pursuit of power.

The Vatican grounds—with parks, graceful palaces, and solemn Swiss Guards as rigid as statues in red-, yellow-, and blue-striped breeches and sashed doublets—fanned out from St. Peter's Basilica on the lower slopes of the Vatican Hill. The setting was picturesque; life appeared deceptively simple. The tiny, hundred-acre state had its own firemen, lawyers, carpenters, bakers, gardeners, bricklayers, and a host of other craftsmen. The Do Good Brothers ran the pharmacy. The Sons of St. John Bosco printed confidential documents. Friars of the Little Work of Divine Providence delivered mail. The papacy had its own flag, police force, postage stamps, and even an official photographer, who always wore white tie and tails.

The Pope lived in the Vatican, which was where the Apostle Peter, the first bishop of Rome, had been crucified and buried. In 1925 the Pope was a private citizen, subject to Italian law, as a result of the loss of the papal lands to King Victor Emmanuel in 1870. The yellow-and-white papal flag, with St. Peter's keys under the triple crown, was a reminder of better times. Indeed, monuments and mementos of past greatness were all about. St. Peter's Basilica, Bernini's baroque masterpiece, loomed above the vast St. Peter's Square enclosed by two semicircular colonnades, also built by Bernini in the seventeenth century. With the Sistine Chapel, the Borgia Tower, the Pauline Chapel, and the formal gardens and statues, the Vatican was a jumble of medieval and Renaissance styles reflecting bygone eras and fluctuations in papal power.

When Spellman took up his duties, however, the Vatican was still the Catholic Church's political nerve center and was still cradled in a courtly, Renaissance-like world of rustling silk, hushed conversations, and insults measured in the depths of bishops' bows. Each day vast amounts of information about the Church and its activities around the world flowed through the compound. The information was of a sophisticated political and economic, as well as religious, nature. The Vatican held forth the promise of an intriguing life.

From the beginning, Spellman was an oddity there. Unlike other low-level Vatican functionaries, he didn't reside in one of the rectories or religious institutions around the city. Instead, he moved into a comfortable apartment in the Hotel Minerva, across the Tiber but still within walking distance of the Vatican. Since Church dignitaries occasionally stopped there, the Minerva had a small chapel on the top floor where Spellman could say mass. One of the hotel's obvious attractions was its location in a bustling, convenient part of Rome. The city itself had become more prosperous since a fascist government had come to power after the war. But for Spellman, the Minerva's prime appeal was that he was free. Since he had first entered the North American College fourteen years earlier, the independent-minded Spellman had had to report all of his movements to superiors, who frequently had confined his activities. He was sick of being treated like a child. Living in a hotel would have been impossible for a priest in Boston because Cardinal O'Connell would not have permitted it, but Italian ecclesiastics weren't so rigid in many respects when compared with their North American counterparts. Another practical aspect of the arrangement, as far as Spellman was concerned, was a discreetness that he liked. He could meet with whomever he pleased, without everyone's knowing.

Each day Spellman walked the narrow streets from the Minerva, crossed one of the Tiber bridges, and turned left toward St. Peter's Basilica, the largest church in the world, its immense dome looming in the distance. The duties he was first assigned were hardly onerous. He joined the ranks of priests who were translators. Most were younger than Spellman, practically all were Italian, and most were graduates of the Pontifical Ecclesiastical Academy, the Vatican school of diplomacy. Established in 1701 for ecclesiastics of noble rank, the academy had a reputation sullied by the embarrassing worldliness of some scholars, whose behavior had resulted in its having been closed several times. Not until 1850 was the curriculum revised and the school's usefulness begun. Students were trained for service either in diplomacy or at the curia, the chief administrative body of the Vatican.

The primary lesson learned at the academy was the same that Borgongini-Duca gave to Spellman before he took up his duties. "Discretion," he said, "is everything." But the warning seemed too grave for the work. The introductory tasks assigned to newcomers at the Vatican state department were more tedious than intriguing. They sat at small wooden desks, languidly translating documents of little consequence. For the most part, Spellman's colleagues were bored, bureaucratic, and reserved.

Instead of succumbing to the general ennui, Spellman turned the situation to his advantage. By acting industrious, he was sure to be noted in the sea of lethargy. Thus, Spellman treated the dull tasks much as he had treated his assignment at the *Pilot*. Outwardly, he acted as though each chore were a challenge, and he worked to do his best. He volunteered for extra assignments and offered to help others. Moreover, he struck many people as delightful. He bustled through the ornate palace corridors, cheerfully greeting everyone, the leather heels of his Italian shoes clicking like taps as he hurried by.

Invariably, the prelates wound up in conversation with the American, who prostrated himself lower than most priests when kissing their rings. Surprisingly, he seemed to know a great deal about each of them—their likes, their dislikes, their favorite charities. Bishops even found themselves posing for photographs taken with the camera that Spellman carried. To many of his superiors, Spellman struck a welcome note of change in the somber Vatican atmosphere.

For his part, Spellman wasn't beguiled by the personalities of the Church's most prominent men. He had seen how far the bloated, pompous Cardinal O'Connell had gotten in the Church. Now, he was exposed to the Vatican's elite, such as Gasparri, the secretary of state, who was shrewd but not brilliant, and the Pope himself. Pius XI was a cranky, bullheaded man who, like his recent predecessors, was intent upon merely preserving the papacy, not enhancing it. (None of the recent popes had had the forceful personality of a Pope Gregory VII, who in the eleventh century imperiously declared that *all* worldly goods belonged to the Church and kept the German emperor kneeling in bitter cold for three days and nights for having defied him.[1]) Spellman, a realist, spotted the failings of the men who had risen to the top and those of men who had fallen by the wayside. He recognized the procrastinators, the weak, and those elevated beyond their capacities. Spellman quickly realized the Vatican was a world that he could conquer, but it would take hard work, persistence, brashness, and luck.

Members of the state department usually held two posts, one internal and the other external. Spellman's outside job, on the surface, seemed a joke: He was the playground director for the Knights of Columbus. The position was actually extremely important because the Knights donated a great deal of money to the Church, and Edward L. Hearn, the Knight's European commissioner, was a prime Vatican fund-raiser among wealthy Catholics. Spellman was his assistant. The moment was right for a man such as Spellman. In 1925 the Church was nearly bankrupt and increasingly relied on pragmatic fund-raisers to generate the vast sums needed for the Church's worldwide activities. Spellman quickly identified ways to help. He became a Vatican money-man, a sure path to ecclesiastic power.

The Church's need for money was great, and popes of recent times had continued to spend lavishly, much as when the papal lands and taxes were sources of income. Under Benedict XV, the papacy teetered on the verge of bankruptcy. Benedict liberally dispensed money to schools, convents, hospitals, and other worthy causes. He kept huge sums in desk drawers; anyone who pleaded a just case walked away with a papal blessing and a large amount of cash. Benedict never kept account of how much entered his coffers, and income barely covered what went out. His successor, in 1922, Pope Pius XI, was also a generous but poor money-manager. His second day on the job, for instance, he handed $26,000 to German cardinals to help their countrymen because the value of the mark had plummeted.

He donated $156,000 to aid Russia's hungry, $20,000 for Japanese earthquake victims, and $21,875 to feed Viennese. Finance ministers looked on such gifts as heedless and became ashen with worry. By the time Spellman returned to Rome, the situation had so deteriorated that each Thursday Pius sat down with one of the Vatican accountants and went over the week's bills.[2]

Though at one time in Boston Spellman had taken several accounting courses, which he believed would be invaluable for anyone planning a career as a churchman, he wasn't tapped for the Knights of Columbus post because of such expertise. Rather, he got the job because Hearn knew and liked him. They had met in Boston and Spellman had poured out his tales of woe about O'Connell's mistreatment of him. Knowing what a terror O'Connell could be, Hearn had sympathized and on several occasions had offered to find Spellman a job outside Boston. When the playground post opened, Hearn suggested Spellman. Hearn didn't like dealing with Borgongini-Duca, who was the primary Vatican link to the Knights. Borgongini-Duca, for his part, had had his differences with Hearn and probably was glad to be rid of the task. In any event, Spellman stepped into the slot and he and Hearn worked smoothly together. The job had an added advantage for Spellman. Hearn, a wealthy man in his own right, introduced Spellman to a number of prominent people. The $6-million Knights playground project finally seemed to work as it should.

Spellman, though, quickly became the object of scorn and criticism among other priests. He reserved tennis courts for influential Italian clerics, at the expense of children who were supposed to use them. Moreover, he made it a point to meet American governors, mayors, congressmen, and other figures of prominence who visited the Eternal City. He scoured newspapers daily to note the arrivals of the rich and powerful, and, like a con man setting up a mark, he even paid concierges at the luxury hotels to alert him to the arrival of the kinds of people he wanted to meet. Once he was aware of their presence, Spellman's brazen form of self-promotion was usually the same. He attended their papal audiences, took their pictures, and showed up at their hotel rooms with the finished photos. Knocking on his subjects' doors, Spellman introduced himself and presented the photos. No one could deny the effectiveness of his conduct. Those approached were often flattered. Spellman saw to it that they had a photograph of themselves with the Pope, and he was more than willing to show them around Rome. Spellman thus established a vast network of influential people who would soon enable him to perform unique favors for the Vatican. They were all his "friends," as he liked to say.[3]

Spellman also gained access to the wealthy American community that wintered in Rome. Many rich Catholics were enchanted with the aristocratic world of the Vatican—its ancient traditions, pageantry, and princes. Such laymen were generous to the Church and priests they liked. Spellman's opportunity to break into this circle occurred one morning at St. Peter's when he noticed two members of the American clique seated in the rear despite vacancies in a front pew. He had them moved to the better seats. After the mass the couple, Nicholas and Genevieve Brady, wanted to know whom to thank. It was then that they met the charming Father Frank.

Spellman got to know many rich people, but the Bradys helped him the most during his seven years in Rome. Nicholas Brady, the scion of a public-utilities entrepreneur, was generous. But it wasn't simply the Brady wealth that made the couple so attractive to Spellman. The large, self-assured Mrs. Brady was a woman of great influence who could help a clever young priest. She became Spellman's patron, introducing him to people worth knowing both inside and outside the Church; she also gave him money and counseled him on career moves. For his part, Spellman fussed over her, was there whenever she wanted his presence, and treated her as though, next to God, she were the most important being in his life.

The Bradys wintered on an estate, on the Janiculum Hill, that was known to everyone simply as Casa del Sole. The view of St. Peter's stretching below was breathtaking. The formal gardens were exquisite, the tennis courts perfect, the stately cedars appeared to be groomed. The Bradys' dazzling parties were as well known for their culinary delights as for drawing the most powerful men at the Vatican. Theirs was a world that Spellman coveted. Overnight, it seemed, he was a regular at their banquets, meeting churchmen and wealthy Americans whom he hadn't yet had a chance to photograph. Often, he played tennis with Brady, who, after their matches, pressed a hundred-dollar bill onto the joking, sweating, half-protesting Father Frank. It then occurred to Spellman that the Bradys should have their own private chaplain, and he offered his services.

As Spellman was exposed to a widening circle of Italian bishops and cardinals, word spread in high ecclesiastic ranks that he was a most unusual man. While all ambitious priests were anxious to please, Spellman outdid his counterparts. He was a marvelous source of worldly goods. Whereas members of the hierarchy liked to maintain their dignity while hinting about what they wanted, Spellman had no such inhibitions. He bluntly interceded on their behalf. In June 1926, for instance, Brady drove Spellman, Cardinal Gasparri, Borgongini-Duca, and Monsignor Giuseppe Pizzardo into the country. At lunch Spellman turned to his benefactor.

"Will you give Cardinal Gasparri a limousine?" he asked.

"Sure," Brady replied.

"Both the cardinal and Mr. Brady are delighted," Spellman wrote home.[4] He himself was delighted. None other than Gasparri, the Vatican secretary of state, was in his debt. And so was Brady.

When the glistening black limousine arrived, Gasparri, in a moment of elation, burst into Spellman's work area, and, as other star-tled translators watched, the cardinal pulled the American outside and had him driven around with him. The cardinal knew that such a wonderful gift didn't come without strings, and Spellman suggested the way Gasparri could repay the Bradys. The pair had long coveted papal titles, thus showing that people had changed little over the centuries. For hundreds of years the papacy had bestowed noble rank upon people who performed favors for the Church, and church-men always wondered at how much people were willing to do for so little. Gasparri agreed to the request. A short while later Brady was made a Knight of the Supreme Order of Christ, an honor usually reserved for Catholic heads of state; his wife was made a papal duchess. Spellman was taken care of as well.[5]

Spellman's critics dismissed him as a social climber, but they missed the significance of his actions. His Sergeant Bilko-like be-havior made him before long an almost indispensable source of fa-vors. Just as important, he became known as a man who could be depended upon to achieve what he set out to do. Through wealthy Americans, he wheedled money, artworks, and, of course, auto-mobiles for members of the Italian hierarchy, who loved to race fast cars through the countryside. Even the Pope turned to him. "The Holy Father told Monsignor Borgongini to ask me about three au-tomobiles," he wrote home. "So I am getting Bob Graham, who went to school with me in Fordham and who now makes the Graham-Paige car, to give them."[6]

In 1926, only a year after his arrival in Rome, Spellman himself was rewarded: he was elevated to the rank of monsignor. The achievement was considerable in light of the short time he had spent at the Vatican. The few monsignors in Boston were all cronies of Cardinal O'Connell. The title gave the holder no new powers, but O'Connell nonetheless was angered. Spellman was officially still his subordinate, yet once again the cardinal hadn't been consulted. But he held his tongue. The Pope himself had ordered Spellman's ac-colade.

As Spellman's ability to get things done became well known, he earned a reputation as "the American back-door to the Vatican."[7] He enabled wealthy Americans to gain access to cardinals and bish-ops, saw to it that they had invitations to special church services, and guaranteed them papal audiences. Not just American but also Italian laymen approached him for favors: they wanted visas to America and favors for family members in the United States. And penniless noblemen optimistically beseeched Spellman to arrange marriages for them with rich American girls, a task beyond even Father Frank's abilities. There was always a circus side to the Vat-ican, and Spellman was a star attraction.

Spellman received a great deal of money for his extracurricular activities. He peppered his diary with references to his receipt of hundreds and thousands of dollars. He received a $1,200-a-year salary from the Knights of Columbus, and that was smaller than many gifts. The Bradys routinely handed him thousands of dollars. There were references in the diary to his receiving thousands more from such people as Mrs. Evelyn Mendelssohn, Mrs. Leminger, and Bishop O'Leary. By 1929 his financial holdings were so great that Spellman's diary noted he bought a thousand shares of Warner Brothers Pictures stock for $54,190. On March 11, 1930, he excitedly recorded in his diary, "Warner Bros at 72."

The Pope himself now personally asked Spellman for favors. For instance, Spellman recorded on February 8, 1929: "Holy Father asked me for three autos." In a demonstration of his own wealth Spellman added: "I shall give one myself." Apparently much pleased with Spellman's not finding the limousines a challenge, the Pope escalated his order. Spellman next recorded: "Holy Father asked me to get him a train." Daunting as the request sounded, Spellman was little perturbed. "First he wanted four cars," Spellman wrote to his mother. "But I explained [that] one car with three or four bedrooms and bath and dining room and sitting room and chapel would be sufficient. . . . So I am now on the hunt for a nice car."[8]

Before Pope Pius XI came to rely upon Spellman, the priest took a major gamble to bring his enterprising abilities to the pontiff's attention. The situation arose when the Pope sought $45,000 for a project at the Vatican library. As Hearn's subordinate, Spellman should have informed the knight about the Pope's request. Instead, Spellman solicited the money without Hearn's knowledge. The risk was great, but the reward could be enormous. Spellman approached the millionaire industrialist John J. Raskob for the donation. Spellman had met the former General Motors chairman in Rome, but Spellman didn't realize that Raskob was a friend of Hearn's. When Raskob routinely sent a copy of Spellman's begging letter to the knight, Hearn was furious. "The result was like the encounter of the U-boat with the *Lusitania*," Spellman wrote his mother. His ironic wit came only after the fact. At the moment Spellman didn't find his being unmasked amusing; he nearly panicked. His impolitic behavior may have offended the generous Raskob as well. If both men ganged up on him, the Pope might be embarrassed. Spellman might even be ordered home. "Heard that Mr. Hearn does not wish me here anymore," he reported in his diary.

Spellman pursued two courses of action. First he roused sentiment against Hearn. He worked on Borgongini-Duca, who had disagreed with Hearn in the past. Spellman whipped his friend into such a state that the American could confidently record in his diary that Borgongini-Duca "wouldn't mind an argument" with Hearn, who was unaware of what was happening. The second phase of his strategy was to write people to pressure Raskob into giving the money. He appealed to the Bradys in particular, knowing that they were ever grateful for his part in getting them their papal titles. He also realized that if he didn't get the money, he had lost a dangerous game.

Anxiously, for several long days, Spellman awaited his fate. Finally, he managed to squirm out of his difficulties. Raskob sent a check for the full amount, and Spellman emerged from the experience stronger than ever. He had displayed the spirit of *Romanita* so appreciated in the highest Vatican circles. The Pope himself actually referred to Spellman as "Monsignor Precious." The American pressed his advantage by exacerbating the differences between Hearn and Borgongini-Duca. Soon, it was understood at the Vatican that Hearn was no longer welcome. The knight, of course, felt betrayed. The man who had behaved improperly was rewarded while Hearn was criticized. But the knight knew that he was left few choices; he angrily departed. A lay Vatican official, Count Enrico Galeazzi, smoothly moved into Hearn's job in Rome. Galeazzi and Spellman understood each other, and the count appreciated the clever way the American removed his enemy. Spellman wrote coolly in his diary, "Mr. Hearn left for Paris. He has high blood pressure."[9]

The exposure he received in the Vatican worked to Spellman's advantage in many ways. Ranking ecclesiastics slowly came around to Borgongini-Duca's assessment of his protégé that he was far shrewder than he at first appeared to be. One very special Vatican diplomat who agreed was Eugenio Pacelli, the papal ambassador, or nuncio, first in Munich and then Berlin, and the man destined to become the next pope. Spellman had met the temperamental, highly skilled diplomat in Germany during one of the American's own diplomatic missions. Pacelli was the kind of man whom Spellman instinctively tried to know, but at the time even he didn't realize the momentousness of their meeting and friendship.

When they first met in 1927, Pacelli, at age fifty, was thirteen years older than Spellman. To date, their careers were very different. The studious and frail Pacelli had been favored in ecclesiastic circles from his youth. Because of ill health, this son of a noble family had been permitted to study at his home in Rome, and after his ordination in 1899 he was swept up in the life of a career Vatican diplomat. Pacelli was sent to Germany in the early years of the Weimar Republic, where he had witnessed a crumbled Germany's attempt to rebuild itself; he watched Germany rebuff a Communist attempt at a takeover, and he viewed the rise of Hitler and his brownshirts and the Third Reich. Pacelli became enamored of Germany, its people, and its Prussian sense of orderliness, which was so far from the chaotic style of Italians, including many who worked at the Vatican. More important, Pacelli's years in Germany gave him a fear of Communism that would dominate his diplomatic strategies for the rest of his life, especially his years as Pope Pius XII.

The Pacelli stories floating around the Vatican made him out to be a remarkable man. There was the time in 1919, for instance, when German Communists in Munich had declared a short-lived Bavarian Socialist Republic. Pacelli's residence was shot at, and the nuncio himself was warned to leave the city because a handful of citizens had already been assassinated. The next morning, armed thugs broke into the delegate's house, demanded food and money, and threatened to kill him. Pacelli was unflappable, disdainfully ignoring their requests and ordering them to leave. "I, too, have a weapon I always carry with me, my friends," he said. "This!" Pacelli held up a crucifix. The tale ended with the men leaving and the nuncio unharmed.[10]

Pacelli was obsessed with Marxism. He read all Marx's works at the University of Berlin and he visited the philosopher's home and places where he had met with kindred souls, such as the Young Hegelians. To Pacelli, the theory of Communism was bad enough. He found Marxism in practice a nightmare, and there was little wonder why. Between 1918 and 1923 the Bolsheviks indulged in a crude inquisition to purge Russia of religion. Thousands of priests, monks, nuns, and religious lay people were sentenced to die or were exiled to Siberia. The persecution of the Catholic Church abated, but the message was clear: Pacelli was convinced that Marxism posed the greatest danger of all time to the Church. That became his guiding political principle when he became Pope Pius XII. Germany, he believed, was a necessary bulwark against the Soviet threat.[11]

Pacelli considered himself a student of the world. Though an admirer of Germany, he remained a staunch nationalist, in spite of his fellow countrymen's less-than-Prussian ways. Nonetheless, he surrounded himself with German priests who were precise, intellectual, and cold. He always distrusted the British and French, and he found the Spanish too fanatical. Like many men within the Vatican, he dismissed Americans as politically naive children with a shallow culture and little understanding of a spiritual life.[12]

In Spellman, Pacelli saw the same lack of cultural sophistication that he found in other Americans, but he was impressed by Spellman's energy, cleverness, and drive. He liked anyone who got a job done quickly in the turgid seas of the Vatican bureaucracy. And according to the reports he received about Spellman, the American was effective. "Italians just eat and sleep and cause trouble," Pacelli supposedly remarked on one occasion.

For his part, Spellman recognized in Pacelli something that he hadn't seen in other Vatican powers. The nuncio had a mark of greatness about him. He was regal and imperious, but not in the blustering manner of a Cardinal O'Connell. A man used to commanding a court, Pacelli wasn't simply a ghost of a bygone era. He was a man much aware of the world, who avidly read magazines and newspapers, in which he circled stories to keep for his files, and who followed diplomatic intrigue. Pacelli had a global view of power and its use, and Spellman would learn much from him. For Spellman the only jarring note within the man's conservative philosophy was Pacelli's contempt for America. Spellman had seen little in Europe that justified continental churchmen's sneering at America. Europe's glory was of the past. When around churchmen who downgraded the United States, Spellman diplomatically held his tongue.

Surprisingly, the Spellman-Pacelli relationship proved a strong one, and a genuine friendship developed between them. A distant personality with an explosive temper, Pacelli had few close friends. Although a very formal man himself, Pacelli liked Spellman's natural informality. The American rarely put on airs, even later when he himself became a prince of the Church; he unselfconsciously walked into a kitchen in a house in order to wash his hands, and he helped people on and off with their coats. Accustomed to churchmen who loved to be waited on for everything, Pacelli found Spellman refreshing. Soon they were traveling companions who spent holidays hiking through the northern Italian countryside, where they visited convents and monasteries. Spellman assisted Pacelli when the nuncio said mass, and the American became one of the Italian's few confidants. Spellman knew how to relax the tense Pacelli; the American was cheerful while Pacelli brooded. With Spellman, the nuncio unwound, even joking as his friend kept up a steady stream of banter.

The only other person who appeared to soothe the churchman was Mother Pascalina. A beautiful nun who ran the nuncio's household, Pascalina was a formidable figure who, like Spellman, guarded Pacelli against his enemies. In time, she and Spellman formed an alliance based on their service to Pacelli.[13]

Through Pacelli, Spellman formed yet another close and valuable friendship. This was with Count Enrico Galeazzi, the lean, hooded-eyed Vatican functionary who had replaced Hearn as the Knights of Columbus's main European contact. With his classic looks and secretive manner, Galeazzi seemed to have stepped out of a portrait of a Renaissance courtier. A shrewd financial adviser, who bore the misleading title "Vatican architect," Galeazzi had received his noble title from the Vatican. He was destined to become the most influential layman at the Vatican and would be in charge of the Vatican bank, overseeing major financial transactions.

On the evening of June 29, 1931, Spellman stood anxiously in the private library of the Pope's apartment, where he had been summoned moments earlier. Overlooking St. Peter's Square the library, with its high ceilings, book-lined walls, and Italian provincial furniture, was where Pope Pius XI had written the encyclical *Non Abbiamo Bisogno* ("We Have No Need"), a condemnation of Benito Mussolini. Spellman was asked to smuggle the document to Paris and deliver it to the press.

With two prominent mentors, Borgongini-Duca and Pacelli, now standing behind him, Spellman's responsibilities had broadened greatly. Not just high Vatican officials but the Pope himself sought his assistance in matters far beyond procuring money or gifts. As Spellman well knew, the Vatican constantly needed loyal, talented men who could promote the Church's interests internationally. When offered the opportunity, Spellman showed both devotion to the papacy and a flair for international intrigue. Thus, the American hastened his rise to prominence by combining highly valued traits seldom found in one churchman: he was both an astute money-man and a politician with an understanding of international affairs. The mission the Pope assigned him on this occasion was considered vital. Two years earlier the Vatican had trusted Mussolini, but now the Pope, who never cared for the fascist on a personal basis, was furious with the dictator for going back on his word. The pontiff was intent on embarrassing *Il Duce* before the world, and Spellman would help him do it.

The background that led up to this turn of events is intriguing. In 1929, after years of cautiously courting one another, the Vatican and the fascist government had signed the Lateran Treaty, which was meant to defuse the bitterness that had existed between Church and State since the demise of the Papal States and that found expression in an anticlericalism of Italian liberals. In 1870 the Pope had rejected an offer of personal protection from the victorious King Victor Emmanuel as a devious attempt to destroy papal sovereignty; he shut himself off from the world in a dramatic show of moral anguish. By the 1920s, Europe had changed dramatically. More than a half-million Italians died during World War I. Fear of Communism pervaded the Vatican. Socialist rumblings made Italy appear all too vulnerable to a Communist revolution, and to Catholic churchmen, such signs were everywhere. For instance, a small church near Bologna was invaded by socialists singing "The Red Flag," and midnight mass was disrupted at another. The fascist Mussolini had brought order to an economically sapped nation that had been routinely torn by strikes, and he was anti-Communist. Thus, in a new age, the Church decided to settle the issue of compensation for Italy's expropriation of papal lands. The impetus for the move was twofold: politics and money.

Pope Pius XI, from the time he took office in 1922, had tried to improve relations with Italy, and he was willing to accommodate Mussolini. If nothing else *Il Duce* had pulled the country together. Despite his history of anticlericalism, Mussolini and his fascists showed a respect for the Church, but it was based on self-interest rather than genuine regard. In 1920, Mussolini cynically had summarized his attitude: "I think that Catholicism could be used as one of our strongest national forces for the expression of our Italian identity in the world." But churchmen looked only at the olive branch Mussolini extended once he assumed power: "Catholicism is a great spiritual and moral power and I trust that relations between the Italian State and the Vatican from now on will be very friendly."

Negotiations for the Lateran Treaty began in 1924 between Mussolini and Cardinal Gasparri. The fascist leader, intent on an agreement, made many concessions to the Church, in terms of both the State and his private life. Freemasonry was outlawed; State funds were allocated to help the nearly bankrupt Church banks, and the clergy was exempted from taxation. When the Pope proclaimed 1925 a Holy Year, Mussolini promoted the event by restricting the activities of Protestant missions in Italy and blocking plans for the construction of a mosque in Rome.

Mussolini reversed many of his stands to conform with Church positions. The onetime proponent of artificial contraception declared a national campaign to increase the birthrate. The ideal number of children, he declared, was twelve. He proposed a tax on childless couples, prescribed severe punishment for adultery, and made infliction with syphilis a crime. He railed against short skirts and certain bathing suits, and wanted women to abandon "negro dances" imported from the United States. (The Vatican enhanced the antifeminist theme by urging women to stop participating in sports: "If a woman's hand must be uplifted, we hope and pray that it will be lifted only in prayer or for acts of beneficence.") In order to ingratiate himself even further, Mussolini launched a campaign depicting himself as a model Christian. He had his children baptized and his marriage legitimized in the eyes of the Catholic Church. *Il Duce* appeared in photographs looking devout, and, according to some enthusiasts, he bore a remarkable resemblance to St. Ignatius of Loyola, founder of the Jesuits.

The Church had cause to be satisfied by Mussolini's actions in foreign affairs as well. He forced the Orthodox Church in Albania to renounce allegiance to the patriarch of Constantinople and pledge itself to Rome. He took up the Church's cause in Palestine, where it opposed the Orthodox patriarch and the British and wanted unobstructed visiting rights to holy places. Finally, in 1929, the Vatican and the government signed the Lateran Treaty, named after the palace where the accord was ratified. Both Mussolini and the Church hailed the pact as a great victory. The Church soon had cause to regret Mussolini's subsequent behavior, but at the moment the agreement benefited both sides.

The public received the concordat with tremendous enthusiasm, lionizing Mussolini, who had settled what for generations had been known in Italy as "the Roman Question." Cardinal Gasparri and his chief aide, Borgongini-Duca, received both international and national recognition as well. For Spellman, who had made some suggestions that were adopted in the treaty—such as letting a Church marriage fulfill civil requirements—the negotiations had been a lesson: the Church and State should both give and take to the benefit of everyone. The Church and the State could lean on one another and both become more powerful. That was an accommodation that men who became strong churchmen understood well, and one that Borgongini-Duca taught his friend from America.

Spellman noted in his diary that his mentor was sure to become nuncio to Italy, the politically sensitive post of dealing directly with the fascist government. He also believed Borgongini-Duca would quickly become a cardinal. He was right on the first supposition but not the second. "Monsignor Borgongini has become a world figure over night," Spellman told his diary, "and if Cardinal Gasparri lasts a couple of years, I do not see how it is possible for Monsignor Borgongini not to be the next secretary of state."

Indeed, the shrewd Gasparri was getting on in years, and there was talk of his being replaced. But Spellman was wrong about whom Pius had in mind for the important job. A year after the Lateran Treaty, the Pope bypassed Borgongini-Duca and gave the coveted post to a longtime favorite, Eugenio Pacelli, the nuncio to Berlin, whom the Pope had proposed publicly as his successor. The news elated Spellman even more than if the post had been filled by Borgongini-Duca. Pacelli was far cleverer than Borgongini-Duca. He would be back in Rome, where he and Spellman could spend much more time together. Spellman himself was bound to become that much closer to the Pope as a result of his relationship with Pacelli.

A mark of Spellman's growing prestige was his attendance at the signing of the historic treaty. The elegant old Lateran Palace was jammed with dignitaries gathered for a brief ceremony. Gasparri, in the medieval splendor of his purple robes, signed the document as bishops and government dignitaries hovered above the table. The cardinal turned to Mussolini, resplendent in morning clothes, at his left, and *Il Duce* signed. Immediately afterward Mussolini strode to his limousine and, in the midst of a flag-festooned caravan, sped away.

On a practical level the Church had many reasons to celebrate. Catholicism formally became the State religion. Catholic religious instruction was permitted in public schools, divorce was banned, and competing religions were restricted in their attempts to proselytize. The Church received a further major concession that members of the hierarchy didn't take pains to highlight: the Vatican received $90 million in payment for the confiscated papal lands. The Church was once again independent financially.

The millions were entrusted to Bernardino Nogara, a relative of the archbishop of Udine and a man whose financial acumen swiftly earned him the sobriquet "gnome of the Vatican." For the next thirty years, Nogara invested the Lateran money in stocks and bonds. The Church became the controlling partner in dozens of major businesses, active in banking, railroads, utilities, textiles, cement, agriculture, and credit. Nogara even saw to it that the Church gained the controlling interest in Italgas, the sole supplier of home-heating gas in most of Italy's major cities.[14] The Vatican's preoccupation was no longer the difficulties of a shortage of money, but the problems of making money work. Whenever anyone questioned the Church's new corporate conglomerate status, Spellman, who wholeheartedly approved of what was taking place, had a quick answer: "By investing we have that much more to give to the poor." He was right, of course. And many churchmen were kept in splendor as well.

The trade-off for the Church was costly in another way. The Pope was viewed as a supporter of fascism. Authoritarian by nature and in a position of supreme ruler himself, Pius would have been unusual if he had been unsympathetic to dictatorships. Moreover, Mussolini was anti-Communist. The Pope's attitude toward fascism, however, wasn't clear-cut. As an Italian, he appreciated much of what Mussolini did. The archbishop of Messina was believed to be speaking for the Holy See when he declared in March 1923: "I feel it is my duty to send my greeting also to him who is leading Italy along the right road, to him who is imbuing the nation with new vigor—I mean, to the head of the government." But if national pride drove Italian churchmen to speak out, they weren't alone in their sentiments. In Boston, Cardinal O'Connell, also in 1923, espoused what could only have been Vatican thought when he said: "Italy has undergone a profound moral, economic, and social transformation since Mussolini was named Prime Minister. . . . There is order, loyalty, industrial development, and cleanliness everywhere." That same year George V visited Italy and decorated Mussolini with the Order of the Bath; the king referred to the "wise guidance of a strong ruler." The American ambassador to Italy had even noted the nation's helping the "moral progress of the whole world by raising on high the ideals of human courage, discipline, and responsibility."

Mussolini needed the Catholic Church's imprimatur to impress foreign leaders who suspected his demagoguery and to reassure Italian Catholics, who had long wanted the reconciliation of Church and State. Once he had the Church's support, Mussolini's old anticlerical attitudes quickly resurfaced. Until the end of his regime, many Italian churchmen rotated between admiration and fear, attitudes spun by nationalism and anticlericalism.[15]

By June 1931, when the Pope summoned Spellman to his apartment, Mussolini was intent upon crushing Catholic Action, a social organization the Pope had founded to enhance Catholicism. Ostensibly, Catholic Action wasn't supposed to be political, but its members could be active in other associations whose aims were political. In the fascist crackdown, Catholic newspapers that were even mildly critical of the regime were confiscated, demonstrations were held throughout the country against the Pope, and the clergy was no longer safe as Catholic Action and fascist gangs fought in the streets. Spellman noted in his diary that his friend Pizzardo and another priest had been threatened.[16] The Pope's pleas to the government to deplore insults directed at him were made in vain.

Pius XI tried various methods to defuse the tensions, turning at times to just about anyone for assistance. Thus, when Spellman brought the Boston politician Jim Curley for an audience, the pontiff anxiously asked Curley to intercede with Mussolini for him. Curley did what he could, but it wasn't much. He took up the case with Mussolini, and Spellman accompanied him.[17] Later, the monsignor reported back to the Pope that little had been accomplished by the Curley intervention. When the Pope tried to take a public stand, his effectiveness was blunted. He verbally denounced the "pagan worship of the State," but he did not openly confront Mussolini. In any event, the fascists refused to permit the publication of his antigovernment statement. As a last resort, Pius drafted his encyclical. His priests and bishops still blessed the homes of the Fasci, those who died for the fascist cause, and addressed fascist conferences. But the Pope demanded that his voice be heard.

Spellman received the encyclical at ten o'clock that evening and worked at translating it until the early morning hours when he fell asleep. By 5 A.M. he was translating again, taking time out only to wire Paris that he wanted two stenographers standing by when he arrived. Leaving Rome under the guise of a diplomatic courier, Spellman carried several letters to the apostolic delegate in Paris. For his return to Rome, he had documents certifying that he carried mail from the nuncio in Paris to Cardinal Pacelli. Before boarding the train, Spellman asked John Evans, the Associated Press bureau chief in Rome, for a letter of introduction to his Paris press colleagues. Spellman minimized chances for anything to go wrong.

Here accounts of Spellman's trip differ. His official biography states that the trip was uneventful. But Spellman himself later recounted that the journey had ominous overtones. He said that two hulking secret policemen followed him onto the train and monitored his every move. Finally, Spellman decided to bluff. He walked up to the pair—this wasn't out of character—and delivered an ultimatum: "If you are following me, you had better arrest me," he snapped. "Otherwise, leave me alone." The police, caught off guard, sheepishly moved off to a more discreet distance.[18]

Whatever the case, Spellman fulfilled his mission. He gave the document to the Associated Press and a half-dozen other international news services with Paris offices. When the stories appeared Spellman was pleased to be identified as the bearer of the important encyclical. Pius did not condemn outright either Mussolini or the Fascist Party, but he spoke of a "real and true persecution" and protested "the irreverences, oftentimes of an impious and blasphemous character, and the acts of violence and vandalism committed against places, things, and persons throughout the country and in Our very episcopal city." He denied that Catholic Action was political, and he repeated the warning against "pagan worship of the State."

The Pope's dramatic move paid off. The world witnessed the Church's having to smuggle a document out of fascist Italy; the story was front-page news around the world. The selection of Spellman for the task probably had as much to do with his being an American as being a favorite of Pacelli. Having an American as a principal in the intrigue helped ensure even greater coverage of the story in the United States, where millions of Italian Americans had friends and relatives still living in Italy. Letters condemning *Il Duce* poured into Italy from America. On a more personal level, the action raised Spellman's esteem in the Church: his name was on the lips of churchmen in both Rome and the United States.

When he returned to Rome, Spellman was congratulated by ranking Vatican officials and inundated with letters from admiring friends, relatives, wealthy acquaintances, and politicians. The fascist press inadvertently added to his prestige within the Church. Editorials and cartoons mocked him. One cartoon depicted a blind man who was asking for help—the monsignor handed him an encyclical. Another showed a man saying, "Hurry up—come quick; there is a man dying!" The cartoon Spellman's response was: "Tell him to wait a few hours because I have a few hundred more encyclicals to distribute!"[19] For one of the few times in his life, Spellman enjoyed being criticized in the press, and he laughed at the heavy-handed attempts to discredit him. As he knew, he could well afford to take the insults lightly. Fascists had learned that the Vatican was more clever than Mussolini had believed, thanks at least in part to Father Spellman.

In light of the publicity surrounding the encyclical, the anticlerical campaign subsided. Pacelli met with Mussolini and a compromise was reached. The government revoked a ban against Catholic youth organizations; the Church restricted the political activities of Catholic Action, and antifascist activists were excluded from holding office in Catholic Action. Mussolini was received by the Pope, who awarded him the Papal Order of the Golden Spur. Cardinal Gasparri, in turn, was awarded Italy's highest decoration, the order of Annunziata. Fascism and the Church again were on friendly terms.[20]

The Vatican's attitude toward fascism was never clear. Three months after Mussolini invaded Abyssinia in October 1935, the Pope issued an ambiguous statement, which some interpreted to mean that the Lateran Treaty had diluted the moral authority of the Church and others that the Pope wasn't out of sympathy with the action. Indeed, Pius seemed to view Italy's expansion as an opportunity for Catholic missionary activity. Vatican officials, who became known as "clerical fascists," took pride in the Italian conquests. Bishops and priests blessed departing troops, and nationalism was rampant among Roman churchmen. The bishop of Siena publicly praised "Italy, our great duce, and the soldiers who are about to win a victory for truth and righteousness," while the bishop of San Miniato claimed that "the Italian clergy are ready to melt down the gold of the churches and the bronze of bells" to aid the invasion. Cardinal Schuster, the archconservative bishop of Milan, roused his parishioners to aid "in this national and Catholic work . . . on the plains of Ethiopia, the Italian standard carries forward in triumph the Cross of Christ, smashes the chains of slavery, and opens the way for missionaries of the gospel."[21]

The formation of the Rome-Berlin Axis brought little outcry from the Vatican. Few bishops spoke out when Mussolini aligned his domestic as well as foreign policies with those of Hitler, even shifting his attitude toward Jews, who had enjoyed an official tolerance under the fascist constitution. Some bishops decried anti-Semitism, but others favored it. There were still churchmen who officially considered Jews "Christ killers." In January 1939, Agostino Gemelli, a Franciscan friar and a noted experimental psychologist, publicly denounced Jews as "the deicide people," whose "blood and religion" prevented them from being a "part of this magnificent country."[22]

By the time Mussolini began his empire-building, Spellman was back in his own country and glad to be there. Nationalism within the Vatican had always grated on him. At the start of Italy's expansionist period in the mid-1930s, the atmosphere in Rome was stifling, and Spellman looked with scorn on what was happening there. He never believed that the new Roman Empire was about to rise from the broken roots of Italy's once-powerful past. No, Spellman looked to America as the next world conqueror. He read about Mussolini's ventures and heard the pride in the voices of his colleagues in Rome. For the time being, he said nothing; he was still focused on his career. Eventually, he would raise his voice—in the name of the American empire. Everything, he knew, was a matter of timing.

The longer he remained in Rome, the more powerful Spellman became. He was singled out for additional honors by the Pope, and his duties expanded so that he had more contact with the American embassy, the press, and the fascist government. He fell into a pattern that marked his years as a churchman—his life was his work. Inevitably, he was to be sent back to the United States as a man of influence and a trusted Vatican official. Restlessly, he bided his time until the right position came along.

The American hierarchy received another indication of Spellman's importance shortly before he smuggled the encyclical to Paris. Early in 1931, Pius decided to deliver a radio message to the United States, a historic first. Pacelli suggested that afterward Spellman should deliver a capsulized translation of the papal address. The pontiff was enthusiastic. He was so captivated by radio that Guglielmo Marconi, the inventor of the wireless telegraphy, had installed a station at the Vatican. The curia had been under the impression that Marconi would pay for construction of the station, and publicly the inventor fostered that notion. The Vatican finance men were angered when he didn't. The Pope, however, not only willingly paid for the project but lavished money on a huge staff and related expenditures. Now, he would be heard around the world.

Thus, on February 12, 1931, millions of Americans heard the voice of the head of the Roman Catholic Church. They also listened to an American monsignor, Francis Spellman. Through a mixup, the first words aired from Rome by the National Broadcasting Company were Spellman's. Monsignor Stephen J. Donahue, a representative of the New York archbishop, Patrick Cardinal Hayes, stood by at the network's New York studio. Neither he nor Spellman realized their voices could be heard when they exchanged greetings:

"Hello, Steve."

"Hello, Frank."

When off the air, Donahue asked if there was anything he could do for Spellman. He had already thoughtfully contacted Spellman's parents to make sure they were prepared to listen to their son. Donahue apparently assumed that Spellman wanted him to make another reassuring call to Whitman with a special message. Instead Spellman replied, "Give my best to Mrs. Brady," his rich friend who had an estate on Long Island.

The Pope gave the kind of stylized address that was expected: "To All Creation: Having in God's mysterious designs become the successor of the Prince of the Apostles—whose doctrine and preaching were by divine command destined for all nations and for every creature—being the first Pope to make use of this truly wonderful Marconian invention . . . " Spellman's translation was smooth. His flat Massachusetts accent filled the airwaves.

Afterward, Spellman received an unusually kind note from Cardinal O'Connell, who occasionally asked Spellman to buy silk for ceremonial robes and perform other demeaning tasks a Vatican servant could do. The Boston cardinal, probably because the Pope was so intimately involved, was gracious enough to tell Spellman that he had performed well. The opening was one that Spellman had long awaited. He gave vent to the bitterness that had been building in him for years and that he was afraid to discuss among European churchmen. He told O'Connell that his patriotism was offended at the Vatican.

Spellman put his complaint in concrete terms by giving an account of the aftermath of a visit to America by the general of the Dominicans, who, after being wined and dined, cosseted and praised, returned to Rome with the kind of disdain for the United States that was so often heard at the Vatican. The Frenchman, who "was feted wherever he went, and learned many things confidentially by reason of his office, displays extremely bad taste by speaking critically of us," Spellman wrote. The general disparaged Americans for being crass materialists, a charge that always made Spellman's blood boil. The monsignor found the insult ironic in light of the money, cars, and unending stream of other goods members of the European hierarchy asked from him. "We may be materialistic, but no nation that I know of has any monopoly on spirituality and I do not notice any one of them that as a national characteristic could despise any material things coming their way," Spellman noted.[23]

Spellman was maddened further. After sneering at America in front of him, the arrogant general had asked Spellman to raise money for him. Spellman apparently didn't want to lift a finger for the churchman, but he diplomatically hid his feelings and kept a smile on his lips. "I could have answered that I have no one to ask for such a some [sic] but I preferred to answer that the persons I would ask were not disposed to contribute because of remarks the Master General made about America's materialism," he wrote O'Connell.[24]

The issue touched a raw nerve with the Boston cardinal, as Spellman knew. The prelate had been exposed to European churchmen's insensitivity and disdain toward America during his years as rector of the North American College and had held his tongue in order to get ahead. The irony in Spellman's case was that he wasn't as materialistic as most of the churchmen around him. Although he occasionally indulged in luxuries, he had little use for the lifestyle of a Renaissance doge that so many bishops and cardinals craved. To him, grandeur had great symbolic importance: he equated riches with power, not simply pleasure.

There were many unwholesome aspects of life at the Holy See that Spellman found difficult to condone. Thus, the Frenchman's sneering at the United States was that much more galling. At the Vatican, Spellman saw venality, greed, and corruption, and for a brief period, he recorded in his diary many of the sordid aspects of life there. In February 1932, for example, he wrote that men such as Pacelli, Pizzardo, and the powerful Monsignor Alfredo Ottaviani were "afraid to tell [the] Pope of great abuses, because it will do not [sic] good. It will make [the] Pope angry and he will be angry with them." The abuses to which he referred were many and varied. Some of the criticism that Spellman bitterly noted in his diary had to do with gross extravagances, such as the squandering of 100,000 lira on a bathroom for a ranking ecclesiastic. Spellman complained of "Spending money for new apartments, luxurious apartments for lay people in [the] Vatican who already receive exhorbitant [sic] salaries." And there were the "Parochial Houses built by [the] Holy Father in Southern Italy and Sicily [that are] all out of proportion to needs."[25]

Other charges were more serious. One had to do with the collapse of the Vatican library because of the "negligence" of the builder, "who would have gone to jail if it had occurred in Italy" instead of the Vatican State. "But instead every effort is being made to exonerate him," Spellman noted. "The commission reported against him so that it was discharged and a new commission reformed. The Pope *personally told me* as he told others that [the collapse] was due to his predecessor Sixtus V" [Spellman's emphasis].[26] The Pope's excuse itself was contemptuous. Sixtus V had commissioned the library three centuries earlier. Pius XI had had an addition built which, because of faulty construction, undermined the library. Spellman's sense of outrage was legitimate. Raised a thrifty Yankee, he pinched pennies and looked on waste as a real sin. He would never reward a contractor who had done slipshod work.

The most disturbing diary report concerned the "Murder of [a] boy in [the] Institute Pius IX . . . by [a] Christian Brother [who was] already accused of [the] crime and yet permitted to be in charge of [a] dormitory where more than 50 boys slept."[27] Spellman's manner of recording the matter makes it clear he was dismayed, probably disgusted. Spellman was no reformer and was not about to do anything to upset his carefully nurtured career. He lost himself in his work, and considering his many activities, this wasn't hard to do.

One of Spellman's jobs was acting as the liaison between American and Vatican officials. He arranged meetings between ranking churchmen and embassy personnel, or set up audiences with the Pope for visiting congressmen and other Americans of note. Sometimes, he used his vast number of contacts to help embassy personnel with practical problems. Once, a petty fascist bureaucrat blocked delivery of a shipment of coal to an embassy office building. Spellman, asked to rectify the problem, as usual wasted little time. He ran to the scene, confronted the bureaucrat, and chewed him out while the man cringed. "I thought I had heard every word in the book until Monsignor Spellman began blistering that little Italian," Earl Brennan, the military attaché at the embassy, would recall.[28]

Somehow, the whirlwind Spellman even found time in his busy schedule to restructure the Vatican press department. Vatican officials neither liked, understood, nor trusted the press, and the prevailing attitude toward journalists was condescension. Often, encyclicals and other materials were handed out only in Latin, long after the event. Only a few trusted Italian journalists were granted interviews, and even those were rare. Spellman was never shy about getting his name in newspapers, and there was a further benefit in being the press liaison that wasn't to be found elsewhere: the range of issues gave him official access to a much broader cross section of Church officials than he met through the Vatican state department.

Taking the job seriously, Spellman initiated a number of practical and helpful measures. He introduced mimeograph machines, tried to get material to reporters on time, and often had the material translated for them. The monsignor even wrote press releases, something that had never been done at the Vatican before. That in itself was enough to earn him the gratitude of the press corps. Spellman also made it a point to be on the newsmen's good side by treating reporters with the same congeniality shown his wealthy friends and ranking churchmen. He gave them background briefings and a few well-screened but tantalizing bits of gossip and information that made the journalists his friends forever. For a press corps used to being stonewalled, Spellman was a breath of fresh air.

Spellman used the office in a further clever fashion. He hired the beautiful nun Pascalina, who, Spellman well knew, needed a friend. Although Pacelli had brought her into the Vatican, she was treated badly by many other members of the hierarchy, most of whom deeply resented her influential position. She repeatedly clashed with men such as the tall, arrogant Eugene Cardinal Tisserant, who groused about her outspokenness and the way she jealously guarded access to Pacelli. In addition, the nun was confronted by a chauvinist tradition that dated back to the Apostles. The power she wielded was unique and resented in the male-dominated institution. It was she who claimed credit for Pius's acting as his own secretary of state and it was she who urged him to do something for the Jews during the war (the evident result being the Pontifical Relief Committee that did aid Jews). Pascalina was in constant touch with Spellman by telephone and cable during the reign of Pius. Spellman was one of the few churchmen she trusted.[29]

From the start, Spellman courted Pascalina as a valuable ally. Spellman, the realist, knew Pacelli wasn't about to get rid of the woman who had served him for many years. And Spellman believed he would be a fool not to exploit the situation. When he first offered her a job, Pascalina demurred. She finally accepted, and soon she was glad she had. The work was stimulating and gave her a unique view of the inner workings of the Vatican. And, as Spellman knew from the outset, she was in a position to help him. It was obvious that the time was drawing near for him to move on to something big, and the more people speaking on his behalf to Pacelli, the better.

The issue of what to do for Spellman was forced by O'Connell in 1932. The bishop of Portland, Maine, died, and the Boston prelate pressed Rome to name Spellman the successor. Portland was far from the most significant post in the American hierarchy, but O'Connell knew that Spellman was being groomed for greater things, probably his own job. If Spellman became the Portland bishop, he would have to report to O'Connell. The prelate still wanted revenge against Spellman for the shabby way that O'Connell was treated at the Vatican, and he possibly could halt Spellman's rapid career rise.

Spellman was unsure of his next move, and his career was much debated among his supporters. Borgongini-Duca and Pizzardo urged him to take the Portland post. Then the possibility of his becoming bishop of Manchester, New Hampshire, was raised. Both posts reported to Boston and either one could place Spellman in line to succeed O'Connell. Cardinal Gasparri and Monsignor Ottaviani, however, told him to press to be an auxiliary bishop in Boston itself.[30] By doing so he could make his presence felt to a much greater degree in the important archdiocese. No one had any illusions about Cardinal O'Connell's reaction no matter where Spellman landed. In any event, the cardinal had squandered his authority in Rome long ago.

In a letter home, Spellman wrote: "I do everything I can for the Church and for the Holy Father with the proper motives. I have absolutely no ambitions to be anything else but a good priest."[31] But his notes to himself in his diary belied the notion that he was without ambition. He charted his career as carefully as a mapmaker. "Cardinal Gasparri said at dinner that it is almost certain that I was to take a big step soon," he painstakingly recorded in May 1932.

On Monday evening July 25, Pacelli asked Spellman to come to the cardinal's apartment. There Spellman learned that the Pope had made him auxiliary bishop of Boston. Pizzardo came by to congratulate him, and the three churchmen talked at length about the implications of the move. Spellman was now one of the Church's elite, entitled to wear the red robes of power. He was forty-three years old and had many influential friends and many powerful enemies. The mere mention of his name in Vatican corridors sparked whispers about his overwhelming ambition. Spellman epitomized a joke that often made the rounds when a monsignor was elevated. "Is he any good?" one priest asked. "How can he be," the other replied. "They made him a bishop."

To the world at large if not to churchmen, it appeared Spellman had been rewarded for his goodness. The public rarely, if ever, glimpsed the egos, the power plays, the intrigue, and the bitter feuds that were part of the rarefied atmosphere of Church politics. The humble face that Spellman exposed to the world was assumed to be his only face. Thus, his parents offered the sentiment that was shared by most Catholics. "May God bless and guide our boy and keep him kind and humble is the prayer of mother and father," they cabled their son when they heard the news.

As expected, O'Connell raged against the appointment, which was yet another humiliation. Not only was Spellman forced upon him as an auxiliary, but Spellman had been given the right to succeed the Boston cardinal. Spellman, knowing O'Connell's reaction, went through certain formalities, sending the cardinal an ironic note of thanks. "I know that your Eminence is chiefly responsible for this great honor. I know that without your Eminence's intercessions, such an honor or any similar honor would have been absolutely impossible. . . . My first act is to pledge to Your Eminence my fullest wholehearted loyal cooperation and to assure Your Eminence of my deep unswerving devotion at all times."[32]

Before going home, Spellman received yet another great honor from his Italian friends. He asked Pacelli to consecrate him as a bishop in St. Peter's, and the cardinal agreed to the request, making Spellman the first American ever to be so rewarded. Spellman's friends were overjoyed and, of all of them, the recently widowed Mrs. Brady appeared the most delighted. Before his consecration, Spellman stayed with her at Casa del Sole, and Borgongini-Duca came three times daily to tutor his friend on the points on which he was to meditate.

On September 8, Spellman stood before the Altar of the Chair, so-called because the wooden seat of St. Peter was hung in a sunburst of gold above the altar. Clad in shimmering silver vestments, which Pacelli himself had worn fifteen years earlier when he was made a bishop, Spellman blessed the audience. Because his mother was ailing, Spellman's parents and sisters had remained home, but his brothers, Martin and John, were in the basilica. Also present was his old classmate from the North American College, Father Edward Quinn. Spellman's new importance was evident from the presence of the entire diplomatic corps and the crowd of priests, seminarians, and wealthy Catholics who filled the enormous apse of the basilica.

The powerful Cardinal Pacelli performed the ceremony and was assisted by two other men of prominence, Pizzardo and Borgongini-Duca, who had taken the trouble to devise a coat of arms for Spellman. The shield was emblazoned with a likeness of Columbus's ship the *Santa Maria*, its sails billowing against an azure sea. The Pope provided the motto, *Sequere Deum* ("Follow God").

CHAPTER FOUR

Reaching for Power

IN LATE SEPTEMBER 1932, BISHOP SPELLMAN BOARDED THE
50,000-ton Italian steamer *Rex* for the United States. There
had been farewell parties, a lot of unsolicited advice, and much
speculation as to what kind of reception awaited him in Boston. None
of the scenarios was appetizing. No one doubted that Cardinal
O'Connell hated him. The prelate had gone so far as to issue a press
release minimizing Spellman's importance:

> There have been so many exaggerated press statements in relation to
> the recent appointment of Msgr. Spellman as Auxiliary to His Em-
> inence, the Cardinal, that the office of secretary to Cardinal O'Connell
> wishes to make a plain statement about the facts of the matter.
>
> Some years ago Cardinal O'Connell was consulted regarding the
> charge of appointing someone who could assist in the Secretary of
> State's office in Rome in the work of translating English documents
> into Italian and vice versa. . . . His task was merely to do the usual
> work given a cleric. . . . As soon as possible after consecration Bishop
> Spellman will return to Boston to take up whatever work Cardinal
> O'Connell designates for him to do in regard to the confirming of chil-
> dren in the archdiocese. . . .[1]

The steamer's crossing was uneventful. Spellman had much
catching up to do. There were American experiences that one

couldn't fully appreciate when viewed from afar. Spellman had missed much of the impact of Prohibition on America, the election campaign of Al Smith, the stock market crash (which he noted in his diary on October 2, 1930, had cost him more than $40,000), and the onset of the Depression. He had read a great deal about each, of course, but living through them was another matter. Moreover, he would catch only the tail end of the presidential campaign of Franklin Delano Roosevelt, who would have a tremendous influence on Spellman's career.

Before the *Rex* docked in the United States, Spellman received a terse cablegram from O'Connell written in the contemptuous tone that the old cardinal would use to address his subordinate in the coming years:

WELCOME HOME. CONFIRMATIONS BEGIN MONDAY OCTOBER TENTH. YOU ARE EXPECTED TO BE THERE.[2]

When Spellman arrived in Boston two days later, he realized the cable hadn't been passing querulousness. O'Connell refused to receive him and forbade him access to the cathedral rectory, forcing Spellman to stay at St. John's Seminary. Such pettiness went on for months. O'Connell refused to assign Spellman to a parish of his own for half a year while Spellman stewed. When he returned to Whitman to officiate at the Church of the Holy Ghost, his hometown parish, he was treated like a celebrity, but, acting under orders from O'Connell, the pastor kept press photographers away from the new bishop.

Spellman explained to his mother, brothers, sisters, and father about the pressure the cardinal put on him. But his family noticed that on his return from Rome the priest in the family had become more sophisticated. He was surer of himself, less concerned with what O'Connell thought or did. Bishop Spellman talked with his father about business, not as a son groping for something to discuss with a father but as a man excited by the subject. The bishop rattled off an impressive knowledge of stocks and bonds, investment strategies, and the government's attitude toward business at the time of the Depression. And from his brothers, John and Martin, who had become doctors, Spellman picked up an interest in medicine that remained with him the rest of his life.

Spellman, as usual, spent what free time he had with his family. His mother, who was in her late sixties, was in poor health; indeed, it was soon apparent that she was dying. By 1935 she was so ill that she couldn't be moved. Her son, the bishop, called upon her whenever he could and said mass in her bedroom. She died on July 28, 1935, and her funeral was an important occasion in Whitman, with the mayor, the governor, the lieutenant governor, and scores of priests and bishops in attendance. O'Connell failed to attend, and the cardinal later obliquely critcized priests who went to the funerals of people whom they had not known. "He obviously meant mother's funeral," Spellman bitterly recorded in his diary, and he never forgave the cardinal.

When O'Connell finally gave Spellman a parish of his own, the choice was yet another insult. He was appointed pastor of Sacred Heart in Newton Center, a backwater hamlet. Spellman was normally careful about expressing himself in writing other than in his diary and had spent years trying to control his temper. Now his self-discipline crumbled and he became the maddened insubordinate he had been years earlier. Spellman wrote O'Connell that he preferred not to take the job but would be pleased to go to Roslindale, a wealthy parish. "I shall endure the humiliation of seeing some priest appointed to a better parish than the auxiliary bishop," Spellman wrote. Several days later he recorded a victory in his diary: "Heard that [the] Cardinal is furious against me for my letter to him."[3]

Spellman's pastoral duties were a minor part of his life. He quickly settled into the role that befitted him—a Church politician. Renewing old acquaintances from Rome, he used them to meet even more people of prominence. Rapidly, U.S. politicians became aware that Spellman was one of the Vatican's political voices for American affairs and they turned to him for advice and favors. He wrote letters on behalf of men who wanted to be judges or hold federal office, and when Jim Curley wanted to be ambassador to Italy in 1933, it wasn't O'Connell to whom he went but Spellman.

The worried Curley heard that his ambassadorial aspirations were jeopardized because the Vatican did not want a Catholic appointed. The only possible reason for such a position was the absence of an American ambassador at the Holy See, and Vatican officials might have believed that a Catholic ambassador to Italy would preclude the appointment of one to the Vatican. Spellman investigated and determined the Holy See had no position on Curley or any other Catholic getting the job. The source of the rumor was Cardinal O'Connell, who had never liked Curley and tried to undermine him. Spellman supported Curley, but he failed to get the post. In noting his disappointment in his diary, Spellman wrote: "President Roosevelt and Postmaster General Farley had heard that I was displeased."[4]

That the President considered what the Boston bishop thought would have surprised few churchmen in Rome or Boston. Spellman knew how to make his presence felt. In the case of Roosevelt, Spellman's contact was Thomas G. Corcoran, one of the President's key aides. Spellman's and Corcoran's mothers had come from the same small Massachusetts town, and the bishop had used this common ground as an excuse to approach Corcoran.[5]

Spellman first surfaced publicly as one of the Church's political voices in 1934. There was a storm of Catholic protest over a statement by Joseph Daniels, the American ambassador to Mexico, who had praised General Elias Calles, an enemy of the Church. Mexico was an explosive issue among Catholics because of the anti-Catholic nature of the 1917 revolution. Between 1926 and 1929, Church schools were shut down and Church services were prohibited. Catholics saw what they thought was another Russian Revolution in the making. (Less than a year earlier, in 1933, they had been embittered when Roosevelt had recognized the Soviet Union.) In Daniels's case, Catholics thought he was slighting their Church when he quoted Calles in a speech on the importance of State-supported education in helping the revolution to "take possession of the minds of the children. . . ." Daniels commented that Calles's ideal was "the only one that can give Mexico the high place envisioned for it by its statesman." The ambassador was denounced from pulpits, and the White House was pressured to recall him. "Millions of Americans—Protestants, Jews, and Catholics—may well ask themselves how soon they are going to meet the same fate as their fellow religionists are suffering in Russia, Germany, and Mexico," stated *Commonweal*, the Catholic journal of opinion. Bishop Michael Curley of Baltimore and the Knights of Columbus were in the ranks of those demanding Daniels's head. Spellman, George Cardinal Mundelein of Chicago, and John F. O'Hara, president of Notre Dame, were voices of moderation. The issue subsided, but only after causing the White House to worry. Religion was a political powder keg in America, and Catholics numbered among Roosevelt's greatest supporters.

Mexico was an important issue to Spellman. Although he had left Rome he had not left the Vatican state department, and one of his jobs was to keep an eye on the Church in Latin America. Latin American countries had huge Catholic populations, but the state of the Church there wasn't robust. Long before the Mexican Revolution, for instance, the Catholic Church's activities had been curtailed in Guatemala. Spellman was sent on a fact-finding mission throughout Latin America and the Caribbean to get a feel for the Church's position. There were fears in Rome that the area was ripe for Communism. Throughout the region, the Church was aligned with dictatorships and oligarchies, but the effectiveness of the institution in some countries was blunted because of a poor, illiterate clergy. ". . . In Venezuela and in some other countries, there is a sad situation," Spellman wrote to Galeazzi. "The people do not assist the priests. . . . Naturally, their standard of living and culture is not very high, and then the people blame the priests when they themselves do not support them."[6] In coming years, Spellman would be the Church's primary American responsible for Latin America. When he could, he used that position for the common benefit of the Vatican and the U.S. State Department.

As Spellman's influence seeped through so many layers of the American Church, he inevitably became the object of a great deal of resentment. In Boston the rumor mill branded him as an unethical man who was so ambitious that he let nothing stand in his way. Stories were traded about the way he rose to power, about his wooing churchmen, the rich, and the politically prominent. Spellman became aware of the talk and, characteristically, he wanted to know its exact nature so he could best protect himself. He went to his old friend, Harry O'Connor.

"Will you tell me when anybody is criticizing me?" Spellman asked.

O'Connor replied that he would, but he imposed one condition: "I'll tell you what is said, but I won't tell you who said it."

The arrangement worked well. One day, O'Connor reported a particularly vicious attack, and Spellman became incensed. "Who said it?" the bishop demanded. "Tell me the name!"

O'Connor refused. When Spellman insisted, O'Connor brusquely turned him aside. "I've had it with you," O'Connor would recall saying. He left Spellman standing where he was.

The next day the agitated Spellman called on O'Connor at the cathedral rectory. He apologized for the outburst and asked if they could go back to their original agreement. O'Connor relented. Until the end of Spellman's life, O'Connor related criticisms of the churchman in Boston, New York, and Rome. Priests saw a great deal of the Janus face that the public seldom glimpsed.[7]

What could not be criticized was the energy with which Spellman attacked the problems of his parish in Newton Center. O'Connell apparently gave him Sacred Heart because the parish was $43,000 in debt. Spellman accepted the challenge for what it was. If he failed to turn the parish around financially, as O'Connell hoped, Rome might not consider him worthy of greater responsibility. If anything, O'Connell's hostility spurred Spellman to great action, just as it had done years earlier. The bishop launched creative fund-raising drives and turned to the wealthy Bostonians and politicians he had cultivated in Rome. One family opened its estate so Spellman could hold a horse race whose proceeds went to the Church. Elsewhere, he held carnivals with gambling, including mouse racing—people bet on numbered mice that scurried toward cheese, a game, some priests noted, only Spellman would have thought up. Announcements of the Sacred Heart parish benefits were sent even to wealthy people who lived such great distances away that they couldn't possibly attend. As Spellman expected, many sent money anyway. Not missing a trick, he produced programs for his events and sold advertising for $100 a page to men of prominence, including Governor Curley. Curley made sure he attended the Church affairs, where he pitched pennies, spun the wheel of furtune, and bet on the mouse races until he had spent several hundred dollars.

As a bishop, Spellman was now treated as royalty, with access to just about anyone. He came to know every wealthy Catholic family in the area, who delighted in having him visit their homes, a sign of status within the Catholic community. He married their sons and daughters, was routinely invited on their yachts, was given big donations, and helped with problems at his parish. The most valuable of these wealthy men was Joseph P. Kennedy.

Spellman and Kennedy were drawn together like magnets. Kennedy, the eldest son of a prosperous Boston politician and tavern owner, graduated from Harvard in 1912, the year after Spellman entered the North American College. But whereas Spellman's career raced along at a breathless pace only during the past seven years, Kennedy's life was a dizzying roller-coaster ride from the day he left school. He had been engaged in banking, real estate, shipbuilding, investment banking, and motion picture distribution and production before President Roosevelt named him chairman of the newly formed Securities and Exchange Commission in 1934. When Roosevelt appointed Kennedy to the post, he allegedly was asked why he put such a shark in the job. "It takes one to catch one," Roosevelt reportedly replied.

Stories about Kennedy's financial exploits were legion. In 1924, for instance, he holed up at New York's Waldorf-Astoria, where he fended off an attack by corporate raiders on the Yellow Cab Company. For a month, he orchestrated a series of buy-and-sell stock manipulations that confounded the raiders and made him a fortune. Several months later the stock fell and one of the principals involved blamed Kennedy for taking advantage of the company's weakened position and going to the other side of the street. He threatened to punch Kennedy in the nose when they met again. Kennedy also made a fortune in the movie industry, first as a theater owner and then as a producer. In Hollywood, he cranked out low-budget pictures, bought and merged companies, and befriended beautiful women, including Gloria Swanson.[8]

Like Spellman, Kennedy cultivated the rich and the powerful, the press and politicians, and wanted to be thought of as a man who had a higher calling in life than merely acquiring riches and power for their own sake. His family of eight children was the vehicle he intended to use to create a life of public service as well as power: he viewed his family much the way Spellman viewed the Church. The Church, too, had its place in Kennedy's world. As an Irish Catholic, he had met his share of prejudice, which bound him close to his religion. He helped the Church in whatever ways he could.

A New Deal supporter, Kennedy used his influence at the White House to further Church-related issues, and he had been instrumental in gaining certain freedom-of-worship concessions from the Soviet Union at the time Roosevelt recognized the Communist government. Like Spellman, he was a doer; that was why he had embraced the New Deal.

In his own way Kennedy was serious about his religion, though he saw few practical applications for his daily life. In Spellman he found a churchman who met him on his own terms. Neither man minded being used by the other, as long as both benefited. They were politically attuned in their opposition to Communism and in almost everything else.

Spellman's success in clearing up the financial problems of Sacred Heart and his numerous political duties in Boston, Washington, and abroad may have impressed others, but Cardinal O'Connell never acknowledged the bishop's deeds. It was apparent that whatever Spellman did irritated O'Connell. The cardinal refused to let Spellman accept honorary degrees, derided his fund-raising activities, and criticized his politicking. What particularly irked O'Connell was the stream of important Italian clergymen who called on his auxiliary bishop in Newton Center.

Indeed, Spellman's star glowed in Rome while O'Connell's barely flickered. This was transparent when Spellman's clever friend Tardini, now Vatican assistant secretary of state, visited the United States. He paid scant attention to the cardinal but had Spellman tour the nation with him, visiting Philadelphia, New York, Washington, Cincinnati, Chicago, Detroit, Buffalo, and Scranton. O'Connell was so angry that when Spellman proposed a lavish dinner for Tardini, O'Connell dashed the plans. He argued that the bishop was being audacious and insensitive at a time of national depression, when so many people had next to nothing to eat. O'Connell, who lived like one of the magi, had one of his secretaries respond in a memo: "That His Eminence would be greatly displeased if Bishop Spellman gave a dinner to Monsignor Tardini at Hugo's; that a public banquet would be unseemly; that such affairs were disgusting to the people, particularly in these difficult times; that there would be a lot of talking and that such reflects on the Church, the clergy, and all concerned and that anything like this would detract from his prestige and dignity."[9]

Shaking his head in exasperation, Spellman showed the memo to his guest. Cardinal O'Connell's alternative suggestion was a dinner for Tardini at the seminary, and Spellman had no choice but to accept. It was a dismal affair. O'Connell, sitting at the head of the table, was in an ugly mood. He criticized various Church figures and institutions, such as the Knights of Malta, a sixteenth-century military organization that had evolved into a twentieth-century charitable institution and was under Spellman's aegis in America. O'Connell also denigrated rumors circulating at the Vatican that he was seriously ill. "Rome is a city of false reports," he said.[10] The cardinal expressed the desire never to return to Rome again. He argued that the trip was fatiguing and expensive, but Spellman and Tardini didn't believe him. They knew O'Connell had been humiliated at the Holy See too often to ever want to go back.

The dinner was fraught with tension as the two antagonists sat at the same table. Spellman later wrote in his diary that he believed the cardinal had directed a not-very-veiled hostility toward him during the entire evening. Tardini, well aware of the troublesome situation, tried to salvage the evening. "Boston is the best city in the world," he remarked at one point.

Glaring at Spellman, O'Connell pointedly replied, "At least once you heard the truth!"[11]

Cardinal O'Connell wasn't the only person who tried to discredit Spellman with the Romans. Two Boston priests, Francis A. Burke and Michael J. Splaine, told Vatican officials that Spellman wasn't a man to be trusted. "[They] put the hooks into me in Rome or tried to," Spellman recorded in his diary on August 10. "[They] told Cardinal Pacelli that no one esteemed me here in Boston, that I was a schemer, intriguer and what not . . . the Cardinal answered that I was his real, sincere and true friend and that he had never heard such things before and did not believe them and the interview ended. Holy Father had spoken affectionately of me in public at [a] Boston audience. [The] Daily papers and Catholic papers carried [the] story but [the] *Pilot* was silent. What a Comedy!"[12]

The cardinal's onslaught continued. When Spellman organized the "Ard Righ Horse Show and Festival" of 1935, O'Connell summoned Spellman to his office, telling him he was a fool for involving Governor Curley because the event now looked like a platform for the canny politician rather than a parish fund-raiser. "Curley is a crook, a beggar on horseback," O'Connell raged. "He is being investigated by Federal authorities and will probably be indicted."*[13] At first, the cardinal forbade Spellman to attend the show he had put together. Later he relented.

On another occasion, Spellman was about to be given an honorary degree by Boston College but O'Connell quashed the honor as soon as he learned of it. In a move bound to offend the cardinal, Spellman accepted an honorary degree at Notre Dame instead. South Bend, Indiana was beyond O'Connell's jurisdiction. When O'Connell wrote his memoirs, Spellman, who hadn't read the work, heard through the grapevine that the material was potentially embarrassing. The

---

*Curley was indicted. He was convicted of mail fraud, but not until 1947.

bishop reported the existence of the controversial memoirs to Rome. The Pope wrote to O'Connell about the matter and mentioned that he had heard from Spellman. O'Connell summoned Spellman, demanding to know what he had written. Neither man wanted to give anything away. "He was tricky and I was cagey," Spellman recorded in his diary on June 26, 1934.

Spellman clandestinely obtained a copy of the cardinal's manuscript and found inflammatory material. One section dealt with the Sulpician order of priests, which O'Connell detested. In his youth O'Connell had entered the order but had been forced to leave. It was rumored that the head of the Sulpician seminary had found him effeminate. In any case, O'Connell had been humiliated and vowed vengeance. When he became archbishop of Boston, O'Connell gave vent to his pent-up anger at what had happened many years earlier by drumming the Sulpicians out of his archdiocese.

Spellman secretly sent a copy of the manuscript to his Vatican friends. A copy was given to Monsignor Amleto Cicognani, the apostolic delegate to the United States. Cicognani was "shocked," Spellman wrote in his diary.

Once again Cardinal O'Connell was summoned to Rome by an angry Pope. Spellman alerted Pacelli, Pizzardo, and others whom he knew well. "Had nice letters from Mr. Galeazzi and Mons. Pizzardo saying they are all prepared for Cardinal O'Connell's visit," he recorded in his diary. His preparations bore fruit. After O'Connell saw the Pope, Spellman received letters from the Romans telling him that his own situation had improved. "Monsignor Pizzardo [wrote] saying that [the] Holy Father told Cardinal O'Connell in precise language that I must be treated better," he wrote on November 4. On November 7 he recorded that another monsignor had told him, "I have nothing to fear from [the] Cardinal."

Thus, when Spellman became very involved in the preparations for Cardinal Pacelli's visit to America in 1936, there was little that O'Connell could do but step aside. The Italian was the highest-ranking Vatican figure ever to come to America and had specifically requested Bishop Spellman's assistance. O'Connell knew the high probability of Pacelli's becoming Pope. Talk at the Vatican these days was about what a clever diplomat Pacelli was and how he helped put the Church on an even keel with Mussolini. With Pacelli as Pope, O'Connell knew, with a heavy heart, there would be no stopping Spellman.

On a raw, clear day early in October 1936, Bishop Spellman, a small figure in a black overcoat and homburg, stood on a pier on New York's Hudson River. The luxury liner *Conti di Savoia* from Naples admitted few visitors during the quarantine period and so a great crowd gathered on the dock. Reporters stood in a knot bantering with one another. Senior members of the hierarchy mingled with the group of wealthy Catholics who waited excitedly to see Cardinal Pacelli. Spellman was allowed aboard before any of the others.

The visit was a historic one. Pacelli, who in less than three years would become Pope Pius XII, had come to meet and talk with American churchmen on their own soil. Of greater significance, the cardinal was scheduled to confer with President Roosevelt, a man of rising importance to Europeans as the clouds of war swirled. For the moment, the President and the Vatican secretary of state had matters to discuss, in addition to Europe's problems, that showed religion's influence on politics in the United States was greater than Roosevelt liked. Spellman's role during the visit was critical. He and Joe Kennedy had done a great deal to establish the Vatican-Washington connection, as well as arrange the rest of the visit. For Spellman, the occasion certified publicly the esteem in which he was held by Rome; he functioned as the right hand of the man destined to rule the Roman Catholic Church.

The bishop, ever conscious of public appearance, carried aboard a small valise containing a black priest's suit for the cardinal. In Europe, Pacelli always wore a clerical gown without trousers. In America, Spellman mistakenly assumed, the diplomat would want to dress like other priests.[14] Spellman hurried into Pacelli's cabin, elated to see his friend after so long. The two embraced, and the bishop turned and warmly greeted Count Galeazzi. The third person present was a surprise to Spellman. Mother Pascalina, at the last moment, had decided to come. The moments the four friends shared were the last quiet time they had during the hectic visit.

Pacelli told the press he was simply on vacation. It was a gross understatement. Thanks largely to Spellman, the cardinal had a number of important items on his agenda, but few people other than Galeazzi and Spellman knew what they were. The two had secretly worked out a strategy for Pacelli and their planning undermined prominent Church figures, including New York's Cardinal Hayes, who wanted to loom large in the pageantry and excitement surrounding the event. Instead of vacationing, Pacelli was bent on shoring up U.S.-Vatican relations. Rome was worried because the United States had recognized the Soviet Union three years earlier. Now, uppermost on Pacelli's mind was getting Roosevelt to send an ambassador to the Holy See. Since the early 1930s the Vatican had pressed to safeguard its position around the world and to extend its influence where possible. A number of concordats had been signed with foreign governments, including one Pacelli himself had negotiated to try to protect Church rights in Nazi Germany. Many countries had ambassadors to the Vatican. Pacelli and the Pope sought one from the United States as a way of developing closer ties between the two. Everyone knew that the issue was an extremely sensitive one in America, where separation of Church and State was held sacred.

For his part, Roosevelt wanted Pacelli to help him with another thorny religious problem. He wanted him to silence an American priest who was creating havoc. The problem priest was the notorious Charles Coughlin, whose anti–New Deal radio program had a nationwide audience of thirty million. The demagogic priest was considered a major enemy. A year before Pacelli's visit, Hugh Johnson, the National Recovery administrator, had publicly warned, "You can laugh at Father Coughlin, you can snort at Huey Long, but this country was never under a greater threat."

Coughlin was one of the more bizarre oddities of American political life. Born in 1891 to a Canadian seamstress and an American seaman, he had attended the University of Toronto, where he avidly studied social Catholicism, and he accepted the premise of *Rerum Novarum*, an encyclical by Pope Leo XIII. This document spoke of the obligation of the State to provide social justice, the immorality of usury, the need for government regulation of working conditions, the sanctity of private property, and called for harmony between capital and labor. By 1936, Coughlin was the pastor of Little Flower Church in Royal Oak, a Detroit suburb, known as a bastion of the Ku Klux Klan. A good friend of Joe Kennedy and an early New Deal supporter, Coughlin had even had Roosevelt name Frank Murphy as ambassador to the Philippines. At one point sixty-six congressmen had signed a petition asking the President to make Coughlin one of his economic advisers. The President and the priest had a falling out over Coughlin's personal financial deals. Though he routinely denounced international bankers and Wall Street speculators, Coughlin spent country weekends at the homes of Wall Street financiers, as well as much time with Joe Kennedy. More that that, he secretly speculated in silver though he publicly railed against profiteers. In 1934, Henry Morgenthau gave a list of prominent silver speculators to Congress. Among them was the secretary-treasurer of the Radio League of the Little Flower, who obviously had invested some of Coughlin's money for him. Roosevelt could have saved the priest a great deal of embarrassment by taking his name off the list, but he didn't, thereby making a vicious enemy.[15]

Coughlin retaliated by attacking Roosevelt in his broadcasts. Kennedy, who continued to be fascinated by the charisma of the priest and the power he wielded, disagreed with his political and economic stances; the millionaire wasn't above jokingly calling Coughlin a "jackass" to his face. But to the President, the priest was no laughing matter. In 1936, Coughlin blamed the nation's ills on Roosevelt, Jews, Communists, and "godless capitalists." The ominous message of his bigoted broadcasts had been taken up by the Christian Front, a private army of storm troopers that had widespread support in Boston and Brooklyn. In 1936, an election year, legions of Americans found it difficult to believe that better times were on the horizon. Millions were jobless, mortgages were foreclosed routinely, starvation was a reality. People across the country turned on their radio sets every Sunday afternoon at three o'clock and clung to the words of the Catholic priest with the mellifluous brogue. He offered scapegoats for what was bothering them. And in this election year he had formed a third major political party, with William Lemke of North Dakota as his presidential candidate. There was little doubt that Roosevelt wanted Coughlin muzzled.

To date the Vatican had done little about the controversial priest, and there was still a great deal of uncertainty in Washington as to how much support he had in Rome as well as America. An editorial in the Vatican newspaper *L'Osservatore Romano* had chastised Coughlin but had done little to mute speculation about whom he represented within the Church. It was known that he had the support of a number of members of the Church hierarchy in America, especially Michael Gallagher, the archbishop of Detroit, who had appointed Coughlin to Royal Oak.

Prior to Pacelli's visit, Spellman had visited the President at Hyde Park and Roosevelt had complained about Coughlin. Normally, the President's primary political contact with the Church was George Cardinal Mundelein of Chicago, a suave man who loved the elegant lifestyle of his office. But it was the blunt, hard-nosed Spellman who informed Amleto Cicognani, the apostolic delegate in Washington, that Roosevelt wanted Coughlin silenced.

Cicognani posed another problem to Spellman because neither Spellman nor Pacelli respected him. When Spellman presented him with the thorny Coughlin issue, the timid little Cicognani, predictably and to Spellman's disgust, retreated into paralysis. He indicated there was nothing he could do. The delegate was "weak and frightened and I am sure that he is suspicious and too cautious," Spellman noted in his diary.[16] Cicognani didn't want to confront the American hierarchy. The only ranking cleric to speak out against Coughlin to date had been Boston's Cardinal O'Connell and he had been curtly informed by midwestern ecclesiastics that his jurisdiction didn't extend to Coughlin. So disgusted was Spellman with Cicognani's weakness that he didn't even bother informing him about Pacelli's visit.

When the Vatican announced the cardinal's trip to America, Cicognani was put out, but he wasn't the only one. Another was Spellman's guardian angel, Duchess Brady. She had known for months about the impending visit, but she had operated under the assumption that Pacelli was to spend most of his time at her Long Island estate, Inisfada, as indeed the cardinal had assured her he would. When Vatican dispatches failed to mention that he would be her houseguest, she became frantic as she tried to find out what had gone wrong. Anxiously, she cabled Rome for an explanation of the oversight. She also demanded information from American churchmen, including Spellman, about why her painstaking plans were disrupted. None of the churchmen gave her a satisfactory answer. Of all of them, Spellman knew—but he never told her—that Pacelli's social visit had shifted gears and was now a diplomatic mission. Instead of being truthful with her, he was deceitful; and his actions destroyed their once strong friendship. Despite his declarations of devotion to her, Spellman had never liked the duchess. When he learned of her phone calls to churchmen, he was contemptuous. "She is such a nut," he wrote in his diary on September 30, 1936.

One reason Spellman was reluctant to tell her the truth was that it was he who had sabotaged the duchess's plans. He believed Pacelli's time was too precious to be squandered at Inisfada, where Mrs. Brady had lived alone since her husband's death a few years earlier. Spellman had arranged for the busy Pacelli to spend a limited amount of time with her. Spellman's motive was self-serving as well as practical. The bishop wanted to heighten his own importance during the visit, and there was only so much room at center stage.

Spellman's changes in the Pacelli itinerary were apparently to have been presented to Mrs. Brady and Cardinal Hayes by Count Galeazzi as Pacelli's own. The deception almost succeeded, but at the last moment Spellman blundered. While at Hayes's New York residence, Spellman lost a memorandum of a telephone conversation with Galeazzi. The memo, which outlined his intrigue, was brought to Hayes's attention. He, in turn, informed Mrs. Brady and Cicognani.

Beside himself when he realized his slip, Spellman ran back to the residence and tried to retrieve his notes. But he was thwarted. "Decided to go to Cardinal Hayes and Apostolic Delegate and ask [for] my lost memorandum back," Spellman recorded in his diary on October 9. "Both denied having it or knowing anything about it. They are both liars, so is Mons. [J. Francis A.] McIntyre." Later, Hayes and Mrs. Brady knew so much about what he was doing that Spellman believed a spy from the New York chancery had entered his hotel room in Manhattan and read his correspondence. The lost memo didn't have all the information that was thrown back at him. "Nobody but one person could have told [the] Duchess all she knows, unless my diary and my letters here have been read in my hotel room," he told his diary on October 12. That person was Galeazzi, his partner in intrigue.

On the surface, Pacelli's visit went smoothly. Crowds thronged sidewalks for miles in Manhattan when the cardinal appeared in a motorcade. Cheers erupted as he passed, and the devout made the sign of the cross in his shadow. The press dogged his footsteps and wrote reams of clichéd copy about the ascetic-looking Italian wrapped in the magnificent robes of his office who tirelessly blessed crowds, received bouquets of flowers from small children, and stirred the hearts and spirit of the faithful. He was gracious with one and all, but reporters were unable to ask him questions of importance because Spellman shielded the cardinal from them.

Even before Pacelli's arrival, there was much speculation in the press about the true nature of his visit. On October 2, *The New York Times* reported: "According to reports freely circulating in the Vatican today, Cardinal Pacelli wishes in the first place to enlist the support of President Roosevelt and the United States for the anti-Communist campaign the Pope has been waging for some time. . . . It is thought that Cardinal Pacelli wishes in the second place to invite the Washington government to establish formal diplomatic relations with the Vatican. . . . Finally, it is thought that Cardinal Pacelli wishes to convey to President Roosevelt formal assurances that the attacks made against him by the Rev. Charles E. Coughlin have received no encouragement from the Vatican. . . ." But reporters could never raise those issues. The tight-lipped Spellman always kept them at bay.

At Inisfada, Mrs. Brady had been severely put out by the change in plans, but she wasn't angry at Pacelli. She directed her hostility where it belonged, at Spellman. The duchess put on a cordial front as the party toured her house and grounds. But when they finally dined, the duchess's anger was transparent. "Tension at [the] luncheon [was] terrible," Spellman noted in his diary.

When he tried to talk to Mrs. Brady, Spellman was attacked. The duchess recounted all of the favors she had done for him over the years—the contacts she had enabled him to make, the good word she had dropped on his behalf in high Vatican circles when he was still a lowly priest, the countless thousands of dollars she and her husband had given him. Now, she bitterly announced that she intended to cut him from her will. She accused him, he confided in his diary, of "treachery." Spellman, who for years had expected to benefit from her death, tried to appease her. He begged her pardon, and he told her his version of events. But Mrs. Brady was beyond being placated. Spellman had lost an influential friend.

The battle with the duchess broke into the open several times. She marshaled a great deal of opposition to Spellman. There was "increased violence," he lamented in his diary, "and different friends of hers are jumping into the fray." Pacelli, however, remained firmly behind Spellman. He defended his bishop against much of the abuse and himself comforted Spellman. At one point the cardinal embraced Spellman and told him that he liked him more than ever. Nonetheless, Spellman spent sleepless nights as a result of the experience. "The shock of losing the friendship of the Duchess and in incurring her violent enmity is something I cannot throw off," he wrote.

The affairs of the moment distracted the bishop. The cardinal was scheduled to see America, so Spellman was constantly on the phone making arrangements, lining up prominent cardinals, bishops, and priests, helping in the preparation of speeches, and translating for the cardinal. The press had to be constantly fed innocuous interviews and pictures. Thus, the weeks went by in an endless blur of cities, churches, lunches, dinners, speeches, meetings, shrines, schools, and hospitals. Pacelli visited Boston, Philadelphia, Baltimore, Washington, South Bend, Cleveland, St. Paul, Cincinnati, Detroit, Chicago, San Francisco, Los Angeles, and St. Louis. Typical was Philadelphia, where the party visited with Cardinal Dougherty and had lunch with him, then drove to see the Liberty Bell, visited Rosemont College, Mercy Hospital, a Catholic girls high school, and a seminary where Pacelli was to speak. Everywhere the cardinal went, the reception was tremendous, crowds gathered, and the press reported the festive nature of his visits.

Once back in New York, both Spellman and Pacelli had once again to face the fallout of Spellman's deviousness. The retaliation was hidden from the public eye. Mrs. Brady gave a reception for the cardinal that was as grand as anything she and her husband had given in Rome. Inisfada glowed from the soft light of candles that illuminated the immense driveway which led up to her Georgian-style house. As guests entered, the first floor was filled with organ music, vases of long-stemmed roses were everywhere, and cardinals and bishops in their watered-satin robes mingled with the formally attired laymen and bejeweled women. The imperious duchess and the aristocratic Pacelli received guests in a vast hall dominated by a blazing fireplace large enough to burn unsplit tree trunks. But Spellman had to have the scene reconstructed for him, because the duchess hadn't invited him.

Cardinal Hayes followed suit. When Pacelli spoke at Fordham, for instance, Spellman wasn't allowed to be present. *"My own college,"* Spellman complained in his diary. When Hayes gave Pacelli a dinner, he told Bishop Stephen Donahue and Chancellor McIntyre that there was no room for Spellman at the table; Hayes didn't even want him in the chancery. Thus, when Spellman came to the affair with the cardinal, he was confronted by the bony, tough McIntyre, who relished such assignments. Unhesitatingly, McIntyre yanked the Boston bishop aside as he was about to enter. The chancellor brusquely told Spellman that he wasn't wanted, and he threw him out. "Another awful day!" Spellman wrote.

Meanwhile, Joe Kennedy, acting as Spellman's agent, had arranged for Pacelli to visit Roosevelt at Hyde Park right after the election. Spellman's behind-the-scenes dealings with the White House on this and other matters continued to upset Cicognani, who witnessed the rapid erosion of his own power. The nuncio hadn't known until after the fact that Kennedy and Spellman had arranged the Pacelli-Roosevelt meeting.[17] As the apostolic delegate knew, he had been made to look foolish; he had been trying to arrange such a meeting on his own.

On November 5 a private railway car containing Pacelli's entourage traveled to Hyde Park. The press was out in full force. Photographers ran across the expansive lawns and lengthy driveways while reporters kept trying to get to Pacelli, but Spellman firmly barred interviews. Thus, the world at large was deprived of information about what happened at Hyde Park with regard to such important issues as Communism, Coughlin, and the U.S. representation at the Vatican that the Church desperately wanted. Overall, however, the press greatly contributed to the success of Pacelli's visit. He had swept across the country on a wave of enthusiasm that had never before been shown in the United States to a Catholic churchman. His somber countenance had appeared in most daily newspapers in the country. Moreover, he had discussed matters of mutual concern with the President.

Though Pacelli couldn't have been delighted with certain aspects of Spellman's handling of the trip, he didn't rebuke his friend. Spellman, as was obvious, was useful. He got a job done quickly, did whatever was asked of him, and was discreet. Shortly after he left the United States, Pacelli asked a favor of Spellman. "Cardinal Pacelli sent me $113,000 to take care of for himself," Spellman wrote in his diary.[18] The bishop had grown accustomed to churchmen possessing great riches. Since being elevated to his lofty rank, Spellman, who had been well on his way to making a fortune while at the Vatican, received increasingly valuable gifts from wealthy patrons. Mrs. Evelyn Mendelssohn, a rich Detroit dowager, for instance, "bought 20,000 bushels of wheat for me at $6.29," Spellman wrote.[19]

The bishop may have felt an even greater satisfaction than usual in such a gift. When Mrs. Brady died a short while later, she had been true to her word: she had cut Spellman from her will. Spellman carefully recorded the name of each person that the duchess rewarded and how much she gave each. Archbishop Murray received $250,000; Pacelli, $100,000; the brilliant orator Monsignor Fulton J. Sheen of Washington, $100,000; and so on. During the Depression such sums were staggering. Spellman noted in his diary that he had been in her will for seven years, until her love turned to hate. "I was to receive $100,000," he wrote, smugly adding, "I have no regrets."[20]

Truthful or not, he had little reason to complain. He was rich. He was an intimate of such men as Massachusetts Senator David Walsh and John W. McCormack, who was destined to be the Speaker of the House. He was in with Joe Kennedy, and he could pick up the phone and ask for the President and get through. Most important, his friend Pacelli was destined for greater things.

The only thorn in Spellman's side was Cardinal O'Connell and his routine lessons in humility. After Pacelli's visit, the cardinal accused Spellman of being a conniver who sullied the red robes of his office by acting like a ward heeler. The charge was ironic in light of his own career, but O'Connell wasn't an introspective man. At one point, he sent Spellman a note telling him to stay away from a local political gathering the bishop was about to attend.

"It is my distinct wish that Your Excellency keep away from this and similar celebrations inasmuch as they are purely political gatherings and at the present time it is more prudence [sic] for an ecclesiastic in your position not to be present at them," the cardinal's note stated.[21]

O'Connell knew by now that he couldn't checkmate Spellman. The bishop, though, was shrewder than his superior, and O'Connell, old and his power enervated, could no longer hold him back. This became obvious to all when Cardinal Hayes of New York died, and Spellman moved into high gear.

Upon hearing of Hayes's death in September 1938, Spellman realized that a golden opportunity was at hand. Although he was to succeed O'Connell one day, that day seemed no closer than it had been when he returned from Rome six years earlier. He was nearly fifty years old and time was flying by. Spellman decided to gamble. Besides, New York was the most important archdiocese in America.

Once he made up his mind, Spellman telephoned Count Galeazzi and told him he was interested in the New York job. As Spellman knew he would, Galeazzi did the rest. The count told Pacelli, Pizzardo, and other Spellman supporters what Spellman wanted. As everyone knew, including Spellman himself, he was a dark horse. He had enemies in Rome and O'Connell could still muster some opposition to him among old friends. But there was always a chance, and Spellman had nothing to lose. Soon newspaper accounts mentioned that Spellman was among the candidates for archbishop, but it was also pointed out that there were more likely men for the post. "Since there is 'no chance,' I don't suppose there can be any harm done except the reaction after the appointment is made and I am considered an 'unsuccessful candidate,' " he wrote in his diary on November 6, 1938. "But what of it?"

Candidates who were considered stronger than Spellman were New York Bishop Stephen Donahue, the man groomed for the job by Hayes himself; and John T. McNicholas, the archbishop of Cincinnati who was promoted by a Vatican faction that believed he was ready for a more important position. Finally, word seeped out that McNicholas had been offered the job. But just as Spellman resigned himself to remaining in Boston, the unexpected happened. Before McNicholas was confirmed, Pope Pius XI died. As Spellman delightedly noted, the cards had changed. "Guess there is a lot of excitement and speculation around *new Pope—and new Archbishop* of New York," Spellman nervously wrote in his diary.*[22]

Nineteen thirty-nine was similar to other years in which a pope died, for Rome became more alive. Everyone fed on rumors. Like Washington, the Vatican was a political center filled with fluid alliances. Men rose and fell from power. Influence shifted with the deaths of the high and mighty. Powerful forces sparred with one another, wooed each other, and blocked one another in efforts to become stronger. The only difference in 1939 was that the American cardinals would arrive on time. Transportation was faster, and, thanks to Cardinal O'Connell's bitter encounter with Cardinal Gasparri after the Bostonian's late arrival in 1922, the allotted traveling time to a conclave had been extended.

Thus, O'Connell was among the ranks of cardinals from around the world who descended on Rome in February like foreign potentates, with their vast retinues of assistants and servants, piles of trunks, and mounds of gold, silver, and bejeweled gifts for friends, favorites, peers, and, of course, the man destined to be Pope. They stayed at the Vatican or the city's luxury hotels until it was time for them to seclude themselves from the world in a conclave, where they fought, bartered, and formed alliances until they were so moved by the will of God to select a Pope. On this occasion, though, the leading candidate had few rivals. He was Pacelli, Pius XI's handpicked successor and a man well-versed in the Byzantine ways of international diplomacy. With the rise of Hitler, Mussolini, and Communism, few cardinals doubted that they needed a man at the helm who could steer the Church through the roiling seas of international warfare.

Spellman had desperately wanted to go to the election, but he had been persuaded to stay home. O'Connell, of course, didn't want Spellman's presence to mar that of his own in the Eternal City, but the Boston prelate had no bearing on Spellman's decision. Surprisingly, the man who asked him not to go was his dear friend Pacelli. The Vatican secretary of state had been warned that Spellman's presence could harm him, and Pacelli was not about to see the crowning glory of his career elude him because he was foolish enough to have the controversial Spellman at his side. Spellman noted in his diary that Cardinal Marchetti had advised Pacelli that having Spellman in Rome might "cause a bad impression." His own presence "might hurt him in [the] conclave," Spellman quoted Marchetti as telling Pacelli.[23]

Spellman restlessly went to Cuba and then to Florida, but he did not enjoy either place, as he was so preoccupied with the unfolding

---

*Spellman's emphasis.

events. He read every newspaper account of what was happening and he called Galeazzi and others to get firsthand information. Though he was almost certain that Pacelli would get the nod, there was never a guarantee. An adage in Rome stated: "Many Popes enter a conclave, but many Cardinals leave." To his immense relief, the fretting proved ill-founded. "Cardinal Pacelli elected Pope Pius XII!!!!!!!!!!!!!!" Spellman excitedly recorded on Thursday, March 2.

The bishop remained secluded in Florida so that he didn't have to deal with telephones, reporters, and messages of congratulations. One man, however, always knew where to reach him. Almost immediately after his election, Pope Pius XII sent Spellman a telegram at the Everglades Hotel. Suddenly, Spellman had become the most important churchman in America. He was the good friend of the leader of the world's 600 million Catholics, and evidence of his new status swiftly made itself known. The Apostolic Delegate Cicognani, for instance, swallowed his pride and wired Spellman in order to humbly ask *him* for the new Pope's coat of arms. Moreover, the White House tried for two days to locate him. Spellman loved his new position as the confidant of a most powerful man. As he well knew, the likelihood of his being handed more power himself was almost inevitable. The New York job was still open. "I suppose I am back 'on the list' again," Spellman noted on March 8.

Spellman had reason to gloat. New York was one of the major items on the new Pope's agenda. The position had been vacant since September. Spellman was almost certain that McNicholas was out of the running since Pacelli hadn't immediately confirmed his appointment. Nothing was certain, of course, but Spellman was reasonably confident of getting the job. He wrote that there were at least three cardinals who opposed him, but, as he well knew, the odds were in his favor. A pope can act on his own.

Spellman had to watch the deft maneuvering from afar, however frustrating that was. It was much too soon for him to go to Rome. Fortunately, his friend Joe Kennedy, who a year earlier had become ambassador to Great Britain, represented the United States at the funeral of Pius XI and stayed on for the conclave. Now, Kennedy talked by telephone with Spellman and kept him abreast of the power plays that affected the bishop's career. With his long-coveted prize almost within his grasp, Spellman was in turmoil. "I am feeling well but the magnitude of all the happenings produces such a conflict of emotions that I am overcome with joy, apprehension and I don't know how many other things," Spellman wrote.

By mid-March the bishop received a personally signed blessing in a telegram from the Pope, a sign that all was well. Then he received an important letter from the Vatican that apparently was about the New York job and whether he was sure he wanted it. Spellman rushed back his response, leaving no doubt. "Answered [by] telegram 'supplicating,' " he wrote in the diary. Even so, he knew that Pacelli had to stand against many people in order to promote his friend over the heads of more deserving churchmen. "Evidently [the] fight is on again with a new target," he told his diary.[24]

While Spellman nervously waited, Joe Kennedy called. The millionaire boasted of the honors that he himself had received from the Pope. Kennedy also told Spellman that Cardinal O'Connell was opposed to recognition of the Vatican by the United States. Both Spellman and Kennedy were actively lobbying for such recognition, but, at the moment, Spellman couldn't share Kennedy's indignation. Finally, Kennedy told him something that Spellman wanted to hear. "Enrico is in there fighting for you all the time."[25]

The words were comforting. Spellman knew what a shrewd operator Galeazzi was. If anyone could help Pacelli steer the controversial appointment through the maze of objections to Spellman, the count was the man.

The days dragged on. Spellman was increasingly on edge. On April 4, more than a month after Pacelli was elected Pope, the worried Spellman was still uncertain about his fate. "There is an eloquent silence from Rome and Washington," he glumly reported.

On April 12 the tension broke. Spellman received a special-delivery letter in Boston stating that he was to be appointed archbishop of New York. When the news broke, Spellman and his family were besieged by reporters, well-wishers, and friends from whom they hadn't heard for years. The morning after, nuns who attended Spellman's mass came up to him with tears of joy in their eyes. They knew nothing of Church politics and always treated themselves as the servants of priests. That a man they had served under for years was about to become the archbishop of New York had them nearly speechless. The significance of the move wasn't lost on the press. Newspapers across the nation carried the story, and the press accounts were typical examples of the way that churchmen were generally perceived. "In this city [Boston] he is well liked because of his spirituality, his democratic attitude, and, now, because of his unwillingness to let the honor that has come to him change his belief that, whatever his title, he is always the parish priest," noted a story about him in *The New York Times* on May 7, 1939.

But not everyone viewed the appointment that way. A group of New York priests had lobbied in Rome for Bishop Donahue and they were resentful. Other priests, such as Joseph Fitzgerald, who had monitored Spellman's career from their seminary days, thought he was unworthy because of his duplicitous nature. Still others, such as the Bostonians Burke and Splaine, opposed him for political reasons. "Francis is an example of what happens when you teach a bookkeeper how to read," Cardinal O'Connell noted dryly when informed.

Now that Spellman was moving on, however, O'Connell was predisposed to be momentarily magnanimous. He invited Spellman to his residence, and the bishop warily accepted. Spellman's relationship with the cardinal always led him to expect the worst from the man; all he had gotten over the years from him was criticism. O'Connell had never acknowledged the work that Spellman had done to ease the way toward having the United States seriously consider sending an ambassador to Rome nor even his work in pulling the Newton Center church out of debt. But O'Connell merely wanted to offer some words of advice, including, as Spellman told his diary, advising Spellman he would be wise to remove some of the key men from Hayes's staff. They were bound to resent the newcomer, O'Connell said, and some of them might sabotage his plans.

As Spellman was leaving, O'Connell couldn't resist a last dig. "Don't be so humble," the cardinal noted ironically. "It doesn't get you anywhere." Spellman later wrote, "I said to myself, 'O, Yes'!"[26]

The truce with O'Connell was short-lived once the cardinal found out that Spellman was still working against him behind his back. Spellman had promoted a Boston priest to his friends in Rome as the man who should succeed him as auxiliary bishop and pastor of Newton Center, which was now, due to the prominence Spellman brought to it, a much desired post. Spellman's candidate was a friend, Richard Cushing, a big, gregarious man who looked like a tough Irish cop.

A plainspoken man with no pretensions, Cushing relied upon Spellman's knowledge of Church politics. Cushing had gone to a Boston seminary, so he didn't speak Italian or have mentors in Rome. Nonetheless, he had come to the attention of Vatican officials who, like Spellman, were impressed with Cushing's phenomenal fundraising abilities. Spellman was forever seeking out able administrators or strong fund-raisers. With Spellman's endorsement, Cushing was made the auxiliary bishop. Though O'Connell too had promoted Cushing, he was maddened by Spellman's last-minute meddling in the Boston archdiocese. When Cushing was consecrated a bishop, the cardinal refused to let Spellman participate in the ceremonies. "I would like to have taken part if I had been invited," Spellman reported in his diary. "However, I had part enough in the whole affair to satisfy me."

To the end, O'Connell maintained the policy that the public face of the Church was one of decorum. Thus, before members of the press, the cardinal went through the motions of being overjoyed with his bishop's good fortune. Newspapers everywhere carried photographs of O'Connell and Spellman standing side by side. Spellman was quoted as saying his success was due entirely to the cardinal. O'Connell reciprocated by saying Boston's great loss was New York's great gain. Oddly, O'Connell stood next to Spellman during press conferences but didn't read his own statement, a chore that fell to one of his secretaries. Apparently, he again wasn't on speaking terms with Spellman.

During one press conference Spellman was near tears when he looked up at O'Connell. His voice quavering, he told the gathering of his seven wonderful years as an auxiliary bishop to a marvelous cardinal: "I should like to say at this time, Your Eminence, that I have been very happy in Boston as a student, a priest, and a bishop working with you. You have been faithful, helpful, considerate, and sympathetic."

Tears rolled down his cheeks when he finished. They could have been tears of laughter or joy at his finally breaking away from the aged tyrant. If he hadn't left Boston, Spellman would have spent five more years under O'Connell before he died. Now Spellman had his own subordinates with whom he had to deal.

The drive from New York to Boston was tense and unpleasant for both Bishop Stephen Donahue and Monsignor Francis McIntyre. Though they had worked in the same chancery for years, they didn't care for each other. Their personalities clashed. A rigid, flinty man who confused piety with goodness, McIntyre ran the day-to-day business of the archdiocese of New York with ruthless efficiency. The handsome Donahue, whose intellect was seldom praised, could barely balance a checkbook. They were about to present their resignations to their new boss, Archbishop Spellman. The manner in which Spellman dealt with them illustrated the pragmatic way he would deal with New York's priests for nearly three decades. He rewarded those who were loyal, useful, and politically attuned to him. Others he ignored or discarded.

The strain between Donahue and McIntyre had heightened after Hayes's death. Donahue had been selected by the archdiocesan consultors, an advisory body to the archbishop, to be the see's acting administrator. Presumptuously, he had moved into Hayes's apartment in the archbishop's residence, apparently assuming that as Hayes's longtime favorite he would succeed his mentor. He had even taken it upon himself, at the suggestion of several influential monsignors, to appoint a number of pastors. Rome had upset his ambitions, and Donahue had reason to blame McIntyre. The chancellor had written to the Vatican that Donahue was ill-suited for the job, that Hayes's reputation for financial mismanagement would only be compounded.

What few New Yorkers realized until later was that McIntyre's letter had had little bearing on the choice of archbishop. If anything, it only reinforced a generally held belief in Rome, where there was long criticism of Hayes. The "Cardinal of Charity," as Hayes had been known, had opened soup kitchens and given a great deal of money to the poor during the endless days of the Depression. In doing so, he had plunged the archdiocese even more deeply into debt. Instead of redressing the situation, he had increased his charitable outlays. Hayes himself had known of the Vatican's disappointment. "I'm criticized for not knowing enough bankers," he had said ruefully. It was a charge that would never be brought against Spellman.

Both Donahue and McIntyre had been Hayes men, and this made them vulnerable when a new archbishop took over. The fact that the man was Spellman gave them reason to believe that their careers were finished. They had both been instrumental in acting out Hayes's reprisals against Spellman during the Pacelli visit three years earlier. No one had emerged from the nasty business looking very good. Now, to their surprise, Spellman greeted them with extreme cordiality. He rejected their resignations and actually worked at laying aside their fears. The past, he said, was the past; all was forgiven. Thus, Spellman rejected the advice O'Connell had offered. Spellman told them he needed their help. "You will be invaluable to me," he said.

Donahue later found Spellman's words hollow. Donahue, whose primary qualification for even having been considered for the top job was that he *looked* good, had no discernible talents. He wasn't an outstanding administrator, hadn't proven himself an able fundraiser, and wasn't good with budgets, nor was he especially adept at finding rich men and women who would leave fortunes to the archdiocese when they died. Spellman looked unblinkingly at the man and found he had little use for him. Donahue, who had spent his life in the Church from the time he had entered a seminary at age fourteen, soon found his position deteriorating. His career was over.

McIntyre was a different story. A street-tough New Yorker, he didn't enter the priesthood until he was twenty-nine years old, a step he had postponed until he believed he no longer had any family obligations to hold him back. As a young man he started as a runner on the New York Curb Exchange and went to night school. A relentless worker with a good head for business, McIntyre rose to the position of office manager of a stock-exchange firm. His mother was dead and he tended his father at home. Just as he was offered a partnership in a brokerage house, his father died. McIntyre felt he had no choice left but to enter the seminary, and because of his age and experience, he had whisked through his studies in a few years.

To many priests, McIntyre was an enigma. He spent long stretches on his knees obviously praying fervently, but when he stood up, the grace he had tried to summon drained out of him. He was a mean-spirited, vindictive man who rationalized his conduct as always being for the good of the Church. His rise in the New York chancery was as fast as his rise in the business world, for the same reason. Hayes had needed to depend on someone who had an intimate knowledge of finance. Running an archdiocese was like running a corporation and meant dealing with realtors, bankers, portfolio managers, and platoons of other businessmen for myriad services.

Spellman appreciated the chancellor's business acumen but was equally impressed with other qualities in McIntyre's character. The chancellor was tough and unswervingly loyal. Later, Spellman discussed with McIntyre the treatment that he himself had received during the Pacelli visit.

"Will you show the same loyalty to me that you did to Cardinal Hayes?" Spellman asked.

"I am your obedient servant," McIntyre replied. And he meant it. For the next decade, the chancellor would act as Spellman's surrogate in running the day-to-day business of the archdiocese. Moreover, he hounded priests the archbishop didn't like, made sure pastors fell in line behind Spellman's programs, and generally put the fear of God into priests who were out of step with "the Boss," as Spellman was known among his priests.

There was little doubt that Spellman needed all the administrative help he could get. The New York archdiocese was one of the Church's most demanding assignments. Geographically, the see included New York City (except for Brooklyn and Queens) as well as Dutchess, Orange, Putnam, Rockland, Sullivan, Ulster, and Westchester counties. There were nearly two million Catholics in the archdiocese, in a general population in 1939 of five million. There were four hundred parishes, as well as Catholic schools, hospitals, orphanages, and old-age homes, scattered over the archdiocese's 4,717 square miles. When religious orders such as the Jesuits were added to the diocesan priests, Spellman was served by some twenty-five hundred priests. There were also some ten thousand nuns and brothers, as well as an untold number of lay people who worked for Spellman. On top of everything else, the archdiocese was heavily in debt—$26 million. "I'll never have a moment of peace," Spellman told Harry O'Connor.[27]

Though intimidating, the post appealed to Spellman. New York was potentially the richest diocese in the world. Access to men and women of prominence in every field was now open to him. New York City was the nation's financial center and the world media capital, and the front doors of the archbishop's residence opened into the heart of it. The job was made for a man such as Spellman. Yet, as he prepared to go to New York, Spellman was defensive, for a reason that had little to do with the kind of challenge the city itself posed. He knew the archdiocese was a closed shop as far as priests were concerned, just as Boston was. He was the outsider; he had displaced Donahue, one of their own. Moreover, Spellman was aware that his reputation as an intriguer and political operator had doubtless preceded him.

Thus, Spellman was wary when, according to tradition, he was escorted across the boundary of his see by ranking New York clerics. The day was dark and threatened rain. When the party—which had gathered at Manresa, a Jesuit retreat near South Norwalk, Connecticut—reached the perimeter of the archdiocese, the standard rituals and official greetings were hurriedly executed.

Despite the gathering storm, thousands of schoolchildren lined the twenty-mile route that the entourage took to reach the archbishop's residence on Madison Avenue. The music of marching bands and the cheers of children rose above the claps of thunder and the cracks of lightning. Snug inside the chancery limousine, Spellman looked through the windows and realized that he had entered the ranks of the most honored men on earth. He turned his humble face to the cheering throng that had gathered outside his new residence. The new archbishop had arrived.

PART II

THE POWER AND THE GLORY

CHAPTER FIVE

The Archbishop
Takes Charge

THE MORNING WAS RAW AND THE OLDER PRIESTS, MONSI-gnors, and bishops had donned sweaters or topcoats over their robes to keep out the damp late-spring chill. Nearly two thousand clerics in all, wearing the medieval plumage of their orders, walked slowly behind three altar boys, the middle one bearing a long, slender bronze cross. Few members of the New York clergy, by far the largest group represented, knew what to expect of the new archbishop whom they were honoring this day, May 23, 1939.

The procession began shortly before 10 A.M. in front of the arch-bishop's residence, just north of Fiftieth Street at Madison Avenue. The line snaked around the block before seeping into St. Patrick's Cathedral, the Gothic church on Fifth Avenue. The largest of its kind in New York's history, the procession included fifty-one members of the hierarchy of the Roman Catholic Church. Most of the influential churchmen were Americans, but representatives of the Church had come from Italy, Mexico, Spain, Canada, and even China. They, as well as some fifty thousand people who had gathered outside the cathedral, came to witness the installation of Francis Joseph Spellman as head of the archdiocese of New York.

The day's ceremonies were an odd amalgam of New York in the twentieth century and the Church of the Middle Ages. The liturgical music, the beautiful silk-brocade vestments tinted with every color of the rainbow, and the pageantry were of a bygone age. Reminders that it was 1939 were the loudspeakers placed outside St. Patrick's so the huge throng spilling over the sidewalks could hear the service, the presence of microphones in the church so that radio networks could broadcast the event around the nation, and a cablegram from the Pope bestowing his apostolic blessing on those who were present.

On Fifth Avenue, a detail of fifty khaki-clad men from the New York National Guard, the famed "Fighting Irish," led the procession. Behind them trailed Jesuits in barrister-like black gowns, Dominicans in white tunics and black capes with hoods, and Paulists in plain black cassocks and starched white collars. Bearded Franciscans and Capuchins wore coarse brown habits; Carmalites, their white wool mantles with brown hoods; Augustinians, white-sleeved tunics with capes, hoods, and black leather belts; Redemptorists, black cassocks, cloaks, and birettas. The Passionists stood out in their rough, mantled tunics with a heart embroidered on the breast. The Trappists wore startling white wool habits; the Josephites were in deathly black. There were Salesians, Marists, Fathers of Mercy, and other orders. Many people in the crowd had never seen some of the orders before.

Prominent laymen added to the pageantry. More than sixty representatives of papal orders, looking more like lords of the British admiralty than the businessmen and politicians they were, filled pews in the front of the cathedral. They included Marquis George MacDonald, the financier; former Governor Al Smith; and John Burke, president of the B. Altman department store. They were among the privy chamberlains of the Cape and Sword and were attired in red military jackets, black dress trousers, and dress swords. There were knights of Malta, knights of the Holy Sepulchre, and knights of St. Gregory.

Politicians, although not officially one of the Church's military orders, were out in force. Governor Herbert Lehman, Mayor Fiorello La Guardia, and Senators Robert F. Wagner, Henry Cabot Lodge, and David Walsh were among those present. The contingent of Bostonians included Mayor Tobin, Governor Curley, and U.S. Attorney General Edmund J. Brandon. They were all men Spellman knew well.

As the procession entered the cathedral, three choirs sang strains of "Ecce Sacerdos Magnus." "Behold the high priest, whose life has pleased God," the hymn rang out. "Therefore the Lord hath promised that he shall become great among his people." Onlookers were enthralled by the grandness of the occasion. Admiring murmurs swept through the crowd as the colorful procession continued wending its way inside. The strains of organ music and the swelling voices of the choirs seeped through the church's windows, walls, and doors. People were overcome with emotion; tears flooded their eyes as they surveyed the grandeur of their religion. Nonetheless, New Yorkers who had seen only pictures of Spellman were taken aback when they saw him in person. He seemed so small for such greatness. Everyone stared at him, and they may well have done so even if he weren't the man being honored this day. The sound of the hard leather heels of his Italian shoes clicking loudly in the vaulted cathedral drew attention his way. According to ritual, Spellman walked along a path through the crowd. He approached a green-covered footstool placed before the altar of the Sacred Heart at the right of the sanctuary, where he knelt in silent prayer. Then he rose and walked steadily to the throne, at the right side of the altar.

Glaringly absent from the ceremonies was Cardinal O'Connell. Spellman had asked him to officiate, as protocol demanded, but the cardinal refused. The honor went instead to Amleto Cicognani, the apostolic delegate, who probably now wished he had had nerve enough to decline as well, as the investiture lasted a full three hours. Other than O'Connell's absence, the only awkwardness was a cry of anguish from Monsignor Michael J. Lavelle, the cathedral rector, who, in his eighties, could be excused because of his age. Spellman took no notice of the disturbance. The archbishop pledged to "sow the seed of the gospel" and to rely on a "zealous clergy, the self-sacrificing religious, and the devoted faithful of the laity."

Nothing detracted from the enthusiasm of the crowd. Like their counterparts in Boston, New York's Catholics were mostly of Irish heritage. They were far removed from the politics of the hierarchy. To most of them, the Church was the local priest who helped people in times of trouble, ministered to the sick and dying, and acted as God's representative who gave them the sacraments. To such people, an archbishop was simply a better priest. They gave little thought to the ambition that went into the pursuit of such a position, nor did they consider the many responsibilities it held, such as raising the enormous sums needed for schools, churches, charities, and other activities. The laity generally saw members of the hierarchy only on special occasions, such as confirmations, high school and college graduations, and, of course, St. Patrick's Day parades.

St. Patrick's Cathedral itself was a monument to the faith of a people who had turned to the Catholic Church as their major solace when they arrived in a new land far from family and friends. The church had been built largely with the nickels and dimes of poor Irish servant girls, who unquestioningly obeyed their Church's representatives. Their children and grandchildren accepted the Church as a normal and major part of their lives. Bishops and the archbishop were their royalty; they were men of God. This was why people humbled themselves by kneeling and kissing their rings. The men who wore the bishop's red or the cardinal's purple were held in awe.

When Spellman left the cathedral he was greeted by a burst of thunderous applause. He walked through the multitude, smiling benignly. Traffic on Fifth Avenue slowed to a crawl as drivers and their passengers gawked. People in buses and cars smiled, waved, and cheered, and Spellman waved back. The new regime moved smoothly into place. Tradition remained unbroken. Behind the closed doors of the chancery, however, it became readily apparent that Archbishop Spellman was different from Archbishop Hayes, and different from his benign public persona. Many people outside St. Patrick's would have had trouble recognizing that the steely executive who took charge of the archdiocese was the same smiling, affable man who waved to one and all.

Spellman was determined to succeed in his new assignment. The enormous difficulties of the posting were obvious, but he had leaped at the opportunity with his eyes wide open. One of his reasons was the mounting influence of the United States. He was convinced that his nation verged on being the most powerful, in spite of Hitler and Mussolini and their thirst for power. When that happened, New York would be the most powerful archdiocese.

To set his new house in order, Spellman underwent a dramatic change. Long the subservient Vatican man who had spent years in a defensive battle with Cardinal O'Connell, Spellman now wanted to be perceived as a man who knew how to command. Thus, he modeled his behavior on that of the two churchmen he had most recently served, Pacelli and O'Connell. Spellman adopted Pacelli's aloofness, a distance that always generated respect in the clergy. He took from his adversary O'Connell a stern, patriarchal attitude toward his priests. In the realm of politics, he adopted, in some cases, Pacelli's continental, behind-the-scenes manipulation, while, in others, he pursued a vigorously partisan O'Connell-like approach. The archbishop was a man of many moods and many faces. And, like both Pacelli and O'Connell, in private he no longer tried to control his anger.

At age fifty Spellman looked cherubic. His face was perfectly round and he was bald with the exception of a wispy fringe of gray hair. Gold wire-rimmed glasses added to his benign look. The archbishop, however, was intent on showing the clerical establishment that, despite gossip to the contrary, the New York job wasn't too big for a little man who didn't look tough enough for the demanding post.

The first group exposed to executive Spellman was the archdiocesan consultors, the archbishop's advisory board of twenty-seven experts on such matters as education, health care, real estate, banking, and law. The consultors met in a vast elegant room in the chancery. The ceiling was twenty feet high, the walls adorned with intricately carved walnut panels. The glistening conference table stretched down the center of the room. The chamber could have been a room in a Roman palace, but the atmosphere was strictly business. Meeting Spellman, the consultors found they served a cool, pragmatic, and demanding manager who wanted to know everything. A priest whose budget for hospital supplies was short, for instance, found himself singled out. "I see that adding figures in a column is beyond your grasp," Spellman said. "Isn't it, Father?" As the others sat in uncomfortable silence, the man stared, shamefaced, at the floor.

Spellman immediately challenged Father George Waring and Guglielmo Arcessi, a slight, Rome-trained monsignor. Both men had become forces behind the throne in New York. Hayes, who had not gone to the North American College and did not speak Italian, increasingly relied on these men, especially after becoming seriously ill several years before his death. They had influenced the consultors in naming Donahue the acting administrator. Like Hayes, Donahue depended on them.

After demanding Donahue's resignation publicly, Spellman expressed anger with Donahue for having appointed certain pastors, as though he were archbishop. Spellman rescinded the appointments and then renamed the same men. Donahue had acted on Waring's advice and moved into the archbishop's suite at the instigation of Arcessi, a nephew of Cardinal Gasparri. Spellman let the pastors know that they were now in his debt. The lines of power were clearly drawn. Arcessi and Waring lost face. Later Donahue bitterly complained about the shabby way Spellman treated him. The bishop lost all authority and was reduced to performing ceremonial tasks. But when he complained to Cicognani, he found little solace in the apostolic delegate. "Look at the way he treats *me!*" Cicognani replied.[1]

Spellman's imprint on priests wasn't felt just at the top. He shook the entire clerical establishment, which, by 1939, was characterized by a high degree of complacency. New York priests had little to do. A small proportion taught in schools or at the seminary, or were active in organizing labor. But, for the most part, many priests' responsibilities didn't extend beyond the routine duties of their parishes: they said mass, heard confessions, visited the sick and dying, and gave the other sacraments. Nuns tended most schools, orphanages, hospitals, and old-age homes. Housekeepers cooked for priests and cleaned up after them. Priests had a great deal of leisure time, and many of them knew their way around country-club golf courses better than the recesses of their parishes.

The same situation had been true in Boston, and Spellman, who was always active, couldn't stand to see priests waste so much time. Now that he was boss, he was determined to get a day's work for a day's pay out of his underlings. He cleverly established a method of keeping priests off balance by personally calling unexpectedly on rectories, something an archbishop hadn't done before. If a pastor was out and he didn't have what Spellman believed was a good reason, Spellman was cool. "When you see him," he would tell the housekeeper, "tell him the archbishop was here." On other occasions he sat in a pastor's confessional box on Saturday afternoon until the man finally showed up and Spellman could dress down the delinquent. The method was effective. Word spread quickly: "Be on your toes with Spellman."

Not only did priests learn that they had to watch their hours, but Spellman kept a surveillance on his subordinates' politics and friendships in a way that Hayes had never done. Spellman brooked no mavericks. In his insistence that priests toe his line, Spellman demanded loyalty to his conservative political and social philosophy as well as to himself. The priests who suffered most were liberals: they found themselves on the archbishop's enemies list. Spellman carried on the old antiliberal traditions he had learned in the seminary. About the only liberal priests he tolerated were those who aided the labor movement; their work was seen as building an alternative to Communism.

The suspicious Spellman asked McIntyre to identify the archdiocese's troublemakers. At the top of McIntyre's list was a liberal the chancellor despised, George Barry Ford, pastor of Corpus Christi parish and the chaplain at Columbia University.

The elegant Father Ford was an oddity in New York and the kind of priest Spellman instinctively disliked. Ford was a man of taste who enjoyed art and music. His character flaw, in the chancery's view, was his independence: he wore his hair longish like an Anglican minister, dressed in tailored suits from Brooks Brothers, and rode a bicycle. Worse than his appearance, as far as Spellman was concerned, were the man's liberal views. He had Protestant and Jewish friends at a time when most priests were insular and conservative. Whenever liberals needed a priest to sign a petition, sit on a panel, or say a prayer, they turned to Ford. Thus, the second day on the job, Spellman called Ford and said he was coming to see him. The ostensible reason was that Ford had been a character witness during the trial of a U.S. Circuit Court judge who had been convicted of conspiracy. When Spellman confronted Ford he told him he shouldn't have testified. Ford didn't back down.

"I respectfully disagree," he replied. "A priest is always in character when engaged in an act of charity."

Spellman was incensed, but for some reason, the archbishop called Ford the next day and told him to forget the encounter. However, that wasn't the end of the affair. Spellman wasn't about to let Ford's answering back go unchallenged. Instead of personally meting out retribution, Spellman turned Ford's case over to McIntyre, and for years, Ford was harassed by McIntyre's "Gestapo" tactics, as Ford referred to them. Ford was periodically summoned to the chancery, where he was berated, threatened, and accused of being everything from a subversive to a crypto-Communist.[2]

For his part, Ford's natural inclinations continued infuriating Spellman and McIntyre. Neither the archbishop nor the chancellor, for instance, had much use for labor organizations, even those sanctioned by the Church. Ford, however, allowed workers, such as five hundred employees of Consolidated Edison, the use of his parish hall as a meeting place to discuss grievances. The Powerhouse became angered when Ford's monthly parish bulletin denounced two well-known companies for underpaying their workers. In response, McIntyre demanded that future copies of the bulletin be censored by the chancery and that the statement about the companies be retracted. Ford refused, and his life was made more miserable. "Our concern was a matter of social justice, while that of the Chancery was solely a fear that one of the firms, and perhaps both, would cut off contributions to Catholic charities," Ford wrote of the incident in his autobiography, *A Degree of Difference*.

McIntyre was such an insular man that he was shocked when Ford sent flowers to an Episcopalian minister friend at Riverside Church to use in the sanctuary. Neither Spellman nor McIntyre believed in Catholics' mingling with people of other religions. Thus, the morning after Ford's gesture was noted in the press, the pastor received a special-delivery letter from McIntyre accusing Ford of being on thin ice: sending flowers was close to *communicatio in sacris*, an evil by which a Catholic participated in a divine worship with non-Catholics. The chancellor took Ford to task for a series of "crimes," such as having had the fire escape on one of his parish buildings painted without asking permission. When Ford dared nominate a woman for a trustee opening on the parish board, he was flatly rejected. Eventually, the harassment proved too much: Ford resigned his pastorship and the chaplain's job at Columbia.

The resignation should have solved a problem for Spellman, but it did not. Ford was extremely popular among his parishioners. He had, for instance, brought the quality of the parish choir to nearly professional level. The grade school was probably the best in the archdiocese. Ford had removed the nuns who had taught there when he first arrived and imported from Wisconsin noted teachers who had trained at non-Catholic institutions; the pastor didn't believe that the quality of Catholic-trained teachers was high. Although Spellman resented Ford's attitude, the bottom line was that he was a popular pastor and a strong fund-raiser who had pulled his parish out of debt. Spellman later had to ask him to return to Corpus Christi to keep the parish running smoothly. But neither he nor McIntyre stopped trying to belittle the priest. They launched a smear campaign against Ford, contending that the man was a fool or simply crazy. His parish became a dumping ground for other liberals and assorted other priests whose careers were sidetracked because they had run afoul of Spellman. "Ford is just a nut," Spellman was fond of saying.[3]

The saddest side of the Ford episode was that many of his clerical friends fell away. They had ambitions and associating with Ford could only harm them. Years later, Philip Furlong, who became a bishop, considered having spurned his onetime friend Ford one of his life's regrets. "I too turned my back on Father Ford," he would recall.[4] Like so many other ambitious priests, he wasn't about to incur Spellman's displeasure.

In light of the archbishop's attacks against liberals, his priests were confused when Spellman failed to move against Dorothy Day and her radical worker movement, which was based in New York. Her newspaper, the *Catholic Worker*, addressed problems of race, labor, housing, and hunger, and her solutions ran counter to Spellman's conservative philosophy. The archbishop believed the Church's duty to the less fortunate ended with raising funds for charitable institutions. She believed in changing society itself to help those who needed it, and she became a heroine to young Catholics in a later age.

Spellman, however, wasn't a man who looked for trouble. He shrewdly realized that censuring Dorothy Day would create more problems than it would solve. Though her newspaper had a circulation of 150,000, the number of people active in her movement was small; their numbers and influence might increase if he focused more attention on her. Moreover, such a move wouldn't be popular in the Church. Chancellor McIntyre almost superstitiously gave money to Day's selfless cause. She was a reminder of what many priests had once intended doing with their lives. When asked why he didn't silence her, Spellman appeared momentarily startled. "She might be a saint," he replied.

For her part, Day loved her Church in spite of some of the men who governed it. She was in the Church, she noted in her work *The Long Loneliness*, "not for itself, because it was so often a scandal to me," but for the "Cross on which Christ was crucified." What she lamented was "the scandal of businesslike priests, of collective wealth, the lack of sense of responsibility for the poor, the worker, the Negro, the Mexican, the Filipino, and even the oppression of these, and the consenting to the oppression of them by our industrialist capitalist order—these made me feel often that priests were more like Cain than Abel." Spellman paid no attention to her sentiments. The institution, he knew, would survive her, just as she knew it would survive him.

Spellman always struck his priests as an oddity. He was warm and attentive with men and women of power and prominence, but with his priests he was most often abrupt and cold, and could be quite ruthless. Although a conservative, he tolerated the most radical Catholic woman in the nation propagandizing under his nose. What made him appear stranger still was the way he changed completely with a priest who approached him with a personal problem such as alcohol, women, men, or money. In such cases Spellman was genuinely compassionate. He could empathize with troubled priests. His advice was usually "Stop!"

In New York, many priests said they were surprised when he obviously favored young priests or seminarians. To the public at large, Spellman was often a stern moralist who offered little comfort to sinners. Only within the special brotherhood of the priesthood could he be forgiving.

In November 1939, Spellman engaged in an act of mercy to a priest that became a legend in the archdiocese. He visited the town of Millbrook, some eighty miles from New York City. The business at hand was seeing to the transfer of an estate that had been donated to the Church. While there, Spellman remedied a long-standing problem. A man named Bonaventure Broderick living near Millbrook had once been a Roman Catholic bishop. Now, he ran a gas station. Broderick's fall from grace had had to do with money. At one point in his career, he had been sent to Cuba to settle Catholic Church claims against the U.S. government for damage done to Church property during the Spanish-American War. What happened next is hazy. It was rumored that he had used his influence to see that a huge government contract to install sewers in Havana was awarded to his brother. Whatever transpired, his superiors were incensed by what he had done. Broderick left the Church in disgrace. Now, the Vatican had asked Spellman to rehabilitate him. Why the Vatican decided to do so at this late date is open to speculation. The Romans responsible for his punishment may simply have died off or finally forgiven him.

Spellman willingly undertook the task. While he held priests generally in no special regard, the brotherhood of the priesthood meant a great deal to him. He knew all too well the difficulties of trying to live up to the demanding lifestyle. What had happened to Broderick, he well knew, could easily have happened to him—and almost did— many times during his career. Spellman went to Broderick's home and told him that all was forgiven. He was once again Bishop Broderick and was to be chaplain of a hospital in Riverdale, New York. His thirty years of exile were over.[5]

There were other stories of Spellman earnestly trying to talk men out of leaving the priesthood and, on one occasion, he traveled to Ohio to do so. In rejecting the priesthood, these priests were turning their backs on everything for which Spellman stood, and he found that intolerable.

Spellman's day-to-day running of the archdiocese was similar to Pope Pius XII's running of the Church. The archbishop, like Pacelli, had two secretaries who were on call twenty-four hours a day. They were his primary liaisons with the men who ran the various departments under him. The secretaries often started their day at 7:30 by eating breakfast with the archbishop and discussing the day's agenda with him. They wrote his speeches and letters, and transcribed the numerous memorandums, sermons, and reports he dictated at all hours of the day or night into a tape recorder.

A man who easily delegated authority, Spellman demanded a weekly report from his department heads. If one received a note with a small cross next to his signature, it meant that the archbishop wanted to see him—and that usually meant something was wrong. Spellman drove his secretaries relentlessly. Some couldn't maintain the pace and fell by the wayside; over the years a few had nervous breakdowns that other priests attributed to the driving pace the archbishop maintained and expected others to keep. A workaholic, Spellman wanted the men around him to be the same.

Spellman took over the same flat-topped walnut desk used by Cardinal Hayes. On it he placed his dictating machine. The desk also contained a Mercator globe that the archbishop frequently fingered and a small American flag. No religious symbols cluttered the top. Two telephones, each with two lines, were to his right. To the left was a five-deck workbasket marked: Vicar-General, Chancellor Secretaries, Catholic Charities, Military Ordinariate. The archbishop worked from a yellow notepad, checking the reports in front of him and clipping sheets of memo paper to them with directions—"For whatever action you consider appropriate" or "Please prepare draft of suggested reply."

The archbishop's secretaries inhabited a large office across the hall from his. The secretaries handled the constant stream of incoming phone calls, arranged his appointments, carried out his orders, met people for him, assisted at his masses, and often traveled with him. Their job was extremely demanding, but they had an opportunity to demonstrate their abilities to the man who, more than any other, could accelerate their careers and introduce them to people worth knowing both inside and outside the Church. An ambitious man couldn't be better positioned, if he could stand the pace.

Spellman's days were crammed with meetings, and he thrived on them, a secretary always at his side. The archbishop loved rushing in and out of conferences, moving from one department to another. The topic of one meeting might be fund-raising for a hospital, while the next concerned an education bill before Congress and a third had to do with real estate. When traveling between public functions, Spellman catnapped in the back of the limousine; he fell asleep immediately and awoke the moment he arrived at his destination, his batteries recharged.

The archbishop labored mightily at maintaining a benign yet forceful public image. Each spring he received a blizzard of requests from Catholic colleges to speak at their commencements, and he accepted as many as he could. During every season he attended banquets and receptions practically every day. And he always worked at being well prepared. If his planning was disrupted, he resented it. Spellman's short fuse ignited if a vase of flowers wasn't sitting on an altar to his satisfaction or if he showed up too late or too early for a function. Once while appearing at a police communion breakfast, he found the officers hadn't yet entered the room at the time he was scheduled to speak. The men were still gathered outside talking and joking. "Now what am I supposed to do?" he asked in a withering tone as he turned to Monsignor Joseph Dunn, the police chaplain.[6] Once in the limousine, he berated his aides, even though such offenses often were beyond their control.

Actually, Spellman treated Dunn better than most of his priests because he admired him. A no-nonsense man of military bearing, Dunn had been wounded while a chaplain during the Korean War. Spellman liked chaplains and boasted to people about Dunn's Purple Heart. Spellman found that manly—he was always trying to show that priests were real men.

Spellman's secretaries weren't subjected to the same abuse other priests received. The archbishop needed them—they had to spend up to sixteen hours a day with him—so he couldn't afford to have them sulking. The secretaries' job, however, was exciting. There were always important visitors from the government, the Vatican, or foreign nations at the Powerhouse. The secretaries met rich people who took them to concerts, invited them to their estates, and gave them money. Those who could meet Spellman's demands learned the inner workings of a strange world that was far different on the inside than it was perceived to be from the outside. They saw the clashes of personalities and power within the hierarchy, and the shrewder among them learned how to maneuver deftly for power of their own—and were sometimes rewarded by becoming bishops.

Although the secretaries were privy to a great deal, they weren't aware of everything the archbishop did. Spellman was an extremely secretive man. He often immediately burned letters and telegrams from government officials, the Vatican, and politicians. He held muffled telephone conversations with the Pope, congressmen, the President, and other men of note, so that even his most trusted aides were never certain about the nature of everything in which he was involved. Over the years, Spellman had his hand in so many clandestine affairs that his staff was never sure where he was going or whether his frequent trips were vacations or special missions for the Vatican or the U.S. government.

There was a restlessness about Spellman that affected the entire chancery. The atmosphere wasn't simply a result of the energy he poured into his work, but almost a kind of mania. Spellman hated to be alone and hated having nothing to do. Sometimes his secretaries even had to go for walks with him, not to talk but simply so he was with someone. He required motion. He would demand that the limousine take him and a secretary or another priest or two to Staten Island, just to have someplace to go. At other times, he flew to Paris for several days just to go somewhere, to lose himself in travel. Most often, however, his trips were planned and his missions were secret. A familiar sight was Spellman sitting in his office, a map spread open on the desk in front of him and a packet of airline, ship, and train schedules by his side.

That Spellman was far more important than Hayes was not lost on anyone. Hayes's influence had been restricted to New York; the people he had known well were those who lived within the perimeter of the archdiocese. On the other hand, Spellman seemed to know everyone, or soon did. The archbishop invited to lunch at the residence men of great influence such as Joe Kennedy and Bernard Baruch, Senator Walsh and Congressman McCormack, bankers and Wall Street speculators, city, state and Tammany Hall politicians, entertainers, ambassadors, heads of state, and churchmen. "It was like working for the President," Patrick Ahern, a Spellman secretary who became a bishop, would recall.[7]

The chancery staff was amused by Spellman's loving to refer to himself as a simple parish priest. Around the residence he even wore an old black cassock that was rusty with age, the kind of dress a village priest might have worn. The irony was lost on no one.

Hectic as it was, Spellman loved his life. After decades of doing everyone else's bidding, he was now the man in charge. Everyone deferred to him, and power was a rich reward. Not surprisingly, Spellman wanted to help old friends who had stuck with him along the way. At the lower levels of the ecclesiastic world, there weren't too many of them. Thus, when Harry O'Connor showed up at the residence one day, Spellman was delighted. He introduced the Boston priest to his maids, pretty Irish girls who cleaned and cooked and waited table. Then he paraded O'Connor through the parlor with its floor-to-ceiling gold curtains, red-velvet chairs, Persian rug, and paintings of past archbishops. They strolled into the throne room, where Spellman raced forward and sat on the throne that rose above the other chairs in the second-floor parlor which was used for special, formal presentations. There was the dining room with its heavy dark furniture and the archbishop's study, decorated with comfortable stuffed chairs and a large fireplace.

"What do you want, Harry?" Spellman asked with a satisfied air.

O'Connor, who had never shared Spellman's lust for power, replied that he wanted nothing. The priest derived a certain satisfaction in seeing men such as Spellman relentlessly racing after ever more power. It made him that much more certain it wasn't a life he ever wanted. "I have no great ambitions," he replied. "I just want to be a parish priest."

As he knew, the answer was bound to irritate Spellman, who in his humbler public moments liked to look wistful and say that all he had ever wanted out of life was to be a simple parish priest, implying he had reluctantly assumed the burdens of office that somehow had fallen on his shoulders. Spellman shook his head in disgust at O'Connor's reply. "Don't be stupid, Harry," he said.

O'Connor knew Spellman too well to be offended. He did, however, repeat a warning that he had offered shortly before Spellman took over the reins of New York. "When you left Boston, I told you that eighty-five percent of what you hear will be bullshit from people trying to flatter you or get on your good side," he said. "That's always been the problem of American bishops."[8] That wasn't a warning Spellman really needed. He quickly sized up people, knowing who was trying to use him and why. A master of flattery, Spellman wasn't about to succumb to flatterers himself. He did, however, continue relying on O'Connor to tell him what others said behind his back. His defenses were always ready.

Though his critics continued denigrating his politics, they didn't criticize Spellman's administrative abilities. It soon became obvious that he was able to perform far better than anyone expected. He was tough enough for New York, and, as though heeding his father's advice, he surrounded himself with people smarter than himself. Men who were good at their jobs were left alone while others were replaced. Though his subordinates resented his caustic wit and unbridled anger, they appreciated his quick decision making. On occasion, he even listened to advice if a priest was persistent, could aggressively support his position, and presented his views in a way that was palatable to Spellman. The archbishop, though, was usually difficult to deal with once he had made up his mind. He was obstinate and iron-fisted. That was something learned not just by churchmen, but also by New York's movers and shakers.

Weakness was not to be pitied in New York's financial circles, but to be exploited. The Church was no exception. For years the city's ruthless bankers had treated the New York archdiocese as an easy mark. A major factor in their advantage was that the Church presented no unified financial front. Each pastor dealt with bankers on his own, and this, in many cases, made them easy pickings for financial men. The interest rates charged on church loans were usually not only higher than commercial loan rates but often as high as the traffic would bear. The interest rates on mortgaged Church property were a major reason that the Hayes administration had suffered such heavy debt. Typically, Spellman didn't rue what had happened in the past. He efficiently waded through the archdiocese's financial problems and sized up the situation for what it was. His course of action was to centralize the archdiocese's business. In the process, he established New York as a model of financial management and enhanced his own reputation as the first modern Church money-manager in America. One way the archbishop achieved this goal was by bringing the city's bankers to heel.

Thus Walter M. Bennett, the president of the Emigrant Savings Bank, one of the city's leading lending institutions, sat startled in Spellman's office and tried to make sure that he had heard correctly. He had—the banker had just been threatened. Spellman told Bennett that he wanted all the mortgages Emigrant held on Catholic Church property to be renegotiated at a much more favorable interest rate. At first Bennett dismissed the request as the kind of plea he heard from worried men all too often, no matter what their line of business. Hayes, for instance, had always wanted the bank to give the arch-diocese a break, but Bennett always explained the impossibility of such an action. Business, after all, was business. Chancellor McIntyre on such occasions used to lecture Bennett on banking practices, but McIntyre got so carried away by his own erudition that he failed to notice bank rates stayed the same. Bennett, however, learned the hard way that Spellman wasn't ignorant about finance as Hayes had been, nor did he have McIntyre's weakness of being easily distracted. After making his request Spellman got tough: he threatened to yank all of the archdiocesan business from Bennett's bank and place it with Boston banks. The threat wasn't an idle one. Through Joe Kennedy, Spellman had already lined up the Boston banks. The threat was far worse than it at first appeared. If news of such action occurred, many of the bank's substantial number of Catholic depositors would most likely bolt.

A grim-faced Spellman sat waiting for the banker's response. The archbishop had carefully chosen his strategy and was perfectly willing to carry out the threat. Reducing the mortgage rate would go a long way toward erasing the staggering debt he had inherited from Hayes. But, just as important, Spellman wanted to teach Bennett a lesson that would spread around town: the new head of the archdiocese wasn't a financial incompetent who could be flattered, cajoled, bullied, or deluded; Hayes was dead and so was his era. The new arch-bishop knew how to deal with business barracudas. He could stand toe-to-toe with financial men and give as well as he took.

Bennett had brought the threat on himself. He had unwittingly antagonized Spellman before he even met him. Among the bouquets of flowers, letters, and telegrams welcoming Spellman to New York had been a note from the banker, who hadn't wasted time in coming to the point. His welcoming note had mentioned a concern with the Church's debt. Emigrant, he noted, held substantial mortgages on Church property at interest rates ranging between three and six percent. While the archbishop was still reeling from the crush of business facing him on his new job, the banker apparently had contemplated raising all the rates to the highest level. When the two sat down, Spellman dispensed with small talk and made his pitch for lower rates. Emigrant, in the end, gave the archbishop the terms he wanted—two percent. Spellman had cleverly used his office. No banker wanted to be known as an exploiter of the Catholic Church in New York. Other banks followed suit.[9]

Banking was only one aspect of the archdiocese that Spellman wanted to overhaul. He thought that archdioceses generally were managed as though the Church were in a financial dark ages. The accounting he had studied in Boston and the practical experience he had gained in Rome and in running his own parish had given him a solid understanding of business. The gross disorganization of the archdiocese dismayed him. Each parish was an autonomous unit that established not only its own banking arrangement, but also insurance policies, and contracts for repairs, heating oil, coal, and much else. The only thing that made any sense to Spellman was centralization. He believed he could not only save a fortune but also concentrate more power in his own hands. Thus, the businessman Spellman installed innovative financial controls in his see. No longer would individual pastors deal with banks on their own. Spellman established the chancery as the central banker. The archdiocese borrowed money at two percent and loaned it to parishes at two-and-a-half percent. Overnight, a huge proportion of the $46-million debt he had inherited disappeared.

Spellman applied the same logic to other areas. He consolidated the insurance coverage for Church property so that the business was in the hands of a few companies that gave favorable rates for dealing in big numbers, instead of the four hundred different insurers, including one or two in Ireland, that previously shared the business. Moreover, he created the Institutional Commodities Services, which bought bulk quantities of everything from automobiles to altar candles, resulting in a saving of at least $1 million a year.

There was no doubt that the new measures were pragmatic, but, in many cases, they took a human toll, and some pastors tried to get Spellman to look beyond dollars and cents. While certain pastors resented giving up their autonomy to the archbishop, others worried because many of their former suppliers were small-business owners who were parishioners. Pastors had placed their insurance policies mainly with local insurance dealers. Cars were bought from local car dealers. In the case of some local firms, such as small home-heating oil and coal companies, the parish was their biggest customer and the loss of its business created hardship. Spellman, however, was single-minded in his intent to shave costs wherever he could, and he was deaf to pleas to the contrary. When some pastors balked at complying with some of the new financial measures, Spellman used McIntyre to help them change their minds. McIntyre was always effective.

Spellman was pleased with the results. He was the first Church administrator in the nation to introduce such practical cost savings, and one of the benefits was his growing reputation as a financial genius. "The Catholic Church never had a greater executive than Cardinal Spellman," said Jonah J. Goldstein, a Republican politician in New York. "If there was a merger of AT&T, U.S. Steel, Westinghouse, General Electric, and General Motors—and if you were asked to pick a president of that merged corporation, and he was not a priest—I'd suggest Francis Spellman."[10]

In part, Spellman succeeded because he drew on the expertise of sophisticated financial men. He relied, for instance, on McIntyre's judgment and, at times, McIntyre could be quite creative. When he was named archbishop of Los Angeles, McIntyre formed great plans to buy up city land to build huge shopping malls. Other men to whom Spellman turned were Burke of B. Altman and John Coleman, the brilliant stockbroker who became chairman of the New York Stock Exchange and Spellman's chief emissary to the financial community. Like Joe Kennedy, Coleman was invaluable to Spellman.

Coleman was a New York City success story. The son of a New York policeman, he had grown up street savvy in a tough neighborhood on Manhattan's West Side and carried that toughness into business. Like McIntyre he was a man of little formal education who had started as a runner on Wall Street. By the age of twenty-one, Coleman was a stockbroker. In his second year as a trader, he borrowed $81,000 to buy a seat on the exchange. On the floor of the exchange, he had a reputation for remaining as cool as a British colonel under fire and had actually made money when the market collapsed in 1929. Every day of his work life, he went down to the trading floor to participate in the clamoring, hectic atmosphere.

By the time Spellman met him, the broad-shouldered Irishman with dark hair and a hooked nose was known as "the speculator's speculator," a man who loved taking risks in the high-flying world of the stock market. The broker's advice to Spellman was profitable. Spellman invested millions of dollars of Vatican as well as New York archdiocesan money in the market. The Church invested in major U.S. corporations, such as General Foods, Procter & Gamble, Westinghouse, RCA, Colgate-Palmolive, Firestone, and Goodyear. In one $30-million transaction, Coleman invested Church money in Lockheed, Boeing, Curtiss-Wright, and Douglas Aircraft.[11]

Coleman was helpful to Spellman in other ways. A fervid Catholic who went to mass and communion each morning, Coleman was generous with the Church in terms of both his time and money. In 1920, when only nineteen years old, he was already a member of the archdiocese Committee of the Laity, which solicited financial gifts. He himself always made huge contributions to the Church's many charities, and he was rewarded in the traditional manner. Two years before Spellman's arrival, Coleman had been appointed a knight of St. Gregory the Great. After the archbishop took over, Coleman collected more honors than the Duke of Windsor. He was named a knight of Malta and a papal chamberlain—the latter meant he could serve mass at the Vatican—and was awarded thirteen honorary degrees by Catholic schools, including Fordham and Notre Dame. In 1966, Spellman even named a high school in Kingston, New York, after Coleman.

The allure of Church titles was great among well-off Catholics. While some organizations, such as the Knights of Columbus, took one and all, others, such as the Knights of Malta, were fairly selective, and Spellman was in charge of determining who among Americans was to be admitted. The initiation fee was a donation of $5,000 or so, although some men apparently were willing to pay much more. Knowing well the fund-raising potential of the Knights of Malta, Spellman encouraged many wealthy men to join. Moreover, men who were generous to the Church posed with the archbishop for photographs that Spellman signed with warm words. The Jewish head of a New York music-recording company who posed for such a picture after donating $2,500 to Catholic Charities joked that he placed it face-out on his desk whenever Internal Revenue Service agents visited his office. "It worked," he told his friends. "They'd be in awe of me because I was a friend of the archbishop."

Yet another New Yorker Spellman came to rely on was John J. Reynolds, an aggressive Bronx Irishman who handled the archdiocese's real-estate transactions. Early on, Spellman had asked McIntyre to name the shrewdest real-estate broker in town, and McIntyre immediately suggested Reynolds. A racetrack habitué and stage door Johnny who had married a Ziegfeld girl, Reynolds was big, gregarious, hard-drinking, and ruthless. He took commissions from both ends of a deal whenever he could. Although he considered himself a staunch Catholic, the bluff Reynolds didn't let his religion stand in the way of profits. The archdiocese received the same treatment as his other clients. "When a pastor called and said he had a piece of property he wanted to buy, I'd tell him, 'Don't tell the Cardinal because he'll just get Reynolds involved and you'll wind up paying more than it costs now,' " one of Spellman's secretaries would remember.

Occasionally, Spellman bawled out Reynolds, but not because the broker embarrassed him by constantly hanging around racetracks or failing to get better property deals. Spellman was furious when Reynolds missed meetings because he was hung over. Nevertheless, the archbishop had reason to forgive his repentant realtor time and again. The broker was amazing—he wrapped up deals quickly, scared off rivals from property in which the Church was interested, knew how to slip through the tricky city bureaucracy, and dealt in cash.

The Spellman-Reynolds real-estate wheeling and dealing became the stuff of legends, and when, on occasion, a few details of their collaborative efforts became known the reason that Spellman tolerated Reynolds was obvious. In one of the shrewder transactions they negotiated, the city paid the archdiocese $8.8 million for land and buildings owned by Manhattanville College. The actual value of the property was estimated as only a fraction of that amount—$2.9 million. The two then turned around and acquired land in Purchase, New York, for $500,000 for a new campus for the school; the rest of the money was used to build a much larger and more sophisticated campus than the one they had abandoned.[12] In another transaction, a property Reynolds acquired for Spellman for $275,000 on Madison Avenue was sold six years later for $1.35 million.[13] The Church became the biggest private real-estate holder in the city.

Reynolds, however, was also a shrewd stock investor who put the archbishop on to a number of advantageous deals. It was he who interested Spellman in oil wells as investment opportunities that generated substantial income for the archdiocese. Thus, Spellman considered Reynolds's taking commissions from both ends as small payment for the man's usefulness. Spellman even let the wealthy Reynolds live rent-free in a Church-owned mansion in Riverdale, an exclusive neighborhood in the Bronx. The gracious home in a parklike setting had its own tennis court.

So impressed was he with Reynolds that Spellman made sure that he shared him with Joe Kennedy, who, like the archbishop, was always seeking out clever men who could help him build his fortune. When he met the realtor Kennedy didn't waste any time in getting down to business. "Do you think I could make some money in real estate?" he asked.

Reynolds shot back the kind of answer both Kennedy and Spellman loved to hear: "We both could."[14]

Kennedy and Reynolds embarked on a buying spree of New York real estate during the Second World War and immediately afterward that Reynolds estimated made Kennedy about $100 million. Never satisfied, Kennedy raised the rents of the commercial properties in which he invested, often doubling the rates charged. There were so many complaints from outraged tenants that New York imposed commercial rent controls which remained in effect for twenty years. Though Kennedy hated the bad publicity his rent-gouging caused, he could never fault Reynolds. The shrewdest purchase Reynolds made for Kennedy wasn't in Manhattan but Chicago, where he acquired the huge Merchandising Mart for $12.5 million, less than half the mart's original $30-million construction cost. Marshall Field, who had opened the mart in 1930, no longer needed space at the ninety-three-acre center and was worried about low rents paid by government offices housed in the complex. Reynolds bought just as the demand for such space turned up. Soon, the mart increased in value and became Kennedy's biggest asset.

The archbishop tried to help Kennedy in other ways. Marriage between Catholics and non-Catholics wasn't simply frowned on but was considered anathema in the Church. Yet when Kennedy's daughter Kathleen announced that she wanted to marry a Protestant—Billy Hartington, son of the Duke of Cavendish—Spellman took her request a good deal less to heart than her own family did. Spellman didn't tell the Kennedys that their daughter shouldn't marry the Protestant, which is what priests routinely advised in such situations. Rather, he first tried to get some sort of dispensation for the union from the Vatican. And when that failed, he still saw little reason to make a fuss. Joe Kennedy, Jr., Kathleen's closest confidant in the family, visited the archbishop to discuss the impending marriage and the family's hand wringing over going against the dictates of the Church. "His attitude seemed to be that if they loved each other a lot, then marry outside the Church," Kennedy wrote to his father. "He didn't seem to be disturbed about its creating a bad example."[15] Spellman was too worldly to take such matters seriously.

Indeed, Spellman was glad that Kennedy owed him another favor for having taken Kathleen's case to the Vatican. Several years later he called in the debt. The chancery needed new offices, and as the archbishop knew, Kennedy had bought a block of houses on Madison Avenue across from the archbishop's residence. Spellman wanted the buildings at favorable terms and got them. "It pays to have friends," he said. *Romanita*.

A people long discriminated against, Irish Catholics found that even when they had money they still weren't accepted socially. That had always been true in Boston and Philadelphia, but by the time Spellman arrived in New York Catholics were just beginning to move with ease among the Protestant rich. Kennedy, for instance, moved to New York not simply for his financial health but so his family could circulate in a much broader social milieu than was possible in Boston. Nonetheless, the parallel social institutions that had grown up in the wealthy Irish Catholic circles were still strong. Because religion was the reason for such institutions' existence, there was a fierce allegiance to the archbishop of New York. Thus, Spellman moved into a special world where he was looked upon as a social leader. He was part of the Church's royalty, and this authenticated the social strivings of the rich people who flocked around him.

The families who made up the hub of the New York Irish social set were the McDonnells, the Murrays, and the Cuddihys, who, in their heyday, helped transform Southampton into a sort of Irish Riviera because they weren't welcome at Newport. The McDonnells owned one of New York's most respected brokerage houses. The Murrays' money was based on the enterprise of Thomas F. Murray, an inventor who held numerous patents in the electrical field. The Cuddihys were in publishing. They socialized and intermarried with zeal and were devoted to their Church.

Spellman attended their parties, spent weekends at their summer homes, and married their children. He quite enjoyed the special role he played in their lives, so they were assured papal audiences when they visited Rome and were received by bishops and cardinals elsewhere when they traveled throughout Europe. Spellman turned to the more financially astute among them, such as T. Murray Mc-Donnell, who became one of the archbishop's major financial advisers and managed a great deal of the archdiocese's funds as well as his considerable family wealth. The Fifth Avenue apartment of James Francis McDonnell, for instance, was at one point the largest in New York and quite amply accommodated himself, his wife, the former Anna Murray, and their fourteen children. The dining room chandelier alone was valued at $100,000, which an unfortunate insurance company had to pay for one day after it crashed to the floor. The McDonnells' Southampton home had a retinue of sixteen servants, one for each member of the family. There were stables, limousines, yachts, and a polo field.

When attending any of the social set's functions, Spellman was always the center of attention. The event he liked the most was the Gotham Ball, which was New York's leading Catholic debutante affair. Usually held at the Plaza, the event was the outgrowth of the Gotham Dances, which had been started in 1912 for debutantes and private school boys of "good" Catholic stock. At the ball, held to benefit the Church-run Foundling Hospital, the girls were presented to Spellman. He was in a good humor as he buzzed among his wealthy friends, and, on several occasions, he made a dramatic entrance by bursting through huge garlands of red roses.

The most pious among this wealthy band was Thomas Murray, Jr., who considered himself the family conscience and maintained private chapels, one in New York and the other in Southampton. He had received three papal decorations for services rendered to the Church. Not all such Catholics shared Murray's attitudes toward the Church. His brother Joe and brother-in-law Lester Cuddihy, for instance, would duck out of mass before the sermon in order to smoke. Moreover, Cuddihy argued with Tom Murray over the merits of a Catholic education, which Tom told everyone was the only true education. Cuddihy felt Catholic schools were inferior and whenever he encountered a Jesuit he demanded to know, "Why don't you have *one* college that doesn't have to bow its head in the names of Yale and Harvard and Princeton?"[16]

Unlike most of his family members, Cuddihy didn't stand in awe of Spellman and his office. Once, for instance, he attended an affair at the home of Mrs. Robert L. Hoguet. As usual, Spellman was at the front of the receiving line. Cuddihy had new dentures and as he bent forward to kiss Spellman's ring the archbishop noted, "Ah, Lester, I see you have some new teeth." The furious Cuddihy hissed, "I'll teach you to call attention to my new teeth!"[17] He bit the archbishop's finger while Spellman, in pain, tried to keep a smile on his face.

New York City's politicians as well as financiers were forced to reassess their relationship with the archbishop of New York. Unlike Hayes, who occasionally wielded power in political affairs, Spellman wanted a permanent voice in city matters that interested him. And those were many. In time, Spellman's influence in New York City seemed so pervasive that no one was sure how much power he actually commanded. Few people willingly challenged him in order to find out.

The fact that an archbishop of New York exerted political force wasn't remarkable. Because of the size of the city's Catholic population, from the nineteenth century to the time Spellman took office, the Church had always been a factor politicians had to take into account. New York's first archbishop, John Hughes, known as "Dagger John" because he assigned a stiletto-like cross next to his signature, had even formed a slate of candidates to run for city elections when the anti-Catholic Know-Nothing movement was riding high. Over the years, the Church's political positions generally reflected moral stands. On November 14, 1921, for instance, *The New York Times* printed a story demonstrating that muscle. The headline stated, BIRTH CONTROL RAID MADE BY POLICE ON ARCHBISHOP'S ORDERS. Three years later, Cardinal Hayes joined Boston's Cardinal O'Connell in opposing the Child Labor Amendment to the federal constitution. Hayes also smashed the flamboyant Jimmy Walker's hopes of running again for mayor in the 1930s. Hayes had a priest read a statement, at a prominent politician's funeral, that left little doubt the Church would oppose the flagrantly immoral Walker.

As in Boston, the Church in New York was forced to rely on machine politics, for the same reasons. The Church and Tammany Hall were the sources of social welfare for immigrants. Because of the willingness of Tammany to provide them with food, clothing, and fuel in emergencies and to aid those who ran afoul of the law, these new Americans became devoted to the machine. The Church, as often as not, was willing to ignore the graft, corruption, and fraudulent voting practices because Tammany Hall was so effective in helping people. Also, politics in New York as in Boston was a path of upward mobility for the economically blocked Catholics. Tammany Hall became dominated by men who were usually Catholic and Irish, and the Church, as did many citizens, benefited from their favors.

There had been repeated efforts to clean up New York's political corruption. The abuses of William M. ("Boss") Tweed in the latter half of the nineteenth century had led to reform, but Tammany returned to power under John Kelly. By the 1890s, big bossism was again firmly entrenched, with Tammany Hall once more a source of food, clothing, jobs, and access to hospitals. By the time Spellman arrived in New York, however, there had been an effective purge of political corruption. Moveover, there wasn't the same need for the old power structure. Immigration had slowed and older immigrants were being rapidly assimilated. Literacy was growing, the government was moving into the social-welfare areas that were once the preserve of the Church and the political party, and civil-service requirements were reducing people's reliance on the machine for jobs.

Spellman recognized the new realities but differed from his predecessors in that he did not limit his intrusion to occasional public stands involving the welfare or morality of the faithful. Spellman wanted to be a power broker. His seeking such a role was in keeping with what he had learned in both Boston and Rome, where he had witnessed the interplay of Church and governments. He supported certain candidates for office and deterred others. He was consulted on who ran for mayor, sat on court benches, and governed the public school board. Though his actions were seldom on public display, there was little doubt that he was involved. Eventually, his influence seemed so pervasive that a new expression, "Check it with the Powerhouse," became part of the city's political vocabulary.

When Spellman took up his duties as archbishop in 1939, the times were ripe for such a man. The Church operated a sophisticated system of cultural and moral controls that were evident for all to see. It held sway over its members' lives to such a degree that most of them unquestioningly avoided certain books, magazines, plays, movies, and anything else that the priests condemned. Few politicians doubted that Catholics—New York's biggest voting bloc—could just as easily be mobilized behind any legislation or political candidates that a Church leader embraced.

Spellman was fortunate in many respects. Though Tammany Hall had lost much of its clout, Irish Catholicism had not. Most of the city's police, labor, and political bosses were Catholic, and Church leaders enjoyed a privileged position among them. Nationally recognized New York Democrats such as Al Smith, Jim Farley, and Edward Flynn were devoted to their Church; Farley, for instance, was an usher at St. Patrick's on Sunday mornings. Such men naturally had an interest in helping their archbishop. Thus, when a churchman who relished manipulating political affairs appeared on the scene, there were many men to whom he could turn. They could see to it that his views were not only heard but often obeyed.

But Spellman was too shrewd to rely solely on Catholics to advance his many causes. As he had in Rome, he quickly identified the most prominent people in the city and began cultivating them. Before long he had formed a powerful, ever-expanding alliance that included Robert Moses, Bernard Baruch, and Tom Dewey. His tactics didn't change from his days in Rome, but now they were even more effective. He was a figure whom other leaders wanted to cultivate as well.

In the case of Al Smith, Spellman, dressed in a priest's black suit and white clerical collar, came to the former governor's front door. The man who answered yelled to Smith, "Some priest's here, Al." When the smiling archbishop identified himself, Smith apologized profusely. Spellman should have been shown more courtesy, he said. "No," Spellman replied. "I'm just a simple parish priest."[18] Spellman captivated Smith, just as he did so many other people of prominence. He was always so cheerful and gracious with them.

To some of his priests, Spellman seemed like two different people, a "Dr. Jekyll and Mr. Hyde," said one of his department heads, who went so far as to take a sample of the archbishop's penmanship to a handwriting analyst to determine the kind of person Spellman was. Prominent New Yorkers met only Dr. Jekyll, not Mr. Hyde. Spellman inquired about their health and their families. He remembered their birthdays and anniversaries, and had his secretaries send them copies of his sermons and speeches, and notes for all occasions. The archbishop realized that people were flattered simply because he knew them. It mattered little what he said or wrote to them. He had the same litany of little jokes, told over and over, that were usually turned on himself. A day didn't seem to go by that he didn't tell someone that his father had told him to surround himself with people smarter than himself. "And they shouldn't be hard to find," he always quoted his father in the same self-deprecating way. "He was a wonderful man," recalled Abraham Beame, who rose through the city bureaucracy to become mayor in 1972. "He sent me a note of congratulations on the very first speech I gave."

Since the archbishop seldom revealed his political role publicly, he used emissaries, or "conveyor belts," as some politicians cynically called Spellman's men. They included both priests and laymen. Among the latter were John Burke of the B. Altman department store; Frank Folsom, of RCA, who was another link to the business community; and the Stock Exchange's Coleman. Then there was John Connorton, a health-care executive who became a deputy mayor because of his Powerhouse ties, and Charlie Silver, "Spelly's Jew," who raised funds and provided political and economic contacts in the Jewish community and also became a deputy mayor. In Congress, John McCormack was known as "the bishop," because he promoted so much Spellman-inspired legislation.

Eventually, it struck some priests at the chancery that the archbishop's political power in New York knew few limits. But even they were baffled by the ways in which Spellman managed to maneuver behind the scenes. "As far as I was concerned, he controlled Tammany Hall," said the Reverend Albert Nevins, who worked in New York for twenty years. "He made judges and other appointments, but you could never prove it. There was never anything on paper in New York politics. It was always done through the back door."[19] Politicians themselves were soon awestruck by the muscle Spellman flexed. Herbert Brownell, who became a powerful national political figure himself when he served as President Eisenhower's attorney general, found that Spellman was like a Renaissance cardinal in New York; "he was very, very powerful."[20]

Politicians were amused that Spellman publicly created the impression—or at least tried to do so—that he was above politics. When he first arrived in New York, he was asked to join the Grand Street Boys, a social organization whose membership included a number of politicians as well as the previous archbishop. Spellman rejected the offer. He piously replied that he had nothing to do with politics and joined "no organization outside of the Church." Bostonians would have roared with laughter if they had heard the statement, but at the time the New Yorkers who asked him didn't know his history. It was only in retrospect that they found the incident amusing.

One politician who was wary of Spellman from the outset was Fiorello La Guardia. Formally, the mayor and the archbishop had little in common. An Episcopalian and a Mason, the flamboyant mayor was half Jewish and half Italian. He was also extremely liberal. What they shared were naked ambition and a lack of conscience about appealing more to their constituents' emotions than to their reason. "I can out-demagogue the best of demagogues," La Guardia once boasted. The mayor, too, was feisty and backed down from few men, except when it was politically expedient. He periodically found himself in that position with Spellman. The product of New York tenements, La Guardia possessed the sharp instincts of a street politician and was smart enough to know that, even as mayor, he was in no position to take on the archbishop of New York. He tried to maintain a formal relationship with Spellman that, he found to his chagrin, wasn't always possible. "On several occasions La Guardia went to the archbishop and said he didn't want preaching in Church about politics," Frederick Cuneo, once La Guardia's law secretary, recollected.[21] La Guardia should have saved his breath. The mayor swiftly found out he was up against the most political churchman in American history.

Spellman routinely pressured the mayor for sundry matters that sometimes had to do with the Church and sometimes did not. For instance, Spellman had both La Guardia and Robert Moses discuss with him his prospects for free public transportation for Catholic schoolchildren to visit museums. This was the first educational issue in which the archbishop became involved that bore on separation of Church and State, and the matter was straightforward. Spellman got what he wanted, and it proved the easiest victory in the State-Church arena that he would ever win. He also had city officials keep him abreast of developments in planning for housing, hospitals, and schools since such city efforts paralleled his own large-scale plans for Church-run facilities.[22]

Trouble arose not in such concrete areas that bureaucrats and politicians could readily understand, but when the archbishop chose to subject secular forces to his moral dictates. The archbishop's authority, as everyone knew, wasn't respected because he controlled a building budget, but because he was the primary moral voice of Catholicism in the region. La Guardia felt the full force of this fierce weapon in the case of Bertrand Russell, when the outspoken philosopher was hired in 1940 as a professor at City College. There was an immediate barrage of criticism, overwhelmingly Catholic in origin, because of Russell's unorthodox views. Spellman, in particular, ranted about Russell's book *Marriage and Morals,* in which Russell expressed libertine views in opposition to the Church's teachings.

Russell was fired, and he publicly scolded the Catholic hierarchy for bringing about his demise. Though Spellman was held responsible, it couldn't be proven that he was. "It was generally believed that Spellman got Russell fired, but La Guardia wouldn't talk about it," Cuneo recalled.[23]

For Spellman, he was merely doing his job as he saw fit. There was no issue of freedom of speech or democracy involved, as far as the archbishop was concerned. To Spellman, who saw many issues in black and white, Russell had no rights. Spellman indirectly commented on the Russell case when addressing a Catholic girls' high school a short while later. His May 1, 1940, speech left little doubt as to the archbishop's sense of righteousness: "Catholic education, believing in the objectivity of truth, challenged the wisdom of subsidizing the dissemination of falsehood under the guise of liberty. Falsehood, whatever its sphere, has no more legitimate claim to be freely disseminated than have the germs of disease a right to formal cultivation in the bloodstream of the individual."

Though La Guardia may not have cared for Spellman's meddling, there was little he could do to prevent it. The archbishop had a say at the White House as well as in New York, and his influence in the city grew larger and larger as he intruded on an ever-widening pool of concerns ranging from motion pictures to labor strikes. In 1942, for instance, Spellman was called on to intervene in a bitter labor dispute involving the city's transit employees. Michael Quill, the burly, loudmouthed president of the Transport Workers Union, had challenged La Guardia by calling a strike over higher wages. La Guardia stubbornly dug in his heels rather than be bullied by Quill. A citizens' committee frantically tried to find a compromise. Quill's suggestion about what to do next indicated the city's growing consciousness of Spellman's role in public affairs. "What about calling the cathedral and seeing where the Catholic Church stands on this?" Quill said.

The others agreed. Quill made an appointment with Spellman. Though Spellman privately detested unions, if he could find a solution to the impasse, both the unions and La Guardia would be in his debt. Spellman called the mayor in Quill's presence. He was blunt, continuing his harangue until he received some sort of concession from La Guardia. "When it was over, he said he would be in touch with me in a few days," Quill said.

A short while later, Spellman announced a compromise. A committee was appointed to investigate city relations with subway workers. Spellman had broken the deadlock. He saw to it that he maintained a position of strength in the outcome of the dispute. The new committee was headed by one of his men, Ignatius M. Wilkinson, dean of the Fordham Law School. Spellman hadn't missed an angle. After the Wilkinson report was submitted, workers received raises and the city's labor policy with the union was revised.[24] Moreover, Mike Quill, a major labor leader, was indebted to Spellman while politicians were warier than ever of him.

The source of Spellman's power was his position as a moral leader of the Church. Catholics viewed themselves as an embattled minority and their archbishop as their standard-bearer. Most Catholics listened to him intently and obeyed his commands unquestioningly. Spellman's moral concerns were almost always of a sexual nature—rarely did he condemn such sins as lying, cheating, or hypocrisy. He sought to punish those who publicly flaunted sexuality. While other bishops and religious organizations voiced similar complaints at times, Spellman's voice was the most shrill. When, on November 26, 1941, Spellman exerted moral authority over his flock, the move wasn't inconsequential. On that date he began his first moral crusade, against the motion picture *Two-Faced Woman*, which starred Greta Garbo.

Two-Faced Woman had already been condemned by the Legion of Decency because Garbo wore low-cut gowns and made passionate love in one scene. Since its founding in 1934, the legion had become a much-dreaded institution in motion-picture circles; Hollywood soon realized that the legion's criticisms hurt the box office. Spellman, who hadn't seen the film, nonetheless issued a pastoral letter that was read from parish pulpits throughout his see during each mass that Sunday. He found the film had an "immoral and indecent" attitude toward marriage and "suggestive" scenes, dialogue, and costumes. In the presence of many people, in fact, the Cardinal was a prim and prissy man who was uncomfortable with the subject of sex. (Shortly before denouncing the Garbo film, Spellman had linked sex to the war in Europe. "All of us," he said, "are victims of war, the war of Satan, the war of the flesh. . . .") He never tolerated off-color jokes or language in his presence, so that even salty Joe Kennedy bit his tongue on occasion.

For years rumors abounded about Cardinal Spellman being a homosexual. As a result, many felt—and continue to feel—that Spellman the public moralist may well have been a contradiction of the man of the flesh. Numerous priests and others interviewed took his homosexuality for granted.[25] Others within the Church and outside have steadfastly dismissed such claims. Finally, to make an absolute statement about Spellman's sexual activities is to invite an irresolvable debate and to deflect attention from his words and deeds.

But without question, Spellman was a rabid public moralist. He ranted against movies, plays, and films that treated sex even lightly, let alone those that exploited sexuality as a major theme. What was perhaps even stranger, Spellman castigated such entertainment without actually seeing many of the productions he condemned. Censorship was something he demanded. In a national radio address on March 23, 1942, he said: "The 'fifth column' of saboteurs of our factories and public utilities has its counterpart in the 'fifth column' of those who piously shout 'censorship' if they are not permitted freely to exercise their venal, venomous, diabolical debauching of our boys and girls. . . ." Shortly thereafter, while addressing the New York City Police Department's Anchor Club at Memorial Day services at St. Patrick's, Spellman roundly condemned the immorality of the Broadway stage. Broadway, Spellman declared, "would drag the name of New York down to be synonymous with Sodom and Gomorrah." He claimed to have recently stormed out of a theater "in horror and shame" because he was so revolted by what he had witnessed.

At times, Spellman insisted that others be punished for innocuous sexual fare. The police were his weapon. Predominantly Irish Catholics, they revered any man who sat on the archbishop's throne. They responded to Spellman's clarion. Within a day after his self-righteous attack, police barged through the door of the Ambassador Theater, at Forty-ninth Street and Broadway, and served summonses on the manager and producers of *Wine, Women and Song,* a relatively tame burlesque show featuring a fan dancer and a comic. The production had been listed in the archdiocesan newspaper, *Catholic News,* by the Catholic Theater Movement as "wholly objectionable." The movement was a group of Catholic actors, actresses, and priests who were intent on bringing morality back to the stage. Because of their Irish Catholic culture, many of the city's leaders and citizens saw little wrong and a great deal right in the action. Mayor LaGuardia tried to sidestep it. When asked about the show, he was evasive. "The title was very misleading," he replied with a straight face. "The public thought it was a Viennese musical."

Finally, most people were hardly taken up with the question of whether Spellman had a sex life. They were far more concerned about other things. What offended Gore Vidal, for instance, was the archbishop's politics: "The serious crimes of Spellman were not sexual."[26]

CHAPTER SIX

The War Years

O N OCTOBER 24, 1939, ARCHBISHOP SPELLMAN WENT TO THE White House at the request of President Roosevelt. Their relationship was about to enter a new phase that would lead to closer ties between Washington and the Vatican than had ever existed before. Over the course of the next several decades the foreign policy goals of the United States and the Holy See would prove to be the same, and, in the process, make Spellman an international power broker.

Cardinal Mundelein, who had acted as Roosevelt's primary representative to the Vatican, had died several weeks earlier, at the age of sixty-seven. He had been a rarity in the Catholic hierarchy—a liberal and a supporter of the New Deal. Spellman was neither, but he had a background in international affairs, from his years at the Vatican state department, that Mundelein had lacked. Moreover, Spellman had better Vatican contacts than Mundelein had had and knew more of the Vatican thinking. Roosevelt would find such qualities useful, especially when the United States entered the war in Europe.

The passing of the mantle to Spellman wasn't unexpected. During the past few years Spellman had increasingly represented Vatican positions in Washington, and, as a result of his friendship with Roosevelt's son James, Spellman had become a familiar figure at both the White House and Hyde Park. In 1936, Spellman had said mass in the Monroe Room at the White House, the first priest ever to do so. After Pacelli's visit, Roosevelt even felt out Spellman about the possibility of his representing the Church in Washington, apparently on a full-time basis. The intermediaries had been Judge John Joseph Burns and Tommy Corcoran, who had first brought the then Boston bishop to Roosevelt's attention. At the time, Spellman had immediately dismissed the suggestion. He wanted to be an archbishop and then a cardinal, and Boston had already been promised to him. "Impractical and impossible," was his assessment of the President's proposal.

Roosevelt may have wanted Spellman in Washington because he realized how little confidence Rome placed in Cicognani. Technically, the apostolic delegate was a religious representative with no diplomatic status, since the United States and the Vatican had no formal relations. But in practice, the delegate could have a great deal of quiet, unofficial influence as a representative of one of the most powerful organizations in the world. Early on, Spellman obviously had seized much of Cicognani's potential power.

Now, in 1939, not many of Roosevelt's men were happy that Spellman was succeeding Mundelein. They found the archbishop, if anything, far too political, "a hard-boiled politician," in the words of columnist Drew Pearson. Spellman alternated between his Janus faces when with the President's men. At times he was the humble bishop and at other times he was abrasive, devious, and arrogant. Mentioning Spellman one day, Roosevelt himself noted that the administration's best-known Catholic, Postmaster Farley, "doesn't like Spellman." "Nobody liked Spellman," James Rowe, a Roosevelt aide who later became a Washington attorney, reminisced. Yet when the archbishop spoke, whether about Vatican-U.S. relations, Franco's Spain, or Hitler's Germany, "everyone listened very closely," Rowe said.[1]

A political atmosphere conducive to the Spellman appointment was actually introduced by Cardinal Mundelein. Mundelein had died only a day after completing work on a radio address praising the administration. The speech, delivered instead by the cardinal's right-hand man, Bishop Bernard Sheil, became both a eulogy for Mundelein and a firm signal of support for the President: "In these critical years in Europe, we have the matchless political leadership in foreign affairs of President Roosevelt. . . ."

The tribute was considered necessary because of opposition largely by Irish and Italian Catholics in the United States to the administration's revised neutrality laws, a step toward aiding the British. In terms of Church politics, the Mundelein statement was considered an accommodation necessary to encourage Roosevelt to send a representative to the Vatican. There was fear that Catholic opposition to the President's foreign policy would jeopardize the plans that Spellman and Joe Kennedy, in particular, had carefully nurtured. Thus, *L'Osservatore Romano,* the Vatican newspaper, quoted passages from Sheil's speech, an act that was viewed in Washington as papal support for Roosevelt.

Such support had the desired effect. A short while later, Roosevelt told Spellman that plans for a special mission to the Holy See were finally jelled. The New York archbishop, who had worked toward this for years, was gratified. He was heartened to see a level of understanding develop between the Holy See and his country, and he hoped that it would undercut the Vatican's disdainful attitude toward America. An increased reliance on the United States, he believed, would go a long way toward deflecting the negative sentiment. Thus, for the first time in more than seventy years, the United States would have formal relations with the Church. Spellman knew that Roosevelt was taking a substantial risk, but one that had been well considered.

The appointment was a potential political minefield. It meant bucking the Protestant establishment, which could prove disastrous for any politician. There was still a large body of anti-Catholic sentiment, as the President knew, if only from his wife. Eleanor half-believed stories about papist plots and she adhered to some of the bigoted propaganda against Catholics that had been part of her upbringing. For all her sophistication and intolerance of most forms of prejudice, she was wary of Catholics and she especially disliked Spellman, who personified to her the worst political aspects of the Church. "Eleanor still believed the anti-Catholic nonsense she heard during her childhood," recalled Joseph Alsop, political columnist and Eleanor's cousin.[2]

This issue of a Vatican representative was clouded by an unfortunate history. From 1848 until 1868 the United States had sent ministers and chargés d'affaires to the Papal States. Appropriations for those legations had been discontinued because of a belief in certain quarters that the Pope had Confederate sympathies and because Protestants had been outraged when, in 1868, a Protestant minister was forced to hold church services outside Rome. Moreover, political developments in Washington resulted in the severing of the Vatican links. By the mid-nineteenth century, some congressmen were so overtly hostile to Catholicism that the sins of the Pope were actually debated in Congress. The Know-Nothing movement, which espoused the goal of destroying papal power in America, had sent eight senators and dozens of representatives to Washington in 1854.

Though the Vatican had pursued closer links with the United States since the early 1930s, the need for such a relationship was seen in Rome as being greater than ever as a result of what was happening in Europe. The Pope was making many efforts to preserve the peace. He had even proposed a conference to be attended by

Britain, France, Germany, Italy, and Poland to determine how to avoid war. The suggestion was ignored and, as German threats to Poland grew more ferocious, the Pope was urged by the French ambassador to condemn Hitler. The Pope's response was indirect and established a pattern of behavior on the part of the papacy that led to charges that the Church was morally leaderless. On August 24, Pius made his last appeal for peace, in which he uttered the often-repeated phrase: "Nothing is lost with peace: everything may be lost with war." Nazism wasn't mentioned. Pope Pius XII, a man raised in the world of the Vatican state department, where shadings of meaning were often expressed in the faintest pastels, was incapable of taking a bold position. As the war progressed, the Vatican looked more like a tiny secular state jockeying to maintain its neutrality than like a moral leader. Because of the persecution of the Church in Poland, the Vatican Radio carried reports on atrocities committed there, and later there were reports on religious conditions in Germany. But in 1941 the Vatican Radio ceased making references to Germany. The British believed the Pope had been bullied into halting the broadcasts by the Germans, but the Holy See said the action taken by the Pope had nothing to do with Germany.[3] One possible reason was the Nazi distortion of Vatican broadcasts for their own propaganda purposes. In any event, the Pope wanted to have diplomatic relations with as many countries as possible, especially the United States, as an outward sign of his neutrality.

Roosevelt didn't resume relations with the Vatican as a favor to Catholics. He was far too astute a politician to underestimate the pitfalls of what he contemplated. But Secretary of State Cordell Hull and his assistant Sumner Welles urged the recognition that Rome wanted. Religion, they argued, wasn't the key factor. The Vatican was a prime listening post for the entire continent. If the United States were drawn into war, information gathered in Rome could be vital. The move turned out to be wise.

Roosevelt told Spellman that, in a deft maneuver, he intended to establish the U.S. mission to the Vatican during a congressional break—though it would not require congressional approval. Congress was expected to recess in November, after revising the Neutrality Act, and stay out until January. Potentially embarrassing counterforces wouldn't be given time to muster. In an attempt to deflect criticism, the head of the mission would be called a representative, not an ambassador, but this would be a distinction that fooled few. The men Roosevelt mentioned as candidates for the post were Myron Taylor, former chairman of United States Steel Corporation, who was working on the problem of displaced refugees in Europe; and Breckinridge Long, the former U.S. ambassador to Italy. Both men were well-known Protestants, which was expected to ease the acceptance of whomever Roosevelt chose.

Spellman marveled at Roosevelt's own deviousness, and the next day he submitted a report on his meeting with the President to Luigi Cardinal Maglione, the papal secretary of state. In writing directly to Maglione, Spellman bypassed Cicognani, who, because of his position, was supposed to be a party to all Vatican dealings with the administration. That the apostolic delegate was angered by the slight was obvious when he wrote Spellman a letter saying the Pope was pleased. Observing protocol, the Pope had passed his response through the delegate. Cicognani pointedly added that the Pope hoped that "Your Excellency as well as I will make opportune overtures to the President, that he may carry out his proposal." Thus, Cicognani made it clear that he wanted to have a hand in future negotiations. Spellman craftily rewrote the delegate's letter, deleting any references to Cicognani playing a role and focusing on the Holy See's pleasure with the progress to date. Then he took Cicognani's letter to the President, thereby undermining the apostolic delegate once again.[4]

The next Spellman-Roosevelt meeting was scheduled for December 7. To avoid any speculation about what the New York archbishop was doing in Washington, Roosevelt left word that Spellman should "come in the back way." As the Church politician and the President huddled together at the appointed time, Roosevelt said he probably would announce the Vatican mission on Christmas Day, when goodwill should be running high. The archbishop gave the President confirmation of the Vatican support. Spellman had a right to consider that he had performed well. He had completed one of the major assignments the Pope had given him. Moreover, he had solidified his relationship with the President and bound the Vatican and his country closer together. He had made an even bigger fool out of Cicognani.

"The President was wonderful to me," Spellman wrote in his diary on December 7 and 8. "Luncheon lasted 1 hour and a half and he agreed to recognize Vatican and send either Myron Taylor or Harry Woodring as Ambassador. He agreed to make announcement himself at Xmas as my letter from the Delegate which I left with the President was sufficient to give official assent of the Holy See. It was a wonderful day!!"

Two days before Christmas, Spellman was once again at the White House. Roosevelt handed Spellman a handwritten letter to the Pope announcing Myron Taylor as the personal representative to the Vatican. Spellman, circumventing Cicognani once again, sent the text of the note to the Vatican by telegraph.

When publicizing the move, Roosevelt tried to diminish some of the impact. He sent letters on Christmas Eve to George A. Buttrick, president of the Federal Council of the Churches of Christ in America, and Rabbi Cyrus Adler, president of the Jewish Theological

Seminary of America. He wrote about the need for cooperation among churches to promote peace. Those letters were released to the press along with the disclosure about the Vatican mission. The move didn't muffle the roar of outrage. Protestant organizations around the nation fired off letters and telegrams of protest. The President was denounced from pulpits, especially in the South. Outwardly, Roosevelt appeared unflappable in face of the backlash. Privately, he vented his spleen. For instance, he wrote to North Carolina Senator Josiah Bailey, a leading Baptist layman, that ". . . if some of my good Baptist brothers in Georgia had done a little preaching from the pulpit against the Ku Klux Klan in the 1920s, I would have a little more . . . respect for their Christianity."

Spellman jumped into the fray as soon as the story was released. Chancellor McIntyre issued a press release to newsmen, who had been alerted that something was in the wind. The archbishop's message was an inextricable lumping together of Americanism and Catholicism, of the sort that would mark Spellman's career. At this stage of his life, he was determined that the goals of his nation and the Vatican be one and the same: "As an American, living, working and willing to die for the welfare of my countrymen, all of them, I am very happy that President Roosevelt has harmonized the voice of Pope Pius XII with his own clarion call for peace among nations and peoples. . . ."

The archbishop wasn't willing either to ignore or try to quell the storm of controversy. He established a lifelong pattern of behavior. Spellman lashed out at his critics and, in turn, became a target of criticism. He fanned the flames of bigotry and the fear that Catholics wanted to subvert the American government. In the coming years, Spellman's face came to represent what for many people was formerly a faceless religious enemy.

On March 12, 1940, Spellman was invested with the pallium, a sacred wool vestment symbolizing the office of archbishop. He used the occasion to talk of Taylor's appointment. St. Patrick's Cathedral was jammed once again with some fifty-five hundred bishops, priests, monsignors, papal knights, and politicians. The archbishop spoke as the voice of his Church, the political voice that was meant to reflect the will of the nation's twenty-one million Catholics. Clad in the silver robes he had worn when consecrated a bishop, Spellman expressed gratitude that Roosevelt had appointed Taylor to the Vatican. But he made it seem that his critics opposed a far greater issue than an American official's presence at the papal court; they opposed world peace. Then Spellman said something that was bound to incite his critics even more. He scoffed at the separation of Church and State, discounting the importance of that concept to the nation: "The only reason non-approvalists seem to have for their position is the shibboleth of separation of Church and State."

Spellman never would recognize such a division. His position touched off a round of bitter criticism. Ministers across the country denounced him. Typical was the response of Louis D. Newton, associate secretary of the Baptist World Alliance: "Your apparent ridicule of us in holding this 'shibboleth' will serve, I fancy, to stir many an American to yet firmer conviction regarding the priceless and precious principle of religious liberty." Spellman was little bothered by his critics. By speaking out in such a fashion, he intended to chip away at the wall of Church and State in America until it was leveled.

Roosevelt publicly stayed as far above the conflict as he could. Privately, he tried to gain from the controversial appointment. He wanted leverage in his position with the Vatican. The President himself briefed Taylor for his first meeting with the Pope and Cardinal Maglione. The delegate was to convey a stern message. Taylor, the President said, "might express the thought that there is a great deal of anti-Jewish feeling in the archdioceses of Brooklyn, Baltimore, and Detroit and that this feeling is said to be encouraged by the Church."[5] The message was clear to anyone who knew anything about Church-State politics. The bishops of those sees were all anti-Roosevelt. In Brooklyn and Baltimore, they were Irish-American isolationists who opposed attempts to aid the British. The Detroit archbishop protected Father Coughlin, who was still broadcasting his anti–New Deal venom.

Roosevelt's motives, however, were more complex than simply wanting to curb criticism. The President made tentative gestures to play a hand in Church appointments. He wanted a voice in picking the man who would succeed Mundelein in Chicago. As Roosevelt well knew, the conservative Church hierarchy wanted a conservative in the job. Roosevelt wanted someone who would welcome his own brand of politics. Thus, he asked Frank Walker, the only Catholic in the cabinet, to let Spellman know that the White House thought Sheil would make a good candidate.

"There will be an active and militant Irish-Catholic reactionism in this country for at least a generation if the wrong man is appointed archbishop of Chicago," Harold Ickes, the secretary of the interior, warned the President. Sheil, Ickes noted, "has always seen social and economic questions through Mundelein's eyes. He is about the only prominent churchman in the country who has even a faint coloration of liberalism."[6]

The issue of heads of state appointing Church hierarchy had been a thorny one in Rome for centuries. The leaders of most Latin American countries nominated bishops and cardinals, as did such European powers as Spain, Portugal, and Italy. The Pope didn't want to grant that power to Washington if he could help it. Besides, Sheil was considered too liberal in Vatican circles to be elevated. Thus, the Pope dismissed Roosevelt's wishes. Bishop Samuel Stritch of Milwaukee received the nod, and this dented Roosevelt's prestige. "Well, you and I have had a pretty severe blow today in Chicago," he told Ickes, over lunch in the Oval Office.[7]

Ickes, of course, was upset. He faulted Roosevelt for not pushing Rome harder. "I do not think that the Vatican would have dared turn him (the President) down if he had made strong representations," Ickes recorded in his diary. In going over what happened, Ickes was clear on one issue. Roosevelt hadn't wasted his time trying to get Spellman to lead the Sheil bandwagon. "The President said he could not depend on Archbishop Spellman," Ickes recorded. "Spellman was much too concerned with his own red hat."[8]

What now maddened the President was a report that Stritch was not only a conservative but even favorably disposed toward Coughlin. Spellman, who had warily watched Roosevelt's reaction to the Chicago appointment, now rushed to place himself at the President's disposal. He hastened to reassure Roosevelt that all was well. On February 5, 1940, he wrote Roosevelt: "Quite naturally I was upset at these reports and I assumed to telephone to Milwaukee to ask Archbishop Stritch the precise question whether or not he was unfavorable to your administration. He categorically and emphatically denied it. . . . In all sincerity and frankness I believe him to be a supporter of your administration as *I certainly am proud and privileged to be.*"*

Next, Roosevelt tried to have Sheil named archbishop of Washington as a way of undercutting Baltimore Archbishop Michael J. Curley, an anti–New Dealer who had Washington as part of his see. When Myron Taylor broached the subject with the shrewd Cardinal Maglione, the issue was deftly avoided. Maglione, feigning helplessness, said that such appointments were in the hands of the Sacred Consistorial Congregation.[9] In reality, the man who moved on such matters was the Pope. Pacelli, probably with Spellman's encouragement, wasn't about to give Sheil anything that would bring him closer to the President. Spellman wanted the path to the White House clear for himself.

As far as Roosevelt was concerned, he received few benefits and a lot of criticism for having done the Vatican the favor of placing a representative there. He lost twice on the Sheil moves. Certain bishops still opposed him. Coughlin was not only still on the air but also published a pro-Nazi, anti-Semitic, anti–New Deal magazine, *Social Justice*.

According to several accounts, the President decided that since the Catholic hierarchy needed a greater reason than had been put forth to date to silence Coughlin, he would provide it. Roosevelt evidently turned to New Deal supporter Monsignor Francis J. Haas,

*Spellman's emphasis.

chairman of the sociology department at Catholic University. He sent Haas to tell Spellman that if Coughlin weren't taken off the air once and for all, the Internal Revenue Service would be ready to look into the personal taxes of each of the nation's Roman Catholic archbishops.[10]

Such a prospect would terrify any archbishop. Millions of dollars flowed through their fingers each year; few, if any, archbishops would emerge unsullied from a tax investigation. Their personal finances were in a vague form. Often, gifts to the Church were given directly to them, and many archbishops used the money for personal as well as Church matters. It was difficult to determine where one such use stopped and the other began. All archbishops spent lavishly. Spellman routinely gave presents to friends in Rome; he knew from his Vatican days that Church officials appreciated expensive gifts. He gave gold watches, grand pianos, tapestries, jewels, and, of course, money to the Pope and other men of prominence. Even the Pope's white-and-gold electric shaver came from Spellman. Besides, Spellman had an unusual payroll that his counterparts did not. He was rumored to have a number of informants in Rome, mostly poor monsignors, who kept him abreast of Vatican political undercurrents in return for the thousands of dollars he gave them as "donations."

Thus, Coughlin went off the air in 1940. In the end, the priest said he had "bowed to the orders of superiors."

Roosevelt had reason to be sensitive about the radio priest. Nineteen forty was an election year and the President had cause to worry about the Catholic vote. Jim Farley had walked out on the President over the third-term issue. Moreover, the Vatican, talking through Spellman, expressed its unhappiness with Roosevelt's trying to meddle in Church politics. The method Spellman chose was one that Roosevelt could easily understand. It was an example of one calculating politician's striking out at another.

Shortly after arriving in New York, Spellman started having private lunches at his residence with prominent guests. They were often businessmen, politicians, diplomats, military leaders, and even entertainers such as Gene Kelly and Loretta Young. Spellman, when dining with a guest who could help him or his Church in the political arena, always had a specialist from his staff at the table to question the person in order to glean as much information as possible. So that people spoke freely, he insisted that such encounters were off the record.

On August 23, 1940, the rule against going public was broken as a warning to Roosevelt. The guest was the Republican presidential candidate Wendell Willkie. Spellman had made it very plain that he wanted Willkie to visit the Powerhouse, even sending a personal emissary to the candidate when he was campaigning in Colorado Springs. After the lunch Spellman told the Republican he could tell the press about their meeting.

When Willkie made his announcement, the implications were startling. The New York *Daily News,* considered the newspaper of most of the city's Catholics, prominently printed a story on page two that began: "At a meeting of deep political significance, Wendell Willkie, Republican candidate for President, was the guest yesterday of Francis J. Spellman, at the Madison Avenue residence of the Vatican's trusted adviser and confidant. . . ." The story noted frosty relations of late between the Vatican and Roosevelt. "Willkie's supporters were spreading the hopeful wish last night that Catholic support, long a powerful bulwark of F.D.R.'s political strength, would swerve from the New Deal and give its strength to Willkie," the report stated.

Roosevelt recognized a power play when he saw one. He knew well the respect with which Catholics held their archbishops and that the gesture couldn't be treated lightly. The message wasn't lost on other politicians either. Spellman was a man on whose good side they wanted to remain. The President hastened to neutralize the impression that Spellman had created. Just what he did to placate Spellman wasn't clear. For his part, Spellman probably believed Roosevelt was going to win, and he wanted to stick with a winner. In any case, only five days after the Willkie visit, the President had Spellman to lunch at Hyde Park. The press was told well in advance about the archbishop's coming.

Thus, the archbishop and the President were helping each other again as the late afternoon sky darkened over Fordham University on Saturday, October 29, 1940. Excitement swirled through the brisk, autumn air as thousands of people gathered around the open field in front of the school. In the center of the grassy expanse, the five hundred twenty-five members of the university's Reserve Officers Training Corps stood stiffly at attention. They faced a black limousine convertible containing Spellman and Roosevelt. Roosevelt's voice rang over a public-address system as he told the cadets how proud he was that they were learning "how best to defend America." Spellman, who had replaced Governor Lehman in the seat of honor next to the President as soon as the presidential party had arrived, sat smiling.

Roosevelt's presence at the small Catholic college was vivid testimony to the political skills of both men and the high regard that the administration placed on the Catholic vote. Each man got what he wanted. Roosevelt publicly received the archbishop's blessing for his controversial third-term candidacy. In turn, Spellman's influence with the White House was made obvious to political observers across the nation. The archbishop and the President basked in the publicity, as news photographers furiously snapped pictures of them together.

Soon, the importance of Spellman's domestic role would be forever overshadowed by the one the President cast for him as a key American figure who shaped the international affairs of his nation, his Church, and other countries. More than any other aspect of his career, Spellman's influence as an international power broker contributed the most to his rise and fall as a master politician both in his country and his Church. For the next quarter-century, he was destined to be the celebrated prelate who blessed the crusades of the American empire—a figure who both publicly and clandestinely worked actively to expand his country's influence around the globe.

In March 1942, Spellman was angry. The Vatican cast him in an untenable position with Roosevelt and touched off a wave of anti-Catholic sentiment in the United States. Only four months after Pearl Harbor, a Japanese mission was accredited to the Holy See, an action that caught the archbishop flatfooted. Spellman had to respond in a way that neither offended the Pope nor riled the White House further. Ironically, only three months earlier, Spellman, a staunch patriot, had praised Catholics for being "outstanding in their loyalty to American ideals." Now it seemed to him that he had to start from scratch. He had to face the age-old issue of whether American Catholics owed their allegiance to Rome or to their homeland. He began constantly looking for ways to prove himself—and his religion—to the President.

The Holy See's action wasn't its first to embarrass the Church in America and elsewhere in the world. In his intense desire to appear neutral, the Pope—to the shock of many Americans—had in the previous year received the murderous Anté Pavelic, the Nazi puppet who had seized power in Croatia. To his credit, Pius had initially intervened to stop a Pavelic plan to send all the nation's Jews to Germany and thus some people were spared. But the Pope did all too little. The Pavelic regime slaughtered hundreds of thousands of Orthodox Serbs, who refused to convert to the Catholic Church, while the Pope remained silent. The archbishop of Zagreb, Aloysius Stepinac, belatedly criticized the government in 1943 for policies that had taken place for several years. Stepinac's role in the reign of terror was questionable and there were Catholic priests who had participated in the massacres.[11]

Spellman became aware of the Vatican-Japanese agreement only a day before Roosevelt, when he received a memorandum from Rome that outlined the rationale for the controversial step: ". . . the presence in the Vatican of missions of various belligerent countries which are at war with each other does not diminish but rather emphasizes the strictest impartiality of the Holy See."[12] As Spellman realized, the act could only embitter Americans in general and Roosevelt in particular. The next day Spellman received a letter expressing the President's disgust. Roosevelt said a "great error of judgment was made . . . there must have been a dosen [sic] ways of deferring the action, for one reason or another, at this time." The President wearily concluded, "I shall say nothing officially, in all probability, but my heart is torn because it is bound to get out and there will be definitely a bad reaction to thus [sic] unnecessary move."[13] Spellman's heart was torn as well. At this stage of his life, he spent his days proving his country and his Church worthy of one another, while the Vatican and Washington looked upon each other suspiciously. The archbishop of New York had to strike a balance between the two.

Though angry, Roosevelt wasn't vexed at Spellman. To date, the archbishop had been one of his biggest boosters on the war effort. He couldn't blame Spellman for the insensitivity of Vatican politics. Only the previous fall, Spellman had bucked isolationists within the hierarchy and firmly supported Roosevelt's controversial military draft. On the eve of the first drawing of Selective Service System numbers, the President had once again made a highly publicized trip to Fordham, where he reviewed the ROTC units with Spellman at his elbow. When Roosevelt pulled the first SSS number the next day, he read a message from a rabbi, a minister, and a priest. The Catholic statement—Spellman's—was the most militant: "I do believe it is better to have protection and not need it than to need protection and not have it.

"We really can no longer afford to be moles who cannot see or ostriches who will not see. . . . We Americans want peace and we shall be prepared for a peace, but not a peace whose definition is slavery or death."

The words contained hints of the Cold War warrior that Spellman one day would become, but in 1941 these words were of great encouragement to a President trying to gain support for an unpopular war buildup. The President took such outward displays of confidence into account when settling his debts with Spellman. Through Representative John McCormack, for instance, Spellman asked Roosevelt to help get a shipload of goods through British blockades to the Vatican; Roosevelt saw to it that the mission was carried out.[14] On occasion, the President even involved himself in trivial concerns of the archbishop's. The President dropped a note to Donald M. Nelson, chairman of the War Production Board, telling him to fix Spellman's furnace: "A little bird tells me that the furnace at 51st Street and Madison Avenue, New York City, really does need repairs. It happens to be the residence of Archbishop Spellman, and I hear this repair has been turned down for priority. . . . Don't say anything about it to anyone, but I really think the Archbishop ought to be kept warm during the winter!"[15]

Spellman remained the primary conduit between the Vatican and Washington, despite Myron Taylor's new position at the Holy See. The archbishop, more than Taylor, had the contacts and the instincts to be of help to both the President and the Pope whenever the occasion arose. As war fever swept the country, the demands on Spellman's time increased exponentially. The Pope appointed him military vicar of the armed forces in the United States, a demanding job, and one that Spellman took most seriously. The thirst for military adventure that he had sought when he applied to become a chaplain years before had been postponed, not forgotten. Now, he was the greatest chaplain of them all. Rapidly, he beefed up their ranks and personally toured military bases in North America to understand better the needs of the men who served him.

As his duties escalated, Spellman hired men to help him. He appointed John O'Hara, the former president of Notre Dame, as his auxiliary bishop in charge of the military. O'Hara was a good organizer and administrator, and Spellman liked his conservatism. Though initially reluctant about coming to work for Spellman, O'Hara found himself well rewarded by being made a bishop and given juicy assignments. One of his earliest missions was war-related and bore on Spellman's role as overseer of the Church in Latin America. The task reflected the archbishop's long pent-up nationalism and the level of cooperation he gave to his government.

Shortly after Spellman became archbishop of New York, the archbishop of Colombia, Ismael Perdomo, issued an anti-American pastoral letter declaring that the United States would swallow the whole of Latin America and was funding Protestant missionaries to convert Latin Catholics. The matter was brought to Spellman's attention by the U.S. minister to Colombia, Spruille Braden, who had his hands full with anti-American Catholic priests, especially "subversive" Jesuits: "We had a problem in Colombia, which one gets whenever there is a Spanish priesthood in Latin America . . . they were tied in with the Nazis and doing some pretty bad subversive espionage down there."[16]

Whether Spellman assisted Braden with the pro-Axis Jesuits isn't known, but his nationalism was pricked by the Perdomo letter. After years of listening to his country downgraded in Rome, Spellman was in a position to strike a blow for America. He turned to O'Hara, an archconservative who had been born in Latin America and spoke excellent Spanish. O'Hara was sent by Spellman to Bogotá as a guest of the U.S. embassy. As an emissary of the powerful Spellman, O'Hara had a devastating effect on Perdomo. In Braden's presence, O'Hara humiliatingly censured the Latin archbishop. Anything Perdomo wrote about the United States henceforth had to be shown to Braden before being released. "You're to submit it to the ambassador for his review and approval first before it is to be made public in any way, shape, or manner," O'Hara told him.[17]

Braden found it strange that an American priest could give orders to a Latin archbishop. Nonetheless, he was pleased, just as he enjoyed O'Hara's making protocol visits with him. "It was good theater," Braden remarked.[18] Spellman enjoyed the display even more. The American Church had asserted itself.

With his growing infiuence, Spellman realized that he needed an international affairs expert on his staff. O'Hara's expertise was confined to Latin America. He plucked from the Brooklyn archdiocese—over the objections of Archbishop Thomas E. Molloy—a priest named James H. Griffiths, who was an unlikely Spellman man. The heavyset, red-faced Griffiths was brilliant. Rome-educated, he spoke a half-dozen languages fluently and had a passion for law and international affairs. He also had a passion for brandy and was a raconteur who held other priests spellbound with his stories. Griffiths was an oddity in more ways than one. He couldn't work during the morning or do anything else but sleep. He awakened at noon and worked through the night.

Griffiths proved invaluable. He instinctively understood diplomatic subtlety, and the position papers he drafted for Spellman on topics as wide-ranging as the internationalization of Jerusalem and the postwar election prospects of Italy were so well done that he earned the respect of the Office of Strategic Services. More important, he gained Spellman's respect. A stickler for orderliness, Spellman liked his chancery and his schedule run like clockwork. Yet he put up with Griffiths's erratic behavior because he recognized what an asset the priest was.

Thus, when Spellman was offered an unprecedented opportunity by Roosevelt that would necessitate leaving his archdiocese for months on end, Spellman felt comfortable in accepting the challenge. Chancellor McIntyre, always a reliable workhorse, could run the routine business of the archdiocese while he would be away. Griffiths would be in place to assist him with international affairs. The astounding proposal Roosevelt put forth was that Spellman act as a clandestine agent for him in the far corners of the world. It would be the archbishop's job to contact chiefs of state in the Middle East, Europe, Asia, and Africa. He would carry messages for the President, present the American point of view—forcefully when necessary—and act as Roosevelt's eyes and ears.

The President made the astonishing proposal for a number of reasons: Spellman's Church office would mask the nature of his White House role. As military vicar, Spellman had an excuse to meet with generals and enlisted men, and to travel in war zones. As a ranking churchman, he could visit the Vatican frequently and possibly enter nations where American diplomats could not. Yet another factor must have entered into Roosevelt's calculations. Spellman was tough: he made a beeline for whatever was his objective, letting little stand in his way. Finally, the archbishop didn't have to stand on the protocol that often inhibited official diplomats.

The President knew his man. The assignment appealed to Spellman on a number of levels. He relished the intrigue, similar to that of his days at the Vatican secretariat of state. Of greater importance, the President offered him an opportunity to wield more power than any other American religious figure had ever had. Spellman would move as an equal among the greatest figures on the world political stage. While the assignment appealed to Spellman's Americanism, it also dazzled him as a churchman. He saw no division between his nationalism and his religion. He believed he could be the President's eyes and ears while serving the same function for the Pope. Thus, he was offered an exceptional opportunity to help both his country and his Church, and to profit in both realms simultaneously.

Thus, in 1943, Spellman embarked on a lengthy journey that took him to Europe, Africa, and the Middle East. In the process, he became a celebrity and a subject of mystery both at home and abroad. In the ensuing months, there were newsreels, radio reports, and reams of newspaper and magazine articles about his travels. He was shown in planes, troop ships, trucks, jeeps, and horse carts, facing hazards of all kinds. Press photographers captured him saying mass in ruins and on runways, visiting the wounded in hospitals, and blessing doughboys in the trenches as well as their bombs, tanks, machine guns, and bullets. But few people were certain about what the archbishop did during his far-flung travels. His clandestine work raised questions at home about the role of a religious figure involved deeply in government affairs, and abroad he was a source of worry for the Axis.

On February 16, 1943, Spellman was escorted by a Spanish soldier into the large, airy waiting room in the old Pardo Palace in Madrid. He had come to see Generalissimo Francisco Franco, who had set up his controversial government in this bastion of Old World aristocracy that smelled of centuries of court intrigue. The reception room was decorated with antiques, ornate mirrored walls, and rock-crystal chandeliers. The carpet on which Spellman stood was designed for the dimensions of the room and bore the date 1825.

The meeting with Franco was typical of those that Spellman had with the world leaders he approached for Roosevelt. Spellman usually conveyed a message that Roosevelt was unhappy, very unhappy. The archbishop's assignment was to stab fear into Franco's heart. Their conversation ranged over the many aspects of the raging war: Spanish and American attitudes; military, economic, and religious matters. Franco was in favor of a negotiated peace with Germany, but Spellman told him this was an impossibility. The archbishop, as he later related to Roosevelt, presented "clearly to him our American position and our realistic appreciation that we knew the terrors, devastation, and sorrows and sufferings of war, but we realized, too, that we had no alternative."[19]

Roosevelt wanted to worry Franco. It was time the Spaniard started thinking about hard realities, not what he would like to see happen. It was Spellman's job to get Franco to wonder what would become of him when the war ended and the United States had won. Franco, as Spellman pointed out to the Spaniard, wasn't America's friend. The President wanted Franco to disavow Germany, and he wanted anti-American propaganda ended. German military successes were treated in the Spanish press in heroic proportions but Allied successes were dismissed. In light of the aid that Germany gave to Franco during the Spanish Civil War, that favoritism wasn't surprising. But Spellman conveyed to *Il Caudillo* that to continue such behavior was unwise. The archbishop reported to the President that his mission was successful. "There will be a gradual modification of the misleading headlines in the papers, and I trust that I presented to him . . . America's attitude toward the war," Spellman wrote.[20]

When the meeting ended Spellman rushed back to the American embassy and dictated his version of the encounter, which was forwarded to the White House. Evident from his dispatch was that, while he was up to his neck in the policies of his government, he was still very much the churchman. He cleverly promoted Vatican policies with Roosevelt, just as he promoted the President's policies with others. Franco had the Church's firm support. Barring a return of the Spanish monarchy, the Church wanted to see the generalissimo in power. The Vatican's motives were obvious: Franco had granted many religious concessions to the Church and he was rabidly anti-Communist.

Thus, when filing his report Spellman presented the Vatican line on Franco to Roosevelt: "My impressions of him are in accordance with his reputation as a very sincere, serious and healthy middle-aged man," who, Spellman lamented, "could not understand America's attitude toward Russia." He repeated for the President the Spaniard's "solemn textual words when he said: 'The only thing that can make Spain fight is Communism.' "[21] The archbishop remained a staunch Franco defender, just as his Church was. After all, as *Time* magazine pointed out in its February 23, 1943, edition, the generalissimo ran a "Fascist dictatorship which claimed that the Spanish Civil War was a crusade for the Roman Catholic Church."

When he flew from Madrid to Rome across the red-and-gold Spanish soil, there was a great deal of speculation within the diplomatic corps about the nature of Spellman's assignment, which was picked up in the international press. *Time,* for example, noted that it was "possible that he had been called to discuss political problems involving the servants of the Church. Whatever his mission, Archbishop Spellman's visit concentrated the attention of world diplomats on the Vatican. . . ." Such stories generated letters to the State Department about Spellman's activities. "Was Archbishop Spellman at the Vatican on a personal mission or did his visit purely concern religious matters?'' a typical letter asked. Warily, the State Department formulated a vague reply: "It is my understanding that the Archbishop's journey was undertaken as Military Vicar of the United States Army. . . . His trip was not sponsored nor undertaken on behalf of the State Department.'' Technically, the reply was true; Spellman reported directly to the President.

Spellman remained in Rome for two weeks. The first few days, he disappeared each morning into the Pope's top-floor apartment. There they talked quietly in Pius's private office, whose great windows overlooked St. Peter's Square. The meetings, which sometimes lasted until 9 P.M., were so private that not even the Pope's chamberlain was admitted. Such clandestine behavior only heightened gossip. The Japanese, who, like Roosevelt, had wanted a mission at the Vatican to serve as a listening post, were especially concerned. On February 13, Ken Harada, Japan's envoy to the Holy See, was instructed by Tokyo to "find out what Spellman is after and what he does.''[22]

Harada's task wasn't easy. Rumors flourished and official Vatican sources were useless. When Vatican Secretary of State Maglione "sincerely assured" Harada that Spellman was "not charged with any political mission,'' Harada continued tapping all the sources he could muster. Finally, he reported what seemed the most logical reason for Spellman's visit. "The Finnish minister told me that he heard from a spy that Spellman was trying to divorce the Axis countries, so I am watching for anything that would indicate this,'' Harada secretly cabled Tokyo.[23]

While moving mysteriously through Vatican corridors, Spellman met with an intriguing variety of diplomats and churchmen, including Prince Erwin Lobkowicz, the representative to the Holy See from Pavelic's Croatia, and the Italians who were conspiring to overthrow Mussolini. Despite Maglione's soothing words to Harada, Spellman was obviously wading in the turbulent waters of international intrigue.

Before he left Rome, Spellman was charged by the Pope with yet another responsibility. The archbishop must do what he could to help Italy now that it was so obvious the country was a loser in war. The Pope's nationalism was evident in a controversial letter of regret he sent to Luigi Cardinal Lavitrano, the archbishop of Palermo, which had been bombed by the Allies a week before Spellman arrived in Rome. Pius hadn't sent similar letters to Church leaders in foreign towns or cities that were destroyed by fascist bombs. While Spellman ignored such favoritism, not all American priests could. Vincent A. McCormick, an American Jesuit working in Rome, was disgusted by what he viewed as papal hypocrisy. Like Spellman and O'Connell years earlier, McCormick was subjected to more than his share of anti-Americanism at the Vatican, and he now bitterly resented the Vatican's partisanship.

"Holy See seems to manifest very keen interest in sufferings of

[the] civilian population when the population is Italian," McCormick noted in his diary. The priest recounted how high-level ecclesiastics were "fully aware of what cruel sufferings" Italians had inflicted on Greece, Croatia, and Slovenia, including the "burning of whole towns, [and] murder of innocent hostages in revenge." There were no letters in those cases, McCormick lamented: "Would that I were miles away from here, in some place where I could forget it all!"[24]

The Pope, who remained silent about Nazi and fascist atrocities, wanted his homeland to emerge from defeat as unscathed as possible. At the Pope's instigation Spellman sent a long letter to Roosevelt pleading the Italian case. The Italians, the archbishop wrote, were desperately awaiting their liberation by America and were "suffering tremendously." Anti-German feelings among Italians, he said, were rampant. "The only obstacles to peace that I see are Mussolini and the fact that if peace were obtained, then Germans would retaliate by bombing Rome," he added. Spellman, however, apparently had already done what he could to help remove the first obstacle: Mussolini would soon crash down from the heights of power.[25]

When Spellman left Rome, he was shrouded in mystery. Armed with presidential letters to Allied commanders, he was assured a royal welcome wherever he went and access to whomever he wanted to meet. For a man such as Spellman, all this was the answer to a dream. The archbishop relished the special attention, publicity, and cloak-and-dagger aura that surrounded him, and he juggled his many roles with ease. Effortlessly, Spellman the churchman became Spellman the diplomat, and then he was Spellman the military vicar.

The latter was the most visible of his assignments. When Spellman visited troops they were quite moved that a man of his lofty office had come to see them. He was the highest-ranking religious figure of any faith to visit front lines, and the gesture was more than appreciated. Wherever he went, hundreds of men gathered around him, wanting to say a word, or even just to touch him so they could write home that they had met the archbishop. At times his masses were attended by thousands, and they were often said within the sight of lazy clouds of smoke from bombs and punctuated by screams and muffled explosions. At Spellman's direction, chaplains who accompanied him took down the names and addresses of the young men Spellman met; his secretaries in New York later sent their families notes saying the archbishop had met their sons. Spellman dressed in military fatigues and often gave away articles of his clothing. He had bags of campaign hats that he gave to soldiers, sailors, and marines. At times, he took off his field jacket and gave it to a soldier, while an aide ran to fetch him another.

The archbishop, however, didn't spend all his time with the men in the foxholes. He made sure he met Dwight Eisenhower, Mark Clark, George Patton, and the other military leaders who ran the

Allied war effort. The archbishop used his letters of introduction, which had an astonishing effect on the military leaders. The presidential letters produced a deference that Spellman quite enjoyed, but then his own office often had much the same effect on these men. In the archbishop, the officers found a passionate supporter of the military.

Spellman admired men of war, and he liked chaplains because they exposed themselves to the heat of battle and ministered to the needs of men who could die at any moment. Spellman also loved to discuss military and political strategy with ranking officers. His conservative philosophy, belief in the righteousness of America, and deep suspicions of the Russians were shared by many of the military men he met, and they appreciated his enthusiasm for what they did. "The military vicar was a very sophisticated military and political thinker," General Albert C. Wedemeyer would recall. "He thought in terms of what happened in one country in one part of the world and how it affected another on the other side of the world."[26]

Spellman saw war in black-and-white terms, and there was no doubt that he believed God was on the American side. Before he had even left the United States, he had done much to cast the Allied effort as a Christian crusade. "The abandonment of Christ and His teachings, in personal life, in social life, in civic life and in international life, has brought us to the end of the world we have known," he stated. "Morale means courage, readiness to serve, high purpose. Morals is the sense of right and wrong, divinely taught, which makes a man strong in his duty to God, and morale makes him strong in his duty to country. . . . Religion and patriotism support and strengthen each other. . . ." This fusion of religion and patriotism worked well during World War II, when Spellman could denounce Hitler as the "anti-Christ," giving an ominous religious overtone to the Allied effort.

In late March 1943, Spellman appeared in London. His visits to military encampments had been cut short by the death of Arthur Cardinal Hinsley, the ranking Catholic churchman in England. On March 23, Spellman was among the six thousand people, including representatives of presidents, kings, foreign armies, and the Church, who filled Westminster Cathedral for the solemn funeral mass. Among the notables were men whom Spellman already knew or soon came to know. Some were men Spellman had long wanted to meet, including Winston Churchill and Charles de Gaulle.

Several days later, Spellman dined with Churchill at 10 Downing Street. The guests included the Prime Minister's wife, his daughter Mary, and Brendan Bracken, British minister of information. As Spellman sat back, the first question Churchill posed was, "May I without irreverence ask you if you are a 'short snorter?'" The term referred to someone who crossed the ocean by air, still a rare feat in 1943. Upon crossing, passengers signed their names on a dollar bill, which was supposed to be kept on one's person. If any passenger was challenged to produce the bill but couldn't, he had to buy everyone else a round of drinks, or short snorts. Spellman produced his dollar with a wonderful smile. He loved to collect everything from stamps to mementos of important occasions. There was little chance he would not have the bill.

There were no records of Spellman's conversations with Churchill, except for innocuous exchanges that Spellman later wrote for magazines. The talks, however, must have touched upon the controversial matters of the Free French and the government of Ireland, both of which posed problems for Washington and London. While in London, Spellman was told to confront de Gaulle and read him Roosevelt's riot act. Since the Casablanca Conference, which Roosevelt had attended earlier in the year, the President was put out by de Gaulle's squabbling with General Henri Giraud about leadership of the Free French and what they should be doing next. Both Roosevelt and Churchill believed that too many important issues were at stake for the two Frenchmen to air their petty feuds publicly. Thus Roosevelt asked Spellman to shape up the general. The President knew Spellman wouldn't balk at taking on a prima donna like de Gaulle.

With the strength of the U.S. government and his own considerable ecclesiastic power looming behind him, the stubby Spellman met with the towering, imperious de Gaulle. Neither man said what transpired, but there was little doubt that Spellman was tough when he delivered Roosevelt's message. After the confrontation de Gaulle, at least temporarily, patched up his differences with Giraud. A military intelligence report on the confrontation noted that Spellman "very forcefully brought home to General de Gaulle the American feeling on need for unity among French and that certain compromises were essential. . . ." The report described de Gaulle as "noticeably affected. . . . This opinion as to constructive effect shared by Ambassador [A.J.D.] Biddle."[27]

Meanwhile, Ambassador Biddle cabled Roosevelt, asking if the President wanted to send Spellman to Ireland. The answer was yes. Thus Spellman's next mission was to try to ease Ireland's hostility toward England and to help the Allied effort. The job was practically impossible, but Spellman undertook it anyway. In Ireland, Spellman was feted wherever he went. Because of the strength of the Church there, Spellman's ecclesiastic rank and his background an an Irish-American made him an exceptionally exalted figure. Spellman was pleased by the Irish press—which dogged his footsteps and wrote warm stories about his visit, including colorful accounts of the masses he celebrated—and by the huge crowds and entourages of important officials.

While leading a very public life there, Spellman bided his time until he could put forth Roosevelt's cause. He seized an opportunity during a dinner given by the American minister to Ireland, David Gray, on the evening of March 30. The guests were Prime Minister Eamon de Valera; his deputy, Sean T. O'Kelly; the archbishop of Dublin, John C. McQuaid; a ranking British official, John Haffey; the Canadian high minister, John O' Kearney; and Monsignor Enriei, secretary to the nuncio of Ireland. Noticeably missing was Cardinal MacRory, the eighty-two-year-old archbishop of Armagh in Ulster. The old cardinal was widely respected by his people but, according to U.S. intelligence reports, was considered "extremely dangerous," because of the ease with which he whipped anti-British sentiment to a fever pitch.[28]

Even without MacRory, Spellman had his work cut out for him. The archbishop probably was given access to the U.S. intelligence profiles of the guests, and the summaries weren't encouraging. De Valera, for instance, was the opposite of the hard-headed Spellman. A mystic, the Prime Minister was obsessed with the wrongs done to Ireland over the centuries. "While clever," the intelligence report concluded, "[he is] believed incapable of being influenced by practical considerations or requirements." McQuaid, who had tremendous influence over de Valera, was considered "difficult."[29]

Undaunted, Spellman talked about the size and scope of the U.S. war effort. As de Valera sat in stony silence, Spellman firmly said that the United States intended to "prosecute war vigorously to a final and definite victory." The next day the archbishop met privately with the Prime Minister. Once again, he forcefully presented Roosevelt's case to a leader of a foreign government. Unlike Franco, the Prime Minister could see little to gain by moving closer to the Allies. Spellman was frustrated, but he wasn't about to drop the issue. That evening de Valera gave a dinner at Ivegh House, the seat of the Irish government. Warily, the Prime Minister steered the conversation away from politics, and he tried to keep the tone of the evening light by welcoming Spellman as a man of Irish ancestry. Irked by de Valera's unresponsiveness earlier in the day, Spellman proposed a toast: "To the President of the United States and the cause he serves!"[30]

Glasses were raised. With forced smiles, the Irish hosts participated. That was Spellman's only victory in Ireland.

Undismayed, Spellman returned to North Africa. The debts Roosevelt owed him were rapidly piling up, and the archbishop called in some of those presidential I.O.U.s. The Vatican wanted Spellman to pressure Roosevelt into helping Italian priests who were incarcerated in British prisons in Egypt. The diplomat Spellman was again churchman Spellman. The British apparently had imprisoned the priests because they had worked for the Axis, a situation not unlike that of the Jesuits Spruille Braden had complained about in Colombia. Spellman, though, said the priests were victims of a grave misunderstanding. The archbishop visited the jailed men and contended they were "treated not only arbitrarily and unfairly but also with unnecessary harshness."

Armed with Roosevelt's authorization, Spellman pressed his case upon Allied diplomats and military men in Cairo. To dramatize the priests' plight and generate sympathy in the press, Spellman personally dined with the prisoners on May 2. Because of the publicity and the favors he owed Spellman, Roosevelt pressured Churchill into seeing that the priests were released and allowed to leave the country.

During his travels, Spellman's high-level contacts expanded rapidly. In Baghdad he was presented to the Prince Regent, Abdoul Ilah, while in Iran he had an audience with King Mohammed Riza Shah Pahlevi, who sought his "permission to enter the war on the side of the Allies." In Egypt he was with King Farouk, and in Ethiopia with Haile Selassie. He spent three months traveling through the Middle East, speaking at times for Roosevelt and at other times for the Church, and, on occasion, for both. In Baghdad, for instance, he discussed Zionist control versus the internationalization of Palestine, an issue of interest in both Washington and Rome. "Spellman let it be known his sentiments did not favor overlordship by Jews in Palestine," a confidential embassy report to Washington stated.[31]

Toward the end of his sojourn, Spellman surfaced in Istanbul at a critical time. Axis forces had surrendered in North Africa. It appeared that neutral Turkey might join the Allies, just as Axis forces were trying to rally a new Balkan invasion. Spellman's presence fueled speculation that the archbishop would try to hasten Turkey's entry into the war, but it wasn't clear what he actually did.

While in Istanbul, Spellman made a protocol visit to a churchman he had known in Rome, Archbishop Angelo Roncalli, the earthy apostolic delegate to Turkey. If Spellman had been told that, in fifteen years, Roncalli would succeed Pacelli as Pope, he would have found the notion preposterous. In 1943 the two were a study in contrasts: Spellman gloried in moving among the elite like the religious leader of a medieval crusade who publicly blessed the troops while privately whispering secrets into the ears of kings. Roncalli was preoccupied with the suffering caused by war. He quietly helped thousands of Jews escape Nazi tyranny by issuing safe-conduct passes to them, certifying that the bearers were Catholics so they could stay in neutral Turkey until arranging passage to Palestine.

In Rome, Spellman was admired and feared as a man who could exert his influence at the highest level, whereas the worldly Vatican diplomats found Roncalli an embarrassment, an opinion that didn't change for years. Instead of maintaining a clear picture of world power and of how the Vatican could best improve its position, as did Spellman, Roncalli wrote impassioned letters to the Pope asking him to speak out on behalf of the Jews. Roncalli wanted the Pope to exercise his moral authority, not his diplomatic skills. Neither Spellman nor Pacelli understood Roncalli. Following custom, Spellman and Roncalli exchanged gifts; the delegate gave Spellman a silver tray with his name and seal, which, when he returned to New York, the archbishop put in the basement of the chancery, where it gathered dust.

When Spellman finally returned to the United States on August 1, 1943, the world had changed dramatically. Less than a month earlier, Allied forces had invaded Italy, and Mussolini had resigned only six days before, on July 26. Spellman was confident that he had handled his assignment well. The archbishop flew to Washington, where he fittingly was greeted by officials of the two worlds he had served so ably for the past six months: the State Department and the National Catholic Welfare Conference, the Church's U.S. lobbying arm. The President, who was attending the Quebec Conference to discuss the war in the Pacific, had left word for Spellman to meet with Secretary of State Hull.

Spellman immediately went to the residence of the apostolic delegate, where he prepared an innocuous press release that failed to address the rumors that he had helped overthrow Mussolini and arrange an Italian armistice. He returned to New York that evening and the next morning gave his statement to the press. At the press conference, Spellman, clad in a cassock with red piping and sash and with his pectoral cross dangling from his neck, showed no signs of the rigors of the past six months. Ever conscious of publicity, he defused possible resentment over his not answering questions by making sure that he shook hands with each reporter, asking the name of each man's newspaper and saying something pleasant to him.[32]

A month elapsed before the archbishop met with Roosevelt. On the evening of September 2, he sat in the White House with Roosevelt and Winston Churchill, who had traveled with the President from the Quebec Conference. As Spellman was about to learn, the foreign policy objectives of the United States and the Vatican were worlds apart. He could do little but walk a tightrope between country and Church. Pragmatically, he didn't choose sides, but later he devised ways of reconciling the Vatican's desire to grow stronger with the goals of the expanding American empire.

Spellman had two matters on his agenda of great importance to the Pope. The first concerned Allied bombing of Rome, which had made the Pope bitterly angry. Just before the Allies had invaded

Sicily, Roosevelt had assured the pontiff that "churches and religious institutions will, to the extent that is within our power, be spared the devastations of war during the struggle ahead."[33] Yet, the Basilica of San Lorenzo was partially destroyed and worshipers were killed during an attack on Rome. Also damaged was the cemetery of Campo Verano, where the Pacelli family—Pope Pius XII's own family— was buried.

The President was well aware of the problem. He had received a formal complaint from the Vatican about the San Lorenzo incident. The background of the Pope's letter to Roosevelt illustrated the peculiar mind of Vatican churchmen, who always put the institutional Church above all else. The day after the attack, Tardini, the shrewd Vatican assistant secretary of state, had drafted a version of a complaint to Roosevelt and presented it to the American Jesuit McCormick, who, like Spellman years earlier, was a translator. The American found the document cold-blooded. Tardini had emphasized the destruction of the basilica, not the human suffering. McCormick rewrote the draft, reversing the emphasis. ". . . I did not wish to give the appearance that the Vatican was more interested in the material than in the spiritual, in churches than in the Church," he wrote.[34]

In responding to the rebuke, Tardini summarized the philosophy that governed the Vatican: "A church has a spiritual value, and its loss may be greater than that of human life." He coolly rationalized his stand by saying the Allies had acknowledged the inevitability that civilians would be killed in war but had committed themselves to bombing military targets around Rome without destroying Church property. The final version of the letter to Roosevelt, a compromise, expressed the Pope's dismay at seeing "the harrowing scene of death leaping from the skies and stalking pitilessly through unsuspecting homes, striking down women and children. The Papal basilica of St. Lawrence, one of the most treasured and loved sanctuaries of Romans, especially close to the heart of all Supreme Pontiffs . . ." was partially destroyed.[35]

The letter was given to Myron Taylor's assistant, Harold Tittman, who regretted to McCormick that the Pope hadn't protested the bombing of German cities. Tittman cynically told McCormick the Vatican was upset about the bombing of Rome because it would have been a "feather in their caps for them, if the war ended without Rome being bombed," and the Vatican could take credit, McCormick noted in his diary. "So they are bitterly disappointed, ripping mad."[36]

The other issue Spellman mentioned to the President was the Pope's hope that all the Allies would now work with the Reich to settle the war in Europe. In his obsession with Communism, the Pope wanted Germany kept intact as a major roadblock to Soviet expansion. The Pope had sent Galeazzi to Spellman in August with that message. Spellman shared Pacelli's fear of Communism, but unknown to Pope or archbishop, Germany's fate had already been decided.

Roosevelt hadn't any encouragement to offer on either of the Pope's concerns. He told Spellman that the Rome bombings were based on military objectives and that such bombings couldn't be as precise as everyone would like. As for Germany, the Pope sought the impossible. By now, the President treated the archbishop as a trusted member of the diplomatic community. He frankly told him that the Soviet Union was a major player in international affairs, a power with which the Vatican would have to live. Roosevelt went into great detail about the likely state of geopolitics after the war. The picture he painted was bound to make the Vatican shudder.

After the meeting Spellman prepared a two-page, single-spaced memorandum that he sent to the Vatican, demoralizing the Pope further. Roosevelt had said the world would be divided into spheres of influence. Britain and Russia would get Europe and Africa; the United States, the Pacific; China, the Far East. The League of Nations wasn't considered successful because small states were allowed to exert undue influence. A future league would be controlled by the Big Four powers; smaller nations would have only consultative powers, not the right to decide issues or even vote. There would be no opposition to a Russian-dominated regime in Austria. Germany would be disarmed and divided into several states under the domination of the Big Four, mostly Russia.[37] The message was clear: the Vatican and Spellman had better adapt to new world realities. For his part, Spellman thought Roosevelt was a fool for giving so much away. The United States, he believed, should take the world for itself.

Although enmeshed in global affairs, Spellman still cultivated people who could help him. Under McIntyre the archdiocese was running well, even with the disruptions caused by war. The number of priests was reduced because of military service, collection baskets were skimpier with so many men in uniform, and there weren't enough workmen to tend to the maintenance of churches, schools, convents, and other institutions. The kind of help Spellman sought, however, had less to do with the Church than with himself. Always conscious of publicity, Spellman found that he was now a celebrity as a result of his highly publicized trip overseas. He was well known across the nation as well as in foreign lands. Not wanting to lose the momentum, he sought ways of heightening his image even more.

Thus Spellman introduced to the chancery an unlikely member of his staff named Gertrude Algase, who was the aggressive literary agent for the popular writer and lecturer Monsignor Fulton Sheen. Large and stocky, she had long, straight, jet-black hair, and priests around the chancery immediately dubbed her "Mortal Sin." She struck many of them as looking decadent and Spellman treated her as seriously as sin. She was given a secretary and an office near the archbishop's. Her job was to promote Spellman as a literary figure by making book and magazine deals and editing the results of Spellman's bouts with writing. Swiftly, she came to exert a great influence over Spellman, who listened to her for purely practical reasons. She was successful, and Spellman always appreciated successful people no matter what their other qualities.

Spellman's interest in writing was another extension of his ego. Churchmen had long written inspirational books and prayers, and Spellman did as well. But being highly pragmatic, he turned to magazine articles, and eventually even a novel, as means of increasing his prestige. Mrs. Algase's first success came with a series of articles she edited about Spellman's experiences during his six months overseas. The results were published in *Collier's* magazine several months after his return home; she later repackaged them as a book, *Action This Day*. The articles were wartime travelogues, jammed with innocuous anecdotes about countries, points of interest, and the names of the high and mighty. There was little about Spellman's adventures on behalf of the Pope or the President. The articles revealed the archbishop as an innocent abroad, a kindly, even holy man going about God's work.

The articles also underscored the political points Spellman wanted to make. Each article was supposed to be a letter addressed to his father and began, "My Dear Father." His father learned, for instance, that Franco was sincere, intelligent, and decent. "Whatever criticism has been made of General Franco (and it has been considerable), I can not doubt that he is a man loyal to his God, devoted to his country's welfare and definitely willing to sacrifice himself in any capacity and to any extent for Spain," Spellman asserted. The dictator's enemies, Spellman found, were inspired by a "hatred of religion." The archbishop ignored the unpleasant side of Franco's repressive regime, and the saccharine portrayal of the dictator's exploits resulted in a round of criticism.

A group of prominent, exiled Spanish professors was so appalled by what Spellman had written that they wrote an open letter to the archbishop. Arguing that his articles contained "a large quantity of false data which damage the reputations of honorable people," they noted the brevity of Spellman's trip to their country and his lack of intimate knowledge of Spain. They said he had drawn conclusions "without a knowledge of what the Spanish people are and wish to be, in spite of the scrupulous respect of Your Eminence for the Eighth Commandment of the Law of God. . . ."[38]

The Vatican had a vested interest in Spain, and what Spellman had written was merely the Church's view of Franco, or at least the

one that the Vatican would have liked to see prevail. The generalissimo had restored many privileges to the Church, especially in the
area of education, and eventually would even give control over motion-picture censorship in the nation to the Church. At the Vatican,
Spain became the model for Church-State relations.

When the letter from the Spanish professors appeared in the liberal
publication *PM* in 1943, Spellman was furious. This was the first
time he had been attacked publicly since the announcement of the
Myron Taylor mission, and he resented it intensely, evidently believing a man of his preeminent position should be beyond reproach.
"What can you expect of a paper like this but garbage," he said of
PM.

Nonetheless, the archbishop retreated when the articles appeared
as the book, *Action This Day*. Many of the offending passages were
either toned down or deleted. The spunky *PM* then managed to rile
Spellman again. The newspaper delighted in running excerpts from
the *Collier's* pieces and showing how they were watered down in
the book version. Moreover, *Christian Century,* the prominent Protestant publication, also published a withering attack, the first of many
scathing commentaries on Spellman. It wrote that Spellman "makes
statements of alleged fact that are contrary to the evidence that was
easily accessible to him," adding, "But all of this is rather an old
story—this glaring misrepresentation of events in Spain by apologists
for the Roman Catholic Church."

Less controversial were several volumes of clumsy poems that
Mrs. Algase helped Spellman write. The poems, which sold well,
were mostly about patriotism and religion and contained echoes of
Joyce Kilmer, the Catholic battlefield poet of World War I. Spellman's "Prayer for America" began:

O God, Father of America
Thou hast formed this Union of States, easing it with high destiny,
That our nation be light to all peoples in their dark despair,
Life to all peoples in their fear of death,
Love to all peoples under their yoke of hate.

For this destiny, Thou dost teach us to fly as an eagle
    Girding us with lightning and thunder,
    Enriching us with treasures in field and fold.

Spellman had little time to share with the muse of poetry. He
constantly shuttled to Washington to confer with the President and
State or War Department officials. The archdiocese demanded his
attention and his military vicar's role kept him occupied with many
details. His most nagging demands, however, came from the Pope.
Pius, feeling burdened with the weight of his office, wanted Spellman
back in Rome to help him.

A series of events conspired to make Pacelli turn increasingly to Spellman. The New York archbishop had established himself as an international statesman and now Vatican Secretary of State Maglione was seriously ill. The United States, as Spellman always believed was inevitable, had emerged as the key player in the Allied war effort, and it was obvious that Germany would be defeated ignominiously. Moreover, Pius trusted his friend Spellman, who always appeared in command of himself. Thus in June 1944, Spellman was once again in Rome, because the Pope wanted him by his side.

Spellman found Pius more tense and nervous than ever before, and the archbishop was worried. Though cold as ice in public, Pacelli in private had always been high-strung, but now he appeared distraught. On his first meeting with Spellman, the Pope "wept."[39] One reason for the Pope's state was frustration. As the pace of the war quickened, he seemed almost forgotten by world powers; his pleas for the cessation of the bombing of Rome were ignored. Even the papal summer villa, Castel Gandolfo, had been partially destroyed by a bomb. Although a minor incident of the war, the Pope found it a humiliating sign of his ineffectiveness. Also, the news that Roosevelt had given Spellman about the likely fates of Germany and the Soviet Union had upset Pacelli terribly.

When Allied soldiers moved onto Italian soil and Nazis were put to flight, the Pope issued a strange public letter to bishops. He lamented the state of the world and called upon bishops to pray. "Dangers of evil are rushing in upon the Christian family of people," Pius stated. His fear of Soviet Communists may have prompted the words, but they sounded strange from the man who had said so little when Nazis and fascists brutalized millions of people. The Jesuit McCormick wondered whether the Pope really felt that way about a German defeat or if it were his nationalism speaking. "The robbed and starving in Greece, in France, in Belgium, Holland, Austria, in concentration camps, religious, priests, seminarians, the enslaved workers—does their liberation mean nothing to the Vat[ican]? Sad, sad," he wrote in his diary.[40]

To be sure, Pope Pius XII's wartime behavior raised criticism in the ranks of diplomats and churchmen alike. As early as June 1940 the French Cardinal Tisserant had noted that since Italy had entered the war, the Holy See had accommodated itself "for its own exclusive advantage—and very little else." And the British representative to the Vatican told Tardini that his Foreign Office viewed the Vatican as a small neutral state where the Pope "for worldly rather than spiritual reasons, has allowed himself, like others, to be bullied."[41] While the Church worked quietly in many instances to help Jews, the Pope was besieged with requests from Catholics, rabbis, and Protestant bishops to speak out against the Nazi atrocities, but Pius said little.

Spellman, if not Pacelli, was concerned about the Pope's appearance now that the war was coming to an end. People might start pointing fingers of blame at those who could have acted more decisively. Thus, while in Rome, Spellman made a half-hour radio address for his old friend General William ("Wild Bill") Donovan, the head of the O.S.S. The purpose of the broadcast was to encourage civil disobedience against the pro-Nazi regime in Hungary. The topic was anti-Semitism: "Abraham is our Patriarch, our ancestor. Anti-Semitism is not compatible with this sublime reality. . . . Spiritually we are Semites. . . . No man can love God and hate his brother. . . ."

After the broadcast Spellman said that he had made it at the urging of the Pope. This may have been true, as the Pope had to do something to indicate dismay at the way the war had turned out. Spellman also had to go on record strongly against anti-Semitism. (Nearly two years earlier, in November 1942, the Church hierarchy of the United States had issued a proclamation denouncing all racial persecutions, citing specifically a "deep sense of revulsion against the cruel indignities heaped on Jews in conquered countries." Spellman hadn't taken a leading role in the movement.)

Thus, Spellman found himself trying, if not to rectify, at least to defuse some of the results of the Church's wartime sins of commission, as well as omission, as he worked for the Pope. One of the more difficult of such assignments was de Gaulle. After Paris was liberated on August 25, 1944, de Gaulle angered the Pope by immediately making an embarrassing issue of the fact that certain members of the hierarchy in France had been collaborators. De Gaulle's main targets were Cardinal Suhard of Paris and Monsignor Valerio Valeri, the apostolic delegate, whom de Gaulle wanted recalled. De Gaulle even talked of prosecuting them, along with several dozen bishops who collaborated. Many priests and bishops had supported the Free French, but all de Gaulle seemed to be able to remember were the times Suhard had posed for photographs with Vichy officials, and he was angry that the Church had recognized the Vichy regime after receiving special educational privileges from the state.[42]

De Gaulle had been insulted when Suhard, immediately after the liberation of Paris, celebrated mass at Notre Dame Cathedral, which many Frenchmen believed to be the heart and soul of France. The cardinal had taken the general by surprise. Suhard had arranged the service directly with a U.S. Army chaplain, who hadn't consulted French authorities. The following Saturday, the Resistance newspaper *Combat* editorialized: "Although many prelates like Msgr. Sallege of Toulouse upheld the honor of their faith and of the country, a minority of dignitaries displayed during the occupation an attitude incompatible with the interests of the nation. In Paris, Cardinal Suhard was one of these."

For his part, the frantic Suhard denied he had helped the Vichy government or even intruded in political matters. The Pope stood by his representatives and, to press their case, apparently sent Spellman to de Gaulle. The next time Suhard said mass at the cathedral, Spellman was on the altar with him. Whatever position Spellman put forward to the general, de Gaulle apparently rejected it.[43] He summoned Valeri and told the delegate his presence in France was "incompatible" with the new government.[44] Then de Gaulle pointedly refused to attend mass at the cathedral, celebrating the festival of St. Joan of Arc, as a snub of Suhard who officiated. Suhard remained in Paris, but the nuncio—not being a lifetime officeholder like a cardinal—was recalled to Rome. Eventually, an accord was reached whereby the Vatican finally recognized the new government.

Smarting from the insults, the Pope wasn't about to let the incident pass lightly. He decided to retaliate by devaluing the post of apostolic delegate to Paris, traditionally an elite appointment. According to some reports, he did this by selecting to succeed the aristocratic Valeri a man whom both the Pope and Spellman considered a ridiculous fellow, someone whose very presence in Paris would be an insult.[45] He was the peasant Angelo Roncalli, the troublesome nuncio in Turkey. (The plan backfired. Roncalli during his Paris years would gain considerable esteem for his handling of many matters, including to a large degree defusing the issue of bishops who had collaborated.)

The most pressing issue the Pope had on his agenda was Italy. Defeated Italy was being cruelly exploited. Retreating Germans had taken whatever they could. Conquering Allies took the rest, and the Allied Military Government of Occupational Territory was woefully inept in dealing with the myriad problems that Italy faced. Black markets, thievery, and prostitution were rampant. Italy's future hung in the balance and the prospects were bleak. Once again Pius turned to Spellman. Both Spellman and Pacelli were worried about the possibility that Communists would take advantage of Italy's weakened position. Unless something was done, Vatican officials lamented, they could one day be surrounded by a Communist nation.

As usual, Spellman quickly decided what to do. Believing the United States had to embrace the Italian cause, he had his international affairs expert draft a position paper on why it was in America's interests to help Italy recover economically. The archbishop took his case to Washington, a precedent that he followed for years whenever it appeared that Communists would make strong inroads if the United States failed to act decisively somewhere. His analysis, actually Griffiths's, struck the right tone for the times. The arguments, similar to those that later launched the Marshall Plan, were compelling:

> Italy cannot be amputated from the European economy; nor can she be sliced up as fair loot. Italy has a surplus of highly efficient tech-

nicians to help her in her own reconstruction if she has the material and tools, and then she can take her place and pay her share among the nations of the world. Italy has the head, heart, and hands to rebuild her economic structure if given the chance. She knows she must make her comeback the hard way, but in clearing away the wreckage strewn by Fascism and war, the road back must not lead to economic and political ruin, making Italy a land of beggars, a land of slavery and a land of slavers. The uprising of the hungry and the unemployed would mean a sweeping victory for Godless Communism and the peace will be lost even as the war is won.

His views prevailed. The United States committed itself to keeping Communism at bay in Italy. Spellman even personally advised the Allies about the kinds of relief programs needed to help the people and rebuild the economy. He also earned the gratitude of the nation, since his efforts were widely publicized in the Italian press; he spoke at a time when Italy had few friends. But he had also achieved a significant political act. The goals of his Church and the rising American empire were the same, and Spellman was the catalyst in getting both parties to recognize the advantage of their working together.

Now, however, he was worried that he might be too successful and that his diplomatic skills might trap him in Rome. "[The Pope] doesn't want me to go away," Spellman wrote in his diary.[46] When Maglione died, the Pope was more explicit about wanting to have Spellman with him permanently. Pius offered to make Spellman his secretary of state, the second most prestigious post at the Vatican and the job that had been Pacelli's last before becoming Pope. The offer was obviously enticing, but, as Spellman knew, the job had many drawbacks while Pacelli was Pope. On some foreign issues, Pius had consulted with Spellman far more often than with Maglione and there was no guarantee the Pope wouldn't turn to someone else in the future. More significant, Pacelli husbanded so much authority that he rarely delegated anything until he absolutely had to do so, and that was a trait Spellman couldn't abide.

As archbishop of New York, Spellman operated free of Vatican constraints and his independence gave him greater power than if he were under the Pope's eye. Now, the Pope had to rely on him for his political prowess in Washington and access to money from New York. When he analyzed the offer Spellman knew he would be in a stronger position if he stayed where he was. Besides, he had long since had his fill of the anti-Americanism that pervaded Vatican corridors. Thus, he asked the Pope to let him postpone making a decision until the end of the war; he didn't want to reject the Pope outright at a time such as this. He later told friends and relatives that he hadn't wanted the job, but he gave Pacelli the kind of diplomatic response a superior loves to hear: "I said I was indifferent, that I would leave New York, family or anything if the Holy Father thought I could serve in any place for the Church," he reported in his diary.[47]

Surprisingly, rumors about Spellman's being considered for the lofty job didn't surface for months. When U.S. intelligence officers looked into the reports, they confirmed them. They also came up with intriguing reasons why the Pope wanted Spellman. Pacelli, the reports stated, wasn't simply trying to reward a faithful friend. An F.B.I. memorandum, dated April 12, 1945, listed three strong reasons for Spellman being under consideration. The informant for much of the material was an Italian cardinal:

—An Italian Cardinal, if appointed, might be accused of having fascist connections, but Archbishop Spellman could not possibly be attacked and his appointment would, to some extent, protect the Vatican against the attacks of Russia.

—Communism will be the most important political problem in the United States after the termination of the war and it would be beneficial to the Vatican if the secretary of state were an American.

—As the United States is the banker of the world, the Vatican would benefit from the appointment of Archbishop Spellman.[48]

When the O.S.S. officers analyzed the situation, they decided that Spellman probably wouldn't get the job because of nationalism. In the end an O.S.S. report concluded: ". . . it seems very improbable that a non-Italian would be nominated to such an office."[49] The O.S.S. analysis was right but for the wrong reason. Spellman could have had the job for the asking. The issue, as far as he was concerned, wasn't the improbability of a non-Italian's rising so far in the curia. He would have accepted if he had sensed the possibility that it would lead to the one position above that of secretary of state. Spellman ultimately didn't accept because he realized the unlikeliness of a non-Italian's becoming Pope. So he stayed where he was and was content to forge tighter bonds between the Church and America. The United States, he knew, was the source of power in the world, and he wanted to have a say in the way that might was used.

Spellman's frequent shuttling in and out of Rome and the secrecy shrouding his activities made him constant grist for the Vatican rumor mills. The most persistent report about him in 1944 had him negotiating peace for smaller nations such as Hungary or for Germany, but a more plausible explanation for his secret missions was just as startling: he was working to thaw relations between the Vatican and Moscow.[50]

Roosevelt pushed for an easing of tension between the two antagonists as a way of helping the war effort. In Rome, Spellman probably first broached the subject for the President not long after Pearl Harbor, but the archbishop was first publicly linked to feelers between Rome and Moscow only in 1943. When Spellman traveled to Teheran, he had arranged a secret meeting with Andrei A. Smirnoff, the Soviet ambassador to Iran. News of the encounter was leaked to the press, perhaps as a way of notifying the world that the two enemies were talking: if a rapprochement did develop, the public would have to be eased into accepting what seemed like the impossible. A dispatch in *The New York Times* on June 16, 1943, noted the Spellman-Smirnoff encounter and said that the two had discussed "United States–Soviet questions." Implicit was the possibility of a relaxation in Vatican-Soviet relations.

Although the Church might gain concessions to rebuild its largely demolished base in Russia, the Vatican was wary of any deals. The Soviet Union stood to gain the most; the Communist government's most vocal critic would be muted. Nonetheless, the Vatican had taken steps as early as 1941 to prepare for possible improved relations with Russia: the Pontifical Commission for Russia, which had been established in 1930 as a result of the persecution of the Church in the Soviet Union, was assigned the task. Just how far along the commission was by the time Spellman met with Smirnoff isn't known. After the meeting in Teheran, however, the Holy See—through an understanding with Washington and London—arranged to have Monsignor Acida Marina, the apostolic delegate in Teheran, meet again with Soviet officials. Talks between them continued throughout 1944.

According to O.S.S. informants, Spellman met with the Pope, several monsignors, Myron Taylor, and Father Zachee Maker, the American assistant to the office of the Jesuit general, to discuss the extremely complex business. Their topics ranged from Russia's reestablishing religion in countries it would liberate to the Soviet role in ending the war in the Pacific.[51]

There appeared little doubt that Moscow was anxious to build bridges to the Church. In 1944 an unknown Polish-American priest, Stanislaus Orelemanski of Springfield, Massachusetts, had suddenly come to international attention, to the dismay of Spellman and other churchmen. Orelemanski, who had organized a pro-Soviet League of Poles in the United States, was invited to Moscow by none other than Stalin himself. The priest accepted the offer and in Moscow spoke twice with Stalin, who indicated a desire for increased contact with Rome and expressed a commitment to religious freedom. When Orelemanski returned home, he gave a statement to the press in which he said Stalin was sincere. Spellman was furious in the wake of the publicity the incident received. The naive priest, he believed, might have jeopardized the work he and others were doing secretly. He wanted Orelemanski silenced. Suddenly, the priest found himself denounced as a "stooge" by Church officials who dismissed his mission as a "burlesque." At first Orelemanski was bitterly angry, but later he recanted. The priest wasn't heard from again. He was banished to a monastery.[52]

According to the so-called Vessell Papers, O.S.S. reports from Vatican informants, the major stumbling block to a Vatican-Moscow accord was Poland. The Vatican was alarmed at the prospect of a Moscow-linked government in Poland, a nation where the Church historically had exerted great influence. Throughout the war, the Vatican had supported the exiled Polish government in London. The accuracy of the Vessell documents has become suspect because of the nature of the strange band of spies—priests, journalists, and others—who had been recruited by James Angleton, the Rome station chief for the O.S.S. and later head of counterintelligence for the organization's successor, the C.I.A. One of Angleton's spies was identified as Monsignor Enrico Pucci, the Vatican press aide who furnished daily briefings to foreign correspondents and moonlighted as an O.S.S. informant. During the war he apparently sold reports to the Axis. The most bizarre of Angleton's operatives was Virgilio Scattolini, a former writer of pornography, who was characterized in an O.S.S. background paper as "unscrupulously mercenary and has no evident political affiliation; is an opportunist and, today, states that he was always an anti-Fascist." It was believed he had also sold information to the Nazis and Japanese. Nonetheless, he was well connected at the Vatican.[53]

The Vessell Papers, however, indicated what was generally known to be the case anyway. The prospects for a civilized Vatican-Moscow relationship were never good. Both the Pope and Spellman were rabidly anti-Communist, and they saw the Church losing if they relaxed their vigilance against Marxism. The Vatican's impetus for seeking any possible accommodation was to gain rights for the Church in Russia and a practical recognition of the importance of the Soviet Union in world affairs, which the Holy See dreaded seeing happening. Thus, both the archbishop and the Pope were dismayed, believing that too many concessions were being made to Russia by the West, and at the Yalta Conference, in February 1945, their fears were borne out. Roosevelt and Churchill traveled to the Soviet Union, rather than meet with Stalin on neutral ground or make him come to them. The outcome seemed inevitable. The Soviets got what they wanted, including Catholic Poland.

Spellman knew that Roosevelt thought he could check Stalin with personal diplomacy. The archbishop thought the President was being naive. Well aware of Vatican fears, Roosevelt sent Democratic leader Ed Flynn first to Moscow and then to the Vatican in an effort to salvage something from the attempts to bring the powers together, but the mission was doomed. Flynn spent a month in Russia but was forced to cut short his time in Rome. The reason was disheartening. Franklin Roosevelt, the man who thought he could checkmate Stalin, died on April 12, 1945.

Spellman recognized the end of an era. With Roosevelt dead he had no illusions about making peace with the Church's ideological enemy. Pacelli had never liked the idea of being flexible with the Russians. The prevailing attitude at the Vatican was summarized in an O.S.S. report of November 1945, six months after Roosevelt's death and three months after the end of World War II. The Vatican was now girding for battle with Communism. Peace was out of the question. The report stated that the Pope had entrusted the Jesuit General de Boynes with determining the level of Soviet aid being given to Italian Communists. It was obvious that the Russians were no longer trying to appease Washington by courting Rome. Pacelli recognized that Communism was on the march and that his beloved Italy was a target. He was determined to thwart Communism wherever he could, and, as the O.S.S. reported, de Boynes was ready to deploy "intelligent and well-trained Jesuits who can travel through Italy without arousing any particular suspicion, in [an] attempt to come into possession of documentary proof of orders given by and financial aid furnished by the Soviet Union to Italian Communists. . . . Father de Boynes says that he has priests capable of this work, who have specialized for years in the bitter struggle against Communism and who have a perfect knowledge of the Russian language."[54]

Thus, the Church embarked on a new crusade that affected the world. The Vatican became the first power to declare the Cold War on the Soviet Union, and Spellman played a key role in the power struggle. He was entrusted with getting the United States to provide the cold steel needed to back up the Church's moral fervor. For this part, Spellman needed no encouragement. As the American Church's political leader, he sought vengeance on the enemy of both Catholicism and the burgeoning American empire. In doing so, he welded his Church and nation to the goal of obliterating Communism wherever it appeared or even threatened to appear. The policy would prove disastrous for the United States, the Church, and Spellman himself. But for two decades Spellman's rabid anti-Communism enhanced his power base at home.

CHAPTER SEVEN

The Cold War Churchman

ARCHBISHOP SPELLMAN SAT IN HIS OFFICE, SPEAKING QUIET-
ly with his visitors. The door was closed so that neither
his secretaries nor Mortal Sin knew with whom he was
meeting. His conservatively dressed visitors respectfully held fedoras
in their hands; they were both apprehensive and deferential in the
presence of a man who, on February 21, 1946, only days away, would
be crowned a prince of his Church. The men were F.B.I. agents,
and they wanted this powerful churchman, a close friend of their
boss, J. Edgar Hoover, to help them.

Spellman didn't have to be asked twice. He prided himself on the
aid he gave to government officials and agencies, a way of showing
how American he and his Church were. In this case, he agreed to
cooperate with the F.B.I. in a crackdown on labor unions believed
to have Communists operating in their ranks. The archbishop left
little doubt among his subordinates that he detested unions. He opposed unionization of archdiocesan workers and referred to unions
as "hotbeds" of Communism and havens for men "who are afraid
of work." Thus, the churchman agreed to help "ferret out and eliminate the Communists and fellow travelers who are in positions of
control in labor unions," an F.B.I. memo on the meeting stated.
Spellman, however, wasn't a fool when it came to such a controversial matter. He wasn't about to antagonize labor itself by letting

word leak that he was instrumental in any purge. "This must never be known to anyone," he warned.[1]

Hoover must have been certain of the reception Spellman would give his men before he sent them. After the war Spellman was a whirlwind of anti-Communist activity. He gave speeches across the country and wrote articles for popular publications such as *Cosmopolitan* and *Good Housekeeping* about the Communist menace. Communists, he believed, had infiltrated America and systematically destroyed his Church abroad. Spellman was determined to battle his foe not just in the propaganda sphere; he was anxious to help clandestine moves by both his Church and his country to halt the Communist onslaught.

Cooperation between law enforcement officers and the Church in New York was nothing new. New York City police had long granted the Catholic Church a special status. Priests, arrested for being drunk and disorderly or caught during a raid on a brothel or in some other crime, weren't booked but were routinely handed over to the Powerhouse. Although federal crimes were of a different nature, Hoover was willing to do likewise because Spellman was willing to do him favors. According to various accounts, priests turned over to Spellman by the F.B.I. during the war had either committed crimes or made themselves vulnerable. A priest of German ancestry, for example, had been arrested on suspicion of being an Axis spy. Another had an intimate relationship with a Washington woman who was a spy; susceptible to blackmail, he too was handed over to Spellman. There were other cases, and Spellman dealt with them all in the way that the Church since medieval times had dealt with problems—the sinners were banished to monasteries.[2]

Now, Spellman anxiously listened to the F.B.I. agents and liked what he heard. They planned to publish a monthly magazine to alert the business community to the dangers of Communism. Another idea was furnishing confidential reports through a special service that the F.B.I. wanted to establish under the guise of a legitimate business. The service would tell companies "how to eliminate Communists" among their employees and the agents already had a client. A major department store was willing to pay $25,000 for such assistance. "Many large employers of labor are willing to spend large sums of money to put . . . persons opposed to Communism, in positions of control in labor unions," the agents told Spellman.[3]

The archbishop, for his part, was willing to provide contacts, quietly talk up the project, and, he told them, even bring it to the attention of the Pope. Once again, however, Spellman insisted that his affiliation be hidden from the public. He didn't want labor unions turning on him, nor did he want to give those who shouted about separation of Church and State whenever he spoke more grist for their mills. (The F.B.I. did launch operations similar to those outlined.[4])

Just what else Spellman did to assist the F.B.I. with the labor movement isn't known, but he broadcast his anti-Communist views through the press and a lecture circuit that had him racing from podium to podium. His message was the same whether in person or in print. In the June 1946 issue of *America,* the Jesuit periodical, he warned: "They try to seduce us into believing that Americans can be Communists, but a true American can be neither a Communist nor a Communist condoner, and we realize that the first Loyalty of every American is vigilantly to weed out and counteract Communism and convert American Communists to Americanism. . . ."

Mrs. Algase included in the *America* piece a photo of Spellman taken as he sat, smiling benignly, with a group of two-year-old children. Implicit was the message that the kindly, loving man was doing his best to protect future generations.

There was a growing market for such sentiment. Roosevelt's attempts at joining hands with the Soviets during the last two years of the war hadn't met much enthusiasm. After the war Americans were anxious about Communism and most wanted the Communist Party banned. There was growing fear that the atomic bomb would fall into Russian hands, and anti-Communism was used as a hot issue by some of the returned veterans who were running for political office. In California, for instance, a young Richard "the Fighting Quaker" Nixon smeared his opponent, Jerry Voorhis, as the candidate of the Kremlin. In Wisconsin, "Tail-Gunner Joe" McCarthy described his senatorial opponent, Howard Murray, as a "pinko." More men than Hoover and Spellman were exploiting the issue.

In private Spellman, as usual, was even blunter about Communism than he was in public. His notion of what to do about the Reds was summarized in *One Lonely Night,* a Mickey Spillane novel. Spellman urged priests around him to read the book, so taken was he with Spillane's solution: "Don't arrest them, don't treat them with the dignity of the democratic process of the courts of law . . . do the same thing they'd do to you! Treat 'em to the inglorious taste of sudden death. . . ."

Spellman's effectiveness was reflected in the Soviet Union's fear of him. His political influence and the enormous respect he commanded made the archbishop a formidable enemy. When it was announced that Spellman was to become a cardinal, the Soviet publication *Izvestia* declared that the Vatican was spreading "reactionary" policies and singled out Spellman for his role.[5] "What can you expect from pigs but grunts?" Spellman replied.

The Papal Throne at St. Peter's Basilica was covered with red damask and stood before the high altar in the long eastern nave. Above the *confesso* leading down to the tomb of St. Peter was a richly brocaded, green-carpeted enclosure in which the new Sacred

College of Cardinals was about to hold its first public assembly, on February 21, 1946. Spellman was finally to be made a cardinal. The years of maneuvering, the countless favors for ranking Churchmen over the years, the hard work and loyalty were to bear fruit. He had expected the honor for years, but the war had kept the red hat just beyond his grasp. Now, he was a prince of the Church, a man entrusted with the selection of the next Pope, a man who was actually in line, at least in theory, to become Pope himself. Spellman was where he had dreamed of being when he walked the streets of Rome thirty-five years earlier as a young, ambitious seminarian.

A few months shy of his fifty-seventh birthday, Spellman still walked at a brisk clip, made decisions quickly, and rotated between his humble and arrogant personalities depending on circumstances. There was now something different about him, however, and it had much to do with a confidence he had gained from his wartime activities. No longer was he defensive about being an American churchman. He had seen how much the world depended on the United States, and this change was reflected in an interesting shift that affected him much more personally. Whereas he had always depended so much on Pacelli, now the Pope had come to depend on him. Just as the leadership of the world had obviously shifted from Europe to America, a less perceptible shift had taken place within the Church. The Vatican now had to look far more than ever before to the United States, for money and political support. And that meant looking to Spellman.

Rome itself was marked by the ravages of war, although not nearly as badly as the other great cities of Europe. In 1946, Ciampino Airport used makeshift runways, and the roads into Rome were pitted with bomb craters, overturned trucks and tanks, and the rubble of smashed buildings. The city itself was still very much a military town, as British and American jeeps edged through legions of shabby, unemployed Italians. The members of the large party of Americans who accompanied the Cardinal-elect were appalled; it was the first time they had seen the destruction of war firsthand. Knowing the scarcity of goods in Rome, Spellman had ordered that his entourage bring most of the food for their stay, a gesture that was noted in the Italian press and appreciated.

As usual, Spellman's days in Rome were hectic. The hours when he wasn't involved in the rituals leading up to the public ceremonies, he spent in conference with the Pope or old friends, such as Galeazzi and Pizzardo. There were papal audiences for two hundred chaplains who were in Rome, and also for Spellman's party. Since members of the New York press had come with his party to cover the historic event, Spellman went to the Rome playground of the Knights of Columbus, where he had worked years ago, and to the North American College, where he posed for pictures. He dined with Mark Clark, the commander in chief of the American Occupation Forces in Austria. And he broadcast a report about his elevation to the high ecclesiastic plateau, which was heard throughout the United States.

While in Rome, Spellman shored up controversial alliances. *The Nation* wryly noted that one evening he attended a state dinner at the Spanish embassy, where he was "knee-deep in anti-democratic politics." Moreover, he was the only one of the four Americans elevated to cardinal who accepted the invitation from Prince Umberto of Italy's outmoded royal family, to a reception at the Quirinal Palace. Umberto's father had been forced to accept Mussolini, a sign of the end of the Italian nobility as a major factor in the country's political life. Even the reception itself was a relic of a Europe of yesteryear. An attendant bearing a candle met each cardinal and escorted him past immense palace guards, booted and wearing picturesque military garb including horsehair plumes on their helmets, as they approached the throne room. A reception supper was served for the cardinals in a Hall of Mirrors. Champagne flowed and blood-red roses were everywhere. The reception was the first by the House of Savoy for the College of Cardinals since the papal lands had been lost and, as it turned out, it was the last. In May the king gave Umberto the throne. Only three months later the new king was in exile.[6]

Long before 9:30 A.M., when public ceremonies investing the cardinals were to begin, the basilica was filled with notables from all corners of the world. The Italian family was represented by Umberto and his wife, Princess Marie Jose. Behind them sat bejeweled members of the nobility, their diamond tiaras, necklaces, and rings flashing lancets of light. Members of the Vatican diplomatic corps, elegant in formal attire, were present en masse, nodding to one another and to members of the clergy or leaning in whispered conversations. Just to the right of the golden papal throne were American military leaders, headed by General Clark. Robert Jackson, chief American prosecutor at the Nuremberg Trials, had traveled from Germany. Opposite them were friends and relatives of the Americans being honored.

Devastated by death during World War II, the Sacred College had shrunk from seventy to thirty-eight. Until the new men were appointed, the United States had only one cardinal—the aged Dennis Dougherty, a man of enormous girth who was jokingly known in Philadelphia as "His Immense." Now, in light of the rising importance of the United States, Spellman, Stritch of Chicago, Mooney of Detroit, and John J. Glennon of St. Louis were added to the list of cardinals, but Spellman's elevation had been the most widely reported in the American press. Already, there was talk that someday he would become the first American-born Pope.

The word "cardinal," Latin for hinge, was appropriate for the churchmen who bore the title. They were the Church's most powerful politicians; success or failure of Vatican policies often did hinge on their actions. They were the major fund-raisers, diplomats, political theoreticians, guardians of doctrine, overseers of Vatican finances, advisers of popes. Their number had been set at seventy in 1586 by Pope Sixtus V; few as they were, they were the Church's true aristocracy. And all were vehemently anti-Communist.

The new cardinals reflected a Church that was coping with new realities. The tradition of continental cardinals had changed. Few were princely patrons of the arts or accomplished party-givers who played beguiling games at diplomatic courts. There were vestiges within the royal ranks of a bygone era, Roman cardinals who maintained palaces at Frascati or in the hills of Abruzzi and who lived with the graciousness of old aristocracy. But most of the newer cardinals, the Americans in particular, were pragmatists who lived the fast-paced lives of the modern world, men more at home in board rooms than salons.

Most of Pius's thirty-two new cardinals were now in Rome. In an age-old tradition, Italians who thronged St. Peter's Square treated the spectacle like a political convention, cheering wildly for their favorites. Spellman received a large ovation as he entered the basilica wearing the royal purple. Newspapers reminded readers that, "even at a time when Italy was most depressed and despised," Spellman had been a friend. The press emphasized what a "great friend" he was to the Pope and how Spellman had been granted a papal audience only three hours after his arrival in Rome, the only cardinal to be so honored.

The cardinal who received the biggest ovation was Clemens Von Galen, a brave Bavarian bishop who had defied the Nazis. The towering, Teutonic-looking Von Galen had spoken out against Hitler and been arrested. The first time that soldiers attempted to seize him, Von Galen had donned his royal robes, grabbed his miter, and said he was ready. The guards had been afraid to lead him through the crowd that had gathered outside the bishop's palace.[7]

At 9:30 the silvery peal of trumpets signaled the entrance into the basilica of the old cardinals, led by the venerable Granito Pignatelli di Belmonte, at age ninety-three the dean of the college. They walked past noble guards, drawn from the ranks of the Italian aristocracy, and the Palantine and Swiss Guards. Suddenly, the sharp turning of heads in the front of the crowd had a ripple effect as all eyes turned on the Pope. Clad in scarlet and gold and carried aloft by twelve scarlet-uniformed Pontifical Guards, Pius imperiously bent his mitered head to left and right and lifted his hand to bestow his blessing. Thunderous applause filled the 400-foot-high domed basilica. When the Pope was placed on his great throne, one by one the old cardinals—to whom the new ones represented defeats or victories—advanced and were greeted by Pius. They moved to the right of the enclosure, where they took their seats while the master of ceremonies sat on the floor before them.

During the ceremonies Spellman's specialness was lost on no one. There was a pleading for elevation to sainthood of Mother Cabrini, the first American to be canonized—a move Spellman promoted. Of far greater significance, the Pope himself personally honored Spellman. Pope Pius XII's baldachin, the flat-brimmed red hat that had been presented to Pacelli when he had been named a cardinal, was placed on Spellman's head. At the end of the rites, the new cardinals followed the Pope from the basilica and met with family and friends. Spellman always loved the pomp and pageantry of his Church and obviously relished the distinctive purple of his new office. If pressed he would have acknowledged the symbolic value of such splendid vestments and the awe they inspired. The man who wore them, no matter what he was like privately, was esteemed publicly. Now, he himself stood before the world in the royal robes of ecclesiastic power.

Reality unexpectedly marred the day. Spellman found himself surrounded by reporters, who questioned him about a report that he was to carry a secret message to Franco on his way home via Madrid and Lisbon. The day's magical spell was broken, and the Cardinal resented it. He angrily said that he had no messages and had a right to go wherever he wanted. "Don't ask foolish questions," he snapped when a reporter for the New York *Herald Tribune* pressed him, as he pushed his way out of the circle of newsmen.

When he finally returned home, on March 5, Spellman was greeted at La Guardia Airport by a crowd of ten thousand that included Mayor William O'Dwyer, state and city officials, bishops, monsignors, and thousands of cheering laymen. Twenty-five police motorcycles festooned with papal, New York City, and American flags escorted his party back to St. Patrick's, which was ablaze with light although it was after midnight. The peal of church bells filled the night air. Spellman ascended his throne, his magnificent new robes spilling around him so that he appeared lost within them. A smile on his face, he hardly looked like America's leading Red-baiter.

The Church was under assault in Eastern Europe. The new leaders of Soviet satellites tried to strip the Church of its lands and influence, and they were as subtle as Stalin. In their bludgeoning of the Church, Communists provided Catholicism with a unique group of martyrs; they were churchmen, autocratic by nature, imbued personally with a taste for martyrdom, and very political. The first of these was the lean sallow Aloysius Stepinac, the archbishop of Zagreb and the Roman Catholic primate of Yugoslavia. Like Spellman, he was a protégé of Pacelli's. When Pavelic established his Croatian dictatorship Stepinac served on its council. During the war he was criticized for not breaking with the government, although on occasion he had spoken out against the slaughter of Jews and Gypsies who refused to convert to Catholicism. When Josip Tito's partisans entered Zagreb in 1945, the archbishop tried to rally townsmen to the defense of the Pavelic state. A British officer who met Stepinac wrote a letter to the *New Statesman* and *The Nation* on October 26, 1946, citing the archbishop's rationale for working with Pavelic: "He and his priests had collaborated with the Germans because the issue of the war was a clear one between Fascism and Communism. He chose the former."

When Tito took power Stepinac was charged with collaborating, provoking racial hatred, and forcing religious conversions. Tito warily considered the archbishop a fanatic with a martyr complex, so he ordered a mere seventeen-day jail sentence for him. But the priest became increasingly troublesome, denouncing Tito and his policies so vociferously that he was arrested again. His trial was a sham, and, with both the Catholic and general public closely following the well-publicized proceedings, the world was shocked by the gross miscarriage of justice. When the churchman was given a sixteen-year sentence at the grim Lepoglava prison, people in the West were appalled. *The New York Times,* for instance, was provoked into editorializing that the Stepinac proceedings had been "clearly a political trial" and that the only reason he hadn't been sentenced to death was that "Tito did not feel quite strong enough to make a new martyr."

In the eyes of many people, including his own, Stepinac was a martyr. "I know why I suffer," he told an American newsman. "It is for the rights of the Catholic Church. I am ready to die each day for the Church. The Catholic Church cannot be, nor will it ever be, the slave of any regime." Stepinac quickly became a rallying point for Catholics. Organizations such as the National Council of Catholic Women and the 200,000-member Catholic War Veterans embraced his cause. Catholic Congressmen John McCormack and John J. Rooney unsuccessfully tried to ram through the House a resolution demanding a formal U.S. protest. The Catholic War Veterans demanded that the President and the State Department take action, as they bitterly assailed "the silence of President Truman" and the sending of aid to Yugoslavia. Catholic college students picketed the Yugoslav embassy.[8]

The most passionate outbursts came from Spellman. Speaking to an enthusiastic crowd at a World Peace Rally in New York on October 6, 1946, he claimed that Stepinac's only crime was "fidelity to God and country!" Elsewhere, he declared that Stepinac was "but one of thousands of martyrs of every faith whom corrupt, ruthless dictators daily betray and befoul as they wield poisoned power and force to achieve their goal of godless government throughout the world." Because of Communism, he said, America was "at this moment at war with its very soul." Ever practical, he used the issue to raise funds for a high school he was planning. He turned the fund drive into a crusade for the new "Archbishop Stepinac High School." Within a year, twice the $2-million goal was raised.

Whenever he spoke out, Spellman reinforced his image as a defender of both Catholicism and Americanism. He vowed that no longer would they be seen as mutually exclusive, the charge made against the Church in the United States for so long. Indeed, in many minds Catholicism became identified with Spellman's Red Crusade, and for good reason. The more the Cardinal lashed out at Communists, the greater the response from his constituents. The Knights of Columbus in 1947 broadcast a series of programs over two hundred twenty-six radio stations to show the "truth about Communism." Spellman was often a guest. When the *Daily Worker* denounced the program as "the biggest and most vicious scare hoax in the history of radio," a Knights spokesman accepted the criticism as a badge of honor for "hitting the Commies where it hurts."[9]

Spellman himself became a fictional martyr to the cause. The Catechetical Guild took a step into the surreal when it printed "Is This Tomorrow?," a four-color comic book that wasn't meant to amuse but to frighten. One of the comics depicted a horde of horrible, crazed Communists who attacked St. Patrick's and nailed an angelic-looking Spellman to the front door. Communists, of course, reacted nonsensically. Instead of chuckling over how closely the propaganda mirrored their own cartoons of bloodthirsty, ogrelike plutocrats, the editors of the *Daily Worker* tried to send the guild publishers to jail. All they did was to attract greater attention to the Spellman comic book; orders for copies flooded the guild.

Nationally, anti-Communism became such a force that Truman felt compelled in 1947 to push legislation creating a Loyalty Board to review federal employees for Communist affiliations. The federal board cost a fortune, disrupted hiring practices, and, after reviewing five million cases, had little to show for the effort. Nonetheless, a number of states approved similar legislation, and, in New York City, Mayor O'Dwyer did as well. Spellman, however, found government doing all too little to stop the Red Menace and he took every opportunity to say so. "Once again while Rome burns . . . the world continues to fiddle," he said of the loyalty boards. "The strings of the fiddle are committees, conversations, and appeasements—to the tune of no action this day."

The Cardinal wanted to wake up America, and he wanted to punish Americans who didn't share his view that the battle with Communism was one of life and death. The Church was losing in Europe; no one was doing anything to prevent Catholicism from being erased in Soviet-dominated countries almost overnight. Catholic publications were filled with the death knell for the Church in Communist countries. Spellman spoke at rally after rally about the necessity of doing something to halt the swiftly spreading Red disease. Such militant cries occasionally found expression in action. Repeatedly, the Catholic War Veterans demanded that the United States move against Communist dictators and finally the group took steps itself. In 1948 its members blocked the loading of the Russian freighter *Chuktoka,* which was moored at a New Jersey dock. The veterans contended the ship carried materials that could be used to wage war on the United States. The angry pickets bore signs stating AMERICAN GOODS FOR AMERICAN DEFENSE and HITLER & MUSSOLINI WERE AMATEURS COMPARED WITH PAL JOEY, a euphemism for Stalin. The Cardinal's brand of anti-Communism had taken hold.

His eyes steely, Cardinal Spellman pugnaciously looked out over the twenty-eight hundred guests gathered in the Grand Ballroom of the Hotel Astor on St. Patrick's Day in 1948. Cheers erupted as the prelate, his satin robes rustling and flashing in the harsh podium lights, excoriated Communism. Fueled by alcohol and fervor, the crowd roared its approval when Spellman warned that war hadn't ended on V-J Day. "America is no safer from mastery by Communism than was any European country," he declared. "There we witnessed the killing and enslavement of whole peoples by Communists, who, with the shedding of blood, became as if drunk with it!"

The occasion was the annual dinner of the Friendly Sons of St. Patrick's, perhaps the oldest social club in the United States. Most members were wealthy, political, and Catholic. The main speaker for the evening wasn't Spellman, but Harry S Truman; nonetheless, the cardinal was always guaranteed a warm reception at the conservative club's affairs. On this evening the Cardinal and the President were working in tandem to condemn Communism in America, just as they collaborated secretly to stem Communism in Europe. Though Spellman and Truman weren't close, they used each other when it was convenient, much as Roosevelt and Spellman had done.

When the Cardinal took his seat, the room crackled with the spirit of crusaders. The reason wasn't Spellman's typically awkward delivery or his strange, Old Testament–style speech; the fact that a man of his office appeared at all was what the men found so inspiring. Thus, when the evening's main speaker followed Spellman to the podium, the President was also greeted with thunderous applause. Truman thanked the Cardinal and proceeded to denounce Henry Wallace, his former secretary of commerce and present presidential rival, as an agent of Communism. "I do not want and I will not accept the political support of Henry Wallace and his Communists," Truman intoned.

A burst of applause filled the emerald-garlanded ballroom. The smiling President stopped speaking until the clapping, cheers, and table-thumping subsided. "If joining them or permitting them to join me is the price of victory," he said, pausing dramatically to survey the faces in the audience, "I recommend defeat!" Roar after roar of approval swept the room. Again, the President's voice rose above the din. "These are the days of high prices for everything, but any price for Wallace and his Communists is too much for me to pay. I'll not buy it!"

Wallace was one of the stranger characters on the American political landscape. An astute businessman, he was a millionaire, but as a politician he was a failure. A faddist who embraced many causes, he was a teetotaler, a vegetarian, a dabbler in the occult, and a wrestler who had turned to the sport in middle age. As secretary of commerce, he had acted more like secretary of state. In 1946 he had given a speech at Madison Square Garden in which he painted a dark picture of the world and said the major powers had to learn to live with one another, a thought that later found expression as "peaceful coexistence." His talk was well received by the Left and resulted in much controversy because he had criticized policies of both the United States and the Soviet Union. Whenever he mentioned the faults of the United States he was cheered, while boos erupted over criticism of the Soviets. Wallace had been forced from the cabinet because of his opposition to Truman's foreign policy. As the presidential candidate of the Progressive Party, he infuriated Truman by charging that the administration was responsible for the Cold War. Spellman disdained Wallace and had spoken against him, but that wasn't the only reason Truman was at the Catholic dinner. Truman had carefully chosen the place to denounce the candidate of Socialists and Communists. Catholics, as a group, were vehemently anti-Communist; the Friendly Sons were most respectably so, and the man at Truman's side was the nation's number-one Red-baiter.

Spellman favored Dewey in the upcoming election, but he was far too shrewd to turn his back on Truman. He and the President weren't nearly as close as Spellman and Roosevelt had been, and he and Truman had had their differences. Just before becoming a cardinal, for instance, Spellman had complained—most likely at the Pope's bidding—about difficulties Catholic missionaries of German, Italian, and Spanish origin were having in American-controlled territories in the Far East and the Pacific. Apparently, American authorities didn't trust such foreign nationals, who may have helped their nations during the war, just as Spellman had helped his. Nonetheless, Spellman wrote indignant letters to Truman, wondering how anyone could believe priests were capable of anything but God's work.[10] Truman responded that "in the Pacific Islands where the United States strategic interest is paramount, it was considered important that missionaries of United States nationality be utilized to the maximum extent possible. The desirability of this practice is, I think, readily apparent."[11] Spellman got the message: he wrote a few more *pro forma* letters and dropped the issue.

That, however, was merely an unpleasant memory. Now, in 1948, the Cardinal and the Truman administration collaborated closely with the Vatican on a matter of far graver importance. At one point, Spellman referred to the issue in his Friendly Sons' speech: "One month from tomorrow as Italy must make her choice of government, I cannot believe that the Italian people, whom I learned to know and love as I spent with them thirteen of the most precious years of my life, will yield their faith and America's friendship to Soviet Russia's Communist pressure and propaganda."

Not just Spellman and the Church, but also the U.S. government, greatly feared the emergence of a Communist Italy. To prevent such an occurrence, Americans and the Vatican had been working hand in glove for more than a year. The U.S. government lavished money on everything from a huge foreign aid program to secretly funding the Vatican for political purposes. A confidential State Department report from the Vatican indicated what the Church did:

Catholic Action intensified its work in 1947. Inevitably as the menace to the Church increased, the mobilization and activity of the laity on behalf of the Church's mission kept pace. Moreover, the political significance of Catholic Action increased especially in those areas where Communism became a more immediate threat to free institutions, that is, western and southern Europe. This political significance derived not only from the efforts of Catholic Action to invigorate people otherwise indifferent to political and social developments but also from encouragement to militant youth groups and worker groups.[12]

The report noted that the Pope had granted more audiences to Americans and added: ". . . the department is well aware of how frequently the subject of discussion related to Communism and the responsibilities of those in a position to combat it." In the fall of 1947 the Pope received eighteen U.S. senators and forty-eight members of the House.[13]

Although nearly a hundred political parties were fighting for power in Italy, most were inconsequential; the Communists were the most organized and dangerous. In some cases, Communists went so far as to post lists of anti-Communists who were to be executed on election day. In response, the Church lavished huge sums and much time building up the Christian Democratic Party and lashed back at a Communist-inspired, anticlerical press. Political propaganda wars raged in the press. As the election neared, a series of anticlerical, whimsically named weekly newspapers emerged: *Don Basilio* (named for the slanderer in *The Barber of Seville*), *Il Pollo* ("The Chicken"), *Il Mercante* ("The Merchant"), and *Il Cantachiaro* ("The Plain Talker"). Apart from such satiric papers, there were the official organs of the Communist, Socialist, Republican, and other anticlerical political parties.

The Vatican retaliated by taking steps to strengthen Italian libel laws. The Pope went further, declaring that anyone having anything to do with the publication of *Don Basilio* was subject to excommunication. An opposition press was started, and the names of these newspapers were as emotional as those of their foes: *Il Rabarbaro* ("The Rhubarb," a name chosen for an Italian rhubarb cure for bile and liver ailments), *Il Brancaleone* (a medieval officer known for his fearlessness and honesty), and *Fra Cristoforo* (the courageous monk in Manzoni's masterpiece, *Promessi Sposi*).

A report from Myron Taylor's office noted that while "these new pro-Catholic newspapers offer a useful anti-Communist weapon," they had their embarrassing side as well. "At times, they have also indulged in passionate political outbursts which have frequently conveyed the idea that the Catholic Church, the Right Wing parties and Fascism have been closely associated in the past," noted Franklin C. Gowen, an assistant to Taylor, in a State Department memo. "Furthermore, some of the controversial outbursts of these papers against the anti-clerical campaign have not been dignified, for they have used a coarse, violent and even threatening language of the very type used by their opponents."[14]

The Vatican found the opposition press particularly vexing when it highlighted the Church's financial holdings. The companies in which the Church had controlling interests were revealed and that Prince Julio Pacelli, the Pope's uncle and an adviser to the Bank of Rome, was on the board of the Church-dominated gas company and other interests. The Church was made to look more like a conglomerate than a saver of souls.

Spellman was directly involved in America's efforts to buy goodwill in Italy. Partly as a result of his petitions, vast amounts of grain, dried milk, and other goods were shipped there. He had his international affairs expert, Griffiths, draft a position paper on Trieste, which the Pope wanted returned to Italy. Trieste had been Italian since World War I, but after World War II Yugoslavia claimed the seaport in the extreme northeast corner of Italy. As a solution the region was placed under the protection of the United Nations Security Council. This gave the Italians an advantage since the Yugoslavs physically held the port.[15]

No one knew how much money Spellman funneled directly to the Vatican, but it must have been considerable. He gained a reputation within the Church of using New York money to fund clandestine Church operations. He made no secret, though, of his partisanship in Italy. The Powerhouse was throbbing. Griffiths dashed about, meeting with State Department, Italian, and American relief officials. He asked Spellman to give a broadcast over the Voice of America during the week before the election and suggested that the Cardinal extend a similar offer to General George Marshall. As the election showdown neared, Griffiths warned Spellman that Italian diplomats were "positively desperate and almost immobilized by the fear which hangs over them for armed revolution in Italy before elections or some other disastrous failure at the polls which will put Italy behind the Iron Curtain."[16]

Spellman knew too well of such jitteriness. He heard the same message from the Pope, who, as usual, was pessimistic. In January, Spellman had insisted that the Pope see an officer of the American embassy in Rome. The Cardinal probably wanted the diplomat to reassure the Pope, but, with the specter of Stepinac and other European setbacks haunting him, Pius couldn't be calmed. The Pope "expressed himself as greatly concerned over [the] election outlook, and felt that Socialist-Communist blocs could very easily win [a] plurality," a State Department memo on the encounter stated. "Net impression given was that he was extremely worried about the election results and in fact had little hope of a success for anti-Communist parties."[17] Later the Pope demanded assurances that the United States would support the anti-Communists right up to the election before he spoke publicly on the matter. There was little chance that the United States would back down. In the 1947–48 fiscal year alone, America poured $350 million into Italy in the form of relief and political payments.

To date, the Pope's speeches on the election had been pointed, but, as usual, not so sharp as they could have been. On September 7 he told more than 300,000 people who jammed St. Peter's Square that "the opposing fronts in the religious and moral fields are becoming ever more clearly defined. . . . Are you ready?" A day later he actually told a Catholic women's organization that it was a sin not to vote,[18] and, in his Christmas Eve broadcast, he made his strongest statement: "He is a deserter and a traitor who would give his material support, his services, his talents, aid or vote to parties and to forces which deny God. . . ."

While Pacelli hid behind vagaries, other ecclesiastics used the full force of religion to scare people away from the Communists. Cardinal Schuster of Milan, for instance, became front-page news when he instructed his diocese that "it is a serious offense for the faithful to give their vote to a candidate or list of candidates manifestly contrary to the Church. . . ." The archbishops of Milan and Palermo instructed the clergy to deny absolution to Communists or Marxist Socialists. The egotistical Cardinal Tisserant declared that Communists and Socialists were to receive no absolution or confession.

"They may not have Christian burial or be buried in holy grounds beneath the sign of the cross," he warned.[19]

In the United States, Spellman spearheaded a Vatican-inspired letter-writing campaign encouraging Italian Americans to urge relatives to vote against Communists. "The fate of Italy depends upon the forthcoming election and the conflict between Communism and Christianity, between slavery and freedom," stated Spellman's pastoral letter. Mail to Italy reached a flood tide. Spellman also, at General Donovan's behest, joined the ranks of prominent Americans, including Frank Sinatra, Bing Crosby, and Gary Cooper, who were making radio broadcasts to be aired in Italy at election time.

From February through election days, April 18 and 19, Italians were bombarded with radio messages from America—words of friendship from the famous and reminders of all that America had done for the nation. The blitz included reprints of articles from U.S. newspapers and magazines about the dangers of Soviet expansion and the Communist seizure of the Hungarian government. Hundreds of photos, depicting Truman's turning over merchant ships to Italy and similar themes, deluged Italian newspapers.

As the election approached, both sides prepared for battle. Boatloads of Yugoslav Communist toughs were smuggled in to beef up Italian cadres. Communist war chests were filled with vote-buying lire. The opposition had shock troops and massive American funding. Seminaries were closed and clerics and students were ordered to do what they could. One priest, a Father Bichierai in northern Italy, organized three hundred youths into a battle unit and had guns at the ready. American money was used to buy jeeps, bedding, and other supplies. Tanks rumbled ominously off American freighters anchored in Naples; under the Truman Plan to stop Communism, they were destined for Greece. The Naples layover was ostensibly to refuel, but in reality it was a display of military muscle to frighten Italian Communists.

On the election days ninety percent of the voters turned out to give the Christian Democrats an overwhelming victory. The fears of the Pope and ranking Italian diplomats had been unfounded. Spellman had done his job, which had begun during the war when he had convinced the Roosevelt administration that Italy shouldn't be allowed to wither in the aftermath of war. During the current campaign, he had increased his activities so that he met with congressmen, senators, business leaders, and others to whom he preached the threat of Communism in Italy. The victory, as much as it belonged to any American, was his. Italy became the first nation in which the U.S. government, the Pope, and Spellman clandestinely combined forces to defeat Communism.

Now that Italy was safe, the Pope turned his attention once again to practical concerns. The Vatican had spent a great deal of money bringing the Christian Democrats to power; the Pope sent Count

Galeazzi to Spellman and Joe Kennedy to find a way to make up the Vatican losses.[20] The Pope didn't expect the money to come from Spellman's seemingly inexhaustible treasury; he didn't see why Church money had to be used at all. He wanted the rich American government to give him the funds. Once again, the Pope expected Spellman to perform the kind of miracle that had helped him in his rise to power. *Romantia*.

Four months after the Italian election, Spellman met quietly with George Marshall, who was now secretary of state. Spellman and Marshall knew each other well, and Marshall went over laundry lists of Vatican concerns with the Cardinal much the way he would with a foreign minister of a European government. Spellman supported the Marshall Plan, which was just getting under way and which would prompt spending more than $12 billion in Europe during the next few years as a practical anti-Communist measure. During this particular encounter Marshall gave Spellman good news. His special pleading for reimbursement of Vatican funds spent on the Italian election was successful. "The Vatican had been promised that American funds would be made available to assist in the presentation of the anti-Communist appeal to the Italian public," Spellman wrote to Rome of his Marshall visit. He added that the U.S. government had secretly "released large sums in 'black currency' in Italy to the Catholic Church."[21]

Spellman's report to Rome emphasized the strict confidentiality of the transaction. One reason for the secrecy, he said, was that "Subversive groups in the United States would grasp this as a very effective pretense for attacking the United States Government for having released money to the Vatican, even though indirectly conveyed."[22] Such a revelation would be political dynamite if it fell into Republican hands. This was an election year, and once again the Catholic issue was creating havoc. Myron Taylor wanted to leave his post, and various Protestant groups were petitioning for the shutdown of the mission. Truman would be doomed if it became known that his administration had secretly funded the Holy See. Spellman's own anti-Communist crusade might be harmed as well.

Lightning flashed across the darkening sky as sheets of chilling rain beat down on the thirty thousand people gathered at New York's Polo Grounds on May Day 1949. Cardinal Spellman was leading a "procession of protests" against Communist repression of the Church in Eastern Europe. Moving slowly across the slippery grass, their heads bowed under the furious rain, were religious figures and politicians, including Vice President Alben W. Barkley, Mayor O'Dwyer, City Council President Vincent Impellitteri, and Monsignor Fulton Sheen, who was as rabidly anti-Communist as Spellman and had a reputation as an orator.

The synthesis of religion and politics that Spellman achieved at his demonstrations produced an odd kind of evangelical Americanism. National, state, and local politicians braved the foul weather so they could be seen by the massive number of Catholic voters who came to be reassured that Communism would be repelled. Any politician worth his salt wanted to be identified as an anti-Communist, because Communism was believed to be corrupting both America and the world at large.

The United States was on an anti-Communist crusade that would become an obsession. The House Un-American Activities Committee was investigating Communism in Hollywood, even though the only flagrantly pro-Soviet picture made there, *Mission to Moscow,* was produced by Jack Warner, the most conservative studio boss in the nation, who used a full-time investigator to check on the patriotism of his employees. The press was filled with the federal grand jury testimony of Elizabeth Bentley, the former mistress of a Soviet agent, who named government employees she contended were agents. Within months, Whittaker Chambers fingered Alger Hiss—from all appearances a pillar of the American establishment, a member of Roosevelt's Yalta team and an organizer of the United Nations Charter—as a member of the Communist network in Washington in the 1930s. Internationally, Communists were oozing across Europe and appeared to be winning in China. Catholics knew well that each Communist gain was a loss for the Church. This was nowhere more apparent than in Hungary, where the Church was provided with its greatest twentieth-century martyr—Josef Cardinal Mindszenty, who had strange ties to Cardinal Spellman.

At the conclusion of the procession, Vice President Barkley strode to a microphone facing a gold-and-white altar in the center of the sopping field. His speech, echoing eerily from loudspeakers, sounded like a page torn from one of Spellman's sermons:

> Life is worthless without liberty. The American trinity of virtues— life, liberty and pursuit of happiness—is being attacked by an ideology and a concept that is in the utter negation of those principles. This concept has been imposed by a totalitarian system and is attempting to make inroads in our own democracy.
>
> We will do well, today, as we enjoy our American liberties, to see to it that this wicked, crawling creeping economic disease, this alien nostrum, shall not be permitted to invade or get a foothold in the United States of America. We should educate our people to the danger that confronts them. . . .

The other main speaker was Monsignor Sheen. A mystical-looking man with deep-set dark eyes and a spellbinding voice, Sheen had a well-deserved reputation as an ardent anti-Communist. In condemning Marxism, he had spewed forth a river of sermons, pamphlets, and books. He viewed Communism as a secular religion, one based on a disastrous view of man that wickedly denied God.

For years, Sheen had been much sought after as an orator. Inevitably, Spellman turned to him to help him in his own anti-Communist onslaught, and the Church's prophet of Communist doom worked his special magic. As Sheen followed Barkley at the microphone, the roiling skies and crackling lightning only accentuated the drama that he naturally exuded when speaking. Raising his voice Sheen declared: "There is not anything to fear from the Church. Communism cannot be judged by its foreign policy. We have been on the record on this from the beginning."

Lowering his voice he added ominously: "And we say that Communism is intrinsically evil!"

Thunder boomed in the background like cannon fire as Sheen urged the audience to pray for Communist oppressors. Their fight, he said, wasn't with the Russian people but with the evils of Communism. Since 1917, he said, the Church had suffered because it insisted on asserting the "supremacy of the soul!" The crowd was mesmerized, but the rally was merely one salvo in Spellman's propaganda war. The Church had suffered major setbacks all over Eastern Europe. He meant to keep the Communist victories constantly before the public. This meant taking the cause to the streets. The day before the rally, a Loyalty Day Parade in Manhattan had drawn more than fifty thousand marchers. The affair was put together by Charlie Silver and the Catholic War Veterans. The grim-faced marchers had been reviewed by Spellman and a host of public officials, including Secretary of Labor Maurice Tobin and Secretary of the Interior Julius Krug. Jim Farley, who turned out for any political gathering, stood with them.

Such events were marked by special contingents who had grievances against Communism: Greeks, Poles, Yugoslavs, and other ethnic groups. They carried signs such as WE'VE LICKED FASCISM AND NAZISM: COMMUNISM IS NEXT and COMMUNISTS SLAUGHTERED 228 PRIESTS IN GREECE. Lately, the rallies were marked by the presence of Hungarians. They carried crepe-draped portraits of Cardinal Mindszenty, the latest churchman victimized by Communists. Other Church leaders, such as Stepinac, were considered martyrs. Czechoslovakia's Archbishop Josef Beran would soon be placed under house arrest and sentenced to the prison castle Rapselov for a dozen years. None of these men, however, achieved the same stature in Church hagiology as Mindszenty, who became the symbol of the Catholic Church's suffering behind the Iron Curtain.

On the night of December 26, 1948, a black limousine had glided up to Mindszenty's palace. Several other cars arrived seconds later. Colonel Desci, the Budapest chief of police, rang the bell while subordinates toting machine guns surrounded the palace. When the door opened, Desci pushed his way inside, climbed the stairs leading to the cardinal's private apartment, and arrested Mindszenty, an outspoken critic of the regime who had been involved in a number of antigovernment activities.[23]

The Communists had long claimed the Church represented a weight of unjust history that crushed the people. They accused the Church of being an exploiter that controlled education, owned vast tracts of land and great wealth, and collaborated with the ruling class to influence the political as well as spiritual lives of its flock. To undermine his authority, Mindszenty was indicted on three charges: treason against the State, espionage, and illegal foreign exchange transactions. The primate of Hungary believed that except for the king, he was the nation's chief spokesman. During the trial Spellman's name surprisingly emerged as one of Mindszenty's collaborators. The Hungarian government claimed that Mindszenty had supplied "reports to Western powers" on Hungarian and Soviet matters, including minutes of cabinet meetings. Moreover, he was charged with organizing, with Spellman, a clandestine royalist movement that would place Otto von Hapsburg, the pretender to the Austro-Hungarian throne, as head of a Federated Central European Kingdom.

When Mindszenty visited New York in 1946, the Hungarian government said, he had consulted with Spellman, who suggested that Mindszenty write the following statement: "I declare that Otto von Hapsburg is authorized with full right to represent the Hungarian Catholics abroad and especially in the United States."

One result of the two cardinals' meeting was certain. They collaborated on keeping the Crown of St. Stephen, a symbol of legitimate rulership in Hungary, out of the government's hands. The Church had given the crown, a thousand years earlier, to the king of Hungary for having converted pagan nobles to Christianity. Near the end of World War II, Hungarian guards of the pro-Nazi regime had absconded with the national treasure and given it to American troops to keep it from the Russians. For his part, Spellman made overtures to the U.S. State Department to prevent the crown from being returned to Budapest from Munich, where the Americans kept it. The Hungarian government had petitioned for the crown's return.[24]

Hungary was in political turmoil after the war. When Prime Minister Ferenc Nagy was secretly approached by U.S. officials about the crown, he surprisingly said he was opposed to the restoration of the property because he feared public reaction. Nagy, who was having problems with the new regime even though he was Prime Minister, asked the Americans to keep the crown. "Saint Stephen's jewelry had deep religious significance and political implications in Hungary which make this request exceptional," a War Department memo noted on February 8, 1947.[25]

During Mindszenty's trial it was revealed that Spellman had given money to the Hungarian cardinal. The government presented the canceled checks, drawn on Chemical Bank in New York. Mindszenty had spent some of the money on two limousines for himself, but the government contended that the rest of the money had been used to finance activities against the regime. The possibility of the validity of the charges against Spellman and Mindszenty was lost in the nature of his trial. Like Stepinac's it was a sham, only worse. At the height of the trial, Mindszenty appeared before the court. No longer robust and domineering, he looked sick. He had obviously been drugged and broken. Meekly confessing his guilt on all counts, he was sentenced to death. Later, the verdict was commuted to life in prison, but did little to subdue the public outcry. Once again, the world was shocked by the lengths to which Communists went. The charges that Spellman himself was implicated seemed like paranoid ravings in light of the mockery of justice. American observers had been refused admittance to the trial. The Vatican had cautioned the world not to believe any confession that might emerge.[26]

Spellman's crusade against Communism intensified. Mindszenty's only crime, he declared, was "the defense of the rights of God and man against Christ-hating Communists whose allegiance is pledged to Satan!" His next step indicated how seriously he took the cause. On February 6, Cardinal Spellman made one of his rare appearances on the pulpit of St. Patrick's, his first since V-E Day nearly four years earlier. His speech presented an almost medieval vision of a hellish world:

> A new god has come to you, my people. His fiery eyes do not flash through clouds of incense or from altar candles. They do not gleam from gold-framed darkened pictures of saints. The new god is not a stone statue worn smooth by the kisses of the faithful—he was not born in heaven. He is not far away, nor is he hidden from us. The new god is born from earth and blood—he strides ahead and under the thunder of his steps the globe trembles from East and West. This is the red god. The Seine shudders at his impact and tries to break its banks. Westminster trembles before him like Jericho and across the green ocean his red shadow falls on the walls of the White House. Hosanna! New God.
>
> My dear friends, you know these words are not mine! They are words of an Hungarian Communist, words that echo the thoughts of men depraved and deranged; men who do not know truth, love, justice or faith; men who as their gods know only Satan and Stalin!

The Cardinal declared "Cardinal Mindszenty Day—a day of prayer and protest." His congregation looked up at his pulpit, awestruck.

"Had I a hundred tongues, a hundred mouths, a voice of iron I could not encompass all the crimes of the 'men of sin,' " he declared.

"I avow that unless the American people, without further ostrich-like actions and pretenses, unite to stop the Communist floodings of our own land, our sons, for the third and last time shall be summoned from the comforts, tranquility and love of their own homes and families to bear arms against those who would desecrate and destroy them. . . . Help save civilization from the world's most fiendish, ghoulish men of slaughter. . . ."

Spellman vocalized what a lot of men thought: war with the Soviet Union was inevitable. In a dangerous power play, the Soviet Union only months earlier had established a blockade of all land and water between West Berlin and West Germany. The United States was leading a massive airlift through three air corridors left open to Western powers.

In light of everything that had happened since the war, politicians at all levels rallied to the Mindszenty cause, reflecting the outrage of their constituents. Mayor O'Dwyer exhorted Secretary of State Acheson to do everything in his power to prevent the"lynching" of Mindszenty. The Senate approved a resolution condemning the injustice done the cardinal. Brooklyn Congressman Andrew L. Sommers went so far as to cable the Hungarian Communist leader Mátyás Rakosi that he personally would "create within your country an underground movement which will mean the eventual destruction of your government."

Ultraright-wing Catholics responded by forming Freedom Foundations and Mindszenty Circles to destroy Communism. They established themselves along the lines of Communist cells and met in secret to pore over Communist propaganda to uncover plots. Looking everywhere for Communist inroads, they usually found them everywhere. The fear at large only served to make Spellman stronger. Letters praising Spellman's crusade appeared not only in the Catholic press but also in major newspapers. The Cardinal, like the crime fighter and fellow Communist-hater J. Edgar Hoover, became a national monument.

The only criticism of Spellman came from Socialist and Communist sources, and was dismissed out of hand by most people. For example, in the *Daily Worker* the novelist Howard Fast responded to a letter praising Spellman that had been sent to a New York newspaper by a Jew, Benjamin Gross. The impact of what Fast said was lost because of his forum and his own Communist involvement, but the novelist made a disturbing point:

> It may be that as a Jew, Mr. Gross was wholly unmoved by the considerable proof of Mindszenty's outspoken anti-Semitism; or again it may be that Mr. Benjamin Gross thinks in such broad and abstract terms of factors of justice that such matters as anti-Semitism do not enter the picture at all. . . . I recall to Mr. Gross a picture that was

prominently displayed in the New York *Herald Tribune* as well as in other places a number of years ago. The picture showed the Chief Rabbi of Berlin sweeping dung from the streets, while brown-shirts prodded and bystanders jeered. And at that time, if Mr. Gross recalls, some 50 other rabbis were dying a slow death in German concentration camps.

Now I submit that Cardinal Spellman's voice was not raised in defense of those rabbis. No whisper of rage came from the Pope in Rome and the Department of State here preserved a dignified silence. Harry Truman, who was then a senator, made no statement concerning these vile indignities, and the newspapers of America contained themselves in modest disapproval. . . .

Americans, however, were frightened. Public-opinion polls revealed that the vast majority of citizens believed that Communism would destroy Christianity if given the chance. The world view held for years by Spellman and Pacelli now prevailed in America. The Cold War was on: the United States provided the cold steel, the Catholic Church the moral force.

Spellman kept up his assaults. The May 24, 1949, issue of *Look* magazine, for instance, printed an article by the Cardinal entitled "The Pope's War on Communism." The article stated that the Pope "has embarked on a spiritual crusade against the atheistic philosophies of Communist Russia." Of course, the piece dealt with Mindszenty. One of its more curious aspects was that Spellman treated the Hungarian as though he were dead. "No harm upon this soul can any atheist inflict," he wrote. Publicly, he began speaking of him in the past tense as well, apparently completing Mindszenty's martyrdom. The photographs accompanying the article were interesting. Though the article was about the "Pope's War," there was only a half-page, black-and-white picture of Pius. Spellman himself warranted a full-page color photo showing him looking overwhelmed by his full ceremonial vestments.

The Pope escalated his war in July when he issued a sweeping decree. Catholics anywhere in the world who "defend and spread the materialistic and anti-Christian doctrine of Communism" were excommunicated. The decree had far-reaching implications for the Cold War. A Central Intelligence Agency analysis of the excommunication decree provided some insight into what was likely to happen:

By this decision, the two most powerful organizations for moving men to act on behalf of a doctrine are brought into open and basic conflict. The possible long-term ramifications of this conflict cannot be easily or comprehensively defined. The decree will be a very powerful factor in the East-West struggle. In Eastern Europe, it implies a struggle to the bitter end. . . . In the East it clearly defines the lines of battle. In many other areas of the world, the decree will exert a powerful and prolonged indirect pressure on both policy and action. Communist governments and Communists generally will have to accept the issue as now posed. Although the Communist governments would obviously have preferred to carry on their anti-church campaign at their own pace, the power of decision has now been taken from them. The conflict can be pressed on them with a speed and comprehensiveness that may well affect the satisfactory development of other Communist policies. . . .

Later in the year Communists tried to counteract the blizzard of bad publicity that the Mindszenty affair had generated. Dmitri Manuilsky, the foreign minister of the Soviet Ukraine, appeared before the United Nations Political Committee to contend that Spellman had given Mindszenty $30,000 in 1947 to help restore Otto von Hapsburg to the throne. The churchmen, he said, weren't all they seemed to be.

Manuilsky had been on the defensive for months. Day after day, it seemed, he had to respond to accusations by Western nations that Communists had violated the human-rights provisions of the peace treaty. Americans, in particular, showed open contempt and hostility toward governments that had dragged religious figures through courtrooms in such a terrible fashion. Anticlericalism had never been part of the American political fabric, because there had never been a State Church. For the most part, Americans found it difficult to believe that religious figures could exert a strong hand in government, let alone try to topple a regime.

Thus, Manuilsky's charges against Spellman were treated as preposterous, a view that Spellman himself fueled. "If for thirty thousand dollars democracy with its freedoms could be secured in any of the countries under the Soviet domination, all our soldiers and their relatives would know that it was the greatest bargain since Manhattan was bought from the Indians," he told reporters with characteristic irony.

Spellman knew that in such a case he could tell the truth to the press and not be believed. The reporters laughed and wrote up their stories, not realizing that the Cardinal meant what he had said. As shown in Italy, the Church and the United States were willing to spend a great deal more than that. If members of the press scoffed at the idea that Spellman was an international power broker, one reason was that he didn't seem to have time for such a role. The Cardinal had become so enmeshed in New York politics that it was difficult to believe he could do more than that. Spellman had his hand in so many matters of public policy that he might well have been a city official. It was said that the mayor himself genuflected when he even heard the word "Powerhouse."

CHAPTER EIGHT

The Powerhouse

SPELLMAN FIRMLY BELIEVED THAT POWER HAD TO BE USED. After the war, he held tremendous power, which he fully intended to exploit in each role that he had carved out for himself: churchman, diplomat, politician, militarist.

His anti-Communist stance brought him greater fame. His influence extended around the globe. Since he spent most of his time in New York, he concentrated most of his immense energy on the city, and brought to bear the full impact of his personality there. New York was the easiest place for him to carry out his ambitions. Unlike Washington, where there was suspicion of his religion, or Rome, where there was disdain for his Americanism, New York was where politicians in particular shared his world view; literally millions of people honored him as a great and holy man. As his power mushroomed Spellman came to believe that he could act with the same impunity in the secular arena as in the ecclesiastic. He was the dynamo who ran the Powerhouse, and he began to attract attention, not just in New York but around the nation, because of the way he used his office.

In the spring of 1945, Spellman and one of his secretaries called on the relatives of Al Smith. The governor had died a year earlier, and Spellman wanted to inform the family that he was establishing a special dinner in Smith's honor to raise money for a St. Vincent's Hospital wing—to be named after Smith. The Cardinal had Gertrude Algase to thank for the idea. She and Spellman routinely kicked around innovative ways to raise money. His financial commitments were enormous: it took millions every year just to run the archdiocese, let alone support the massive building programs, Spellman's trips, and the gifts he lavished on friends, relatives, convents, schools, and Vatican personnel.

That the Alfred E. Smith Memorial Dinner turned into a political extravaganza was beside the point initially. At the time, Spellman simply hoped it would finance yet another of his projects. After a rocky period following the war when the national economy suffered, the Church in America grew stronger than ever. Catholics, like other Americans, generally grew more affluent, and they helped their Church financially. The Church also gained tremendously in terms of the number of young men and women, horrified by war, who entered seminaries and convents. A mood of optimism swept through the clergy like wildfire, and Spellman wasn't immune. Growth was the key word on American churchmen's lips and would remain there for fifteen years following the war. The period was marked by unprecedented construction programs across the country as archdioceses built schools, churches, and other facilities so parishes could keep abreast of the baby boom. In time, many of the projects would become financial drains, but in the 1940s and 1950s it seemed that Church expansion would be unlimited. Nowhere was the growth greater than in New York. A look at the archdiocesan building statistics for the years 1955 to 1959 provides some insight into the magnitude of Spellman's projects: he spent a staggering $168.1 million on the construction of fifteen churches, ninety-four schools, twenty-two rectories, sixty convents, and thirty-four other institutions.

Finding the money for these projects was Spellman's responsibility. Half of the archdiocese's revenues came from the four hundred parishes reporting to him. The rest came from a hodgepodge of foundations and from the archdiocese's stock portfolio, gifts, and legacies. The Cardinal sought out financially shrewd priests to head his various departments and to become pastors, and he constantly urged his staff to come up with new money-making ideas.

Spellman counted on his Committee of the Laity, a legion of well-off businessmen led by John Coleman of the Stock Exchange and John Burke of B. Altman's, as a source of funding. He himself constantly sought rich men and women, whom he pampered in the hope that they would bequeath their fortunes to the Church. During his tenure such gifts to the New York archdiocese and its archbishop went from being the occasional to the usual. One of the earliest of such big donors was Major Edward Bowes, the radio personality, who left the Church $3 million when he died in 1946.

When it was mentioned that a pleasant, eccentric, and very wealthy Protestant woman had in her old age become enamored with the Church, Spellman immediately set aside time to see her. She was Mabel Gilman Corey, a former chorus girl and now the widow of a president of U.S. Steel. Because of her storybook leap to fortune, she was immortalized in the song "She's Only a Bird in a Gilded Cage," which she loathed. Mrs. Corey swiftly learned the joys of being one of the Cardinal's friends. She was invited to lunches and teas and given a special tour of the cathedral by Spellman. He sent her holy pictures and notes, and, when she expressed a bizarre desire to live in a convent, Spellman spent the better part of a night badgering and cajoling mother superiors of convents before moving her into one operated by the Trinitarian Sisters.[1]

Whenever he could, Spellman visited her on the way home from a banquet, grabbing flowers from the head table on the way out as a present for her. When Mrs. Corey took brief vacations to Atlantic City, Spellman made the chancery priests turn out en masse to wave goodbye at the train station. When she returned they were all there to fuss over her. Spellman helped make her life a good deal more pleasant, and later he was rewarded well. When she died in 1960, Mrs. Corey entrusted Spellman with $5 million for the Church.

Though such gifts were greatly desired, they couldn't be counted on as a predictable source of revenue. Thus, Spellman appreciated Mortal Sin's suggestion for a Smith benefit. He thought that she was probably right in believing a Smith affair would generate a good turnout. The Smith name was magic in New York, and the Happy Warrior himself had been a major fund-raiser for Catholic charities. Together, Spellman and Mrs. Algase drafted a plan for the affair until a priest ventured to ask whether the Smith family knew of it. To remedy the oversight, Spellman visited the governor's widow, Catherine; his daughter of the same name; and his daughter's husband, Francis J. Quillinan. The Smith relatives listened with great interest as the Cardinal explained his wonderful plans to bring further glory to the governor's memory. They were appreciative, until they heard that Spellman intended to charge a hundred dollars for a seat at the banquet.

"The price is too high," Quillinan would recall protesting. "It will rule out many of Al's friends." Quillinan never forgot Spellman's reply. The archbishop shrugged and said, "The only way to do it is to find out who will pay the price." Spellman himself wasn't certain how the affair would turn out, but he decided to go for broke. "If they pay, they pay," he said.[2]

The Smith dinner reflected Spellman's unabashed approach toward fund-raising. He invited everyone of prominence. Moreover, he contacted Mrs. Mendelssohn, the wealthy Detroit woman he had known during his Vatican days, and asked her to underwrite the cost of the affair, which she did. As word of the dinner spread around New York, Spellman was approached by a wealthy Jewish textile executive, Charles Silver, who wanted to help.

Silver had begun his life in America as an immigrant on the Lower East Side, and had risen to become vice president of the American Woolen Company. The fact that he one day wound up a friend and confidant of a Roman Catholic cardinal had much to say for his determination, drive, financial health, and political ambitions. Gregarious and generous, Silver loved leading a public life, rubbing shoulders with the well-to-do and the powerful. He inevitably gravitated to Spellman's orbit, and, because he was successful, it was quite natural for the Cardinal to take to Silver. The fact that Silver was a phenomenal fund-raiser made Spellman appreciate him all the more. Before long, Silver had sold hundreds of tickets to the dinner, far more than any other individual, a feat that greatly impressed Spellman. Since Silver sold so many tickets to wealthy Jews, the Cardinal saw him as invaluable: the Jewish community was one that Spellman wanted to know better, at least on a financial basis. Thus, to Silver's everlasting gratitude, Spellman made him chairman of the Alfred E. Smith Memorial Dinner, a position he was to hold for more than thirty-five years.

As Spellman and Silver got to know each other, they used one another well. Each introduced the other to men of influence in their respective religious circles, and they helped one another in many political causes—such as pushing for the recognition of Israel—that seemed, superficially, to have little to do with either of them. But both men knew the world worked in strange ways. For now, both were glad that the Smith dinner was an instant success. Thanks to Spellman, his old friend Governor Dewey was the main speaker, and thanks to Silver, many well-heeled New Yorkers, including a great many textile-company executives, were in attendance. What surprised Smith's friends was the array of wealthy Republicans who came; Smith hadn't much use for them when he was alive, and they had had little use for Smith. Spellman himself became annoyed when someone pointed out the irony that so many former anti-Smith people were present. "The tables are filled, aren't they?" he snapped and walked away.

Money is money and politics is politics, but Spellman always had a knack for bringing them together, much as he brought together Americanism and religion. From the beginning, the Smith dinner was largely a Republican show. Dewey set the tone for the gathering, even more than the wealthy Republicans did. When he ran for the presidency in 1948, Dewey was again the keynote speaker, as was Eisenhower in 1952 and Nixon in 1956. Though the Cardinal was known to have Republican sympathies,which the selection of speakers merely substantiated, Democrats didn't boycott the affair. Some attended because the dinner, after all, honored one of the party's heroes. Others simply hoped to keep Spellman off their backs by supporting his cause.

Frank Adams, who in 1953 became police commissioner of New York, remembered that Spellman, by the time of the first Smith dinner in 1945, had already hurt the Democrats. As finance director for the state Democratic Party a year earlier, Adams had had a tough time raising money from traditional Irish-Catholic groups; phone calls hadn't been returned and checks hadn't been sent in, Adams believed, because Spellman was working against his party. One reason was an alliance state Democrats had formed with the American Labor Party, which Spellman and others believed was infiltrated by Communists. What Adams didn't know was the depth of Vatican anger over the bombing of Rome and the rising influence of the Soviet Union that Roosevelt had outlined to Spellman. The archbishop apparently wasn't going to do anything to help the President's party. "Spellman didn't help us—just the opposite," Adams would recall. He believed, but couldn't prove, that Spellman had asked big contributors to sit on their hands. Unlike most New York politicians, Adams wasn't afraid to criticize the prelate. "He was too pushy and involved in a lot of things he shouldn't have been," Adams asserted.[3]

Publicly, Spellman usually made a fuss over all politicians, no matter what their party affiliation. Thus, when the Democratic mayoral candidate, William O'Dwyer, attended the first Smith dinner, Spellman paid him special attention. The archbishop's relationship with La Guardia had never warmed and he was intent on doing better with O'Dwyer.

O'Dwyer was similar to many men who had risen to become mayor of New York during the previous century. He was gregarious, charming, and corrupt. An immigrant who had joined the police force and gone to law school in his spare time, he had received a great deal of publicity, much the way Governor Dewey had, by going after the sensationally named "Murder Inc." when he was a district attorney. The gangsters O'Dwyer netted, however, proved to be small fry who rarely went to prison. Once the publicity surrounding them had died down, O'Dwyer didn't seem to press his cases with much vigor, nor did he take exceptionally good care of his witnesses. One key witness in protective custody, for example, either jumped, fell, or was helped out of a high window before he could testify.[4]

Several months after the Smith dinner, O'Dwyer was sworn in as mayor. Archbishop Spellman, wearing the scarlet silk robes of his office, gave his blessing at the ceremony. Thereafter, Spellman appeared at nearly every city dedication of a new building, bridge, or tunnel, and unveiling of a monument. He loved the publicity he received on such occasions; he also knew that public perception of him as a man involved in city affairs was a logical outcome of his appearances. Moreover, O'Dwyer started involving Spellman in the selection of judges and politically appointed city officials as well as nominees for elected offices. O'Dwyer also helped Spellman get city jobs for friends and friends of friends. In return, O'Dwyer received the archbishop's blessing in public. The Powerhouse became an important factor in the daily political life of the city.

"If there were several qualified candidates for a job and one of them was close to Spellman, he got the job," remembered Julius Edelstein, who had been an aide to Governor Lehman.[5] The process, though, was a bit more complex. Spellman rarely said outright whom he wanted for an office, but he said whom he didn't want. "The Cardinal didn't say who to pick," recalled Abe Beame.[6] "Three candidates for a job were usually taken to him. If he didn't like any of the candidates, he said so." The man would be withdrawn, but there was a lot of second-guessing before it ever got to that stage. The politicians did their best to pick men acceptable to the Cardinal, who represented such an enormous voting bloc in the city.

Generally, Spellman was courteous toward the men who ran the city. He sent notes, telling how much he enjoyed a speech one gave or asking about the health of another. He appeared at their relatives' wakes and their testimonial dinners. He had his picture taken with them, a sign of his public support of them or their policies. When he was offended he withdrew his support. Spellman played by the rules of Tammany Hall: Do a man a favor and he will do one for you.

On occasion, the Cardinal vented his anger with politicians behind closed doors. In 1946, for instance, O'Dwyer confronted a furious Spellman. A Republican district captain and poll-watcher named Joseph Scottoriggio had turned down a bribe from a mobster to allow fraudulent votes at his polling station. On his way to the polls, he was beaten to death by two thugs. The archbishop was incensed that O'Dwyer had let events in the city get so far out of hand. An election-day murder hadn't occurred in New York for decades and this one shouldn't have either, Spellman contended. Furthermore, Spellman seethed because Vito Marcantonio, a left-wing politician who had built a powerful political machine thanks to a well-greased patronage system, had won the Democratic primary for Congress. Spellman loathed Marcantonio, who adhered to the Communist line while Spellman was crusading against Communism.

The murder received tremendous press coverage. Spellman told O'Dwyer to give the appearance, at least, of trying to clean up the city. "Spellman was furious," according to Warren Moscow, a political reporter for *The New York Times* who later became a deputy mayor. "He chewed out O'Dwyer, and the mayor publicly called for reform."[7]

During the same election, Moscow reflected, Spellman received a call from Governor Dewey, who was backing General Hugh A. Drum in a bitter fight over the Republican nomination for the Senate. Anti-Dewey forces were backing Spellman's old O.S.S. friend Wild Bill Donovan. "Dewey called the Cardinal and apologized, saying it must have been an oversight but there weren't any Catholics on his group's slate of candidates," Moscow said.

Spellman pointedly replied, "You *do* have a Catholic."

"We do?" the perplexed Dewey asked.

"Yes," Spellman replied. Then he mentioned the name of a Catholic politician.[8]

The cobwebs cleared from the governor's brain. The Cardinal's man ran for office.[9]

Spellman's political influence was felt in other ways. After the war production ended, the job pool shrank, and economic uncertainty again beset the nation. The construction industry in New York was pressed especially hard. Pastors reported to Spellman that many construction workers' families were in a bad way. Sunday collection baskets weren't full, and no relief was in sight. Spellman had a possible solution. During the war he had erased the huge debt inherited from Hayes. Now Spellman wanted to embark on a building program, which he believed would shake loose construction plans for a lot of major companies around town that were wary about making large capital investments.

First, he summoned the local labor leaders to his office. He told them that he was considering a large-scale construction program but wanted a guarantee that his projects would be worked on by the most skilled union members and that these workers wouldn't be siphoned off if other construction programs materialized. Once the union leaders agreed, Spellman appeared at a dinner at the Hotel Astor, where he addressed construction company presidents and labor leaders. If contractors gave him reasonable cost estimates, he said, he was ready to embark upon a $25-million building plan, mostly for schools. As he expected, corporations quickly followed suit.[10] Construction companies had as much work as they could handle. Sunday collections in many parishes picked up. Politicians once again recognized Spellman's influence and canniness.

Overall, Spellman spent more than a billion dollars on construction projects during his twenty-eight years in power. After New York City government itself, the Church was the biggest builder in the region. The projects included such diverse institutions as the $11-million Foundling Hospital and a $6-million high school named after Spellman himself. He also constructed a $3-million Cardinal Hayes High School. (Not following the customary alphabetical order, the Spellman school's marching band preceded that of the Hayes school in St. Patrick's Day parades.)

The more successes the Cardinal had, the less tolerant he became of people with ideas at odds with his own. For an unusually pragmatic man, he came to believe that his world view was right and he disdained those who didn't share it. That he became so dogmatic was understandable. He was treated with such deference that it was almost impossible for such a man to be anything but rigid. He was lionized nationally for his anti-Communism; the Pope constantly sought his favor; politicians, from the President down, consulted with him. Spellman grew so secure that when he dropped his humble mask in public on occasion, angrily striking out at figures of prominence, he revealed the kind of man he often was in private. One of the first people he attacked in such fashion was Eleanor Roosevelt.

On June 23, 1949, Cardinal Spellman was in a foul mood, making the chancery staff more skittish than usual. He paced about his office, icily issuing orders, a copy of the New York *World Telegram* clenched in his right hand. The source of his anger was Eleanor Roosevelt's "My Day" column. Schools supported by public taxes, she wrote, should be free of any private or religious control. She didn't deny the contributions that "Catholic, Episcopal, Presbyterian, Methodist or whatever" schools made to the community, but she believed they shouldn't receive any tax support. "The separation of Church and State," she contended, in the first of three columns on State aid to education, "is extremely important to any of us."

She was wrong on the last point. Spellman took her column as a personal rebuke. At the time, the Cardinal was involved in a bitter dispute over legislation proposed by Congressman Graham Barden. The so-called Barden bill was designed to block federal expenditures for nonpublic schools. Spellman had gotten into an ugly name-calling brawl with Barden and his supporters, denouncing them as "bigots." The educational issue was a vital one, in which perhaps billions of dollars of potential aid to Catholic schools—money Spellman desperately wanted—was at stake. Thus, he turned his guns on Mrs. Roosevelt and showed his usually hidden Janus face to the world. The result was shocking. Spellman had his defenders, but he was widely criticized for the vileness of his attack. The unseemly conduct of a prince of the Church even reverberated in Washington and at the Vatican.

The Cardinal's antagonism toward Mrs. Roosevelt went far deeper than the school issue. She personified everything that Spellman detested. He thought the former First Lady was a flaccid liberal who let emotions obscure reason; he was convinced she was a Communist dupe. Worse, he thought she didn't respect him, and in that he was right. Their stands on issues were poles apart. Her favoring birth control, however timorous her position, grossly offended Spellman. Her friendliness to Loyalist Spain had challenged his sycophantic support of Franco; more recently, he blamed her for a United Nations resolution that called for members to break relations with Spain. Her support of organizations in which Communists were represented, such as the American Youth Congress, infuriated him.

Spellman decided to gamble. He made up his mind to attack Mrs. Roosevelt in the media, to throw down a test of power to the former First Lady and her gaggle of liberal supporters, whom he hated as well. Later, it was reported that the Cardinal had shot from the hip when he responded to her in a public letter. The reply was seen as the heated response of a man quick to fly off the handle. In reality, Spellman was being true to his calculating nature. He knew exactly what he was doing, and he was a man who could hold a grudge for years. The first "My Day" column appeared on June 23, 1949. Spellman's reply came, not immediately, but a month later, July 21.

"I want three responses," he told his secretaries. "One moderate. One firm. One tough."[11]

Immediately, he dismissed the more reasonable approaches. His secretaries were nervous about drafting a harsh response to a figure as prominent as Eleanor Roosevelt, but that mattered little. Spellman finally took a draft and rewrote most of it himself. Although his secretaries laughed with the Cardinal about the missive he had prepared, they were privately worried. Spellman's letter was a political time bomb. In part he said:

American freedom not only permits but encourages differences of opinion and I do not question your right to differ with me. But why, I wonder, do you repeatedly plead causes that are anti-Catholic? Even if you cannot find it within your heart to defend the rights of innocent little children and heroic, helpless men like Cardinal Martyr Mindszenty, can you not have the charity not to cast upon them still another stone?

America's Catholic youth fought a long and bitter fight to save all Americans from oppression and persecution. Their broken bodies on the blood-soaked foreign fields were grim and tragic testimony to this fact. I saw them there—on every fighting front—as equally they shared with their fellow fighters all the sacrifice, terror and gore of war—as alike they shared the little good and glory that sometimes comes to men as together they fight and win a brutal battle.

Would you deny equality to these Catholic boys who daily stood at the sad threshold of untimely death and suffered martyrdom that you and I and the world of men might live in liberty and peace? Would you deny their children equal rights and benefits with other sects— rights for which their fathers paid equal taxation with other fathers and fought two bitter wars that all children might forever be free from fear, oppression and religious persecution?

During the war years, you visited the hospitals in many countries, as did I. You too saw America's sons—Catholic, Protestant and Jewish alike—young, battered, scarred, torn and mutilated, dying in agony that we might learn to live in charity with one another. Then how was it that your own heart was not purged of all prejudices by what you saw, these, our sons, suffer?

Now my case is closed. This letter will be released to the public tomorrow after it has been delivered to you by special delivery today. And even though you may again use your columns to attack me and again accuse me of starting a controversy, I shall not again publicly acknowledge you. For, whatever you may say in the future, your record of anti-Catholicism stands for all to see—a record which you yourself wrote on the pages of history which cannot be recalled—documents of discrimination unworthy of an American mother.

Though he had said he wouldn't give his statement to the press until Mrs. Roosevelt had a copy, he wasn't true to his word. Before she received his letter, Mrs. Roosevelt was besieged at Hyde Park by phone calls from reporters. Since she hadn't yet seen the Spellman statement, she had no comment. On July 23, the day she actually received the Cardinal's letter, Mrs. Roosevelt penned a response, saying, in part:

I have no bias against the Roman Catholic Church and I have supported Governor Smith as governor and worked for him as a candidate for the office of President of the United States. I have supported or support for public office many other Roman Catholic candidates.

You speak of the Mindszenty case. I spoke out very clearly against any unfair type of trial and anything anywhere in any country which might seem like an attack on an individual because of his religious beliefs. I cannot, however, say that in European countries the control by the Roman Catholic Church of great areas of land has always led to the happiness of the people of those countries.

I have never visited hospitals and asked or thought about the religion of any boy in any bed. I have never in a military cemetery had any different feeling about the graves of the boys who lay there. All of our boys of every race, creed and color fought for the country and they deserve our help and gratitude.

It is not my wish to deny children anywhere equal rights or benefits. It is, however, the decision of parents when they select a private or denominational school, whether it be Episcopalian, Wesleyan, Jewish or Roman Catholic.

I can assure you that I have no prejudice. I understand the beliefs of the Roman Catholic Church very well. I happen to be a Protestant and I prefer my own church, but that does not make me feel that anyone has any less right to believe as his own convictions guide him.

I have no intention of attacking you personally, nor of attacking the Roman Catholic Church, but I shall, of course, continue to stand for the things in our government which I think are right. They may lead me to be in opposition to you and to other groups within our country. . . .

I assure you I have no sense of being an "unworthy American

mother." The final judgment, my dear Cardinal Spellman, of the un-
worthiness of all human beings is in the hands of God.

The American hierarchy, of course, fell in line behind Spellman;
the bishops had little choice. They too wanted the public money
and, even in the cases where they thought Spellman had gone too
far, couldn't criticize him publicly. It was an issue on which there
could be no perception of a division in the ranks. Spellman's charge
of bigotry was one that other bishops all too easily found to be a
weapon that could be thrown at critics. Methodist Bishop G. Bromley
Oxnam, president of the Federal Council of Churches of Christ in
America, who had crossed swords with Spellman on the Myron
Taylor mission to the Vatican, replied to the Cardinal that the purpose
of the Barden bill wasn't bigotry. Its aim, he said, was to protect
American education "from a prelate with a prehensile hand."

The major stumbling block was the constitutional interpretation
of government aid to Church-supported schools. One side, mostly
Roman Catholic, argued that there was room for such funding under
the First Amendment, even though a State Church was outlawed.
Moreover, they argued that the Fourteenth Amendment, which provided equal protection for all, allowed greater cooperation between
Church and State than existed. On the other side were mainly Protestants, Jews, and humanists, who maintained that the First Amendment created a wall of separation between Church and State that
couldn't be transgressed.

Over the years, Protestants had come to monitor Spellman closely.
His politicking, close ties to government, and refusal to recognize
the separation of Church and State symbolized the side of religion
that American Protestants had rejected long ago. Moreover, Spellman
worried them because he condemned anyone who opposed him as
a bigot, often a difficult charge to refute. Thus, Spellman himself
worked at confirming many Protestants' prejudices. From the earliest
days of America, Protestants had been anti-Catholic. Samuel Adams,
for instance, had stated that "much more is to be dreaded from the
growth of Popery in America than from the Stamp Act."[12] The anti-
Catholic Know-Nothing movement of the nineteenth century was
largely a reaction to the huge Irish-Catholic immigration; it sought
to uphold the "American" view and to combat "foreign" influences.
In the twentieth century Al Smith had run up against anti-Catholic
bigotry while seeking the presidency.

The house organs of Protestantism had long openly encouraged
an anti-Catholic spirit. In the 1920s, for instance, *Christian Century*
called for the taxation of religious institutions as a "rational means
of removing that menace to democratic civilization," the Catholic
Church. When Spellman and his belligerent postures appeared, he
was the embodiment of the Protestant nightmare and a rationalization
that years of prejudice had probably been justified.

When *Christian Century* printed an editorial, "The Cardinal Looks for Trouble," in 1947, readers didn't have to guess the subject's name. Spellman had contended that Protestants were "waging a crusade of bigotry against the Roman Catholic Church," with "*Christian Century* spearheading the attack. . . ." The issue had been Protestant opposition to the use of taxpayers' money for busing parochial-school children. Spellman's demands for payment had been based on his Church's shouldering the costs of educating thousands of children, costs that the State otherwise would have to underwrite. The fact that it was their parents' choice to send them to parochial school was beside the point.

The transportation issue had come to a head with the Elverson case in New Jersey, in which the practice of using state subsidies for busing was challenged. The Supreme Court, in February 1947, had determined by a squeaky five-to-four vote that under its general welfare powers, the state could pay the parochial-school students' busing costs. Spellman immediately pushed for more concessions, such as subsidies for textbooks and public aid for health care and other services. He condemned critics of the Supreme Court decision as "mainly the intolerant who in their failure to win a victory in the court of law seek recourse in the shady corners of bigotry."

What alarmed Protestants more than Spellman's condemnations was his influencing school issues in other ways. The New York public school board, for example, reflected the religious diversity of the city. Traditionally, the nine-member board consisted of three Protestants, three Catholics, and three Jews. But among the city's religious leaders, the Cardinal obviously stood apart. He was routinely consulted on the appointment of prospective board members of all faiths, as well as about board policy. There came a time when he even picked the board president, his friend Charlie Silver.

The Cardinal's influence on the New York educational system was understandable. The school board was naturally wary of offending any religious group, particularly Catholics, because of their numbers and because of the influence Spellman could bring to bear. Thus, the board of superintendents went out of its way to placate him. One such occasion occurred when *The Nation* printed a series of articles that were critical of policies of the hierarchy of the Roman Catholic Church. Written by an iconoclast named Paul Blanshard, the articles attacked the political and social policies of the hierarchy. Spellman, outraged, ordered copies sent to the Vatican as an example of the anti-Catholic prejudice he had to battle. He also declared that *The Nation* contaminated public-school libraries and that he wanted it removed. Canceling the subscriptions was done quietly. Nonetheless, a reporter for the New York *Herald Tribune* found out. Spellman's censorship became a *cause célèbre*.

Acting out of indignation, the poet Archibald MacLeish spearheaded an Ad Hoc Committee to Lift the Ban, which gained the support of several hundred intellectuals. These included Eleanor Roosevelt; former governor Lehman; Robert Hutchins, the chancellor of the University of Chicago; and Charles Seymour, the president of Yale. Not all of them agreed with Blanshard, but they upheld his right to say what he believed and the right of students to decide what they read. Faced with a counter-crusade of which he was the target, Spellman was beside himself. Blanshard had examined conservative Catholic stands on such controversial issues as birth control, abortion, and divorce—and found them wanting. "That man must be stopped," Spellman told his aides.

New York courts upheld the ban, but the censorship issue backfired. Blanshard wound up with a contract to turn his articles into a book, *American Freedom and Catholic Power,* which became a best-seller.

There was little doubt that many issues raised by Blanshard needed examining. Planned Parenthood, for example, had an extremely difficult time in New York as a result of opposition by the Church. Legislation to liberalize contraception laws or abortion laws was routinely killed. After *Look* magazine published a sober, factual article about Planned Parenthood, a letter to the editor from a Catholic, printed in the issue of May 6, 1948, condemned Planned Parenthood for advocating "education in animal functions completely divorced from morality and ethics." Such a practice, the writer was convinced, led people to "be sexually promiscuous with least risk of pregnancy or venereal disease. . . . The Planned Parenthood program assumes that the cure for beastliness is to teach juveniles how to get away with acting like beasts." The letter had been shown to Spellman before being sent to *Look.*

Spellman's lobbyists in the state capital were the Albany bishop and Charles Tobin, a lawyer. A soft-spoken, dreary man, Tobin was as unswervingly conservative as Spellman. He called on legislators whenever an issue arose that affected the Church. "It was taken for granted that you didn't go up against the Powerhouse," Julius Edelstein, the former aide to Governor Lehman, noted.[13]

Spellman's words and actions over the years so worried a number of Protestants that they created an organization designed to stop Spellman called Protestants and Other Americans United for the Separation of Church and State. Its supporters were vigilant lest Spellman come crashing through the wall between Church and State, and the danger seemed greater than ever when he faulted Eleanor Roosevelt.

The intensity of the furor that erupted after Spellman's attack on Mrs. Roosevelt was unlike any other and involved more critics than just Protestants. Bill Hassett, a Catholic and one of Truman's secretaries, called the Cardinal's letter "an appeal to prejudice." William

Phillips, a former ambassador to Italy who had known Spellman there in the 1930s, denounced the Cardinal's remarks as "absurd, but . . . dangerous too." The *Raleigh News Observer* wrote that never before had the nation been "presented with a spectacle of a man behaving with less tolerance, less Christian humility, and more readiness to damn and malign those who disagree with him than that shown by Cardinal Spellman."

Spellman bristled. What he found worse than the criticism was that he was actually mocked. His critics delighted in a poem by Archibald MacLeish titled, "I Shall Not Again Publicly Acknowledge You."

The episode, however, was no joke to politicians. In New York and Washington it was a monumental headache. Mayor O'Dwyer went on vacation immediately after Spellman fired his salvo. When he returned he faced the greatest controversy he had ever witnessed. Privately, he told Mrs. Roosevelt that "it must have been the weather" that had made Spellman react in such a fashion.[14] Publicly, the mayor played the role of mediator: "I have great respect for the Cardinal and I have equally great respect for Mrs. Roosevelt. I can understand the Cardinal's interest in the children in parochial schools. At the same time, knowing Mrs. Roosevelt as well as I do, I cannot believe that any position she would take in the case of children would be the result of bigotry."

At the White House, Truman desperately sought an end to the disgraceful business. He was trapped in an awkward position. He had no great love for Mrs. Roosevelt, but she was a symbol of the New Deal and the most prominent U.S. delegate to the United Nations. As for Spellman, Truman was wary of him and dealt with him only when he must, such as during the Italian election and the troublesome Vatican mission. Now, Spellman was causing even more trouble for Democrats in New York. The word was out that Spellman was blocking Lehman's bid for the Senate because Lehman had opposed the Cardinal on *The Nation* issue and sided with Mrs. Roosevelt.

Wherever he turned Truman failed to find help in solving the mess. O'Dwyer, who was running for re-election, was next to useless. The New York State Democratic chairman, at Spellman's urging, had cooled his support for Lehman. Catholic leaders in Congress, such as Majority Leader McCormack and Senator Brian McMahon of Connecticut, spent a lot of unproductive time in conferences with National Democratic Chairman Howard McGrath, chasing the issue round and round, so afraid were they. The Barden bill itself was lost in the shuffle. John Lesinski, chairman of the House Committee on Labor and Education, was afraid to call a meeting for four months after the Spellman letter, although the bill had been voted out of subcommittee by ten to three. Finally, it died before coming to a vote.

The plight of Washington politicians was perhaps best summarized by New York *Daily News* columnist John O'Donnell in his "Capital Stuff." On July 28 he wrote: "They are not just frightened. This is panic. For the first time the boys who are willing to challenge every foe on earth and spit in Joe Stalin's face don't dare to meet head-on a direct and important domestic issue."

Finally, Truman asked New York Democratic boss Ed Flynn to take the case secretly to the Pope.[15] Flynn, known at the Vatican since Roosevelt had asked him to try to ease tensions between the Vatican and Moscow, made a hasty trip to Rome. Flynn returned with a commitment that Spellman would make a public gesture of reconciliation to Mrs. Roosevelt. The mission was one that Flynn enjoyed. Although forced by circumstances to pretend to like Spellman, Flynn privately didn't care for the Cardinal and resented Spellman's politicking. Though he performed favors for Spellman, Flynn believed the Cardinal had made the Church too political. Also, Flynn's own views were much closer to Mrs. Roosevelt's than to Spellman's.[16]

Upon returning from the Vatican, Flynn received a statement from Spellman that was quite different from the original blast at Mrs. Roosevelt. Spellman seethed when writing what the Pope demanded he do. Next, Flynn had lunch with Mrs. Roosevelt and showed her the Cardinal's draft, asking if it met with her approval. Also, Spellman wanted to know if she would talk to him if he called on her.

"Why Ed," she replied, "I'm not the one who said I would have nothing to do with the Cardinal."[17]

Mrs. Roosevelt enjoyed her position immensely. She had never liked Spellman and had resented his conservative influence at the White House. The churchman, she found, heedlessly embraced causes that could be harmful to the nation. "Spellman represented the worst kind of Church politics to her," said her cousin Joseph Alsop. "But she was a practical politician and he was even more so."[18] Thus, both acted out of expediency. She approved Spellman's draft and agreed to meet him. Flynn had accomplished his mission. As they parted Flynn had a last word at the Cardinal's expense. The contretemps had gained international notoriety, and the Spanish press predictably sided with Spellman, even to the point of making slurs against Mrs. Roosevelt. Flynn told her to raise the Franco issue when she was with Spellman. "Tell him," Flynn said dryly, "the Basque priests fought and are still fighting Franco."[19]

For his part, Spellman—no matter what he told the Vatican—was determined not to apologize. He was humiliated by having to visit the woman he so hated, and he believed that was more than enough of a gesture. Thus, when he arrived at Hyde Park he offered a lame excuse about being in the vicinity. "We've had some misunderstanding," he told Mrs. Roosevelt. Sipping tea and smiling enigmatically, the Cardinal chatted about little of consequence until he finally prepared to leave.[20]

Mrs. Roosevelt, though, wasn't about to let him off the hook so easily. She mentioned the Lehman Senate campaign. She knew what was happening: Lehman and his staff found their campaign stalled. "Word had gone out that Lehman had committed an unforgivable act when he opposed Spellman," according to Edelstein, the Lehman aide.

On July 11, Mrs. Roosevelt herself had written to Lehman: "Someone has just told me that Cardinal Spellman has been foolish enough to say that because you went on the committee to prevent the *Nation* from being banned from public schools, he is going to ask the Catholics of the State to oppose you. . . ."[21]

Therefore, she confronted Spellman as one politician to another. Her words implied a threat, if he didn't recognize their common interests: "Sir, before you go, let me say something. There are rumors that you are opposed to Governor Lehman. My feeling is that if the figures show that the Catholic vote has gone appreciably against Lehman, it will make it impossible for any Catholic to get elected in this state for many years to come. Because a lot of liberals, Jews, and Protestants will be very resentful."[22]

The Cardinal recognized harsh realities. He quickly backpedaled. "Oh, Mrs. Roosevelt," he replied. "I'm not opposed to Governor Lehman! I'll get in touch with Ed Flynn as soon as he returns to town."[23]

Spellman kept his word. Democratic leaders were soon in touch with Lehman, who went on to win the Senate seat. Ironically, the Cardinal's intemperate lashing at Mrs. Roosevelt helped his enemies in a number of ways. He had appeared both nasty and foolish. The Pope had made Spellman humble himself, reminding him of old Roman resentments, and the Cardinal vowed never to humble himself again. Furthermore, his organized enemy, Protestants and Other Americans United for the Separation of Church and State, capitalized on his blunder. Membership ranks swelled, funds poured into the war chest, and the anti-Spellman group was forced to move to larger quarters. All Spellman had really achieved with his rash attack was galvanizing his enemies into a greater force and escalating the level of anti-Catholicism across the nation.

The day after Spellman visited Hyde Park, the chancery issued a statement by the Cardinal and another by Mrs. Roosevelt. Both, for the most part, avoided exacerbating the issue. Spellman noted, "We are not asking for general public support for religious schools," but selective support for auxiliary educational services such as textbooks and health care. Mrs. Roosevelt found the Cardinal's position "clarifying and fair," but she pointedly denied she was a bigot. The former First Lady, however, wasn't about to let the public believe the fight had ended in a draw. In a subsequent "My Day" column, she underscored the fact that Spellman had called on her—the gesture of a loser, as Spellman knew.

Ironically, while the Cardinal and the former First Lady were publicly feuding over a domestic issue, they were working independently toward the same international goal regarding the newly created State of Israel. Their motives, of course, were different. Although both wanted to see Israel accepted as a member of the United Nations, Mrs. Roosevelt firmly believed in the justice of the cause. Spellman was doing a friend a favor.

The Cardinal became enmeshed in Israel's future through Charlie Silver. In April 1949, Israel had signed an armistice with Arab nations and applied for membership in the United Nations. It was widely known that Spellman exerted considerable influence at the United Nations with Catholic countries. It was also widely known that Silver and Spellman were good friends. Silver received a call from a prominent rabbi, Abba Hillel Silver (no relation) of Cleveland, Ohio. "Within the next few weeks, the matter of Israel becoming a member of the United Nations will be presented before the General Assembly," Rabbi Silver said. "What I would like to have you do for us, if at all possible, is to find out from his eminence Cardinal Spellman just what position he will take."[24]

Charlie Silver phoned Spellman and made an appointment to go for a walk with him, a habit the two had fallen into. When they strolled up Fifth Avenue their conversations couldn't be overheard.

Silver himself wasn't sure where Spellman stood on Israel. If he had known about the Cardinal's record to date, he wouldn't have felt optimistic. Just a year earlier, Spellman had broached the subject of Palestine with Secretary of State George Marshall and his stance was anti-Israeli. The Cardinal was president of an organization called the Catholic Near East Welfare Association, which looked after Church interests in the Middle East. According to a U.S. intelligence report, "Problems and Attitudes in the Arab World: Their Implications for U.S. Psychological Strategy," the Vatican had two obvious objectives in the Middle East—the protection of Catholic interests and the strengthening of resistance to Communism. With Marshall, Spellman had demanded free access to holy places for Christians and some guarantees for Christians living in Palestine. Barring internationalization, the Vatican wanted control of Jerusalem placed in the hands of Jordan, not Israel.[25]

Spellman went so far as to lodge a formal Vatican complaint with Marshall, focusing on the desecration of Catholic churches in the

State of Israel. "We have been informed by officials and travelers returning from Palestine that Jewish groups have entered monasteries and convents, necessarily abandoned because of their position in the field of battle, and have deliberately desecrated crucifixes and deliberately mutilated religious statues," he told Marshall.[26]

At the Powerhouse, sentiments were strongly anti-Israel. Priests traded horror stories about Israelis' desecrating religious institutions and humiliating Christians. "On one visit to New York, I was told by priests that Zionists took a group of Christians and told them to defecate on the crucifix," Harry O'Connor recalled.[27] "In one town, they made Christian women walk up and down the street naked." True or not, such tales were believed. Thus when Spellman was approached by Silver, the Cardinal had a history of working against the Israeli cause.

"I've never asked you for a *personal* favor, but I will now," Silver said, as they walked through midtown. He explained that he had been asked to find out what position the Cardinal would take on Israel's admission to the United Nations. "Your statement would mean a great deal to us at this crucial hour," Silver remembered saying.

"Charlie, I'm all for it," Spellman said.

Silver was stunned, but he tried not to show his amazement. "I felt you would be," he said. "Will you issue a statement to that effect?"

Spellman surprised the businessman further by saying that he was willing to do much more than that. What he proposed was vintage Spellman. Instead of taking a public stand, he would operate behind the scenes by "personally calling on every South American country to cast their votes for Israel."[28]

Silver would recall that on that very night Spellman started contacting U.N. delegates and officials of Latin nations. Moshe Tov, who became an Israeli ambassador to the United Nations, later claimed that Latin American cardinals suddenly looked favorably on the cause. Also, Tov was told by Rodriguez Fabregat, the U.N. ambassador from Uruguay, that he had been approached by Spellman on behalf of Zionism.[29]

There was little doubt that Spellman knew U.N. delegates. He routinely wined and dined leaders from Catholic nations, many of whom the State Department considered insignificant. That was part of his Roman training. Leaders were treated courteously unless there was a reason not to.

Obviously, the fact that Spellman helped Silver was strange. One reason may have been that Israel had suddenly become more conciliatory on the matter of Jerusalem. The Vatican had publicly expressed its pleasure when Chaim Weizmann, the president of Israel, remarked in April 1949 that his government was ready to recognize the interests of Christianity regarding protection of holy places. At Truman's behest, Spellman had met with Weizmann and Abba Eban, Israel's U.N. representative. Truman had phoned Spellman and told him Weizmann was disposed to accept the internationalization of Palestine.[30] After the meeting Spellman wrote Truman about his concern with differences between Weizmann and Ben-Gurion. Moreover, Spellman said he was amazed to hear Weizmann claim there were "no refugee problems, since any Arab refugee who wanted to return to Palestine may do so."[31]

Shortly before the U.N. vote, Spellman sent Truman one of Griffiths's detailed reports on Palestine that was highly critical of Israel. He noted that the United States was pushing Israel on the U.N. membership; once again, he protested the Israeli stand on Jerusalem. Thus, the actual role Spellman played was confusing. He may have gone along with Silver just because he recognized that the United States would probably get its own way in any event. He may have played both sides so that he couldn't really lose.

After a bitter struggle, Israel was admitted to the United Nations by a vote of thirty-seven to twelve. The Israelis had turned to a number of men of prominence, including John Foster Dulles, to promote their cause. But Charlie Silver was convinced that Spellman had been the deciding factor, and, for this belief, he had to pay a price. O'Dwyer announced in 1949 that he wasn't running again for mayor. In the upheaval that followed, a number of hats were tossed into the race. One of the first was Silver's. The businessman had always wanted to be an elected official, especially mayor. He was a dark horse, but he believed he had a chance. Abruptly, he withdrew his candidacy, later telling friends that Spellman had asked him to back out.[32] Apparently, the Cardinal wanted a Catholic to clean up O'Dwyer's legacy. In any event, O'Dwyer changed his mind and ran again.

Whether Spellman's friend could have improved on the O'Dwyer image was at least debatable. During the 1950–51 Kefauver Committee hearings on organized crime in America, a wealthy businessman testified that Silver had numbered the gangster Frank Costello as his biggest backer when Silver was a mayoral candidate.[33]

The March 1949 day was raw, and the cold chilled the men pacing slowly in front of the heavy metal gates at the entrance to Calvary Cemetery in the borough of Queens. Others stood in knots around trash cans bright with fire. They were gravediggers, members of United Cemetery Workers Local 293, who had been on strike since mid-January. Suddenly, a large bus rumbled up to the gate. The first person to alight was Cardinal Spellman, his clerical collar peeking above denim overalls, who stood by the front door, impatiently waving his right hand and saying, "Come on! Come on!" Dozens of youths in Windbreakers and khaki pants tumbled into the icy air. They were from St. Joseph's Seminary, at Dunwoodie, Yonkers, and Spellman defiantly led them past the strikers into the cemetery. The Cardinal was using seminarians as scabs.

Spellman's step wasn't undertaken lightly, but he saw the need for dramatic action. Labor was a constant headache for him because the archdiocese was an employer on a monumental scale. Each year, Spellman paid out some $30 million in wages just to the building-trade unions that constructed his many projects. The archdiocese spent millions more on salaries for priests, teachers, hospital workers, groundskeepers, maids, and hosts of other tradespeople. The Cardinal had always been opposed to unions, but, against his better judgment, he had accepted the collective bargaining of the cemetery workers three years earlier when they had joined their local, an affiliate of the Food, Tobacco, Agricultural and Allied Workers Union of America.

Now, when the Church was actually struck, the Cardinal was convinced the whole union business had gotten out of hand. Just a year earlier, he had been embarrassed when the Association of Catholic Trade Unionists had organized a strike for clerical help on Wall Street; John Coleman and others had complained bitterly about Catholics' acting like Communists. Spellman had privately agreed with Coleman, but publicly he remained neutral. The ACTU was an anti-Communist union sanctioned by the Church as an alternative to Communism. Besides, that hadn't been his strike, and this one was. Thus, Spellman decided to break the gravediggers' union as an example to other archdiocesan workers who might be contemplating a union.

Spellman's tactics aroused more hostility toward him among his priests than any of his other actions to date. Some pleaded with him to stay out of the issue; but they were ignored or punished for their advice. Once Spellman's mind was made up, there was little dissuading him.

The Cardinal was encouraged by Monsignor George C. Ehardt, his director of cemeteries. A stocky, balding cynic who always had a cigar jutting from the corner of his mouth, Ehardt was as dogmatic as Spellman. When the workers' contract expired on December 31, Spellman had told him to hold the line on wages. Ehardt had taken that as a mandate to insult the gravediggers as well. When the negotiating team sat down with Ehardt and his assistant, a quiet priest named Henry Cauley, the monsignor placed a crucifix in the middle of the bargaining table. The first union contract had been signed in 1946. Now, three years later, the gravediggers petitioned for more than the $59 a week they earned and a five-day, forty-hour week, instead of their six-day, forty-eight-hour week. The meeting concluded when the men made their demands. It was during the second meeting that Ehardt made the archdiocese's first, and final, offer. Again Cauley was at his side, looking uncomfortable. "The most we can do is a dollar a week," Ehardt said. "Take it or leave it." He added pointedly, "The Cardinal's behind me."[34]

The gravediggers were dumbfounded. At first, they thought the monsignor was joking, but they swiftly realized he was not. Sam Cimaglia, one of the negotiators, began arguing. He believed he had a strong case, since he had read a lot of labor literature, including papal encyclicals, on the rights of workers. "The Pope says that a worker with a family of four should get about sixty-eight dollars a week," he began.

"Where'd you read that?" Ehardt interrupted.

Cimaglia told him in *The Sign,* a publication of the Passionist Fathers.

"The Passionists," Ehardt retorted. "Why do you listen to those guys? They're a bunch of bandits."

Cimaglia and his men were all devout Catholics. Many of them went to mass every morning. Never having heard a priest refer to other priests in such a fashion, they were shocked. "You're a man of God," Cimaglia said. "You can't believe that."

Ehardt answered him cynically: "You read the Bible?"

Cimaglia nodded yes.

"Don't you know then that there is no God?" Ehardt asked.

During the exchange Father Cauley blushed crimson. He kicked Ehardt under the table, trying to get him to shut up. "Only a fool would say there is no God," he said, his voice cracking.

Ehardt didn't heed him. "You guys are so religious, why don't you be like God?" he said. "He worked six days a week."

Stonewalled and dismayed, the workers took the only recourse they believed was available. "Put away your rosary beads and go out," Cimaglia recalled Edward Ruggieri, their leader, saying. The sour experience made them realize an aspect of working for the archdiocese that they hadn't previously accepted. "They are just bosses," Ruggieri stated.

Spellman reacted as if he had been betrayed. Like other churchmen, the Cardinal expressed a certain paternalism for people who worked for him. People should be honored to work for the Church, the sentiment went, and be willing to accept less pay for the privilege. In this case, Spellman was angry because the strikers had challenged not only that notion but also his authority. To Spellman, the insolence he perceived was the direct result of the activities of labor priests who encouraged workers to challenge authority.

The man behind the Catholic labor movement in New York was John Patrick Monaghan, the feisty priest with a rich Irish brogue who had been a Spellman contemporary at the North American College. Monaghan represented a different side of the priesthood than

Spellman. Instead of choosing a political career, Monaghan became a professor of literature at Fordham and a labor organizer—and a thorn in the Cardinal's side. The two were always at loggerheads, a clash of idealism and pragmatism. Monaghan championed the poor and the working class, saying they had to tear from the hands of capitalists what was rightfully theirs. Spellman saw the labor movement as dangerous.

In seeking someone to help him deal with the gravediggers, Spellman didn't call on the labor experts among his priests. Rather, he turned to Godfrey Schmidt, a conservative lawyer and professor at Fordham, to work with him to prevent unions from gaining members at all Church institutions, including schools and hospitals. "What are these labor priests writing and talking about?" Schmidt recalled Spellman asking him when he sat down with the Cardinal. "They act as though they know how to run the companies, but they don't know anything."

Labor priests in the archdiocese had tried to temper Spellman's intention to steamroller the union. Father John Byrne, who knew the gut issues involved, criticized the handling of the dispute and warned the Cardinal to stay away from it. It was simply a matter of more money and shorter hours, issues the labor movement was pressing across the nation. For his trouble, Byrne was removed from his faculty position at the cathedral seminary and banished to live with Father Ford, the outcast at Corpus Christi. He wasn't alone. Priests who had nothing directly to do with the strike found their careers singed by the heat of Spellman's wrath. Father George Kelly, for instance, had written a column in the Catholic press shortly before the strike, espousing the virtues of organized labor. Suddenly, Kelly found that as far as the Powerhouse was concerned, he was persona non grata, a status that remained unchanged for years.[35]

The gravediggers found themselves in a similar position. Their savings quickly evaporated; the help they expected from other unions never materialized, and the lesson they learned was bitter. At first, representatives of labor organizations approached them, including teamsters and stevedores, but they quickly disappeared. The only financial assistance the cemetery workers received was a $5,000 check from the transport workers, and even that was awkward. Mike Quill demanded that the gravediggers keep his union's gift quiet. "We were up against the Powerhouse," Cimaglia related. "Everybody was afraid to touch us." Dorothy Day was one of the few who publicly supported the union. She and some of her staff from the *Catholic Worker* passed out leaflets in front of the Cardinal's residence and were arrested. The police forbade the gravediggers to picket Spellman's house.

Spellman met with Schmidt and Ehardt to determine their best course of action. The result showed how out of touch with reality they were. Schmidt issued a public statement in which he proposed that the dispute should be submitted to "an impartial board of three distinguished moral theologians."

Their next step was much more serious and calculated to lose all sympathy for the union: they accused the local leadership of being Communists. In light of the times, the charge was particularly vicious. A dozen men were on trial, at the federal courthouse at New York's Foley Square, on Communist-conspiracy charges, and their story was headlined almost daily. Paul Robeson's passport had been invalidated; Herb Philbrick was giving sensational press accounts of his years as a Red that would be turned into the book and television series *I Led Three Lives.*

The gravediggers were shocked by the charge and were dismayed when many people apparently believed the Cardinal. Spellman, however, also lost support by the move. Some people who had sympathized with him, thinking him concerned about the families of the mounting numbers of unburied, now thought he acted maliciously. The liberal journal *Commonweal,* for instance, criticized his handling of the strike. "I'll never forgive *Commonweal,"* Spellman said. "Not in this world or the next."[36]

The novelist Ernest Hemingway was so offended that he wrote Spellman a blistering letter.

"My Dear Cardinal, In every picture that I see of you there is more mealy mouthed arrogance, fatness and over-confidence," Hemingway wrote. "As a strike breaker against Catholic workers, as an attacker of Mrs. Roosevelt I feel strongly that you are overextending yourself." The writer contended that Spellman "lied about the Spanish Republic" and noted that in Europe it was rumored Spellman would be "the next and first American Pope," adding "do not keep pressing so hard. You will never be Pope as long as I'm alive."[37]

More meaningful criticism came from the Association of Catholic Trade Unionists, which denied the strike was Communist-inspired: ACTU President John Manning condemned the charge as a red herring and a "vicious attempt to smash the union."

Six weeks into the strike, Spellman sent telegrams to all the union members, with the exception of the five-man negotiating team. He wanted to meet personally with the men, apparently believing that his position within the Church would awe them into submission. Thus, on a snowy day in February, the men gathered at Cathedral High School. The Cardinal met them at the door and was extremely cordial. Dressed in his scarlet robes, he greeted each man as he entered. Each worker awkwardly genuflected and kissed his ring, while Spellman asked if he was married and had children. The strikers were ill at ease, but the men had made a pact that they wouldn't stay there unless the Cardinal let the negotiating team into the gathering. The five negotiators were anxiously waiting outside. When Spellman took his place before the microphone, he didn't get a chance to speak. A big striker with a voice like a bullhorn, Frank Malkowski, immediately asked the Cardinal to admit the negotiators: "Your Eminence, why are our five committee members not here?"

"They are not wanted," Spellman replied.

To a man, the three hundred twenty-five cemetery workers stood up and started leaving the hall. The Cardinal was startled, and, for one of the few times in his life, he lost his composure in public. He started running after the men, stumbling over his floor-length silk garments and yelling, "Wait! Wait!"

"If I talk to the committee will you stay?" the breathless Spellman asked.

The men agreed. The Cardinal went to the front door, met the negotiators, and took them to another room, where he started off tough. "I can't deal with you," he said. "You're Communists."

The men angrily denied the charge. Most of them felt guilty about the strike: they were torn between their family duties and their Church. The Communism charge made them feel worse. Their parent union, the Food, Tobacco, Agricultural and Allied Workers Union of America, doubtless had Communists in it; any number of large unions did. Their local, however, had never had any. The men themselves were bitterly anti-Communist. Some had even gotten into fistfights with Communists who had criticized the Cardinal. Moreover, the men suspected that Spellman was simply using the issue as a cudgel to get his own way. When some adverse publicity erupted over his making the charge, the Cardinal retreated. Instead of saying the men were Communists, he softened the indictment, saying they used "Communist tactics."

Now, outside the cathedral school, Cimaglia told Spellman that raising the Communist charge was "pretty hypocritical," adding: "You signed two contracts with us in the past. If we took a dollar-a-week-raise, you wouldn't think we were Communists."

The Cardinal quickly backed down. He obviously wanted the meeting with the men, so he removed the last obstacle from its being held. "I can see you are not Communists," he abruptly told them.

Ironically, Communists had used an intermediary to approach the union, offering support. If they agreed to align themselves with Communists, the cemetery workers were promised a massive rally at Madison Square Garden as well as strike pay of $65 or $70 a week. The Communists wanted to make a cause out of the Church's exploiting labor. The union leaders had rejected the offer out of hand, but they had kept the encounter to themselves. One reason Spellman was so anxious to meet with the cemetery workers was that he had asked the F.B.I. to monitor the union. He apparently wanted to get something on the record indicating the men were Communists.[38]

Shortly after the negotiators walked into the meeting room, however, Spellman lost control over the proceedings. The men asked him questions, and he couldn't steer the discussion in the direction he wanted it to go. At one point, Spellman was asked why he had finally decided to meet with them after so many weeks. He replied, "Because I love you and your families!"

The questioner looked nonplussed at the Cardinal and shook his head. "God save us from love like that," he said.

Spellman never regained his composure. He returned to his office and told Schmidt that the men had referred to him as "a little runt" and worse. "He told me that they reviled him and called him all kinds of names," Schmidt recalled. "They were a coarse, vulgar group."[39] (The men deny making such remarks.)

"Don't take it to heart," Schmidt told Spellman.

Spellman was next approached by a committee of strikers' wives. They believed that if the Cardinal sat down with them, they could clear up the mess. The women were alarmed at the way the strike had turned out and they believed Spellman had a gross misunderstanding of what kinds of men their husbands were and what they were doing. The Cardinal agreed to see them, and when the meeting was held, the women were in awe. Spellman heightened the effect by sitting on the throne in the reception room in his residence. He was dressed in ermine and scarlet and the sun streamed through a window behind him. "He looked so holy," Mary Czak later told her husband, Siggy, a member of the strike committee.

For the occasion, Spellman was a grave Jehovah. "The men have put their union above their Church," he declared.

"No!" Mrs. Czak replied. "The men are not fighting the Church but they are fighting you as an employer."

The Cardinal focused on the men's disobedience. They refused to bury the dead, and this, he declared, went against the Church's teachings on the corporeal works of mercy. The meeting was fruitless, ending with the following statement by the women: "Because of our Catholic faith, we are deeply aggrieved by the reckless and misguided charge of Communism hurled at our loved ones. . . ."

The women were dejected. They had asked for a decent wage for their husbands, and Spellman had acted as if they wanted the Vatican treasury. Mrs. Czak told the press: "The archbishop promised us nothing. He wants the men to go back to work as individuals, not as union men, and he would not allow members of the strikers committee to go back to work because they were ringleaders. . . . The archbishop was adamant. He promised nothing except that the strikers could return with a small increase, but not as union men. He wants no part of the union. We got no place to go."

Publicly, Spellman expressed nothing but solicitude. "I feel as badly for them as if it were my own mother in the same circumstances," he said. But he added abruptly, "They had nothing to offer me, and I had nothing to offer them."

Thus, when Spellman led the seminarians into the graveyard, there was a great deal of bitterness on both sides. He wanted to see how everything went the first day. The second day, he called in the press; reporters and photographers swarmed over the cemetery, and Spellman always found time for an interview. The strike, he contended, had reached "crisis" proportions. He said he was considering formal burial squads at parishes around the archdiocese. "I could have put an unlimited number of volunteers to work," he claimed, surveying the seminarians as they dug graves. "But this won't be necessary. My boys will return to Calvary daily until the job is finished and everything is normal."

The strikebreaking was extremely controversial; its merits were debated in rectories and by the public. Though many priests condemned Spellman behind his back, few besides John Byrne had the nerve to tell Spellman he was wrong. Seminarians were also distraught: some left the seminary as a result of the experience; most of them took the tips they had received from families of the aggrieved and surreptitiously gave them to the strikers. "Very few seminarians wouldn't go because they were frightened about what would happen if they refused," explained Monsignor Myles Burke, who taught at Dunwoodie at the time.[40]

The Cardinal gained the support of columnists Dorothy Kilgallen and Westbrook Pegler. Pegler found that the use of seminarians as scabs was "a sweet example to other employers" who had to deal with "Communists or fellow travelers . . . usually grim and hateful strangers to the boss and most of the help." The strikers felt the brunt of such antagonism, and they began to back down. While the Cardinal urged on his seminarians, the cemetery workers passed two resolutions: One condemned the anti-union stance of the archdiocese. The other, however, was an anti-Communist oath. Moreover, the local voted to break with the Food, Tobacco, Agricultural and Allied Workers Union of America, as a sign of their good faith. That the men felt compelled to prove their anti-Communism was a sign of how easily a smear campaign worked. Ironically, their union meetings had always had the trappings of Holy Name Society gatherings rather than Communist cells. Such sessions opened with members' reciting the Lord's Prayer, a Hail Mary, and the Workers Prayer of the Association of Catholic Trade Unionists, which began: "Lord Jesus, Carpenter of Nazareth, You were a worker as I am. . . ."

Nonetheless, the gravediggers met at their meeting hall, the Anoroc Democratic Club in Queens, and declared they weren't Reds.

Ed Ruggieri, chairman of the negotiating committee, asked them to repeat the following: "We here as Catholic gentlemen declare that we are opposed to Communism and all it means in all walks of life. Be it recorded, however, that Communism is not the basic issue here."

When Spellman heard of the anti-Communist actions that the union had taken, he wasn't inclined toward forgiveness. He knew that hadn't been the issue. "They're getting repentant kind of late," he said.

In the end, the men couldn't hold out. Their bills mounted, and some of them had sick children and no heat in the house. As the Powerhouse directed, the strikers voted to link with the AFL Building Service Employees Union, which Spellman considered safe. Negotiations were handled by David Sullivan, the international's vice president, who was considered one of Spellman's people. An independent mediator was brought in. Two days later, the strike was settled. The men received a wage increase of 8.33 percent. The issue of shorter hours went to mediation, where it was left unresolved. The reason the Powerhouse liked the new union was evident. Sullivan blamed the strike on irresponsible union leadership. Moreover, he told the Cardinal that no such strike would occur under his leadership.

The Cardinal made a show of sending each of the strikers $65 from his personal funds as a sign that all was forgiven. Privately, the union negotiators were harassed in an effort to get them fired. The only loose end for Spellman was trying to generate some sort of public blessing for his stand, preferably from the holder of the highest public office in the nation. He sent the embarrassed seminarians to Washington to tour the capital as a reward for their assistance. The Cardinal audaciously asked Truman to meet with the young men while they were in town. "I would not expect the President to go through the ordeal of shaking hands with each one, but if a five-minute audience could be arranged, I am sure the honor and privilege would remain with them as an unforgettable memory," Spellman wrote to Matthew Connelly, the President's secretary.[41] The effort was worth making, but it didn't work. There was nothing in it for Truman. The President wasn't about to attempt to pull Spellman's chestnuts out of the fire by offending the labor vote. Truman answered that he would meet with Spellman—alone and in private.[42]

Spellman, however, had the last word: "Thus is brought to a close one of the most difficult, grievous, heartbreaking issues that has ever come within my time as archbishop of New York, and it will be my daily prayer that if ever again the working men of this archdiocese must make their choice between following their faith or faithless leadership, they will, of their own free and immediate choice, choose—God!"

New York's politicians, out of enthusiasm or fear of being branded immoral themselves, flew to Spellman's causes like pigeons to bread crumbs. At a time of national uncertainty, when Joe McCarthy made even the highest government officials seem suspicious, the masses of Catholics clung to the Cardinal's moral campaigns because he identified evils they believed they could do something about. As usual with Spellman, however, there was more to his righteous crusades than met the eye. That was the case when he began battering *The Miracle,* a film that few people had heard about and even fewer had seen. In 1951 the Cardinal ranked among the latter group but nonetheless decided the film was as evil as Communism, and as wicked as pornography.

When he heard the story line, Spellman was appalled. An idiot woman in the thrall of religious fervor was seduced by a stranger who she believed was St. Joseph. Malicious neighbors ridiculed her, convincing her that she had conceived miraculously. She gave birth alone in an empty church.

Spellman ordered his secretaries to draft a pastoral letter condemning the movie. The final version was read during every mass from pulpits in St. Patrick's and the four hundred parishes around the huge archdiocese. Thus, on January 5, 1951, the Cardinal declared that not only were New York's two million Catholics in danger of losing their immortal souls, but so were the rest of the nation's Catholics. They must boycott *The Miracle.* The response to Spellman's dictate revealed how city officials toed the Cardinal's line. Massive pressure was brought to bear upon the distributor of the film as well as the theater at which it was shown. Eventually, the issue became such a mess that the United States Supreme Court had to rule on the constitutionality of the censorship case.

Before Spellman called for his boycott, City License Commissioner Edward T. McCaffrey had said he wanted *The Miracle* withdrawn from distribution, declaring it an "attack" on religious beliefs. But it wasn't until Spellman spoke out that the move to rid New York of the film began in earnest. Reaction to the Cardinal's demand was swift. That very Sunday, members of the Catholic War Veterans and other organizations picketed Manhattan's Paris theater. Wearing heavy overcoats and fedoras or their campaign hats, men carried signs bearing such messages as STAY AWAY FROM THIS THEATER and INSULT TO EVERY WOMAN NOT TO MENTION CHILDREN. As with everything else the Cardinal touched, condemning the film somehow was tied to opposing Communism. There was little surprise when pickets, whose numbers swelled to a thousand as members of the Holy Name Society embraced the cause, shouted, "This is the kind of picture the Communists want!" and "Don't be a Communist— all the Communists are inside."

The Cardinal's action was foolish. Not having seen the film, he acted on the basis of hearsay. The film, directed by the renowned Roberto Rossellini and starring Anna Magnani, was elsewhere considered a moving experience that many critics found profoundly religious. The New York Film Critics had chosen *The Miracle* as the best foreign film of 1950, but that mattered little to the prelate. What upset Spellman was that the film was part of a trilogy called *Ways of Love*. To the Cardinal, that smacked of pornography as well as blasphemy. When an aide tactfully suggested that perhaps the film wasn't "dirty," Spellman remained adamant. He seemed to find no other way to consider sex.

While pickets paced outside the Paris, Fire Commissioner George P. Monaghan issued a number of violations against the theater, without any prior notice. The Paris had opened only two years earlier and been inspected monthly since then. When the theater management accused Monaghan of discrimination, he accused the managers of bribing inspectors to wink at violations. The charge was vigorously denied by Mrs. Lillian Gerard, the managing director, who took a line of defense from Spellman himself. "This is another form of persecution," she said.

Mrs. Gerard had been served with subpoenas twice within ten days. Monaghan, who considered himself a good Catholic, asserted that "persons connected with this theater . . . had generously taken care of the fire inspectors to blink their eyes at the open violation of the fire laws." Monaghan went so far as to reorganize the laws of the Division of License Places of Public Assembly. He assured the press that he had done so only to end a "nefarious system which endangered the lives of theatergoers." The Paris merely happened to be the first theater affected in the reorganization. That wasn't the only form of harassment. Police repeatedly raided the theater, ordering audiences out. They claimed there were a number of bomb scares.

Dr. Hugh Flick, director of the motion-picture division of the state education department, was terrified about being caught in the middle of the controversy. He even refused comment on Spellman's assertion that the state censorship board should be "censured" for licensing the film in the first place. Other state officials, meanwhile, moved quickly to ward off Spellman's attacks. The New York Board of Regents voted unanimously on January 19 to summon the distributors of the picture to a hearing to prove why the film shouldn't be barred on the grounds it was "sacrilegious." The regents supervised the licensing of movies distributed in the state.

The Miracle swiftly became another *cause célèbre*. Liberals were once again outraged at the marshaling of Spellman's conservative might. Predictably, the American Civil Liberties Union urged the Board of Regents not to revoke the film's license. Moreover, novelists, poets, playwrights, and publishers petitioned the board not to censor blindly. Two prominent Protestant clergymen, John Hayes Holmes, who had had a distinguished career as the minister of Community Church, and his successor, Donald Harrington, lent their names to the protest. Their statement read in part: "While groups protesting showing of the film have every right to persuade others not to see the film, they have no right to impose their views upon the rest of the population of the state. Revoking licenses at the insistence of private pressure groups would permit them to dictate what other Americans may or may not see or hear."

The man most bewildered by Spellman's lashing out was Joseph Burstyn, the film's distributor. A talented eccentric, Burstyn selected his films carefully and had a reputation for superb taste. He was shocked when the term "sacrilegious" was bandied about. "What the hell is the Cardinal trying to do?" he kept asking.

Spellman's motives were complex. On one level was his preoccupation with sex. But the Cardinal had another reason to damn this particular film: *The Miracle* was Italian. Spellman saw the movie as a vehicle to demonstrate Italian moral laxity. He was bent on showing the world that American Catholicism was more virtuous. He still resented the criticisms he had heard at the Vatican that the United States was a cultural and spiritual wasteland, and he still smouldered from having been forced by the Pope to kowtow to Mrs. Roosevelt. The Italians, Spellman believed, weren't grateful for all that he and his country had done for them.

Unaware of what was on Spellman's mind, Rossellini fired off a telegram to the Cardinal stating his film differed radically from the narrow-minded misconception that Spellman apparently had. Like Burstyn, Rossellini was trying to understand what was happening. He said his film was produced "with the humble spirit of brotherhood to show that the absence of charity in the hearts of men had given way to an immense darkness and sorrow. . . . In *The Miracle,* men are still without pity because they still have not come back to God but God is already present in the faith, however confused, of that poor persecuted woman. . . . The miracle occurs when, at the birth of the child, the poor demented woman regains her sanity in her maternal love."

Spellman wasn't buying any of it, though several priests in the archdiocese, who had seen the film and been struck by its beauty, tried to get the Cardinal to reconsider. "The film is filth," Spellman said.

Spellman's honor was on the line. He wasn't a man to admit he had ever been wrong, and he wasn't about to start. Though it became increasingly clear to him that he had probably made a mistake, he wasn't going to back down. Thus, the priests around him didn't press him too strongly to reexamine his stand, and they had good reason to be cautious. Frank Getlein, a movie reviewer for the *Catholic*

Messenger of Davenport, Iowa, was fired from his faculty teaching post at the Catholic Fairfield University in Connecticut after his favorable review of *The Miracle* appeared. "Spellman must have picked up the phone," Getlein said later.[43] That was the only reason he could find, since the school refused to give him one. He knew the Cardinal had a reputation for being vindictive. He also believed there wasn't a president of a Catholic college in the nation who wouldn't obey Spellman.

That Spellman should have been alerted to Getlein's review wasn't extraordinary, simply because the review itself was out of the mold of those traditionally found in the Catholic press. Most film reviews in Catholic newspapers were by a syndicated reviewer, William Mooring, an outspoken anti-Communist. Mooring usually sniffed out Communist influences in films and spiced his commentaries with warnings that "thirty-five cents of the price of a forty-cent movie ticket goes right to Moscow."

William P. Clancy, a young English teacher at Notre Dame University, was also fired after he wrote a thoughtful piece in the liberal Catholic journal *Commonweal* entitled "The Catholic as Philistine." Unwisely, he denounced the censorship of *The Miracle* as "semiecclesiastic McCarthyism." After he was sacked Clancy came to New York. The only job he could find was working in a bookstore until he eventually became a *Commonweal* editor. He later entered a seminary and became a priest in Pittsburgh, where for years he regaled listeners with his tale of colliding with Spellman.

Another man who rankled Spellman was a prominent Catholic industrialist, Otto Spaeth. An ebullient patron of the arts, Spaeth was embarrassed by many of the Cardinal's stands and separated Spellman from the Church. The industrialist served on Catholic fundraising committees and participated in other worthy causes, while ignoring Spellman. When *The Miracle* furor erupted Spaeth found himself inadvertently on Spellman's enemies list. When City License Commissioner McCaffrey first moved to ban *The Miracle,* Spaeth wrote an editorial for *Magazine of Art* in which he criticized the official's abuse of his office. The businessman was already well-acquainted with *The Miracle*. Spaeth, who sponsored art projects around the city, had had a special showing of the film at his apartment on Manhattan's fashionable Upper East Side, to which several priests, in addition to family and friends, had been invited. Everyone agreed the film was quite beautiful and stirring. Thus, Spaeth was angered by what he called McCaffrey's "ignorant" stand.

In his editorial, Spaeth likened the commissioner's action to a recent public protest by Catholic War Veterans in New Jersey, who had pressured a television station into removing Charlie Chaplin films from the air because of the comedian's Communist sympathies. Such actions, Spaeth wrote, placed Catholics in "the intolerable position of subverting for others the very liberty which Catholics insist upon." Spaeth had dashed off his piece before Spellman spoke out, but it was published after the Cardinal's blast. The timing made it appear a not-well-veiled criticism of Spellman—or at least Spellman took it that way.

Several years later Spaeth and his wife, Eloise, visited Rome, where, as large contributors to the Church, they were granted a private audience with Pope Pius XII. When Spellman's name came up in conversation, the Pope smiled noncommittally. "We got the feeling that he knew that Spellman didn't like us," Mrs. Spaeth recalled.[44] When a Vatican official introduced Spaeth to the European head of the Knights of Malta, the industrialist became intrigued with the organization. The supreme knight asked if he would consider joining when he got home. Spaeth indicated he would, but an invitation never came. The man in charge of passing on American nominees was, of course, Spellman. Said Mrs. Spaeth, "Otto heard that the Cardinal would not let his name be proposed."

In a letter to *The New York Times* the poet and critic Allen Tate perhaps summarized better than anyone else what had happened with *The Miracle* crusade: "I do not assume that the Catholic Church has acted officially on this matter. What has happened, I believe, is that Catholic individuals and groups have brought pressure upon New York politicians to uphold by force what they believe to be Catholic standards. . . . When we remember that the works of Dante Alighieri were publicly burned in the Fourteenth Century . . . the weapon of repression begins to look ridiculous."

Ridiculous or not, the action frightened many people. While publishers and writers openly condemned the censorship, the film industry remained eerily silent. The business, plagued with federal investigators scouring Hollywood for Communists, was running scared. Movie moguls didn't need to be singled out by anti-Communist Catholics. They bent over backward to appease modern inquisitors such as Spellman and the Legion of Decency.

Films were routinely submitted to the legion, which dictated scene and dialogue cuts. When Spellman declared that no Catholic could see *Forever Amber* with a safe conscience, the producer William Perlberg initially boldly replied that he wouldn't "bowdlerize the film to placate the Roman Catholic Church." A short while later, the objectionable material was deleted and Twentieth Century-Fox cravenly issued a statement "to correct an unfortunate impression" about the rights of religious figures to direct the faithful on moral matters. Besides holding sway as a censor, the Church benefited from the production of a number of pictures such as *Boys Town, Going My Way,* and *Waterfront Priest* that cast Catholicism in an exceptionally flattering light.

Walter Kerr, the drama critic for *Commonweal* in the early 1950s, complained in the essay "Catholics and Hollywood" that the power churchmen wielded may simply have made films worse than ever before. He was disgusted when, in 1952, the most publicized Catholic "art" award was given to *Quo Vadis* because, as the priest who made the presentation noted, the film showed "how a handful of human beings, fired with the love and truth of Christ, were able to overcome the might of Pagan Rome." Kerr said it had received accolades only because there weren't any freshly minted films with Catholic sympathies—"no priest in the pulpit, no nun in the backfield, no early Christian Deborah Kerr in the jaws of a technicolor lion."

In the case of *The Miracle,* few people were surprised when the regents disregarded the liberals' pleas and revoked the license to distribute the film, but it did worry people. "The case of *The Miracle* has now developed past the point where champions of free screen— or even those who would hold the limited freedoms now precariously possessed by films—can afford to permit their friendliest deference or formality to lock their tongues," noted *New York Times* critic Bosley Crowther. "For already the clamps of compulsion have tightened a little more on the screen; a major precedent has been set by the Regents which can be ominous."

In Europe, the spectacle was viewed disdainfully as a ridiculous American sideshow. Although the film had been released in Italy three years before, *L'Osservatore Romano* reviewed *The Miracle* as a result of the furor the Cardinal had created. The critic for the Vatican newspaper, perhaps realizing Spellman's attempt to make American Catholicism appear holier than Italy's, noted that "objections from a religious viewpoint are very grave," but said there were "scenes of undoubted screen value . . . [and] notwithstanding all this, we still believe in Rossellini's art."

Spellman retaliated with a pastoral letter. "Satan alone would dare such perversion," he declared, and went on to write:

> In a secondary way, *The Miracle* is a vicious insult to Italian womanhood. It presents the Italian woman as moronic, neurotic and in matters of religion fanatical. Only a perverted mind could so misrepresent so noble a race as woman.
>
> To those who perpetrate such a crime as *The Miracle* within the law all that we can say is: How long will enemies of decency tear at the heart of America? . . . Divide and conquer is the technique of the greatest enemy of civilization, atheistic communism. God forbid that the producers of racial and religious mockeries should divide and demoralize Americans so that the minions of Moscow might enslave this land of liberty.

What further angered Spellman was that until the boycott was called, the film had fared poorly at the Paris. After Spellman railed against it, the lines for every performance stretched around the block.

And when it wasn't Spellman who kept the controversial film before the public, it was one of the officials working in tandem with him. The *New York Post,* for instance, noted the effect of the publicity in an editorial on January 10, 1951: "License Commissioner McCaffrey refuses to drop the subject; he is pressing his legal fight for authority to ban the production. Each day his frantic follies give the film more free promotion. No movie had a more energetic press agent."

Joe Burstyn fought back after the regents finally had the picture withdrawn. The case dragged through the courts, eventually reaching the Supreme Court, where it became a rallying point for people interested in artistic freedom for the entire entertainment industry— radio, television, and stage as well as film. In May 1952 the Supreme Court found, in effect, that blasphemy was not a criminal offense. "It is not the business of government in our nation," the Supreme Court said, "to suppress real or imagined attacks upon a particular religious doctrine, whether they appear in publications, speeches, or motion pictures." Justice Felix Frankfurter, in a concurring opinion, pointed out that many of the most cherished religious doctrines were once considered blasphemous or sacrilegious. "Blasphemy was the chameleon phrase which meant the criticism of whatever the ruling authority of the moment established as orthodox doctrine," he said.

On Sunday, December 16, 1956, the Cardinal launched his biggest censorship campaign ever. Midway through a solemn mass at St. Patrick's, he mounted the pulpit, for the first time since February 1949, when he had denounced the jailing of Mindszenty. The worshipers immediately knew that his message must be grave. "Dearly beloved in Christ, I have a statement to make," Spellman said. A deadly stillness settled over the church. The Cardinal lamented that he was "anguished." He had learned that a movie was about to be released that "has been responsibly judged to be evil in concept and which is certain to exert an immoral and corrupting influence on those who see it."

The picture was *Baby Doll,* an alternately ponderous and witty look at some of the seemier sides of life in the South. The raciest aspect of the movie, written by Tennessee Williams and directed by Elia Kazan, was its print advertising in which the actress Carroll Baker appeared in a slip. Once again, Spellman hadn't seen the film he condemned, and he appeared surprised when asked if he had. "Must you have an illness to know what it is?" he asked.

The film suffered a number of canceled bookings, but once again the publicity that the Cardinal generated resulted in booming ticket sales. A number of viewers later wondered what all the fuss was about.

Vincent J. Fontana, a handsome young doctor who was Spellman's physician, wanted the prelate to take a more reasonable approach. Fontana knew Joseph Levine, the film's producer, and wanted to bring the two men together.

"I think it would be great if Joe Levine met the Cardinal," Fontana recalled mentioning to one of Spellman's secretaries.[45]

"No way!" Fontana remembered the suddenly worried monsignor replying. "No way!"

In any event, Fontana asked Spellman to invite Levine and his wife to lunch. Out of curiosity, perhaps, or simply because he thought Levine might be of some use to him, Spellman did. "They hit it off," according to Fontana.[46] Spellman wound up giving the producer a pair of cuff links bearing the Cardinal's coat of arms, and his wife a pendant. Levine was flattered. The movie mogul couldn't help being pleased that a man as exalted as a cardinal should embrace him. A pragmatist, Levine knew nothing came without strings. The producer later gave several valuable paintings to the Vatican. Hollywood had just come through a brutal period. Spellman, naturally, had supported the anti-Communist purges. As early as 1945, the Cardinal had been involved in the investigations of Communist penetration into the movie industry, and his stance toward films he disliked sent chilly winds through movie studios.[47] Never again did Spellman rake any of Levine's films over the coals of public criticism. Levine learned that it was better to have the Powerhouse as a friend than as an enemy, even if paying tribute were part of the price of friendship.

An aspect of Spellman's power was the inability of most Catholics to see criticism of the Cardinal as anything but an assault on their religion. Brought up with their defenses ever ready, Catholics saw themselves as a beleaguered minority standing bravely against Protestant onslaughts. Such a position had validity until the 1950s, where in New York in particular it defied reality. Catholics had been in control of the city's politics for as long as anyone could remember, and after the war many were rich enough to join the march to the suburbs, many becoming "country club Catholics," a disparaging term used by John Kennedy for those who opposed his presidential bid. Catholicism was the largest and wealthiest religion in the city. It was difficult to find an area of civic life where the Church's interests weren't well-represented; yet the siege mentality persisted. One of the results was the inability of most Catholics to separate Spellman the man from the Church. Whenever he was criticized Catholics formed ranks around him; this was reflected in the business community as well as in politics. Nowhere was this more apparent than in the case of the *New York Post,* a lively liberal newspaper that routinely questioned the Cardinal's positions.

The ramifications of criticizing Spellman were made abundantly clear to Dorothy Schiff, the *Post*'s publisher, during a disturbing conversation she had with Robert Weil, the president of Macy's. She made up her mind immediately to try to talk to Spellman about her newspaper's losing advertising because of stands taken against him. The subject arose when Weil asked why she thought her newspaper hadn't more department-store advertising. Mrs. Schiff was circumspect in her reply. She explained that the advertising department had made special efforts to get certain department stores to advertise but had been unsuccessful. She mentioned efforts to land B. Altman and said that she herself had tried. "But I couldn't even get in to see Mr. Burke, the president," she said.[48]

"You know why that is, don't you?" Weil asked.

"I have an idea," she replied dryly. Thereupon Weil confirmed her suspicions. "He is controlled by Cardinal Spellman," Weil said.

"Have you got Stern's?" he asked.

"No," she replied.

"Same thing," Weil said.

That very day, January 25, 1952, Mrs. Schiff called the chancery and asked to see Spellman. "The Cardinal doesn't give interviews," a secretary said. Though she wrote a column for her paper, the publisher explained that she wasn't seeking an interview. "There are matters of mutual interest I want to discuss," she said. The secretary called back shortly thereafter to invite her to the Powerhouse for lunch on February 11. As much as anything else, Spellman invited her out of curiosity. They had met only once, at a public dinner. Spellman had asked her to spell her name twice—this was one of his techniques for memorizing—and on the second spelling she had identified herself as the publisher of the *Post*. The warm smile on the Cardinal's face faded.[49]

Of all the city's newspapers, the *Post* was the most critical of Spellman and his policies. Fiercely liberal, the *Post* editorialized that the Cardinal consistently trampled on the principles the *Post* espoused. That was in stark contrast to the Hearst newspapers, the *Mirror* and the *Journal American,* which routinely lauded Spellman's positions and whose conservative columnists, George Sokolsky and Bob Considine, were close to the Cardinal. Spellman had cause to be suspicious of Mrs. Schiff. Her paper had angered him by criticizing his handling of the gravediggers' strike, his flare-up with Mrs. Roosevelt, his support of Franco, and his many censorship activities.

Newspaper stories about the Cardinal tended to focus on his many charities, his fund-raising drives, and the controversies in which he became involved, rather than on his partisan politics, his effect upon legislation, or his methods of running his archdiocese.

The gingerly way the press generally treated the Powerhouse made the *Post*'s stands appear that much bolder. Few editors or publishers wanted to get into a wrangle with any of the city's religious leaders.

Francis Joseph Spellman was ordained a priest in 1916 at the age of twenty-seven. After graduating from Fordham University, he attended the prestigious North American College, a seminary in Rome for many American churchmen who moved into positions of responsibility in the Catholic Church in the United States. While at the seminary, Spellman gained a reputation for being ambitious and strong-willed. He forged friendships with Italian ecclesiastics who later helped his career. The photograph below is of the 1916 class of the North American College. Spellman is in the front row, second from left, with his hand on his knee.

Wide World

Acme

Genevieve Brady, Spellman's patroness in Rome, eased his access to people of prominence. At her Long Island estate, Inisfada, she broke with Spellman after he undermined her plans to entertain Cardinal Pacelli during his historic visit to the United States.

Boston's Cardinal O'Connell, left, a Spellman adversary, stands beside Cardinal Pacelli, who became Pope Pius XII and enabled Spellman to become the most powerful prelate in America.

Spellman and Count Enrico Galeazzi became friends and accomplices in the Byzantine world of Church politics.

A great crowd of laymen and clergy thronged St. Patrick's Cathedral on May 23, 1939, to see Spellman installed as archbishop of the powerful New York diocese. Churchmen came from around the world, and prominent politicians and businessmen filled pews and aisles. New York was one of the Church's most demanding assignments. Few people, though, realized the extent of the behind-the-scenes politicking involved in awarding Spellman the coveted post, nor did they know the resentment it provoked among New York priests.

The New York Times

The close relationship between Spellman and President Roosevelt led to Spellman's becoming a national and international power broker and to covert cooperation between the Vatican and the U.S. government in international affairs.

Wide World

Archbishop Spellman's influence in world affairs was enhanced by his network of powerful contacts, including Winston Churchill, who is shown here with Spellman as they cross Park Avenue to attend a private luncheon.

Acme

During World War II, Spellman visited war zones, where he blessed troops and acted as President Roosevelt's secret agent. Here he dispenses communion to American enlisted men in Italy in 1944.

Wide World

Spellman's source of ecclesiastical power was his good friend Pope Pius XII. The Pope increasingly relied on Spellman, who exhibited his prowess as both an astute financial adviser and a shrewd diplomat.

Spellman's ecclesiastical ambitions were achieved in 1946 when he was elevated to the rank of cardinal. Here he stands (left of center) with head bowed in front of Pope Pius XII, who is sitting on his throne in St. Peter's Basilica, Vatican City. Some thirty thousand people watched the colorful ceremony during which the pontiff placed "red hats" on the heads of the new cardinals. Spellman, who had become a friend of the Pope when both were Vatican diplomats, was acknowledged as being more special than the other new cardinals: He was given the red hat that the Pope himself had worn when he had been made a cardinal. Once a prince of the Church, Spellman became a leading anti-Communist who covertly helped the F.B.I. and the C.I.A. Spellman also began pursuing interests that were at times independent of the Vatican and that brought him into conflict with the Pope.

After gravediggers went on strike in 1949 at the Church-owned Calvary Cemetery, Spellman charged they were Communists, and he forced seminarians (below) to dig graves. The women (above) were strikers' wives who called on Spellman to assure the Cardinal their husbands weren't Communists and only wanted a raise.

The New York Times

Spellman became enmeshed in New York City politics to such a degree that his chancery was known as "the Powerhouse." Here he meets with Governor Al Smith and Mayor Fiorello La Guardia.

Wide World

Spellman poses with General Eisenhower and Governor Dewey at the Alfred E. Smith Memorial Dinner, a showcase of the prelate's political power.

Spellman is shown here with J. Edgar Hoover and James A. Farley. The Cardinal and the F.B.I. director clandestinely traded favors and relentlessly sought Communist influences everywhere.

The Cardinal was a firm supporter of both Joe McCarthy and Roy Cohn. Through Spellman, Cohn became enmeshed in Church affairs.

As military vicar of the U.S. Armed Forces, Spellman visited American military bases around the world during peacetime as well as wartime. He attended Pentagon intelligence briefings, discussed military strategy with generals, and became a figure of awe to enlisted men. The Cardinal closely identified his Church with U.S. military ventures and became a symbol of American military might. During his many trips abroad, Spellman gathered intelligence for the U.S. government and assisted the C.I.A. and F.B.I., and upon his return he was debriefed by the U.S. State Department and other agencies. His patriotism ultimately led him to break with the Vatican.

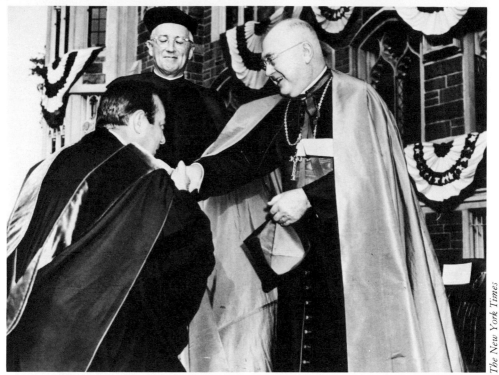

In New York City, Cardinal Spellman's political power seemed boundless. Here Mayor Wagner kneels to kiss the Cardinal's ring while the Rev. Laurence J. McGinley, president of Fordham University, looks on.

The Cardinal raised millions of dollars for charity. His favorite cause was the Foundling Hospital. He held an annual Christmas party for the children and invited politicians and business leaders.

Spellman was the kingmaker in the American Catholic Church. Fifty thousand people attended the celebration at Yankee Stadium marking his twenty-fifth anniversary as a bishop, including Cardinals (from left) Mooney of Detroit, McGuigan of Toronto, Stritch of Chicago, and McIntyre of Los Angeles.

Cardinal McIntyre

Bishop Sheen

Archbishop Cushing

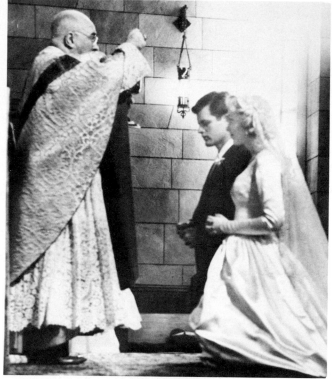

Spellman performed the marriage ceremony for three of the Kennedy children, including Edward Moore Kennedy's marriage to Joan Bennett on November 29, 1958. Spellman and Joseph P. Kennedy formed a close relationship based on the political and financial favors they did for one another and their efforts to bring closer rapport between the Church and the U.S. government. They were active supporters of Senator Joe McCarthy, and it is believed that they tried to make McCarthy President of the United States.

Wide World

Wide World

Spellman stands with presidential candidates John F. Kennedy and Richard Nixon at the 1960 Alfred E. Smith Memorial Dinner. While Kennedy battled Protestants opposed to his candidacy, most of the Church hierarchy, including Spellman, clandestinely opposed him as well. Spellman feared being displaced as the most important American Catholic.

When Pope John XXIII succeeded Pope Pius XII, Spellman resented the liberal turn the Church took. He opposed Pope John's Second Vatican Council and vowed that no liberalization would "get past the Statue of Liberty." With John's emergence, Spellman's power began to wane in ecclesiastical circles much as it did in the secular arena under President Kennedy, who favored Cardinal Cushing.

Spellman with General Anastasio Somoza and his wife and son at St. Patrick's on Easter Sunday, March 26, 1967. Pope John had asked Spellman to refrain from appearing publicly with the Nicaraguan dictator, but the Cardinal did so anyway. As a further slight, Spellman had both his and the Pope's pictures grace Nicaraguan stamps.

Pass the Lord and
PRAISE THE AMMUNITION

Edward Sorel

Spellman's hawkish stance toward American involvement in the Vietnam war brought picketing demonstrators to his residence and the cathedral and a decline in his moral authority. Pope Paul VI sought peace, while Spellman rattled his saber. Finally, Spellman ruptured his relations with the Vatican.

The Cardinal's Vietnam involvement started in the early 1950s when he met Ngo Dinh Diem, then a layman at a Catholic seminary in New York. Spellman helped propel Diem into the leadership of South Vietnam but broke with him before Diem's assassination. He did not, however, lessen his support of the war effort.

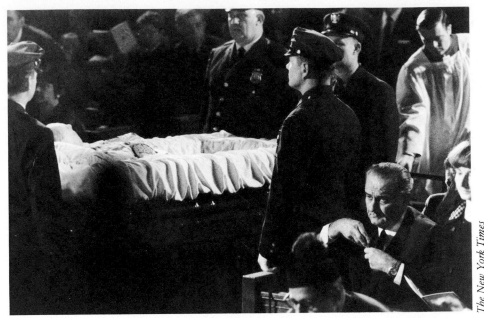

The New York Times

When Spellman died on December 2, 1967, President Johnson lost one of the most ardent backers of his war policy. Johnson's arrival at the funeral was secretive for fear of demonstrations.

UPI

More than three thousand mourners passed Cardinal Spellman's casket each hour until his body was placed in the Archbishop's Crypt beneath the main altar at St. Patrick's. His death marked the end of an era for American Catholicism.

Moreover, the natural skepticism of many reporters melted when it came to the clergy. Everyone knew priests, rabbis, and ministers who worked hard, were decent individuals, and devoted their lives to their fellow man. They assumed that all religious figures had these qualities in common, though they were harder to see in some than in others. Then there was the Catholic Church's special position in New York with its splendid pageantry, stalwart anti-Communism, and accommodation of Irish-Catholic politicians.

And then there was Spellman himself. All of his life he had been image-conscious, and since his Vatican days he was very concerned about how he was cast in press coverage. He hired outside public-relations people, including Ivy Lee, who was one of the best-known PR men in the city, to help him maintain the proper public persona. Generally, the Cardinal went out of his way to be cordial to editors and reporters. Often, he personally returned their telephone calls, flattered them by soliciting their advice, and on occasion gave news tips to select columnists such as Considine. The pugnacious George Sokolsky at times was one of Spellman's conveyor belts for political matters. The Catholic reporters especially revered him and, even in the snow, they knelt to kiss his ring when they met his plane on its return from one of his many visits to Europe or elsewhere. Other reporters had second thoughts about printing anything adverse about the man, simply because religion was a touchy subject, as well as because the Cardinal had such influence that he might simply call a managing editor or a publisher and cause a reporter unwanted grief. "Everybody was a little afraid of him," acknowledged columnist Murray Kempton.[50]

All in all, the Cardinal benefited greatly by his press coverage. Spellman was news, and, even in cases such as his attack on Mrs. Roosevelt, few editorials in the city other than the *New York Post*'s criticized him. Publishers knew of the price to be paid for taking on the Powerhouse. Many readers and advertisers would be outraged, and that could only be bad for business. Dorothy Schiff had found that out.

The publisher arrived at the Cardinal's residence promptly at 12:45 P.M. A servant ushered her into the formal parlor, with its French provincial furniture covered in red velvet. Starched-lace curtains were hung in the windows along with heavy, gold satin drapes. A few minutes later, the Cardinal entered the room, accompanied by Bishop Sheen, who was famous for his converts, such as the columnist Heywood Broun and the feisty conservative Clare Boothe Luce, the latter known as "Fulton's Folly." Five more priests entered, and they all met the publisher.[51]

The luncheon conversation touched on a number of topics, including American representation at the Vatican, an issue again being debated in the press. Taylor had resigned, and there was serious question as to whether Truman would renew the mission. Spellman asked his guest why anyone would object to an ambassador to the Vatican, a question that was routinely asked in the press. To Mrs. Schiff, the answer was obvious, and she didn't mince her words. "I think non-Catholics feel that Catholics would obtain even greater political power in America than they already have," she said matter-of-factly.

The Cardinal's head snapped up. "Catholics have no power!" he declared.

Mrs. Schiff didn't know how to reply. She refrained from laughing outright but became flustered. Then she grew indignant. Something in Spellman's approach made her feel he was about to call her a bigot for even daring to say that Catholics had any political muscle. She didn't believe she had ever been anti-Catholic. "My two best friends as a girl were Catholics," she recalled replying.

Mrs. Schiff had attended the luncheon out of resentment that certain advertisers boycotted her paper. She hoped to convince Spellman to ask his "friends" to place ads in the *Post*. But she wasn't going to let Spellman belittle her. The publisher said she knew of instances of the Church's political power. Carefully, she abstained from citing one of Spellman's power plays. She recounted her experience as a member of a committee of the Women's Trade Union that had promoted a child-labor bill before the New York State Assembly during Cardinal Hayes's reign. "A leading Catholic on my committee—Byrnes MacDonald—and many civic and labor organizations went to Albany and lobbied for the bill, and it was passed by the State Senate," she recalled. "Then it was killed in the Assembly when the Catholic bishop of Albany testified against it. Byrnes MacDonald sent me a telegram saying that he had been forced to withdraw from the Committee." When she finished her story, the priests sat in cold silence.

Inevitably, the conversation shifted to Communism. Mrs. Schiff asked the priests why they thought Communism had such an appeal in Catholic nations such as France and Italy. In his reply, Spellman referred to something that Mrs. Schiff herself had said earlier about the susceptibility of poor and ignorant people to Communist ideology. "The Communists confuse the people by using religious symbols and statues in front of their headquarters," the Cardinal said. "A peasant can go to mass in the morning and a Communist meeting in the afternoon."

"Let me ask you a question now," Spellman added. "How do you think Roosevelt would feel if he could come back to earth today?"

Before Mrs. Schiff could reply, the priests all began talking at once. The topic seemed extremely familiar to them. They bitterly attacked Roosevelt's concessions to the Soviet Union at the Yalta

Conference, as though that had marked the first phase in the end of the world. Mrs. Schiff found their venom unnerving. Finally, she got a chance to speak. "He would be horrified, but he would believe that if he had been here all along, things would never have come to pass," Mrs. Schiff said. "He always believed he could personally influence people like 'Uncle Joe.' " Spellman agreed with her, while the other priests muttered and grumbled. "Yes," the Cardinal said. "I'd heard him say this myself."

The priests then took up the issue of Alger Hiss, who had been convicted of perjury for "betraying" America to the Communists. It was Hiss, they said, who had been the architect of the Yalta Conference. He was also vilified for having written the United Nations Charter, which the priests viewed as another Communist giveaway. The priest on her left, Monsignor Thomas McMahon, was head of the Catholic Near East Welfare Association. He told Mrs. Schiff that, at least, Israel wouldn't go Communist, despite terrible poverty. When she asked what the men thought would be the final outcome of the present world situation, they shrugged. "It's in God's hands," one replied.

Mrs. Schiff had the feeling that the leader of the Catholic Church in America was devoid of solutions, discouraged, and broken in morale. She hadn't realized the depth to which Spellman and his priests felt the defeats of the Church in Eastern Europe, China, and Korea. Several times the priests bitterly complained that they were "persecuted."

After lunch the Cardinal took Mrs. Schiff back to his salon. The priests left with the exception of Sheen. Spellman solicitously asked Mrs. Schiff if she had any personal problems on her mind. She quickly tried to disabuse both men of the notion that they were on the verge of a new conquest.

"No!" she said. "I called on a mad impulse because it was too bad that there was so much distrust between us, [thinking] that probably if we got to know each other, we would find we could be best friends. I have certainly not come to ask you for any favors. I knew that we had been in conflict with Church policy time and again and possibly will be again in the future." As an illustration, she mentioned a Catholic hospital in Poughkeepsie where there was a heated dispute over birth control. Several doctors had been fired for being proponents of Planned Parenthood. The *Post* had deplored that an institution receiving federal funds should have such a policy. "But you don't know the facts," Spellman said. "The doctors had an agreement with the hospital to abide by the rules."

Suddenly, the two were in a confrontation. Spellman denied that doctors had been fired, despite the fact that they had been. Mrs. Schiff took out a pencil and started to take notes. "Please don't do that," Spellman said. He added that the chancery was going to make a statement within a few days about the matter. (The statement was never made.)

Finally, Mrs. Schiff brought up the issue of large department stores with Catholic presidents who refused to advertise in the *Post*. The Cardinal stood firm. He probably had had some inkling about the motive for her visit and was ready. He steadfastly denied that the *Post* was discriminated against. Besides, he probably had never asked Altman's Burke or others to withhold such advertising—he didn't have to.

As she was leaving, Mrs. Schiff asked if she could write a column about the luncheon. The Cardinal vigorously said no. "You come here, everyone comes here," he said. "They never talk about it. After all, this is my private home. If you wrote about it in your column, I would have to change my way of life. I would have to see all the columnists." He rattled off a list of the nation's best-known columnists. At that point, Mrs. Schiff believed the writers he ticked off were frequent visitors to the Powerhouse.

In a parting gesture, the publisher asked Spellman if she could return the luncheon invitation. "No, I don't accept invitations," he replied.

The meeting proved a failure: the *Post* continued its criticism of Spellman, and certain advertising continued to elude the paper. The publisher realized that her paper was actually hurt more than the prelate. The *Post*'s barbs may have wounded the Cardinal's ego, but they had little effect on his attitudes or his public support.

PART III

THE
AMERICAN POPE

CHAPTER NINE

The Rise of Americanism

DRIVEN BY AMBITION, FRANCIS SPELLMAN WAS NO LONGER content to take all of his directives from Rome. Since becoming a cardinal, he wasn't fettered by the constant desire to please other churchmen, not even the Pope, in order to advance his career. He had achieved the highest office—save one—within the Church, and now was more than simply one among seventy princes of the Church. He was the ruler of the archdiocese of New York, the most important see in the world other than Rome. The Pope relied upon him for his political prowess, financial strength, and judgment, but for such a highly independent man, even all that wasn't enough.

Dressed in scarlet, Cardinal Spellman descended the brief flight of steps outside St. Patrick's on April 20, 1951, and walked to the open touring car carrying General Douglas MacArthur. The air was cool and the general's trench coat was buttoned to the neck and his campaign hat firmly in place. Spellman leaned forward slightly while the general reached toward him. They shook hands while the thousands of people who thronged the sidewalk outside the cathedral roared their approval.

The Cardinal had just engaged in a further controversial act, one that displeased both the White House and the Vatican. At a time the Pope was seeking the cooperation of Truman, Spellman had just gone out of his way to antagonize the President. The prelate participated in the lionizing of MacArthur, whom Truman had just ordered home from South Korea. Spellman's display of affection for MacArthur, at least to a degree, was part of a scheme to sabotage the possibility of a permanent United States ambassador to the Holy See. Though nearly twenty years earlier Spellman had worked diligently for such an appointment, he no longer wanted an American official at the Vatican. If an effective ambassador were named to replace Myron Taylor, he would undercut some of the Cardinal's influence, both in Rome and Washington. Spellman had begun to pursue foreign policy interests that were opposed to those of the Holy See; he was starting to break with Rome.

Spellman was prevented only at the last minute from parading through the streets at MacArthur's side. Protests from individuals and Protestant groups had persuaded the Veterans of Foreign Wars—sponsor of the "Loyalty Day"—to withdraw their invitation to the Cardinal. The Cardinal's motivation wasn't purely Machiavellian. He liked and admired MacArthur, whom he had met in Japan after the war. At the time he had been struck by the general's regal bearing, Americanism, and anti-Communism. Spellman had gotten to know him better since the start of the Korean War. The Cardinal had once again donned military fatigues and entered a war zone. As he had during World War II, he toured front lines, this time saying mass at places called Heartbreak Ridge and Pork Chop Hill, and generally rallying the spirits of young soldiers while discussing politics and military strategy with the likes of MacArthur. When Truman recalled MacArthur, Spellman believed it was a grave mistake.

The Cardinal knew that his open display of support for MacArthur would raise Truman's hackles. Spellman still resented the President's refusal to receive the seminarians who had broken the cemetery workers' strike, but the old grudge had little bearing on his current behavior. A hostile Truman might be less disposed toward sending an ambassador to the Vatican.

Publicly, Spellman pressed the Holy See's desire for another American official to succeed Taylor. Later, he told aides he privately opposed the appointment because it meant only the "meddling in Vatican affairs by the American government."[1] He didn't mention the likely diminution of his own role. The Cardinal had known for a year and a half, since the fall of 1949, that Taylor wanted to leave the post. Taylor had asked Spellman for the names of potential candidates to succeed him, but Spellman had failed to produce any. Count Galeazzi, who was in routine contact with Spellman and was also working on the issue, had proposed the wealthy Winthrop Aldrich, whom Spellman rejected on the ground that he was a Republican, someone who wouldn't wash with a Democratic administration.

Thus, when Taylor resigned on January 18, 1950, he left a vacuum.

He himself tried somewhat unenthusiastically to find a replacement and talked of the post being elevated to that of ambassadorial rank. Likewise, Joe Kennedy, who had been instrumental in getting Taylor appointed, offered his assistance to Truman and gave the President a wealth of background information about Roosevelt's opening the post.

Working to Spellman's advantage was Truman's wariness about opening a religious can of worms. Quite possibly Truman was worried that word would get out that he had secretly funded the Vatican's role in the Italian election. Also, since the original purpose of the mission had been as a wartime listening post, Truman may have believed that the purpose had been served. In any event, Truman kept Spellman apprised of his actions, including an initial reluctance to push the matter vigorously. The President said congressional authority might be needed, and noted to Spellman that "everything is in abeyance until I have a report from the State Department" on whether the mission was needed. The State Department concluded that it was, but Truman remained cautious.[2] A new election year was on the horizon, and Protestants once again were revved up.

Christian Century editorialized against renewing the mission and Protestants and Others United rallied its forces to prepare for battle, while a number of ministers across the nation did the same. In Chicago, for instance, J. Ralph McGee, the Methodist resident bishop, urged his pastors to organize. His reason: "The Roman Catholic hierarchy is political-minded." He would have been apoplectic if he had known he was falling into Spellman's game plan.

Faced with the mounting hostility, Cicognani tried to rally a countercampaign. He hurriedly alerted Spellman and Cardinal Samuel Stritch in Chicago that they should be ready to "present the Catholic side." Unwittingly, the delegate asked Spellman for the name of someone to take the Church's case to America. Spellman recommended two men: his international affairs expert Griffiths and a strange, constantly chattering Jesuit, Robert A. Graham, who specialized in Vatican diplomacy; his proposed head for such a lobby was Myron Taylor, who was considered a traitor by many Protestants. But while proposing such measures, Spellman immediately cited their drawbacks. Such a lobby, he noted, would result in a strong backlash from "Blanshard and his secularist group."[3]

The Cardinal personally lobbied for the ambassadorship, but his actions lacked the vigor usually associated with his efforts. For example, he wrote to James F. Byrnes, the former secretary of state, just as Byrnes was to be inaugurated governor of South Carolina, that he thought an American presence at the Vatican would "benefit our country," and, casually, he suggested that if Byrnes thought the mission useful, the Cardinal would appreciate his telling the Senate Foreign Relations Committee so.[4]

In the end, Truman came up with a solution that may have satisfied both himself and Spellman. Through artlessness or design, Truman proposed as an ambassador to the Holy See a candidate so controversial that the likelihood of his ever being approved by Congress was almost nil. On October 20, 1951, Truman nominated General Mark Clark. As both Spellman and Truman must have realized, Clark was anathema to Texas Senator Tom Connally, head of the Foreign Relations Committee, which voted on such ambassadorships. As soon as Clark was proposed, Connally spoke against him. While commander of the United States Army Field Forces, Clark had used the 36th Texas Division at the battle of the Rapido River in Italy. The division was ordered to advance in the face of tremendous odds, and the Texans suffered an enormous number of casualties.[5]

There was a further key element working against the appointment. Truman offended Congress by copying Roosevelt: he put forth the Clark appointment when Congress wasn't sitting, thus rousing the ire of a number of representatives.

Protestant reaction was swift and predictable. Rallies were held. Hundreds of Protestant clergymen converged on Washington to demonstrate outside the White House; they grew angrier when Truman refused to meet their delegates. For months, Clark was vilified, until finally, on January 13, 1952, the general withdrew his nomination.

The furor didn't abate with Clark's departure. Several days later, a pilgrimage of hundreds of clergymen again descended on Washington to protest the naming of an ambassador to the Holy See. Their keynote speaker was the Reverend Carl McIntyre, the extremist president of the International Council of Christian Churches, who excoriated Truman for having "driven a sword deep into the heart of Presbyterian America." The second half of McIntyre's diatribe blistered Spellman. The reactionary minister reflected the worst of Protestant anti-Catholicism. Like Spellman, McIntyre was quick to take to task those he opposed and, like the Cardinal, his prejudices were close to the surface: "Communism is the enemy we are all against. But we have another enemy, too, older, shrewder. It is Roman Catholicism and its bid for world power. In the United States it is called 'Spellmanism.' "

For months the issue raged, and the political repercussions were obvious. On May 14 the president of the Southern Baptist Convention warned that Baptists could not, in good conscience, "countenance any [political] candidate, even one of their own number, who does not make it crystal clear that he opposes any and all missions to the Vatican." Then the American Baptist convention reaffirmed its opposition to "any kind of formal diplomatic relations on the part of our government with the Vatican." As the presidential election neared Truman backed away from the issue. Shortly before the Democratic convention he announced that the question of an envoy was being shelved. When Adlai Stevenson received the nomination he went even further: he said the issue was dead. Such an appointment, Stevenson declared, "would be highly incompatible with the theory of separation of Church and State."

In Rome churchmen frantically wondered what had gone wrong. How could a mission that was expected to be upgraded wind up being demolished? They blamed Spellman. Suddenly, it became clear that the Cardinal hadn't pushed the cause dynamically. Knowing Spellman, the Pope understood the American had some hidden motive for sitting on his hands, and Pius was furious. What further infuriated the Pope was that there was little he could do to strike back. What became clear to him was how much he relied upon Spellman for just about everything—money, political influence, the anti-Communist crusade—even the floor waxers used at the Vatican came from Spellman. Everywhere Pius looked, Spellman was the axle around which many Church wheels spun.

Instead of confronting Spellman directly, the Pope turned to one of his secretaries, a nervous, birdlike man, with large deep-set eyes named Giovanni Battista Montini, whose brilliance was overshadowed by his tentativeness. In 1952, Montini was fifty-five years old and had a passion for politics. He too had been spotted early as a priest destined for high ecclesiastic office, but, unlike Pacelli, Montini was well-liked because of his accessibility and readiness to listen. An intellectual with liberal sympathies, Montini had a major fault—the inability to make up his mind; he always saw both sides of an issue, perhaps too clearly. Later, Pope John XXIII jokingly referred to him as "Amleto," Hamlet-like.

Montini had risen to the heights of papal secretary because of his understanding of Italian and international politics, and his ability to synthesize information rapidly and to put forth declarations in a pithy fashion. It was he who was said to have coined Pacelli's oft-quoted wartime phrase: "Nothing is lost with peace; everything is lost by war." Neither Spellman nor his great ally in the Pacelli camp, Mother Pascalina, had much use for Montini. The other papal secretary was Spellman's old friend Tardini, who with Pascalina and Galeazzi kept him abreast of high Vatican affairs he might not learn directly from the Pope.

Thus, Spellman knew, after Eisenhower took office, that the timid Montini wasn't acting on his own when he sent Spellman a stern letter expressing gross unhappiness with the way the Vatican ambassadorship had been mishandled. The letter decried attacks on the Church in America and smacked of the European sarcasm toward the United States that Spellman always found infuriating. In part, Montini wrote: "In connection with this matter of diplomatic representation and on other occasions in the recent past, there have been repeated, vulgar, bitter and entirely unjustified attacks against the Holy See, with unwarranted deductions and unmerited conclusions that are scarcely compatible with the 'freedoms' of which the United States claims to be the champion and custodian.'' The letter didn't stop there; Spellman himself was chastised for not doing enough to counteract such assaults: "I cannot conceal from Your Eminence that it is felt here that such attacks on the part of non-Catholics did not arouse an adequate reaction to the part of the Catholic community in the United States, and that neither orally nor in the press has there been a sufficient response or any particularly authoritative voice raised in the defense of the Holy See."[6]

Spellman didn't respond to Montini for weeks. In the interim, he ordered the Jesuit historian Graham to New York from Paris, where he was studying. He had Graham collect copies of his speeches, as well as newspaper and magazine articles showing that Spellman had waved the Vatican flag and publicly declared himself for the Clark appointment. "Spellman was furious because the Vatican thought he had sabotaged the appointment of the Vatican representative," Graham recalled.[7] Spellman shipped the press clippings to Montini. He sent a note saying that he was sending them "to save Your Excellency from any inconvenience in locating them in the Vatican archives."[8]

Spellman was especially bitter about the sneering tone used toward the United States. More than half of the funds that the Vatican collected worldwide came from the United States. The Propagation of the Faith in America was the biggest contributor toward Church foreign missions. The War Relief Services had channeled more than $200 million in money, food, clothing, and medicine to needy causes over the past decade. One of the prime beneficiaries of aid from the United States and from himself, Spellman bitterly knew, was Italy.

Obliquely, Spellman referred to another fact that made the letter so galling. If it weren't for the United States, he implied to Montini, the Vatican might well sit in the middle of a Communist nation. Moreover, Italy was gearing up for an election and, undoubtedly, wanted more help from the United States in repelling Communism. Spellman's letter noted, "Your Excellency is well aware of the Communist threats to the Church and her institutions even in countries where the great majority of the people are Catholic."[9]

Indeed, only several weeks after he replied to Montini, the Holy See asked Spellman for help in the coming Italian elections. The Cardinal wrote Galeazzi, venting his anger at the disdainful way that the Vatican treated both him and his nation and then expected both to jump to its defense: "This situation is of particular interest to me since only two weeks ago I wrote to Monsignor Montini defending the Bishops of the United States and myself from the accusation of not supporting the Holy See in the United States, and here now the

Holy See asks the Bishops of America to defend the Holy See in Italy!!!!!!!!!''[10]

Spellman, of course, wrote a letter to the bishops across the nation, asking their aid, and he issued a press release saying he was having certain senators—Pastore of Rhode Island and Kennedy of Massachusetts—and big-city mayors give statements of support to Italy. He launched another letter-writing campaign similar to the one he had that sent a flood of angry letters to Italy in 1948.

Soon after his run-in with Montini, Spellman visited Rome. He carried a small American flag about the city, even taking it into the basilica. The next day, Monsignor Ludwig Kaas, one of Pius's Germans and host of the basilica, issued an order that no national symbols were allowed inside. Later, when walking through the enormous St. Peter's with Spellman at his side, Kaas pointed out markings on the floor that showed how various great cathedrals of Europe compared in length with the basilica, the largest church.

"Where's St. Patrick's?" Spellman queried, and he asked Kaas to mark off the New York cathedral.

Kaas snickered. "Your Eminence," Kaas replied, "you Americans are so proud of bigness that it might be embarrassing to show how small your cathedral is. It might only extend to the altar."

Spellman looked coldly at the German. "Do it!" he ordered.

The American Cardinal felt completely justified in his anger. When he returned to Rome, Spellman found that the criticism of the United States hadn't lessened, but had changed in character. The "ugly American" who visited Europe after the war, with pocketfuls of money, a camera dangling from a cord around his neck, and an ignorance of language, customs, and traditions, was considered as much of a stereotype at the Vatican as elsewhere on the continent. After all, the cartoon American bore an amazing resemblance to "Cardinal Moneybags," as Spellman was now known in the Italian press.

What Europeans found both absurd and frightening, however, was the direction anti-Communism had taken in America, and, here again, Spellman personified the nation whose emotions seemed to have driven away its ability to reason. McCarthyism had seized America, and, from a European perspective, much of what was happening in the United States seemed like paranoia. Privately, the Cardinal was criticized for having embraced the senator from Wisconsin, but publicly the Pope was silent. Spellman was too powerful to chastise, and his anti-Communist activities were of great benefit to the Church. Nonetheless, some of his actions were troublesome.

New York City Police Commissioner Frank Adams was furious and blamed himself. He was seated at the head table in the ballroom of the Hotel Astor, where the communion breakfast of the police department's Holy Name Society was in progress. The more cheering he heard erupting around him, the more Adams, the onetime Democratic Party fund-raiser, wished he had never come.

The source of Adams's irritation and the policemen's cheers was Joe McCarthy. The florid-faced senator had been invited by Cardinal Spellman, who had long given surreptitious support to the nation's most controversial Red-baiter. Today, April 4, 1953, Spellman would give McCarthy his public support, becoming the only ranking churchman to do so openly.

That morning, McCarthy had been to mass with the policemen at St. Patrick's. With the senator in the lead, the men had marched in formation down Fifth Avenue to the hotel, where the police chaplain, Monsignor Joseph McCaffrey, had eulogized McCarthy, as if the senator were about to be canonized. To Adams's shock and dismay and to the delight of the thousands of men in blue, Cardinal Spellman bustled into the ballroom as McCaffrey's glowing tribute wound down. The Cardinal warmly shook the senator's hand, turned to the men in the room, and smiled at their screams of approval. After a few moments Spellman sat at the head table near the senator. Spellman, for all the world to see, gave his imprimatur to McCarthyism.

"I should have gotten up and left, but I didn't," Adams recalled ruefully.[11]

A liberal Catholic, the police commissioner had always been disturbed by what he called the "Cardinal's meddling in politics." To Adams and many others, Spellman had just given McCarthy's dangerous crusade the wholehearted endorsement of the Catholic Church.

The Cardinal's gesture was calculated. Since McCarthy was both Republican and Catholic, Spellman believed it was time he bestowed upon the senator's anti-Communist cause the kind of mixed political and religious blessing only he could offer. To date, Spellman had privately encouraged McCarthy, whose actions were an extension of those that Spellman himself undertook for years. He also fed the senator's ambitions. Indeed, his plans for McCarthy may have been greater than most people suspected. In July 1953 an F.B.I. memo to an agent named A. H. Belmont stated one of the agency's sources had claimed that "Cardinal Spellman is at odds with the Vatican on various foreign issues." The document referred to Spellman as trying "to eventually bring about the election of McCarthy as President."[12]

Thus, on this Sunday morning the Cardinal may have had many motives as he carefully monitored the emotional reactions of the police. The officers seemed to identify with the senator because he was Irish and Catholic and battled an amorphous enemy that seemed a threat to both their country and their Church. The embodiment of their anger and frustration was McCarthy. Buoyed by the enthusiastic reception, McCarthy launched into a diatribe that he stopped a dozen times because of the din of the policemen's applause. He slammed the Pentagon and the failure of the Army to eradicate Communism from its ranks. He inveighed against "bleeding hearts" who tried to put roadblocks in his way when all he wanted was to conduct tough investigations in Washington. In a statement that he may have lifted verbatim from Spellman, McCarthy roared: "We are at war!"

"More! More!" members of the audience chanted.

McCarthy didn't let them down. He warned against professors with "screwy ideas" and declared that a Communist college teacher was "ten times more dangerous" than even a traitor in an atomic plant because he had a "captive audience."

The ballroom erupted into pandemonium. The police whistled, screamed, and stamped. "Give it to them, Joe," men yelled above the roar of applause.

When the noise died down Spellman rose to speak. His statement wasn't rousing, but there was more than enough excitement in the room to sweep him along. The men acted as though Spellman's un-inspired message was fraught with meaning. "I wish to add one word if I may," Spellman said. "Senator McCarthy has told us about the Communists and the Communist methods. I want to say that I'm not only against Communism—but I'm against the methods of Communists."

The police jumped to their feet again, cheering and applauding the churchman who had just lent the full weight of his office in support of the man they so admired. A short while later, Spellman slipped out of the room. He had consecrated McCarthyism.

In light of the Church's stand on Communism, Spellman wasn't alone in his support of McCarthy. Many priests, from the rank and file to cardinals, believed in his cause. In fact, the senator's crusade had been shaped at the outset by a wily Catholic priest. On January 7, 1950, McCarthy had dined at the Colony Restaurant in Washington. At his table were William A. Roberts, a prominent Washington attorney; Charles Kraus, a political science professor at Georgetown University; and Father Edmund Walsh, the dean of Georgetown's foreign service school since 1919. McCarthy mentioned that he needed an issue that would get him reelected. A few ideas were mentioned and discarded, including the St. Lawrence Seaway project, which was considered too dull, and a massive pension plan for the aged, which was scrapped as too costly.

Walsh, who had long strived to mold the American government stance toward Communist Russia, finally came up with the solution. During the 1930s and 1940s he had tried to shape Roosevelt's overtures to the Soviet Union. The priest now suggested that McCarthy raise the issue of Communist subversion in the United States.[13] The

Jesuit was convinced that American traitors had sold out China and were aiding Communists elsewhere in the world. McCarthy seized upon the idea. Earlier in his political career, he had used Red-baiting as one of his tactics against his Democratic opponent. Bishop Sheil had then taken him to task for a smear campaign, but the smear had been effective.

Several weeks after the Washington dinner, in Wheeling, West Virginia, McCarthy charged that two-hundred five Communists had infiltrated the State Department. None of McCarthy's alleged Communists—whose number changed whenever the senator repeated his accusations—were new cases. Most of them had been brought up and discredited during Republican hearings on subversives, and most of the cases had already been scrutinized by the F.B.I. and the Loyalty Board.[14]

One reason for McCarthy's swift acceptance among Catholics was the immediate support he received in the Catholic press. Publications such as Notre Dame's *Ave Maria,* the periodical *Catholic World,* and the newspaper *Our Sunday Visitor* reported the senator's stand in glowing terms. The Church had just come through the purges of Eastern Europe; any anti-Communist appeared to be a friend. McCarthy's most ardent backing came from the *Brooklyn Tablet,* a national publication sold each Sunday morning in the back of churches. PUT UP OR SHUT UP, stated the *Tablet* headline on June 6, 1950. "The time for being naive about the substance of the McCarthy charges is long past," the article said. "The presence of close to a hundred perverts in the State Department—even though Hiss had been forced out and convicted and the perverts fired—justify a complete and thorough search for further evidence of the Communist conspiracy within the departments of our government. . . . It is time for every Congressman and Senator to put up or shut up. If he (or she) cannot offer any better way of reaching and destroying the Communist conspiracy in our government than is being offered by Senator McCarthy, then at least, for the welfare of the United States, let him hold his peace and be silent!''

The *Tablet*'s editor, Patrick Scanlon, had a standing job offer from William Randolph Hearst, who admired his lurid journalistic style. Over the years, Scanlon had supported most of the Cardinal's causes, including Franco and the anti-Communist crusades. One of his brothers was a monsignor who worked at the Powerhouse.

The Catholic press had long painted a world besieged by Communists and cited the examples of Hungary, Czechoslovakia, and Poland, among others. By 1950, however, anti-Church activities in Eastern Europe had diminished considerably. Articles in Catholic publications, though, made it sound as if the pressures were as great as ever before. Moreover, readers were alarmed by the Church's being forced out of China and by the Communist inroads in Korea. McCarthy fed their fears.

Though few in number, liberals in the Church hierarchy detested McCarthy and were dismayed by Spellman. One was Bishop Sheil, who vowed after Spellman's blatant stand with McCarthy that he had to do something to show that the entire Church wasn't behind the senator. Sheil chose to make his stand before the United Auto Workers-CIO. Knowing his address would make news, he worked with the social activist Saul Alinsky to prepare for a large press contingent.

In his speech Sheil made clear that he opposed Communism but equally opposed McCarthyism:

> It is not enough to say that someone is anti-Communist to win my support. As I remember, one of the noisiest anti-Communists of recent history was a man named Adolf Hitler. . . . It is my view that we have been the victims in the last few years of a kind of shell game. We have been treated like country rubes to be taken in by a city slicker from Appleton. . . . We hear there are two hundred five—now we hear eighty-one—now the voice says fifty-seven card-carrying Communists in the State Department. We hear that General Marshall is a traitor, a leader in a black conspiracy that dwarfs every other conspiracy in history . . . who cares about the good name of a venerable general who has given a lifetime of service to his country? The game must go on. . . . Are we safer because the line between a liberal and a nonconformist and a Communist or a subversive is hopelessly blurred? I doubt it. . . . It's time we . . . drop the cops-and-robber game that has been going on.

Spellman was bitter. The implied criticism of him was all too obvious. The *New York Post,* for example, noted that Sheil's remarks had come on the heels of Spellman's support for McCarthy. Moreover, the paper emphasized that it showed a division in Catholic ranks. "Bishop Sheil's eloquent remarks blasted the notion that criticism of Joe McCarthy is tantamount to an attack on a religious group," the *Post* editorialized. Sheil had robbed Spellman of his charge that anyone who challenged him was a bigot.

In retaliation, the editorial writer of the *Post,* James A. Wechsler, who was scheduled to speak at Manhattan College, a Catholic school, was told not to come. The *Post* carried the story, noting: "It was learned, however, that members of the college faculty told students that the meeting was abandoned after the personal intervention of Cardinal Spellman." The chancery denied the story.

As for Sheil, he later "resigned" from his job as director general of the Catholic Youth Organization, which he had founded, and there was much speculation that his political stand had cost him his position. Spellman wasn't alone in having taken umbrage. McCarthy had many friends within the top ranks of the Church. Asked whether his anti-McCarthy speech was the reason for his leaving the C.Y.O.,

Sheil declined comment. "I've already had my say about McCarthy and I have nothing to add," he replied wearily.

The senator's support among the clergy was so widespread that Father Fred McGuire, an anti-McCarthy Vincentian who had come to New York to work for the Propagation of the Faith, was warned that his liberal attitudes would make him unpopular. Mike Prendergast, the New York State Democratic chairman, told McGuire, "All the New York clergy is for McCarthy."[15]

Because of his well-known anti-Communism, Spellman's support of the senator was taken for granted in Washington long before the Cardinal had publicly declared himself. After McCarthy's Wheeling speech, Spellman had a visit from John E. Peurifoy, deputy undersecretary of state for security. Peurifoy later acknowledged that he had discussed with Spellman the senator's charges as well as the issue of a diplomatic mission to the Vatican. They may also have talked about a strange Catholic who was acting as a McCarthy witness. The first person McCarthy had accused of being a Soviet agent was Owen Lattimore, a scholarly China expert; testifying against him was Louis Budenz, a Catholic who had become a Communist and eventually edited the *Daily Worker.* Budenz had made a sensational repentance when he was converted back to his faith by Fulton Sheen.

Though Budenz had spent hundreds of hours giving information to the F.B.I., oddly he had never mentioned Lattimore until McCarthy went after him. An expert witness who testified on just about any matter touching on Communism, Budenz bore witness against Lattimore. The validity of his testimony was called into question by such diverse critics as the Alsop brothers in their column and *The Nation,* which referred in an article to "perjuror" Budenz. Spellman and McCarthy were similar in that they would use a man such as Budenz because he could help them make a point, not necessarily because he was truthful. Both believed that the end justifies the means. In McCarthy's case the end was his political ambitions. In Spellman's it was elimination of Communism—or any non-Communist who had a hand in what Spellman perceived as letting Communism gain advantages.

This was apparent as he traveled around the globe during McCarthy's days of rage. The Cardinal always publicly supported American foreign policy when he agreed with it, but he didn't think the government was firm enough. On his trips Spellman told American Foreign Service personnel and military leaders what they should do and shouldn't have done. A State Department dispatch regarding a Spellman visit to Hong Kong on his way back from Korea quoted the prelate on what the United States should have done in China: "The Cardinal expressed the belief that bold steps were called for immediately after the defeat of Japan, which would have involved

(1) close American supervision of Chinese Nationalist forces to the extent of assigning military personnel at a battalion level and (2) the appointment of American advisers to the Chinese Government on financial and economic matters."

Spellman turned to McCarthy as a solution to a crisis. He realized that the senator had seized the Communist issue as a way to wield political power. But Spellman also realized how effective the senator was.

Until the Holy Name Society communion breakfast, Spellman had kept a careful public distance from McCarthy; he didn't want to have to stand by someone who could momentarily lapse into public disgrace. He often used intermediaries when dealing with the senator and his staff. One, of course, was Joe Kennedy, who gave McCarthy money and advice. Another was Ned Spellman, the Cardinal's nephew, who had recently been discharged from the Navy. Ned Spellman already knew one of McCarthy's young staffers—Robert Kennedy. Through his father's intercession, Bobby Kennedy worked on McCarthy's Permanent Subcommittee on Investigations. One of Ned's assignments was to meet another of McCarthy's aides, the young Roy Cohn, who played a key role in McCarthy's campaign.[16]

The Cardinal wanted to meet Cohn. Indeed, the relationship between the Cardinal and Cohn blossomed into a close one. To Cohn, Spellman extended the mantle of his respectability. He invited the young man to the residence, had their picture taken together, and he even publicly supported Cohn when the lawyer had legal difficulties. Ned Spellman, for example, appeared in court as a character witness for Cohn, and it inevitably came out that he was Cardinal Spellman's nephew. Moreover, Spellman himself publicly congratulated Cohn when he was acquitted after one of his encounters with the law.

McCarthy described Cohn as "the most brilliant young fellow I've ever met," and he was probably right. The only child of a New York State Supreme Court judge and power in the Democratic Party, Cohn graduated from high school at sixteen and crammed college and law school into four years. To strengthen his Permanent Subcommittee on Investigations, which was empowered to investigate the executive branch of government, McCarthy hired Cohn. Only twenty-six, Cohn had sterling credentials, of the kind McCarthy wanted. As an assistant U.S. attorney he had been involved in the prosecution of Communist leaders and the Rosenbergs. In turn, Cohn hired as the subcommittee's "chief consultant" his friend G. David Schine, heir to a hotel fortune, whose only credential consisted of the strange "Definition of Communism," a vanity press pamphlet that mistook Trotsky for Stalin and Lenin for Marx, among the mind-boggling number of errors.[17]

Casting around for something to investigate, Cohn seized on the

State Department's overseas information programs. As McCarthy's right hand, Cohn rampaged through investigations of the State Department and the Voice of America, and, finally, the two took on the Army. This resulted in McCarthy's televised encounter with the courtly Bostonian Joseph N. Welch, the Army's lawyer.

The American public, including Spellman, was glued to the hearings. Most people hadn't seen McCarthy in action, and many were now appalled. The senator began losing sympathy when he called Brigadier General Ralph Zwicker "a disgrace to your uniform." The American Legion and the VFW, for the first time, criticized McCarthy, as did conservative newspapers. Public charges were also made against Cohn and McCarthy that they had sought to secure, through intimidation, special military treatment for Cohn's friend Schine, who had been drafted.[18] Both McCarthy and Cohn denied the Army's charge. But while much of the rest of the country began having doubts about McCarthy and Cohn, Spellman maintained his allegiance to them.

After Cohn parted with McCarthy, the attorney's law firm, Saxe, Bacon and O'Shea, grew quickly; one reason was the respectability that Spellman gave him. Cohn did *pro bono* work for the archdiocese and Spellman introduced the lawyer to men who could use his services. He also became a fight promoter with William Fugazy, a sportsman, Knight of Malta, and limousine service owner.

Initially, Spellman apparently wanted to place Cohn in a political office of great power. "The Cardinal apparently tried to have Cohn become U.S. attorney of New York after I was called to Washington," said Herbert Brownell, who had that post before becoming Eisenhower's attorney general. The go-between in that instance was the politically conservative McCarthy adviser and powerful newspaper columnist George E. Sokolsky, whose work appeared in New York in the Hearst publications the *Mirror* and the *Journal American*. Nothing, however, came of the bid. Cohn was too controversial to put into such a sensitive post, and Brownell said he would fight any such move.[19]

The Cohn-Spellman connection became so close that Cohn even invited prominent people to Church-related functions. For example, J. Edgar Hoover wrote to Cohn, declining an invitation that the lawyer had extended:

> Thank you very much for your thoughtful note of December 1, 1958 and the kind invitation to be the guest of honor at the annual Communion Breakfast of the New York City Police Department next March 18.
>
> I must regretfully decline.
>
> Edgar[20]

Cohn functioned as a unique resource for the Cardinal. Spellman was intrigued by gossip, whether about Vatican figures or American politicians. Well-connected in both Democratic and Republican circles, Cohn related tales to Spellman that never appeared in the press. Saxe, Bacon drafted education and school-prayer legislation for Spellman, and Cohn himself involved Spellman's nephew in a number of business ventures and introduced the Cardinal to people who could be useful. One such man was Lew Rosenstiel, the Schenley liquor king, who had earned a reputation for ruthlessness in the tough liquor business and now sought respectability. Spellman provided Rosenstiel with the social status for which the whiskey baron yearned, and Rosenstiel referred to Spellman as "my best friend." The grateful entrepreneur repaid the Cardinal by lavishing huge donations on Spellman and his causes. Upon the prelate's death, Rosenstiel gave the Cardinal Spellman Memorial Foundation $3.5 million.[21]

Yet another McCarthy supporter Spellman came to know was William Buckley, Jr. They met in the 1950s when young Buckley had been sent on a mission by his father. After family members had been alerted that *Time* magazine was about to print a story that was highly critical of Buckley, Sr., they wanted Spellman to intercede with Luce on their behalf. When Buckley presented his case, the Cardinal gave him one of his humble looks. How, he wondered, could he have any influence on the mighty *Time* publishing empire? Thus, Buckley departed believing that his mission had been aborted. *Time* printed the article but it wasn't nearly as harsh as the Buckleys had expected.

Buckley first heard from the Cardinal when the young entrepreneur established his conservative Christian journal of opinion, *National Review*. Spellman gave him $250 to help launch the publication.[22] To the Cardinal's delight, Buckley was an ardent defender of McCarthy, and the magazine became a McCarthy apologist. That was a role the Cardinal himself assumed as well. Whenever he responded to reporters' questions about the senator, he made it clear that he admired McCarthy's doing something about Communism.

The Cardinal's greatest defense of the senator came in Europe, not America. Spellman's forum, in Brussels, was a Catholic group that sponsored lectures by eminent personalities. The Cardinal's speech was more a defense of America than of McCarthy. It came after the bitterness evoked by Montini's letter, which had simply been the most recent example of the disdain of America that he had heard for years in Europe. At the moment, October 23, 1953, Europe was repelled by the America that had executed Julius and Ethel Rosenberg four months earlier. But, to Spellman, the criticisms he heard sounded all too familiar.

When he spoke out, the Cardinal gave voice to a large segment of America. He believed he was in an ungrateful Europe that, without the help of the United States less than a decade earlier, would have been crushed under Hitler's jackboot.

> It seems, in these latter days, that certain critics in Europe have not honored the canons of constructive criticism in their judgments of America. They see us only in our worst light. Their purpose in criticism seems designed to hurt, not to help. The litany of tired, jaded charges against us is run through with little or no attempt made to understand our true nature as a people. Thus, to such critics we are a grossly materialistic nation. We are vulgar, preoccupied with trivia, possessing neither culture or [sic] soul. We are the New Carthage, all wealth and no spirit. We have no God but money and we have no concern for anyone but ourselves. Such, then, is the picture painted of us by these critics and the conclusion they draw is that since there is little to choose between Russia and America, the plague is pronounced on both our houses.
>
> America's generosity, her desire to share her substance with those less fortunate, springs from a deep evangelical motive. We are not the spirit-less people we are made out to be. Religion for us is something more than the observance of outward forms . . .

Spellman sounded as if he were trying to address all the people who had criticized him over the years. Moreover, he defended both himself and his nation against the European view that the United States had gone mad on the Communist issue and that McCarthyism was the worst symptom to date of that insanity:

> Congressional inquiries into Communist activities in the United States are not the result of any mad legislative whim. There are strong reasons for these inquiries and we thank God that they have begun while there is still time to do something about it. . . . The anguished cries and protests against "McCarthism" [sic] are not going to dissuade Americans from their desire to see Communists exposed and removed from positions where they can carry out their nefarious plans. If American prestige is going to suffer in Europe because of this understandable desire we have to keep our society immune from Communist subversion, then it seems more a reflection of European standards of honor and patriotism rather than ours. . . .

Though aware of the gross injustices of McCarthy, Spellman avoided noting them then or ever. In the speech he was even audacious enough to declare: "No American uncontaminated by Communism has lost his good name because of congressional hearings on un-American activities."

Editorial response was predictable. The reactionary Hearst press praised Spellman. The New York *Journal American,* for example, gushed that the Cardinal had said in "forthright words what should have been said long ago. . . . We think that one of our outstanding churchmen has done this country a great service in speaking out as he did." The *New York Post* reflected the liberal press. Spellman's words "can only enhance the widespread fear abroad that we have succumbed to the McCarthy madness," the *Post* warned. The speech, the newspaper said, was "worthy of Joe McCarthy; it was the senator who long ago proclaimed that those who did not care for him cannot conceivably care for democracy."

McCarthy's support was eroding. Despite attempts by Spellman, Buckley, and others to legitimize the senator's irresponsible charges, criticism of him began growing more voluble across the nation. McCarthy's excesses were no longer excused by many Republicans, and those who had remained silent, including Eisenhower, finally spoke up. The senator had gone too far. On June 1, 1954, Ralph Flanders, the conservative Republican senator from Vermont, addressed his peers. He detailed McCarthy's destructive impact on the nation, noting that the senator had set church against church and "Catholic against Catholic." He cited Spellman's endorsement of McCarthy and Sheil's rebuke of him. "Thus, it became obvious that Dennis the Menace had driven his blundering axe deep into the heart of his own Church," Flanders said.

Spellman once again was angry. Not only was McCarthy criticized, but he himself was held up as an unwitting victim. Questioned about the speech he retorted: "Is Flanders uniting us? That's outside his province." When asked by a reporter about Flanders's remarking that Spellman's appearance with McCarthy had been political, Spellman became sarcastic: "I'm surprised that a New Englander could be that naive."

By the spring of 1954, McCarthy was condemned from Protestant pulpits. Bishop James Pike, dean of the Church of St. John the Divine in New York, for instance, traded pulpits with Francis B. Sayre, Jr., dean of the Washington Cathedral. The liberal Episcopalians' addresses contained oblique condemnations of Catholicism "by hinting that the Catholic hierarchy's silence on the senator was somehow sinister and malignant," stated Donald F. Crosby, a Jesuit who wrote of the incident.

Sayre, the grandson of Woodrow Wilson, declared that "the phenomenon we call 'McCarthyism' is only another of the devil's disguises. . . . He would be nothing without the active support of what has been estimated to be at least one-third of our people. . . ." For his part, Pike condemned large Catholic newspapers, such as the *Tablet,* for being pro-McCarthy. The dean contended that McCarthy represented a "spiritual defect. Our constitutional guarantees and philosophy of government were worked out by men who believed in a moral law which no government or individual should transgress whatever the apparent temporary advantage." "By implication at least," Crosby wrote, "both men were blaming Catholicism for McCarthy."

The following week, on March 28, Pike, from his own pulpit, directly attacked Spellman on the McCarthy issue. Pike, born a Catholic and educated by Jesuits, had converted as a young man. In this sermon, he recalled that a week earlier Spellman, when asked by a reporter about McCarthy, had tried to duck the issue by saying that members of the hierarchy weren't allowed to speak on political matters. "We don't preach sermons on politics," Spellman had told the newsman. Now Pike, his voice ringing through his cathedral, sarcastically reminded his congregation of that statement: "Maybe that's meant as an announcement of future policy, but, up to last week, they [the Catholic hierarchy] were preaching sermons about politics. . . ."

Many Protestant leaders resented Spellman's political clout, which far exceeded their own. Moreover, many ministers disliked the Cardinal's opposition to Protestant and Jewish attempts at ecumenism. Although Spellman had a number of friends and acquaintances among people of other religions, they were primarily for politics and fundraising. Thus, he discouraged his priests from mingling with their counterparts from other faiths. He himself refrained as much as possible from appearing publicly with leaders of other churches. "People might think they're all equal," he said. Spellman didn't want his authority diluted in any fashion. He saw his strength in bending on temporal issues, but remaining firm on religious matters.

Unfortunately, Pike's linking of Catholicism to McCarthy wasn't without reason. The Church appeared to have a great deal invested in the senator. At Spellman's urging, even the Pope had indicated his support for McCarthy. When the senator married his former assistant, Jean Kerr, at St. Matthew's Cathedral in Washington, Pius gave the ceremony his apostolic blessing, an unusual honor widely noted in the press.

The length to which Spellman defended McCarthy was revealed on November 8, 1954, when Edward R. Martin, a former Army chaplain who was the Cardinal's personal representative at the annual communion breakfast of the Catholic War Veterans, made a startling statement. While addressing the seven hundred veterans and their wives, he declared that he personally knew of a $5-million slush fund that had been established to kick McCarthy out of the Senate. The purge, Martin assured his audience, was "solely because of his Catholic ideals."

Spellman stayed away from the breakfast. Martin, a conservative, believed it was an honor to spread this bit of propaganda for the Cardinal. He gave the Cardinal's blessing. At the conclusion of the affair, Martin asked the gathering to carry "the message of your Catholic Church with patience, meekness, fortitude, and courage—

the same type of courage that Senator McCarthy has. Joe is a really sincere Catholic," Martin assured the gathering. "I know this."

The audience cheered lustily. For a brief spell Martin was pleased, but then the roof fell in. His rash remarks were widely publicized. The priest had no proof to back up the extraordinary charge, and everything that happened thereafter made his case look that much worse. Spellman tried to disassociate himself from the ensuing mess. No priest under his jurisdiction made any strong public political statement without the Cardinal's approval. Yet Spellman feigned ignorance. "It's none of my business," he said.

Few people were fooled. Spellman was inundated with mail that ran five-to-one against Martin, and the vast majority of the letter-writers were Catholics. Conrad Hilton, the Catholic hotel-owner, for instance, wrote Spellman that such "wild statements should not be made by a Catholic ecclesiastic."

Seven professors at Colgate University made news when they sent a testy telegram to Spellman: 'We should like to hear from you— Father Martin's superior—that the statements attributed to him do not represent the view of the responsible leaders of the Catholic Church of America. . . . You owe it to all Americans—Catholics, Protestants and Jews—to explain why the movement against the excesses of Senator McCarthy . . . involves an attack on Catholic ideals. You have the obligation to make public the information you have on the $5 million pool. How was it raised? How is it being used?"

The only ecclesiastic to denounce publicly Martin and his slush fund was the priest George Ford. "It is," he said dryly, "a fairy tale."

Spellman was beside himself. His attempt to muddy the McCarthy waters had not only failed but had also soiled his own robes. Pretending to have nothing to do with the matter had likewise boomeranged. He refused now to respond to his questioners, knowing how foolish anything he might say could sound. To make matters worse, McCarthy himself said the Martin speech didn't sound quite right. The senator contended that he knew of groups that raised money to "hamper my work." But he himself doubted that "religion enters into it."

Whatever dreams Spellman may have held for McCarthy were rapidly crumbling. Politically, Spellman found himself in opposition not only to liberals but also to a growing number of conservatives and middle-of-the-road politicians and government leaders. Eisenhower, after trying unsuccessfully to appease the man who had become a ranting demagogue, had finally moved against McCarthy. "Eisenhower finally believed that Spellman and others were trying to make McCarthy President," Herbert Brownell recalled. The White House issued a press release, personally approved by the President, saying that the authority of the executive branch "cannot be usurped by any individual who may seek to set himself above the laws of the land." At the Waldorf-Astoria for the opening of Columbia University's bicentennial celebration, Eisenhower declared that there would be driven from "the temple of freedom all who seek to establish over us thought control—whether they be agents of a foreign state or demagogues thirsty for personal power." In each instance, his aides let it be known that McCarthy was the target.

After he was censured by the Senate, McCarthy collaborated with Spellman on one last effort. The McCarthys had no children, and Joe thought he would like to have one. Though McCarthy was nearly fifty years old, in ill health, and an alcoholic, the Cardinal personally intervened to give him and his wife a five-week-old girl from the Foundling Home in January 1957. Within six months of receiving his adopted daughter directly from Spellman's hands, McCarthy died.[23]

Upon McCarthy's death, memorial services were held at the Cathedral in Washington and St. Patrick's. Each year thereafter, a "McCarthy Mass" was held at St. Patrick's on the anniversary of his death. Spellman never repudiated him. For the Cardinal, McCarthy was always a symbol of the larger issue: fighting the Communist menace.

In his obsession with Communism, Spellman viewed the world at times as an immense chess board where the Communists were on one side and the Church and America were on the other. He saw himself as a master player who shaped intricate plays that took his opponent by surprise. At times, however, the international game he played more closely resembled bowling, as he helped American-made power balls smash into anything that looked like a Soviet tenpin.

His alternate behavior fit neatly into American foreign policy. Since the end of World War II, the American Cold War posture was one of defensiveness. Because there was no strong Western European power that could counterbalance the Soviet presence in Eastern Europe, the job was left to the United States. The policy of preserving the political status quo was called "containment." As originally conceived in 1946 by George Kennan, deputy chief of mission at the American embassy in Moscow, that meant containment of Soviet political threats by political means. But containment came to be interpreted as checking military threat by military means and by quick American response to every sign of Soviet movement. The policy demanded forming a host of alliances with governments, no matter how corrupt, and actively imposing American standards on recalcitrant governments. In time, containment meant that every country threatened with Communism was considered of equal importance, whether it was in Western Europe or in some insignificant corner of the globe.

*   *   *

Eisenhower became President at an opportune time. Europe was steadily reviving; it was the Democrats who had "lost" China, the Soviets already had the atomic bomb (so he couldn't be accused of losing that), Korea was at a stalemate, and Stalin was to die only three months after Eisenhower took office. The Cold War should have started to thaw, but it didn't. Two reasons why the relaxation in tensions didn't occur were the Dulles brothers, John Foster and Allen, respectively the secretary of state and the deputy director of covert operations at the Central Intelligence Agency. Another reason was Cardinal Spellman, who was constantly demanding that Eisenhower come to the defense of nations threatened by Communism.

Of the Dulles brothers, Foster was the most like Spellman in his public attitude toward Communism. The tall, gray-haired, distinguished-looking secretary of state loved moralizing about Communism, denouncing the Soviets, and being involved in power plays and bluffs. Dulles, too, was arrogant and a believer that it was better to do something—anything, and the more dangerous the action the better—than to do nothing. His risky foreign policy came to be known as "brinkmanship." "You have to take chances for peace, just as you have to take chances for war," he liked to say. Through the Dulleses, the United States became involved in a number of highly controversial actions around the world, and the C.I.A. was strengthened.

Spellman admired the foreign policy of Foster Dulles, but not everyone did. *New York Times* columnist James Reston referred to him as "a supreme expert" in the art of "diplomatic blundering . . . he doesn't stumble into booby traps: he digs them to size, studies them carefully, and then jumps." Spellman was usually right behind.

Such was the disturbing case of Guatemala. An official of the Central Intelligence Agency approached Spellman in 1954 with a relatively simple request. The agent wanted him to arrange a "clandestine contact" between one of the C.I.A. men in Guatemala and Archbishop Mariano Rossell Arellano, a ranking churchman there. The contact could be useful "so that we could coordinate our parallel efforts," the official noted.[24] Spellman needed no prodding. Since the Roosevelt administration, he had eagerly cooperated with the U.S. government's covert operations. The F.B.I. routinely turned to him for information about Latin America; often, it had Spellman or his priests gather political intelligence. Spellman, the Cold War churchman, believed any means should be used to stop Communism. Spellman, the American, in time would place the foreign policy goals of his government above those of the Vatican. But in 1954 in Guatemala, they were virtually the same.

During his trips to Latin America, the Cardinal worked, in effect, as an arm of the United States government. Though Secretary of State Dulles had little use for the Catholic Church (even though his son Avery became a convert and then a priest), he was pragmatic enough to recognize its value as a partner in fighting Communism. At one point Spellman's aide Griffiths noted that Dulles "certainly would do nothing if he thought it would benefit the Church."[25] The secretary of state and the Cardinal cultivated one another because of their similar attitudes toward Marxism.

The C.I.A., like the F.B.I., turned to Spellman because of his connections and his prestige throughout Latin nations, where he helped churchmen with money and political advice and rebuked them on occasion. Of greater importance to U.S. officials, Spellman was an avowed supporter of the controversial dictatorships that the American government backed. The Cardinal was wined and dined by Batista in Cuba, Trujillo in the Dominican Republic, Stroessner in Paraguay, and Somoza in Nicaragua, and he accepted their many honors and blessed their regimes.

Spellman saw nothing wrong with his behavior. Generally, the dictators were supported by the hierarchy of their countries. As a churchman, he appreciated their anti-Communist positions. His sense of Americanism was pleased that such leaders toed the U.S. line. Spellman expected little else from a government leader. If asked about some of the brutal policies of Latin dictators, the churchman shrugged. "People often don't do what we would like but they can still be our friends," he said.

Latin officials tended to view Spellman more as a delegate of the United States government than of the Vatican. On his trips he frequently represented American foreign policy and was more than willing to spread American propaganda. While touring Latin America in 1952, for instance, he recorded an address in Peru over "Desfile de Actualidad," the United States embassy's triweekly political-commentary radio program. His statement was mimeographed and five hundred copies were mailed around the country. "It would be almost impossible to overestimate the public-relations value of Cardinal Spellman's visit to Peru," a Foreign Service officer wrote in a report to Washington.[26]

The passionate defense of America that the Cardinal offered in Brussels reflected his true feelings, and he reveled in the role of an American emissary. He saw America not as simply stronger than Europe, but better. As though making up for all the years he had silently listened while his country was derided at the Vatican, the Cardinal was a most vocal patriot.

Thus, when Spellman's trip took him to Bolivia after Peru, his very Americanism made him unwanted. The Cardinal was treated as a ranking U.S. official in Bolivia at a time when relations with the United States were strained over the price of tin. Spellman was told that his scheduled visit with the President was canceled because of the leader's illness. American officials noted, though, that the reason was "Spellman is an American." Despite his illness the President had his picture in the paper; the photo was taken that day while he attended several ceremonies. "The president left La Paz the day of the Cardinal's arrival to recuperate at Copacabana, a hard, five-hour trip by automobile," the embassy dispatch cynically observed. "He is returning today, following the Cardinal's departure, fully recovered!"[27]

On another trip, Spellman landed in Paraguay, where he warmly greeted the dictator Alfredo Stroessner, who had recently effected a military coup. Unlike military dictatorships in Brazil and Chile that at least paid lip service to helping the people, Stroessner made no pretenses. His military and police were rewarded with graft, contraband, and the spoils of lucrative narcotics and prostitution trades. Upon his arrival Spellman went to the general's residence, where he publicly proclaimed what a pleasure it was to be in "the ancient Catholic country of Paraguay."[28] Stroessner, who desired just such a blessing for his regime, thanked the Cardinal profusely.

Spellman took it in stride when he was approached by the C.I.A. about Guatemala. He may even have been expecting the visit. Guatemala had troubled the Church longer than it had Washington. The Church had been limited in its activities in Guatemala longer than anywhere else in Latin America. In 1871 an enlightened despot, Justo Rufino Barrios, had become President. He initiated land and education reforms and checked the influence of the Church by excluding the hierarchy from any active role in national affairs, deporting most foreign priests and threatening other priests caught in political activities. This burst of liberalism ended in 1885 when Rufino was killed in battle. The nation again became dominated by huge landowners and a series of dictators, supported by the United States.[29]

Guatemala's history changed dramatically when, in 1944, a young army officer, Jacobo Arbenz Guzmán, helped lead a revolt against the dictatorship of Jorge Ubico. The way was paved for the first democratic election in the country's history; the following year, Juan José Arévalo became President with more than eighty-five percent of the vote. A schoolteacher who idolized America, Arévalo wanted to institutionalize democracy, protect labor, promote land reform, and improve education, but opposition from the old guard and internal bickering blunted his effectiveness.

In 1950, Arbenz, who had served as Arévalo's minister of defense, was elected his successor. By 1954, the year the C.I.A. approached Spellman, both the Church and the United States government believed their positions in Guatemala had deteriorated. Arbenz enjoyed the support of unions, some of which were Communist-controlled, and this had Spellman and the Vatican worried. To make matters worse, as far as many people in the U.S. government were concerned, Arbenz tried to implement an agrarian-reform program aimed not only at large Guatemalan landowners but also at the powerful United Fruit Company, which, for good reason, was known throughout Latin America as "the Octopus."

United Fruit, while a symbol of Yankee imperialism to many Latins, was esteemed by U.S. lawmakers, including congressmen who routinely demanded that the company's interests be safeguarded. Spellman's good friend John McCormack annually gave speeches on United Fruit and Guatemala, and even read into the *Congressional Record* articles by executives of the company lauding their corporation's contributions to Latin America. The moderate Arbenz program, which would pale considerably when compared with those later introduced by neighboring countries, alarmed United Fruit executives, U.S. officials, and Cardinal Spellman. The company prepared a carefully orchestrated public-relations program against Arbenz, which culminated in covert military intervention by the United States.

Allen Dulles and his C.I.A. subordinates recruited Colonel Castillo Armas as Guatemala's "liberator." United Fruit spent more than a half-million dollars a year for public relations and lobbying to spread the message that Arbenz was up to no good and Castillo Armas was the man to save the day. Foster Dulles had his own reasons for wanting Arbenz stopped, and these went beyond United Fruit. Not only had the Guatemalan challenged an American multinational company, but he had also stood up to the U.S. government. At the Tenth Inter-American Conference, in Caracas, the secretary of state, heavy-handed as usual, had pressured Latin countries into endorsing a resolution condemning Communist infiltration into Latin America. In casting a lone vote in opposition, Guatemala had outraged Dulles.

Thus, Spellman and the Church were swept up in one of the Dulles brothers' efforts at brinkmanship diplomacy. The Church had an opportunity to regain power in Guatemala and stop a man who many churchmen saw as a Communist. Thus, as during the Italian elections, the Church and the U.S. government joined forces. Spellman decided to help the Dulles brothers overthrow the Arbenz government. Little is known about what Spellman actually did, but it was clear that he acted swiftly. After Spellman's meeting with the C.I.A. agent, a pastoral letter was read on April 9, 1954, in all Guatemalan churches. The missive called attention to the presence of Communists within the nation and demanded that the "people of Guatemala . . . rise as a single man against the enemy of God and country." The C.I.A. in Guatemala, under the direction of E. Howard Hunt, capitalized on the letter. Thousands of previously prepared leaflets bearing the message were dropped from airplanes over remote areas of the country.

The high degree of Church cooperation wasn't surprising. Throughout Latin America, the C.I.A. counted on the sympathetic support of Catholic clergymen of all levels. The agency revealed later, during congressional hearings on its activities, that American missionaries of various denominations had been recruited as informers and part-time agents.[30] Spellman was the highest-ranking churchman in such a role.

The Church's support of Castillo Armas was obvious from such actions as a heavily publicized "Mass of Thanksgiving" for the rebel. But though Spellman and other churchmen were willing to support a coup, they were realistic. They had few illusions about the abilities of Castillo Armas. The nuncio in Guatemala, Monsignor Gennaro Verrolino, confided reservations about the rebel's ability to oust Arbenz to John E. Peurifoy, the ambassador to Guatemala. The nuncio matter-of-factly stated that the only way to protect "anti-Communists and Christians" was, most likely, direct intervention by the United States. Peurifoy, a self-styled tough guy who had visited Spellman after McCarthy made his Wheeling speech, needed no encouragement. His mission was either to get Arbenz to heel to American policy or to get rid of him.

An anxious Arbenz was aware of the forces mustering against him. He publicly stated that a heavily financed plot was under way to force him out of office. Among the conspirators was Cardinal Spellman, to whom Arbenz said Castillo Armas and his accomplice, General Miguel Ydigoras Fuentes, had appealed for aid. Spellman's friends Somoza and Trujillo were also implicated. The Cardinal didn't let being unmasked stop him. The number of pastoral messages against Arbenz increased, part of a campaign to make it appear that Arbenz was a Communist. From New York, Spellman arranged to have the clergy in Guatemala hold clandestine meetings with the anti-Arbenz faction. In a futile effort Arbenz turned to the Soviet Union for military aid. The Soviets tried to send six tons of anti-aircraft shells, but Eisenhower enforced a blockade of Guatemala.

The American-engineered coup finally came in June 1954. As Peurifoy jubilantly gave a firsthand account to Washington from his ambassador's office, the capital was strafed while a C.I.A. radio broadcast exaggerated rebels' successes over a "Voice of Liberation." Castillo Armas's ragtag army made some headway. Attempts by the Guatemalan government to get the United Nations Security Council involved resulted in a moral victory for Arbenz but little else. Finally, Arbenz resigned in the face of what seemed like opposing the United States itself. A three-man military junta temporarily took charge, but that government proved short-lived because of Peurifoy; two of the men were apparently bought off for cash and promises of diplomatic posts abroad under a Castillo Armas government.

As president, Castillo Armas immediately dismantled the liberal steps taken by his predecessors. He disenfranchised seventy-five percent of Guatemala's voters by banning illiterates from the electoral process; abolished agrarian reform legislation; restored the secret police; banned political, labor, and peasant organizations; and went on a censorship binge that included burning novels by Dostoevski and Miguel Angel Asturias, a distinguished Guatemalan author and critic of United Fruit. (Asturias, in 1967, would be awarded the Nobel Prize in literature.)

Spellman had reason to rejoice. The new government reestablished long-broken ties with Catholicism. Castillo Armas restored the right of the Church to own property, to give religious instruction in public schools, and to increase the number of foreigners among the clergy. To further enhance the Church's position in Guatemala as well as that of the United States, Spellman saw to it that Catholic Relief Services, the metamorphosis of the War Relief Services, began operating in Guatemala shortly after Arbenz fell. The CRS, which mushroomed to become the largest voluntary relief organization, distributed food, clothing, and medical supplies, most of it U.S. government surplus. The purpose of the CRS was to help the poor and to stem Communism; Spellman saw to it that the countries in which the CRS operated were those in which the American government had parallel programs. Now, Guatemala fell into that category.

Instead of putting Guatemala on the path to prosperity, Spellman and the U.S. officials involved in the Arbenz coup merely set the stage for decades of bloodshed. Guatemala became a financial sinkhole for the United States, which poured some $80 million into the nation in the first three years of the new regime. Little of it filtered down to the poor. By the 1980s, Guatemalan history was marked by a succession of dictatorships and brutally crushed revolts. According to a 1978 report on Guatemala by the World Bank, more than eighty percent of the land was owned by ten percent of the population; the illiteracy rate of seventy percent was the highest in the hemisphere but for Haiti's; the infant mortality rate was also tragically high.

Spellman, however, apparently gave little thought to the consequences of his actions other than having stopped someone whom he suspected of being a Communist. "Arbenz is dangerous for the entire hemisphere," Spellman told his aides.

Reaction to Spellman at the State Department was mixed. The Cardinal willingly shared Church intelligence with American officials, was debriefed by U.S. intelligence agents after his trips to foreign countries, and advised officials on what actions should be taken around the world. "Some people in the State Department thought he was meddling where he shouldn't be, but, with his Vatican sources, his information was sometimes better than what the State Department had," Herbert Brownell, Eisenhower's attorney general, recalled. "Spellman took a part in influencing our foreign policy."[31]

Spellman gained influence with the administration in other areas as well. In 1956, an election year, he came to the White House because he wanted a hand in picking the next member of the Supreme Court. In the presence of Bernard Shanley, Eisenhower's special counsel, the Cardinal told Eisenhower of his dismay with the makeup of the Court. "Mr. President, it isn't that I want a Catholic on the Supreme Court, but I want someone who will represent the interests and views of the Catholic Church," Spellman said. The President shook his head affirmatively and turned to Shanley. "Remind me about what the Cardinal wants when the time comes," the President said.[32]

Given Eisenhower's track record in naming Supreme Court justices, Spellman had reason for concern. The President had placed Earl Warren on the bench in 1953 and John M. Harlan the following year. The shift away from New Deal liberalism that Spellman and other conservatives hoped to see never occurred. Warren, in particular, worried Spellman. He was proving as liberal as anyone Roosevelt had ever appointed, maybe even more so. Shortly after the Cardinal's visit, Justice Sherman Minton retired. Eisenhower whittled his list of candidates down; the man he consulted with most was his attorney general, Brownell. When Shanley reminded the President of his commitment to Spellman, Eisenhower nonchalantly said there was no need to bother him. He and Brownell had made the choice. "It's okay; I've already talked to Herb about it and we've got someone who will suit the Cardinal," Eisenhower replied.

The man the President selected was William J. Brennan, a member of the New Jersey State Supreme Court. He was Irish and Catholic, qualities Eisenhower assumed fit Spellman's bill. Shanley himself was pleased. He and Brennan had grown up together in Newark and had remained friends over the years. "Brennan is the Cardinal's kind of man," Eisenhower told Shanley.

The President was wrong. Eisenhower made the mistake of lumping all Catholics together. As far as Spellman was concerned, Brennan wasn't conservative enough. Of greater importance to the prelate, Brennan wasn't the kind of man who was easily swayed by a member of the Church hierarchy. The first person Brownell called after the selection was Spellman. "The Cardinal was a very powerful political figure in New York," Brownell said. "We wanted him to know that we had selected the Catholic."

Brownell had known Spellman since his days as a campaign strategist for Governor Dewey. He knew of the strong Dewey-Spellman friendship, which, he noted, was a genuine one that "grew out of their common political interests." Although a fierce anti-Communist and an early McCarthy supporter, Brownell had been dismayed by the level of backing Spellman continued to give McCarthy after it was obvious how destructive the senator was. Moreover, Brownell resented the Cardinal's hand in trying to have Roy Cohn replace him as U.S. attorney in New York. Even so, Brownell admired the way Spellman had accrued so much political muscle in New York.

"I don't know him," Spellman said when Brownell called. "Who is his parish priest?" The attorney general, of course, hadn't any idea. The question became a standing joke between him and the Cardinal, who pretended to be shocked at Brownell's ignorance. As far as Brownell was concerned, the matter was closed.[33] Not just Spellman but also other Catholic officials had petitioned Eisenhower to appoint a Catholic to the bench. There hadn't been a Catholic on the Supreme Court since Frank Murphy, an associate justice from 1940 to 1949.

Spellman, however, was disgusted. He hadn't been consulted and hadn't gotten the kind of man he wanted. The Cardinal didn't blame Eisenhower or Brownell—he blamed Shanley. In an effort to help Shanley among both Catholics and his friends in New Jersey, Brownell had spread the word that Shanley had played a key role in Brennan's selection (although Shanley hadn't). Spellman believed Brownell and thought Shanley had betrayed him.

The next thing Shanley knew, Spellman was in his office. Only steps from the Oval Office, Spellman dressed down one of the President's chief aides. "He gave me hell," Shanley remembered. "It was one of the worst things I have ever been through." Shanley declined to specify what Spellman said that cut so deeply. Whatever it was, Shanley was so taken aback by the assault that he couldn't defend himself. A practicing Catholic, Shanley was in awe of Spellman. At one point, the Eisenhower aide tried to explain that he had had nothing to do with Brennan's appointment, but Spellman refused to listen. The Cardinal continued his tongue-lashing until he turned and left.

Shanley kept the confrontation to himself, not wanting to upset Eisenhower. Moreover, he felt humiliated.[34]

Spellman didn't get everything he wanted by presenting his case behind closed doors. There were times when private pleadings simply didn't work, and he sought public forums. To politicians, the Cardinal as a public figure often proved far more dangerous than he was in private. When they stood face to face, politicians could reason with Spellman, or at least try to do so. In public, Spellman played on his followers' emotions to generate support.

Cardinal Spellman stood on the dais of the huge auditorium in the nation's capital. On this muggy day, August 30, 1954, as the main speaker at the American Legion convention, he had the thousands of veterans on the edge of their seats as he angrily denounced the foreign policy of the United States. With evangelical fervor he warned of the possibility of "another Pearl Harbor" and the impossibility of peaceful coexistence between competing political systems, one of which was "continually clawing at the throat of the other." Murmurs of agreement, like the buzzing of angry bees, filled the vast hall. "War to the hilt between Communism and capitalism is inevitable," the Cardinal declared.

Like many men in the audience, Spellman was bitter and frustrated by Communist gains in Korea and China. Just several months earlier he had helped his government destroy the leftist government in Guatemala, but he believed much more had to be done. Spellman thought America was running scared. He cited yet another example of what he perceived as the failure of U.S. foreign policy—a tiny Asian country called Vietnam. Most Americans couldn't even find Vietnam on a map, but in large measure because of Spellman's public and private lobbying, Vietnam would become the leading example of what went wrong when the policy of containment was carried to extremes.

The Cardinal declared that Vietnam was vital to the preservation of the American way of life and Catholicism. In doing so, Spellman helped make the possibility of direct American involvement in Vietnam not only acceptable but desirable to millions of Americans. In the long run, his fervor for the cause would do more to undermine his political power within his Church and his country than any other stance he ever took. In 1954, however, the Cardinal just reacted the way he always did whenever Communism made gains: he moved to obliterate his foe.

For months, Spellman had tried unsuccessfully to pressure the administration into beefing up assistance to the French troops fighting Communist insurgents in Vietnam. The United States, however, had underwritten eighty percent of the French war costs; Eisenhower was reluctant to go further, even though the Dulles brothers also wanted what Spellman pushed. Now Spellman was dismayed. Three months earlier, the Communists had done what had seemed impossible—beaten the French forces with a final major battle at Dienbienphu. The cease-fire negotiated at the just-concluded Geneva Conference called for the partition of Vietnam into halves, with the Communists getting the north. The accord struck Spellman as another example of appeasement of the Reds.

"If Geneva and what was agreed upon there means anything at all, it means that the trumpet which we heard over the fallen garrison at Dienbienphu last May sounded taps and not reveille," the Cardinal told the legionnaires. "Taps for the buried hopes of freedom in Southeast Asia! Now the devilish techniques of brainwashing, forced confessions, and rigged trials have a new locale for their exercise. . . ."

The Cardinal's message was clear. The fall of Vietnam brought the day closer when Communists would dominate the United States. "We shall risk bartering our liberties for lunacies, betraying the sacred trust of our forefathers, becoming serfs and slaves to the Red ruler's godless goons," he swore.

The other speakers needed no introduction: Madame Chiang Kai-shek and Admiral Arthur W. Radford, the chairman of the Joint Chiefs of Staff, who was a familiar figure at the Powerhouse. Both speakers were friends of the Cardinal and shared his conservative views. Madame Chiang lamented that the Soviets had corrupted the "minds and souls of those who became its puppets—the Chinese Communists." Radford asserted that the United States should be ready to police the world. The audience wildly applauded each speaker, but it was Spellman who brought them to their feet in a thunderous ovation. At the conclusion of the meeting, the Cardinal asked the legionnaires to pray for God's intervention. If Eisenhower wouldn't listen to Spellman, perhaps he would heed the Almighty. "Be with us, Blessed Lord," the Cardinal intoned, "lest we forget and surrender to those who have attacked us without cause, those who repaid us with evil for good and hatred for love."

The day after the convention the impact of Spellman's address was noted in the press. New York *Daily News* columnist John O'Donnell, for example, reported: "From a political viewpoint—global, national and New York State—the speech delivered by Cardinal Spellman was by far the most significant and important heard here at the convention. . . ."

Spellman's attack on Ho Chi Minh's revolution was the first sign of his involvement in the politics of Vietnam. Though few people knew this, the Cardinal played a prominent role in creating the political career of a former seminary resident in New York who had just become Premier of South Vietnam, Ngo Dinh Diem. In Diem, Spellman had seen the qualities he desired in any leader: ardent Catholicism and rabid anti-Communism.

Spellman had met Diem in New York in 1950, when the Vietnamese had been at the Maryknoll Seminary in Ossining, New York. A staunch Catholic from a patrician family, Diem was at the seminary at the intercession of his brother, Ngo Din Thuc, a Roman Catholic bishop. A lay celibate and deeply religious, Diem had cut himself off from the world, especially his war-shredded nation, and had been known only to a small, politically active circle in the United States. In his homeland his name had hardly evoked enthusiasm. On an official level in the United States, Diem was an unknown quantity, a situation Spellman helped rectify. Diem's background meant that he inevitably came to the attention of Spellman.

The man responsible for bringing them together was Father Fred McGuire, the anti-McCarthy Vincentian who worked for the Propagation of the Faith. A former missionary to Asia, McGuire's intimate knowledge of the Far East was well known at the State Department. One day the priest was asked by Dean Rusk, then head of the Asian section, to see that Bishop Thuc, who was coming to the United States, met with State Department officials, McGuire recalled. Rusk also expressed an interest in meeting Diem.[35]

McGuire contacted his old friend Bishop Griffiths, who was still Spellman's foreign affairs expert. He asked that Thuc be properly received by the Cardinal, which he was. For the occasion Diem came to the Cardinal's residence from the seminary. The meeting between Spellman and Diem may well have been a historic one. Joseph Buttinger, a prominent worker with refugees in Vietnam, believed the Cardinal was the first American to consider that Diem might go home as the leader of South Vietnam.[36]

In October 1950 the Vietnamese brothers met in Washington at the Mayflower Hotel with State Department officials, including Rusk. Diem and Thuc were accompanied by McGuire as well as by three political churchmen who were working to stop Communism: Father Emmanuel Jacque, Bishop Howard Carroll, and Georgetown's Edmund Walsh. The purpose of the meeting was to ask the brothers about their country and determine their political beliefs. It soon became clear that both Diem and Thuc believed that Diem was destined to rule his nation. The fact that Vietnam's population was only ten percent Catholic mattered little as far as the brothers were concerned.[37] Such a step seemed unlikely. Before World War II Diem had been a civil servant connected loosely with nationalists. Later, he repeatedly refused to accept government offices under Emperor Bao Dai; the job he wanted was Prime Minister, but that had been denied him.

As Diem spoke during the dinner, his two most strongly held positions were readily apparent. He believed in the power of the Catholic Church and he was virulently anti-Communist. The State Department officials must have been impressed. Concerned about Vietnam since Truman first made a financial commitment to helping the French there, they were always on the lookout for strong, anti-Communist leaders as the French faded. After Dienbienphu, Eisenhower wanted to support a broader-based government than that of Emperor Bao Dai, who enjoyed little popular support and had long been considered a puppet of the French and the Americans. Thus U.S. officials wanted a nationalist in high office in South Vietnam to blunt some of Ho Chi Minh's appeal. The result was that Bao Dai offered Diem the job he had always wanted—Prime Minister. Diem's self-proclaimed prophecy was coming true. He returned to Saigon on June 26, 1954, or several weeks after the arrival of Edward Lansdale, the chief of the C.I.A.'s Saigon Military Mission, who was in charge of unconventional warfare. U.S. involvement entered a new stage.

Spellman's Vietnam stance was in accordance with the wishes of the Pope. Malachi Martin, a former Jesuit who worked at the Vatican during the years of the escalating U.S. commitment to Vietnam, said the Pope wanted the United States to back Diem because the Pope had been influenced by Diem's brother, Archbishop Thuc. "The Pope was concerned about Communism making more gains at the expense of the Church," Martin averred. "He turned to Spellman to encourage American commitment to Vietnam."[38]

Thus Spellman embarked on a carefully orchestrated campaign to prop up the Diem regime. Through the press and a Washington lobby, the problems of confronting anti-Communism in Indochina became widely known in America. One of the men Spellman aided in promoting the Diem cause was Buttinger, a former Austrian Socialist who headed the International Rescue Committee, an organization that had helped refugees flee Communism after World War II and now helped people fleeing North Vietnam. The Geneva Accords provided that people moving between the north and south should have three hundred days in which to do so. The refugee problems were enormous. When he visited New York, Buttinger met with Spellman and explained the situation. The Cardinal placed him in touch with Joe Kennedy, who arranged meetings for Buttinger with the editorial boards of major publications such as *Time* and the *Herald Tribune*. Editorials sympathetic to the plight of refugees fleeing Ho Chi Minh's Vietnam began appearing in the American press.

Spellman and Kennedy also helped form a pro-Diem lobby in Washington. The rallying cries were anti-Communism and Catholicism. Through their connections, they soon had a high-powered committee, which was a lumpy blend of intellectuals and conservatives. Two men of national prominence, the former O.S.S. chief "Wild Bill" Donovan and General "Iron Mike" O'Daniel, were co-chairmen. The membership included Senators Kennedy and Richard Neuberger; Representatives Emmanuel Celler and Edna Kelly; and Angier Biddle Duke, Arthur Schlesinger, Jr., Max Lerner, socialist leader Norman Thomas, and conservative Utah Governor Bracken Lee. Spellman's man on the board was Monsignor Harnett, who headed the Cardinal's Catholic Near East Welfare Association and now served as the Vietnam lobby's chief link with the Catholic Relief Services.

To a large extent, many Americans came to believe that Vietnam was a preponderantly Catholic nation. This misimpression resulted partly from Diem's emergence as ruler. With the help of C.I.A.-rigged elections in 1955, Diem abolished the monarchy and Bao Dai was forced to live in exile. The heavily Catholic hue to the Vietnam lobby also accounted for much of the widespread belief. Still another factor was Spellman's identification with the cause.

Then there was the role of a winsome young Catholic doctor working in Vietnam named Tom Dooley. A navy lieutenant who operated out of Haiphong, Dooley worked with refugees. At one point Dooley, a favorite of Spellman, even organized thirty-five thousand Vietnamese Catholics to demand evacuation from the north. Dooley's efforts were perhaps even more successful in the United States than in Vietnam. He churned out newspaper and magazine articles as well as three bestselling books that propagandized both the Catholic and anti-Communist nature of his beliefs. He fabricated stories about the suffering of Catholics at the hands of perverted Communists who beat naked priests on the testicles with clubs, deafened children with chopsticks to prevent them from hearing about God, and disemboweled pregnant women. A graduate of Notre Dame in Indiana, Dooley toured the United States promoting his books and anti-Communism before he died, in 1964, at age thirty-four. One of the last people to visit his sickbed was Cardinal Spellman, who held up the young physician as an inspiration for all—another martyr. Dooley's reputation remained untarnished until a Roman Catholic sainthood investigation in 1979 uncovered his C.I.A. ties.[39]

Dooley had helped the C.I.A. destabilize North Vietnam through his refugee programs. The Catholics who poured into South Vietnam provided Diem with a larger political constituency and were promised U.S.-supported assistance in relocating. The American public largely believed that most Vietnamese were terrified of the cruel and bloodthirsty Viet Minh and looked to the God-fearing Diem for salvation. Many refugees simply feared retaliation because they had supported the French.

Within his first year in office, however, Diem became so closely identified with the United States that American officials grew worried about his effectiveness. This became apparent when Spellman had Harnett arrange travel plans for him to Vietnam. The monsignor contacted General L. Collins, head of U.S. military operations in Vietnam. When he heard of Spellman's proposed visit, the general became concerned. He cabled Foster Dulles that the Cardinal's presence would encourage propaganda within Vietnam that Diem was "an American puppet. . . . The fact that both Diem and the Cardinal are Catholic would give opportunity for false propaganda charges that the U.S. is exerting undue influence on Diem." The general noted, however, that if Spellman came he could serve a useful purpose, "dramatizing once more the great exodus of refugees from the North, the greater part of whom are Catholics." He concluded, though, "I think it would be wiser if he did not come."[40]

Spellman wasn't about to be put off. The Pope had asked him to intervene and he wanted to see the situation firsthand. His physical presence in Saigon, he knew, would place him and the Church firmly in Diem's camp in the public mind. When Spellman arrived at the Saigon airport, he was greeted by a wildly cheering crowd of about five thousand. The sixty-seven-year-old prelate was once again dressed in the army khaki attire that he loved to wear in military zones.

Spellman's propagandizing of the Catholic nature of Diem's regime reinforced a negative image of the Church's position in Vietnam. The sectarian nature of Diem's government and the problems of that government were noted by the writer Graham Greene, himself a Catholic, in a dispatch from Saigon printed in the London *Sunday Times* on April 24, 1955:

> It is Catholicism which has helped ruin the government of Mr. Diem, for his genuine piety . . . has been exploited by his American advisers until the Church is in danger of sharing the unpopularity of the United States. An unfortunate visit by Cardinal Spellman ("He spoke to us," said a Vietnamese priest, "much of the Calf of Gold but less of the Mother of God") has been followed by those of Cardinal Gillroy and the Archbishop of Canberra. Great sums are spent on organizing demonstrations for the visitors, and an impression is given that the Catholic Church is occidental and an ally of the United States in the cold war. On the rare occasions when Mr. Diem has visited the areas formerly held by the Viet Minh, there has been a priest at his side, and usually an American one. . . .
>
> The South, instead of confronting the totalitarian north with the evidences of freedom, has slipped into an inefficient dictatorship: newspapers suppressed, strict censorship, men exiled by administrative order and not by judgment of the courts. It is unfortunate that a government of this kind should be identified with one faith. Mr. Diem may well leave his tolerant country a legacy of anti-Catholicism.

During his visit Spellman presented a check for $100,000 to the Catholic Relief Services, which was active in the refugee-relocation program and later administered a great deal of the U.S. aid program, which closely bound the CRS to the U.S. war effort and later led to the suspicion that the CRS had C.I.A. ties. Turning to the Church to perform such a function was done in Latin America, among other places, but in Vietnam it eventually seemed to bear out Graham Greene's warnings that the Church and the United States were being tied to a cause unpopular among Vietnamese.

The potential for corruption in Vietnam was tremendous and also harmed the CRS's reputation. Drew Pearson estimated that in 1955 alone, the Eisenhower administration pumped more than $20 million in aid into Vietnam for the Catholic refugees. Though it did a great deal of good, the CRS eventually encountered a great deal of resentment. Unavoidably, there was much graft and corruption involved in getting food, medical supplies, and other goods from ships to villages. By 1976 the *National Catholic Reporter,* a hard-nosed weekly newspaper, reported apparent CRS abuses in articles such as one entitled "Vietnam 1965–1975. Catholic Relief Services Role: Christ's Work—or the C.I.A.'s?" The abuses cited included using supplies as a means of proselytizing; giving only Catholics aid meant for everyone; being identified with the military; and giving CRS goods to American and Vietnamese soldiers rather than to the civilians for whom the goods were meant.[41] Moreover, there was much speculation that the CRS leadership in Vietnam had C.I.A. links, although this was never proved.

Long before the *National Catholic Reporter* began its investigations, both the U.S. government and Spellman backed away from the increasingly arrogant and difficult Diem, who, by the early 1960s, lost support among his people almost daily. Buddhists held massive protest marches against the government and clashed in the streets on occasion with Catholics. Finally, on November 2, 1963, Diem was assassinated during a C.I.A.-inspired coup d'etat. Two years after the assassination, Spellman told of his knowledge of Kennedy's involvement to Dorothy Schiff, the *Post* publisher, who again visited him at the chancery. According to her notes: "He [Spellman] knew that President Kennedy had been asked to make a decision as to whether or not Diem would be removed and had decided that it was all right for this to happen—this on a recommendation from American officials in Vietnam. The Cardinal said he knew that Kennedy had thought about it overnight, changed his mind and that he knew that he would have rescinded his decision of the night before had the event not already taken place and Diem been dead."[42]

The publisher was amazed by the revelation, but there was nothing she could do with the information. Once again, she had promised not to reveal what she heard at the Powerhouse. Shortly before the coup Spellman disassociated himself from Diem. When Bishop Thuc visited New York, Spellman refused to see him, and he personally asked Bishop Fulton Sheen not to receive Thuc as well. Spellman and Sheen were feuding. Sheen disregarded Spellman's request and had Thuc to lunch while Spellman simmered.

Though Spellman backed away from Diem, he didn't turn his back on Vietnam any more than the U.S. government did. The Cardinal became one of the most hawkish, arguably the most hawkish, leaders in the United States. By 1965 he clashed with the Pope, who desperately tried to bring peace in Vietnam as Spellman pounded the drums of war.

CHAPTER TEN

The Prince of Power

SPELLMAN EXPECTED DEFERENTIAL TREATMENT NOT ONLY from legions of politicians and millions of laymen but also from other members of the hierarchy. Indisputably, he did more for the Church than all the rest of the American hierarchy combined. His cleverness, contacts, and persistence enabled the Vatican to play a forceful international role, after centuries of limited political power. Spellman was the indispensable source of riches and favors for churchmen in both Rome and America. The Pope depended on Spellman and the Cardinal could get whatever he wanted. At times it seemed impossible to tell where the power of the one left off and that of the other began. It was clear that in America Spellman was the Church's kingmaker. He bestowed the title "monsignor" with the regularity of a commander making battlefield promotions, and he made many bishops in his busy, modern court. If anything, Spellman's power increased after Pius became ill.

The health of a pope is always taken seriously. When it appeared in December 1954 that Pius was dying, Spellman was continually on the telephone to Rome. He had visited the Pope months earlier when Pius was first suffering from violent bouts of hiccuping that left him exhausted and unable to hold food down. Spellman sat by his old friend's side in the Pope's bedroom, with its two windows overlooking St. Peter's Square and its simple furnishings—a brass bed, a chest of drawers, a desk, and a painting of the Virgin. The Pope's situation hadn't improved, and he appeared to have grown weaker. Pascalina, who was in constant attendance, called Spellman whenever there was a change in the Pope's condition. Her calls were never encouraging.

On the morning of December 2, however, Pascalina, the doctors, and others were amazed by the apparent improvement in Pius's health. Pascalina was overjoyed, but she was disturbed by what the Pope told her. He was convinced that he had had a vision in which he had seen Jesus Christ, making him the first Pope since the Apostle Peter to have done so. In his exuberance, the Pope told her the details of his strange encounter, even explaining that the previous day he had heard a voice clearly telling him that he would see a vision. The Pope was seventy-eight years old and had been through a serious illness. Pascalina asked him not to say anything to anyone.[1]

Shortly thereafter Pascalina phoned Spellman, asking him to keep everything as quiet as possible. She warned Spellman that the Pope wanted to make his vision public, and she asked the Cardinal to come to Rome immediately to see if he couldn't get the Pope to temper his remarks.

"Eminence, I am afraid of the consequences," she said.

Spellman too didn't want the Church to appear foolish, so he told her that he would come as quickly as he could. The Pope's behavior could always be excused because of his age and illness, but there was the likelihood that Pius would become a source of mockery. Spellman and Pascalina vowed to keep the whole business so quiet that not even other cardinals were to be alerted. But before Spellman apparently reached Rome the tale was out. The Pope told others and, inevitably, the story was leaked to the press. Much of the reaction was skepticism, and the Vatican issued no comment to members of the press who tried to follow up the story.[2]

In the aftermath Spellman found the Pope that much more dependent upon him. The hardheaded Spellman had been dismayed by the whole affair, but he still considered the Pope a great man, one who had done so much to revive the power of the papacy. Moreover, Spellman remained grateful to Pacelli for all the man had done for him. Even when he began to pursue his own policies, Spellman convinced himself that he did so because Pacelli had gotten older and listened to bad advice. But any difficulties he had with the Pope weren't widely known. Other churchmen saw only Spellman's enormous influence with the Pope and how much power that gave him.

The canopies over the five thrones mounted atop a high platform at Yankee Stadium provided little shade in the hot August sun. One seat was empty, awaiting Cardinal Spellman. Four old men, all North American cardinals, slumped in the others beneath the layers of scarlet silk and white lace that covered them from head to toe. They held their silk birettas in their laps. The cardinals were Edward Mooney of Detroit, Samuel Stritch of Chicago, James Charles McGuigan of Toronto, and the former New Yorker Francis McIntyre, now of Los Angeles. They were the most illustrious of the several thousand members of the clergy who were in attendance. Their ranks included eighteen archbishops, eighty-three bishops, and two abbots. The bleachers and box seats were filled with fifty thousand laymen.

The day was August 30, 1957. The occasion was the twenty-fifth anniversary of Spellman's consecration as a bishop and he wanted to be honored. Cardinal Spellman was at the height of his power within the Church. He was not only the Church's chief political voice but also the Church's primary kingmaker in America. The Church in the United States had undergone a Spellmanization. Though Stritch and Mooney weren't as conservative as Spellman and prevented him from imposing his standards on the Middle West, the New York Cardinal had made his imprint on much of the rest of the country. This would be felt for decades in a rigid conservatism that supported war and nuclear weapons while opposing activism that might redress societal inequities.

Spellman's chancery had become a training ground for the American hierarchy. The formula for success was clear: A priest must adhere to the Cardinal's conservative ideology, pragmatism, and rigid work ethic. He couldn't be an independent Father Ford or an idealistic Dorothy Day. In time, "Spelly's boys," as his protégés were known, moved into positions of responsibility not just in New York but across the nation. The Cardinal, for instance, had his military ordinariate, O'Hara, named archbishop of Philadelphia. McIntyre had gotten Los Angeles. William A. Scully, the assistant executive director of Catholic Charities, became bishop of Albany. The executive director of Catholic Charities, Patrick A. O'Boyle, was made archbishop of Washington. A former Navy chaplain, Christopher J. Weldon, became bishop of Springfield, Massachusetts. Thomas J. McDonnell, national director of the Propagation of the Faith, was the bishop of Wheeling, West Virginia.

There were others, and Spellman's international influence was noted in some of their assignments. Apollinaris V. Baumgartner, pastor of St. John Baptist Church, was made apostolic vicar of Guam. Monsignor Charles A. Brown was named auxiliary bishop of Santa Cruz, Bolivia. Monsignor Vincent I. Kennally was made apostolic vicar of the Caroline and Marshall islands, and Thomas R. Manning was named bishop of Corico, Bolivia. In addition, Spellman had so many auxiliary bishops that they were dubbed "the Twelve Apostles," as they scurried around his court.

Most of his appointees, as well as practically all of the rest of America's churchmen, came to the Cardinal's Yankee Stadium extravaganza. Even Cushing and Sheen, who had long felt the sting of Spellman's vindictiveness, were present. Spellman's secretaries had sent thousands of letters inviting people to the big day, but Spellman himself had personally selected the site for the celebration. The Cardinal enjoyed the Church's pomp and ceremony, and he especially liked wedding Church tradition to what he considered American symbols. The stadium, owned by the Knights of Columbus, suited his taste, lending an informality and a very American character to the day's proceedings.

An altar for an outdoor mass had been constructed on the platform on the baseball field. Forty-eight feet high and one hundred eighty feet long, the platform was dominated by an immense cross that loomed above the altar. Suspended from a girder-like affair, the cross looked like an inverted V centered on second base with enormous arms stretching to first and third. A glass enclosure unnecessarily protected the altar and giant candles from any sudden breezes. Loudspeakers were everywhere.

The ceremonies started at 11:15 sharply. Uniformed police and firemen, members of their departments' Holy Name societies, marched onto the playing field from the left-field bull pen. To great applause, Spellman, escorted by twenty West Point cadets in full-dress uniform, made his entrance from right field. Clad in gold robes trimmed in scarlet, he reviewed a procession that wound around the field. His miter was also gold with scarlet trim. "Behold the Great Priest," intoned the St. Joseph's seminary choir, stationed behind home plate.

When Spellman reached his throne, the choir immediately sang "The Star-Spangled Banner." In little more than a year, the emotions evoked in him by that piece of music would be greater than the music sung in his churches. But on this day, Spellman was satisfied with his position in the Church.

The apostolic delegate, Cicognani, was also on the platform, but his seat was lower than the thrones. Still in Washington and still not a cardinal, Cicognani fretted about his position. The clergy had been appalled just two months earlier when Spellman arrogantly had broken protocol by announcing that Bryan J. McEntegart, a protégé and former rector of Catholic University, had been named archbishop of Brooklyn. Cicognani had wept in mortification because such announcements were supposed to be made by the apostolic delegate.[3]

The nuncio wasn't the only churchman present who resented Spellman. Richard Cushing, archbishop of Boston since World War II, was still not a cardinal, and he had Spellman to blame. Then there was Spellman's old international affairs expert. The brilliant Griffiths was an alcoholic who had embarrassed the Cardinal once in public. Spellman angrily ordered Griffiths back to the obscurity of Brooklyn, where then Archbishop Molloy, having been irritated by the high-handed way Spellman took the priest in the first place, had refused to accept Griffiths. An exasperated Spellman finally made Griffiths pastor of a parish near the United Nations and had little to do with him again. As expected, Griffiths's erratic lifestyle was at odds with the routine of parish work. He couldn't adjust—his drinking worsened until he died.

Of all the priests with whom Spellman had troubles, however, the one he loathed the most was the most popular priest in America, Fulton J. Sheen. The two had become bitter enemies. Though he feared the Cardinal and actually became physically ill when he had to confront him, Sheen refused to back down from Spellman. The orator believed—mistakenly—that he would prevail because God was on his side.

In 1950, Sheen arrived in New York to take on the prestigious post of director of the national office of the Propagation of the Faith, the huge organization that raised money for the Church's foreign missions. The Cardinal was convinced that Sheen's charisma would increase donations and that the presence in his archdiocese of the well-known priest would enhance Spellman's own prestige. The Cardinal always wanted to attract to his archdiocese the kinds of men who had made their mark in the world. Once in his orbit, however, they found Spellman resented them if they continued acting like stars. Sheen, as independent-minded as Spellman, thrived on the limelight.

Born on May 8, 1895, in El Paso, Illinois, a small town about thirty miles from Peoria, Sheen was baptized Peter John. He lived his early years with his grandparents and adopted their name, Fulton. He became a priest in 1919 after studying at St. Paul's Seminary in Minnesota. Recognized for his outstanding scholarship, he was sent to Catholic University in Washington for graduate studies. He continued his education at the University of Louvain in Belgium. While in Europe he made his first convert—a distraught woman who had attempted suicide—and he gained renown for his remarkable intellect.

After receiving his doctorate in philosophy Sheen was offered a rare opportunity—to take yet another degree, an Agrégé en Philosophie, which had been granted to only about ten students in forty years. He studied in London and Rome and went through the ritual of an oral examination before some three hundred of the most learned professors of Europe. After the ordeal the candidate was sent to his room. If he passed he was invited to dinner. The beverage served indicated how well the examination had gone, starting with water. For Sheen, waiters served champagne.[4]

When the elegant, handsome young priest returned to the United States, the president of Columbia University, Nicholas Murray Butler, discussed making Sheen a professor of Thomistic philosophy. Cardinal Bourne of England had suggested that Sheen open a Catholic college at Oxford with Monsignor Ronald Knox. But Sheen had a reputation for arrogance, and his superiors wanted to test his obedience. Back in Peoria, Sheen was assigned duties at a poor inner-city parish. When he accepted, his superiors acknowledged that he had passed his test and he was reassigned to Catholic University.

Although an aloof figure, Sheen became a popular lecturer. He swept dramatically about his classroom, bringing his lessons to life with the magic of a Shakespearean actor. He came to national popularity with a radio program, "The Catholic Hour," which began in 1930 and remained his principal forum until he launched a television career in the 1950s. He used the program to proselytize for the Church and to denounce Communism, and he proved to be a witty, magnetic orator who was much sought after as a speaker. His prestige was enhanced by his success as an author.

The monsignor lived graciously in Washington in a large white brick house with a spectacular circular staircase, two studies, a private chapel, and piped-in Muzak. He held dinner parties that were known for their witty conversation, almost always dominated by Sheen. By 1950, however, Sheen was fifty-five years old and seeking new challenges. Thus, when Spellman offered to make him director of the Propagation and elevate him to the office of bishop, he accepted.

To date, Sheen and Spellman had impressed one another. Sheen admired the Cardinal's vast power and influence and his ability to accomplish so much. For his part, Spellman was taken with Sheen's energy, oratorical skills, and diligence at converting the high and mighty, including Clare Boothe Luce and Henry Ford II. Yet another bond was a virulent hatred of Marxism, the deadly enemy of the Church. In his book *Communism and the Conscience of the West,* Sheen espoused a philosophy that Spellman lived: he urged Christians to adopt the passion of Communists in order to fight them.

What was striking about Spellman and Sheen wasn't their similarities but their differences. Sheen was handsome, articulate, and mystical. He loved public speaking, had little use for the nitty-gritty of politics, and was a terrible administrator who had more passion for saving souls than erecting edifices. Moreover, he loved the roar of the crowd and being courted as a celebrity. At age fifty-five, however, Sheen was long accustomed to getting his own way. His past successes had made him arrogant. There was no room in New York for two prima donnas.

Sheen threw himself into his new work with the intensity that he brought to bear on his earlier activities. To him the Propagation was a rare opportunity, not only to alleviate poverty but also to bring spiritual salvation to millions. The more enmeshed he became in the Propagation's activities, however, the more Spellman, who normally allowed his department heads a great deal of latitude, second-guessed him. Spellman demanded acknowledgment of his authority, but Sheen, either disregarding or oblivious to the signal, refused to bend. When Sheen was consecrated a bishop in May 1951, eight months after taking on his new job, he had the ceremony held in Rome rather than New York. He explained to friends that he didn't want Spellman to officiate.

The Propagation assignment was demanding. The society had one hundred thirty offices scattered throughout the United States and each reported to Sheen. He, in turn, reported to Rome, the international headquarters. Contributions from the United States were by far the most generous; and under Sheen, this funding became greater than ever before. The Propagation's assignment was to help, on an equitable basis, all of the Church's missionary units. Jesuits and White Fathers had nineteen hundred missionaries in Africa alone. Maryknoll and Columbian Fathers had six hundred priests scattered about Latin America, Japan, the Philippines, Burma, Korea, and the Fiji Islands.

Until then, Sheen had never really considered the poverty of the Third World. His life had been insulated from destitution by the seminary and academia and by his moving among people who took money for granted. When he saw the poor, Sheen was horrified. Helping them became as much of an obsession with him as anti-Communism, and he channeled his writings and preachings into what became his new cause. One result of this labor was a sudden disdain for the kinds of people he had long associated with—and Spellman cultivated.

"Is it because the money goes to other parts of the world or because, when they give at home, they can see their names on libraries and gymnasiums?" Sheen sermonized one day. "But they cannot see their names in a leper colony—nor can they be thanked by the poor of India, nor by the victims of Communism in Korea or Vietnam."

In 1952, Sheen made the transition from radio to television. The Dumont Network executives put him on the air more as a time filler than as a dynamic personality able to draw a sizable audience. His time slot, Tuesday at 8 P.M., faced two formidable rivals—Frank Sinatra and Milton Berle, who was known as "Mr. Television." To everyone's amazement, Sheen was an instant success. People were mesmerized by his piercing gaze, wit, and style. Nuns demanded that students watch Sheen's program and quizzed them about it the next morning. Sheen was a born performer who carefully prepared his scripts and monitored everything from the brightness of lights to camera angles. His rich voice ranged from an eerie, ghostly whisper to the thunderous tones of an affronted Jehovah. He swept onto the stage dressed in a black cassock with red piping, a red cape flowing from his shoulders and a gold cross flashing on his chest.

Bowing deeply, he said, "Thank you for allowing me into your home again." Thus began another half-hour of *Life Is Worth Living*.

Like his radio program, Sheen's TV show was a showcase for discussions about the Church, Communism, and personal problems. He also used it as a forum to impart the needs of the poor. He spoke of the slums of Latin America and the African bush. Speaking in an Irish brogue wedded to an amalgam of Oxford and American English, he emotionally moved his audience. So popular did the show become that it moved from Dumont to ABC, where it reached a nationwide audience of twenty-five million by 1954. At first Sheen was paid $10,000 per telecast by the Admiral Corporation, which sponsored the program. By 1955 the figure was $16,500. All the money went to the Propagation.

Inevitably, Sheen's popularity created resentment and jealousy in other priests, some of whom dismissed his rhetoric as theatrics and disdained his selling Admiral radios, televisions, and toasters "like a circus barker," in the words of one monsignor. Among those who resented Sheen most deeply was Spellman. The Cardinal wasn't bothered that his auxiliary bishop plugged merchandise, but he disliked the visibility and greater independence that the show gave Sheen. Spellman and Sheen began quarreling about money, but the real issue was authority. Sheen did what no one else dared: he challenged a cardinal who was supposed to have absolute power.

Spellman was chairman of the Propagation of the Faith in the United States, and he treated the organization as part of his personal fiefdom, much as he did the military ordinariate, Catholic Charities, and the myriad other organizations and departments that fell under his jurisdiction. What Sheen resented was Spellman's habit of helping himself to Propagation money. On his frequent trips, Spellman gave donations to schools, hospitals, priest friends, bishops, cardinals, and other people and causes. On his trips to Rome he arrived laden with presents for all.

Whenever Spellman dipped into Propagation money, Sheen objected. He told the Cardinal the funds were collected for the poor, not Spellman's cronies or pet charities. When rebuked in such a fashion, Spellman went into one of his icy furies and vowed vengeance.

In public, the two attended the same affairs, spoke before the same audiences, and even had their pictures taken together. Privately, their relationship became marked by backbiting and smouldering antagonism. When away from Spellman, Sheen disdainfully referred to the Cardinal as "the Little Man" and "the Red Knave." For his part, Spellman called Sheen a "pathological liar" and tried to pry potentially damaging information about Sheen from Propagation workers. After Propagation board meetings the Cardinal stopped by offices of Sheen's workers and spoke to them about their careers. Spellman knew that Sheen was a difficult man for whom to work, and he wanted to exploit problems the men had with their boss.

For instance, Spellman tried to take advantage of the dismay Fred McGuire, the Vincentian who worked for the Propagation, felt at Sheen's arrogant assumption that he knew everything about missionary work. A veteran missionary, McGuire found his advice ignored by Sheen, who, until he assumed the Propagation post, hadn't had any real notion of what missionaries did.

Sidling up to McGuire, Spellman probed: "I hear that you aren't getting along with the bishop?"

McGuire would mutter noncommittally. "I just wanted to stay out of their feud," he recalled. "They were both strong personalities. I was in a no-win situation."[5]

No matter how much anyone faulted the way Sheen ran the Propagation, few criticized the results. Donations soared; the amount of money generated by the Propagation in America was more than double the total amount collected in the rest of the world. In his sixteen years in office, Sheen raised about $200 million. To Spellman's dismay, Sheen was feted whenever he traveled to Rome, and Vatican Propagation officials liked to say that the bishop was "our right hand." Spellman was forced to view Sheen as an opponent he couldn't easily undermine. It would be difficult for him to criticize the bishop in Rome, where Sheen's star shone brightly; more worrisome was the prospect of Sheen's criticizing him.

The first major issue that Spellman and Sheen fought over was whether the Propagation would temporarily subsidize the costs of shipping goods to foreign lands for the Catholic Relief Services. The CRS was a corporation separate from the Propagation, but both reported to Spellman. When a CRS director needed a loan, he approached Sheen, assuming that one agency would help the other. The director explained that the U.S. government had proposed to reimburse the shipping costs of any religious organization's overseas services in countries in which the State Department had an aid program. Naturally, Spellman enthusiastically endorsed the proposal, which would save the CRS about $1 million a year in shipping costs as well as ally America's and the Church's political efforts in various nations.

Sheen was told of the difficulty in paying the charges for shipping goods. The government subsidy would be delayed for many months. The director wanted Sheen to pay the charges out of Propagation money and be reimbursed when the federal funds were paid to the CRS. The Propagation normally had $2 million or $3 million invested in the United States at any given time because Rome dictated where funds went and the process of clearing the Catholic aid program with foreign governments was often painstakingly slow.

Sheen denied the request. The transfer of funds was probably illegal, but Sheen also believed that it wasn't right to juggle money already committed to a specific charity. When Spellman learned of Sheen's refusal, the Cardinal ordered Sheen to pay the CRS charges. At first Sheen refused, but in the end, he had to abide by Spellman's will. The Cardinal, after all, was chairman of the Propagation. In the aftermath their relationship deteriorated further. Sheen disdained Spellman, who, in turn, belittled Sheen.

In 1957 the antagonism between them boiled over in what became known in the Church as the "Milk Fund Scandal." The U.S. government gave the Church surplus goods, largely powdered milk, which Spellman signed over to Sheen. Spellman contended that he had paid for the goods and demanded hundreds of thousands of dollars in reimbursement from Sheen. Once again, Sheen challenged him. The bishop claimed that Spellman had received the surplus goods gratis. Sheen insisted that he was under no obligation to pay.[6]

Spellman was furious, but he became fearful when he learned that Sheen had taken the case to Rome. The bishop, however, found that he had difficulty getting to see the Pope. His access was blocked by Galeazzi, Pascalina, and Pizzardo, as well as a few others who formed a phalanx around the Pope. Pius had been in ill health since his bout with hiccups several years earlier; he was now in his early eighties and more autocratic and unpredictable than before. The Pope's guardians wanted to spare him stress—and to protect their friend Spellman.

The worried Spellman tried to remove Sheen as director of the Propagation by making him pastor of a new parish. If he had succeeded, Spellman would have killed two birds with one stone. He would have effectively removed Sheen from a forum in which he could make his milk-fund charges, and he would have him as head of a parish that desperately needed a preacher with a strong reputation to attract the crowds and monied Catholics necessary to make it solvent. Recognizing the ploy, Sheen refused.

When the bishop persisted in taking his case to Rome, Spellman became alarmed. He wanted something to discredit Sheen. As Father Daniel P. Noonan, Sheen's chief aide, remembered, Spellman had Sheen's personal life investigated several times. Each time he came up empty-handed. "Sheen was afraid of Spellman," Noonan said.[7]

Eventually, Sheen's determination paid off. He brought his charges before the Pope, apparently through one of the Germans on the pontiff's staff who disliked Spellman. What the Cardinal feared came about. Pius, furious, ordered both men to Rome. The Cardinal and the bishop told the Pope their stories. Spellman insisted that he had paid for the milk. Sheen was equally insistent that Spellman hadn't done so and that the Propagation was under no obligation to pay the enormous sum the Cardinal claimed he was owed. He said Spellman wanted to cheat the Propagation.

Spellman hoped that his long relationship with Pacelli and his own position as cardinal would immediately end the matter in his favor. It did not. The aged Pope was affronted. To Spellman's dismay, the Pope referred the matter to Washington, where it could easily be determined whether Sheen's documentation on the surplus food was valid. Word came back: Sheen spoke the truth.

The Pope was apoplectic. Spellman had committed an unpardonable offense. Not only had he tried to con Sheen out of the money, but he had also lied to the Pope. The matter weighed heavily on Pacelli, whose friendship with Spellman dated back thirty years. Spellman realized that his gamble had been disastrous. He was wounded immeasurably at the Vatican. The long chain of his papal friendship was greatly weakened, if not broken.

"I will get you," Spellman told his bishop. "I will get even with you. It may take six months or ten years, but everyone will know what you are like!"[8]

As word of the tattered Spellman-Sheen relationship spread, the clergy in New York and elsewhere watched closely. A cynical expression circulated among priests who knew them both: "They hate each other for the love of God."

Spellman wasted no time in retaliating. Sheen's TV show was taken off the air, and he was forbidden to speak anywhere in New York. Pastors throughout the archdiocese were warned that they courted the Cardinal's wrath if they allowed the bishop to preach in their churches. Spellman even spoke to students at Dunwoodie seminary about Sheen, telling them the bishop was the vilest kind of priest imaginable. What is more significant, Sheen's career was blocked. When Cardinal Stritch in Chicago died, Sheen was no longer considered the most likely candidate to succeed him. Chicago went instead to Bishop Albert Meyer.

Sheen continued acting independently. At an annual meeting of the Propagation in Rome, Sheen was asked why U.S. Propagation funds were down significantly. During the course of the year Spellman had siphoned off about $400,000 for his own projects. "Cardinal Spellman can better answer where the money is since he took it," Sheen declared. Then, dramatically pointing at Gregory Cardinal Agagianian, the world head of the Propagation, Sheen in his doomsday voice asserted, "You can ask that man about fifty thousand dollars." A friend and former classmate of Spellman, and a powerful Vatican figure, the Cardinal had been given that sum during the year.

Spellman remained immensely powerful in 1958, even after the scandal, but his position within the Church was about to change. He was still recognized as a contributor of vast sums to the Vatican; his political advice would still be sought. But he would become one voice among many. The reason had nothing to do with the Cardinal's losing face. Pope Pius XII, Spellman's mentor, died.

* * *

A tired and upset Spellman arrived in Rome on October 9, 1958, the day Pius died. He insisted upon being driven immediately from Ciampino Airport to Castel Gandolfo, where thousands of mourners were pressed against police cordons, encircling the pontifical summer palace.

Only six days earlier, the Cardinal had led a pilgrimage of six hundred New Yorkers to the Vatican. Rome had been their last stop on a tour that included the shrines at Lourdes in France and Fatima in Portugal. The highlight of their trip had been an audience with the Pope. Spellman had used the trip as an excuse to mollify Pacelli, who had remained bitter after the Sheen business. It was an open secret at the Vatican that the ardor that had marked their friendship had cooled. The Cardinal had spent time alone with Pius: they had come such a long way together that the Pope had probably forgiven Spellman.

When news flashed to the ship carrying the pilgrims, Spellman immediately disembarked and flew back to Rome, where he encountered an embarrassing situation. The aged pontiff's death wasn't shocking, but some stories of the circumstances surrounding his death were. The Communist press in Italy reprinted allegations made by the Polish press agency PAP: the Pope's stroke was caused by his having been terribly upset over a rift with Spellman. When the Cardinal appeared in public a horde of Italian newsmen descended on Spellman asking him if he had killed the Pope.

"Ridiculous!" Spellman replied icily, as reported in the press.

St. Peter's was draped in crepe on October 13, the day of the Pope's funeral. Vatican City swarmed with peddlers selling rosaries, scapulars, and pictures and statues of Pius, Jesus, and the Blessed Mother. Pushcart vendors, hawking sandwiches, snacks, and sodas, were besieged by hungry mourners.

The cavernous basilica overflowed with ranking diplomatic representatives from around the world. Lay and ecclesiastic members of the Vatican court wore their medieval finery. Thousands and thousands of people crammed into the basilica and spilled down the steps into the square. The solemn funeral rites saw the participation of twenty-four cardinals and several hundred patriarchs, archbishops, bishops, and other members of the clergy. The voices of choirs could be heard above the din of the crowd outside. At the end of the ceremonies the cardinals gathered in front of the magnificent papal altar, beneath the 400-foot dome painted by Michelangelo. They solemnly watched the ornate gold casket descend by rope and pulley to the tomb where popes were buried.

The moment of sadness was tinged by excitement. A new pope must be elected. Few if any of the cardinals realized they had witnessed the end of an era. The Pope of Power was about to be replaced by the Pope of Peace.

The year 1958 was very different from the last time a pope had been crowned. In 1939 there had been universal agreement that Pacelli was bound to win; the conclave that elected him had been the shortest in four centuries. Now, no candidate stood out. Late in October, *L'Osservatore Romano* scolded the press for acting like everyone else in Rome. Journalists were treating the election of a pope like any other political contest. Newspaper correspondents wrote reams of copy in which they spelled out the most likely candidates. They noted alliances that were forming and the popularity of particular cardinals. For the first time in ages, foreigners were serious candidates. Mentioned were Agagianian, the patriarch of Armenia and part of the small oriental wing of the Church, and Cardinal Tisserant, the dogmatic Frenchman who was the Vatican expert on the Soviet Union. Then there was Spellman.

The possibility of Spellman becoming Pope was raised in the American and foreign press, but the likelihood of his getting the job was considered impossible because he had many enemies in Rome. He had openly clashed with some powerful Romans, including the extremely conservative Ottaviani for attacking a work by Myles Burke, a liberal canon lawyer in the New York archdiocese. There was also Spellman's run-in with Montini. The former secretary to Pius was the only non-cardinal to be a serious candidate for Pope.

Another strike against Spellman was his nationality. An American Pope would give credence to Communist claims that the Vatican was a tool of the United States. But the biggest problem Spellman faced was his hard-earned reputation, which was exploited by an Italian comedian at the time of the election. "Considering the world situation, I feel that what is needed is a political pope," he joked. "And I feel the one best adapted is Cardinal Spellman."[9]

Most of the candidates were Italian. There was even talk of Roncalli, the former nuncio to Paris, as a compromise candidate if a suitable prospect could not be found. But even that seemed unlikely. The prelate had a wealth of diplomatic experience and had been archbishop of the influential Venice See for the past five years. But when the congenial, dumpy little man was compared with the aloof, elegant Pacelli, the thought of Roncalli as Pope was ridiculous. Moreover, he was seventy-seven years old. No cardinal over the age of seventy had been elected Pope in more than two hundred years.

Most cardinals were present for the conclave, or secret meeting of cardinals. Missing were Stepinac, who now lived in a Yugoslavian village and feared he would not be able to return to his homeland if he left; and Mindszenty, who, since the aborted Hungarian Revolution of 1956, lived as a self-assigned political refugee at the American embassy in Budapest.

In a tradition dating back nearly seven centuries, the cardinals were locked away from the rest of the world to vote in the Sistine Chapel. The only signs the public had of what happened were whisps of smoke that indicated whether they had agreed on a pope: black for no, gray for yes. The practice of quarantining cardinals started in the thirteenth century when Senator Matteo Rosso Orsini, the most powerful layman at the Vatican, forced the election of a pope. There had been so many political factions squabbling for power that the cardinals couldn't agree. After months of bickering, Matteo had the cardinals bound hand and foot, beaten, and thrown into a huge structure on Via Appia. The doors and windows were sealed, and the place was ringed with guards. The senator then ordered them to elect a pope. Rain poured through the roof. Still, it was more than a month before the churchmen concocted a plan to nominate someone who would abdicate immediately after they were freed. An infuriated Matteo saw through their ruse. He threatened to dig up the recently buried Pope and put the cadaver in their midst until they chose his successor. If they didn't, he said, he would kill them. They finally elected Celestine IV.[10]

The conclave of 1958 lacked such high drama. Nonetheless, in its own way it was much more significant to the Church. The cardinals were split along ideological lines. The conservative faction, headed by a group of cardinals known as "the Pentagon," consisted of Canali, Pizzardo, Micara, Ottaviani, and Mimmi. They dominated the curia and adhered to the policies of Pius XII, and they enjoyed Spellman's support. The progressive, or anti-Pentagon, group was largely identified with Cardinals Lercaro and Roncalli and Archbishop Montini. (Four years earlier, Montini had been made archbishop of Milan. In the eyes of many Church politicians, he had been removed from the Vatican and denied the honor of being made a cardinal largely at Spellman's instigation.) Abroad, the anti-Pentagon forces were supported by the Polish Primate Wyszynski, the Indian Cardinal Garcias, and the French cardinals.[11]

Until the time of the conclave, it appeared that the entrenched Pentagon cardinals would have their way. Their candidate, Archbishop Siri of Genoa, was cast in the Pacelli mold and, indeed, had been a protégé of the late Pope. There were, however, a number of cardinals who were concerned with the rigidity of Pius XII's regime, including the overcentralization of the Vatican, the unwillingness to confront problems or engage in reform, and many were troubled by the crusading anti-Communism that had become anachronistic. The progressive cause gained momentum with the arrival of Cardinal Wyszynski, the only cardinal from a Communist country and a sign of a thaw in Communist-Church tensions, one that Pacelli would have chosen to ignore.[12]

Nonetheless, the first rounds of voting showed no one surging into the lead. Neither the conservative candidate, Siri, nor the progressives' man, Montini, could muster the necessary votes. Four times a day—twice in the morning and twice in the afternoon—the cardinals voted. Rather than face a prolonged and fruitless struggle, cardinals began agreeing that they must choose a compromise candidate. Thus, Roncalli, though a progressive, was selected. He was old and little was expected of him. Cardinals of both factions believed they would be given time to rally their forces by the time of the next conclave. As the Roncalli movement gained momentum, Spellman, who sat directly across from Roncalli in the Sistine Chapel, watched the man. Spellman was surprised when he saw no reaction.

After only three days, on the eleventh ballot, Roncalli was elected Pope. If others were surprised, he wasn't. Roncalli calmly reached into his pocket and withdrew a long speech he had written in Latin. With great dignity, he said he would become John XXIII—the first Pope John since the notorious days of the anti-Pope John six centuries earlier. Just as calmly, Roncalli changed his cardinal's scarlet robes for the white worn by a pope.

When John assumed his throne that faced the altar, the cardinals, one by one, approached in order of their seniority to perform the ceremony known as adoration. They humbled themselves on their knees, kissed the Pope's slipper and hand to show obedience, and, in turn, received the kiss of peace. Spellman went through the rituals, but he resented the new Pope. In Pacelli, Spellman saw the power and glory of the Church. In Roncalli he saw a man who would squander the kind of political authority he and Pius XII had spent decades restoring to the papacy. Like most people, Spellman underestimated Roncalli.

Angelo Giuseppe Roncalli was born on November 25, 1881, in Bergamo. His parents were dirt farmers who had five sons and six daughters. At the age of eleven the boy entered a minor seminary, and twelve years later he was ordained. Roncalli's early career was almost indistinguishable from that of other ambitious young clerics. He did the tasks assigned him, worked at finding mentors who could help him, and tried to make sure he didn't offend anyone. The succession of jobs that he held indicated he was career conscious but never had the kind of powerful support as a young man that such "predestined" churchmen as Pacelli and Montini had had. Roncalli served first as a secretary to the bishop of Bergamo, then, successively, as a military chaplain, a president of a Catholic Action group, a professor and spiritual director at the Bergamo seminary, a fundraiser, and a professor in Rome. He led the comfortable life of a churchman. In 1925 his career took a firm step upward when he was assigned to be the apostolic representative in Bulgaria, a post that required he be made a bishop. Roncalli was passed over for the more prestigious post of nuncio in Rumania. Then, in 1934, he was appointed apostolic delegate to Turkey and Greece, with his residence in Istanbul.

What went largely unnoticed in Rome was how popular Roncalli was with the people of the countries where he served. He wasn't a particularly astute diplomat who earned kudos for his cleverness. He didn't impress people as an ambassador of the power and glory of the Vatican. Quite simply, his warmth as a good-hearted man touched people. Roncalli sought human answers to situations, not political responses. He had gone against his training during the war and issued false baptismal certificates to about four thousand Jews, so they could stay in Turkey until they continued on to Palestine or elsewhere. When sent to Paris, he managed to reconcile the disparate political interests and defuse the bitterness toward the Church and bishops who collaborated. As he grew older, Roncalli worried increasingly about his Church. When he was made a cardinal in 1953 and given Venice, he was afraid he would die while the Church continued its fatal course under Pius XII, who saw only power and privilege and confrontation with Communism. Then fate intervened.

Spellman held his tongue in Rome, where it was unwise to be indiscreet about a new pope, but when he returned home, the Cardinal announced his disdain. "He's no Pope," Spellman scoffed to his aides. "He should be selling bananas."

The Cardinal cynically retrieved from his basement the silver tray Roncalli had given him in Turkey during the war. He had it polished and prominently displayed in his dining room. It was bound to impress certain people who would believe his new papal ties were strong. Otherwise, he displayed nothing but contempt for the new Pope. He refused to place John XXIII's coat of arms either at St. Patrick's or the chancery. As a reminder of what he believed a pope should be, Spellman had a life-size wax figure made of Pius XII. Dressed in Pius's clothes, the dummy was set in a glass case in the rear of St. Patrick's. Later, the figure was moved into Spellman's residence, where it brought startled gasps from visitors who found it so lifelike that at first they thought it was a strange priest they hadn't met.

Swiftly Spellman believed he was right to suspect John didn't know what he was doing. The Pope's first encyclical, *Ad Petri Cathedram*, was a rebuke of Spellman's world of privilege, power, and riches. The Pope lamented that "there still remains too great a difference in the distribution of wealth," and he blamed the "concept of the right of private property, which is at times defective and downright unjust, held by those who are interested only in their own benefit and convenience." The public posture of the new papacy was more than rhetoric. To Spellman's disgust, John treated Communism almost casually and didn't bother to launch a strong anti-Communist campaign during the next Italian election. Privately, John tried to build a bridge to Moscow in order to defuse Catholic-Communist tensions.

On a more personal level, Spellman was angry with the Pope.

One of John's first acts was to order Mother Pascalina out of the Vatican; she was given only a few hours to pack her bags. She had gone too far: in a heated confrontation with Tisserant, she had slapped the Cardinal. Then Spellman was outmaneuvered by the Pope. Cushing was made a cardinal, and Cicognani was not only recalled to Rome but also was made a cardinal and Vatican secretary of state. The biggest blow to Spellman came when Egidio Vagnozzi, the new apostolic delegate, was entrusted with the role of loosening Spellman's political grip on the American Church.

After years of exercising unbridled power, Spellman felt himself being reined in. Never a docile follower, the Cardinal refused to be one now. He accepted the attempts to check his power as a challenge.

PART IV

THE DECLINE AND FALL

CHAPTER ELEVEN

The Displaced Prince

JOHN F. KENNEDY'S PRESIDENTIAL CAMPAIGN WAS WONDER-
ful to behold. Slick and snazzy, it was filled with incredibly
bright performers who were telling America to wake up after
the long sleep of the Eisenhower years and forget the nightmare of
the McCarthy era. It was time to turn the nation's face to the future
and follow a dream.

Cardinal Spellman wasn't buying any of it. In 1960 the Cardinal
was seventy-one years old, and one of the realities of his age was
that there barely seemed to be enough time to hold on to the present,
let alone rush to embrace the future. The young Spellman who had
excitedly awaited the emergence of a powerful America and a powerful Church had seen his desires fulfilled as reasonably as possible
in a world where the future could never really be controlled. Now,
Spellman wanted to support a presidential candidate who gave him
guarantees, not slogans about idealism. The fact that one of the candidates was Catholic made no difference to Spellman. The Cardinal
was for Richard M. Nixon.

The Cardinal was on the telephone, and his tone was icy. When
he hung up Spellman turned to one of his secretaries with a baleful
look. "That is a truly evil man," Monsignor Eugene Clark remembered Spellman saying.

Spellman had just hung up on Joe Kennedy. Though the two had much the same world view for nearly thirty years and had worked hand in glove on many occasions, they had broken because of the political ambitions Kennedy harbored for his son Jack. Thus, like a police commissioner who closes ranks when his department is criticized, Spellman took Kennedy's assault on churchmen as a personal attack. He wasn't wrong.

In October 1960, the millionaire had demanded to know why most members of the hierarchy were opposed to his son's candidacy for the presidency. Kennedy wanted to know, indirectly, why Spellman was against Jack. Later, Kennedy barged into the Cardinal's residence and ranted and raved about the bishops being lined up against his boy. "He blew his cork," said Clark, one of Spellman's secretaries. "He was in a foul mood, but he didn't blow his cork at the Cardinal. No one ever dared do that. He didn't take the Cardinal head-on. He spoke about the bishops not supporting his son, but Cardinal Spellman didn't give an inch."[1]

Largely because of Spellman's daunting behavior over the years and their own prejudices, many Protestants and Jews believed that a Catholic in the White House would be a puppet of the Vatican. One of the greatest ironies of the 1960 campaign was the chasm between reality and the public perception of the role that religion played. As Joe Kennedy well knew, Spellman was one of the chief architects of the policy that forced his son to battle the issue of religion. "Naturally most of the hierarchy are extreme conservatives," candidate Kennedy privately remarked. "They are accustomed to everyone bowing to them, to associating with the wealthiest men in the community. They like things as they are—they aren't going to be reformers."[2]

There were, of course, bishops who favored Kennedy, but they were rare. Foremost among them was Cushing. The Boston cardinal was closer to the senator from Massachusetts than any other churchman, and he delighted in helping a candidate whom Spellman opposed. But the Church's political leaders in the United States, primarily Spellman and Apostolic Delegate Vagnozzi, had practical grounds for knocking Kennedy's candidacy. The Democrat had asserted that if he were elected President there would be strict separation of Church and State on all issues. He flatly opposed federal aid to parochial schools, and said he would never appoint an American ambassador to the Vatican, an issue that still rankled Rome.

The united front that Spellman and Vagnozzi presented on the Kennedy issue was unusual. Since replacing Cicognani, Vagnozzi had crossed swords with Spellman on several occasions. He intruded into the affairs of archdioceses around the nation, including New York, and was carving out a larger role for himself in Washington that directly challenged Spellman. They both, however, saw Nixon as the Church's choice. Paul Hofmann, a *New York Times* reporter, drafted a memorandum to Arthur Krock, the *Times* columnist, regarding an off-the-record talk he had with Vagnozzi about the campaign. Vagnozzi made it clear to Hofmann that "a sophisticated current among Roman Catholics in the U.S. and in the Vatican feels that a Roman Catholic in the White House at this moment might do more harm than good to the Church."[3]

Vagnozzi, an aide at the apostolic delegation in Washington from 1932 to 1942, was an astute student of American politics. He outlined why the Church might benefit from a Kennedy defeat. The delegate recalled that after Al Smith's defeat, "many Protestants afterwards felt sorry" for Smith and his co-religionists, and this apparently had been turned to the Church's benefit. Hofmann summarized Vagnozzi's attitude by stating that "the Vatican and Pope John must receive a very favorable appraisal of Nixon and a rather cool one of Kennedy."[4]

For form's sake, the delegate told Hofmann that the Vatican "expected the Roman Catholic bishops individually and collectively to stay out of the electoral campaign." Reality contradicted such a sentiment. The Vatican itself took a lightly veiled stand against Kennedy in *L'Osservatore Romano* on May 17. The candidate had indicated that the hierarchy held sway over Catholics' souls, not their politics. Thus the Vatican paper, without actually naming Kennedy, warned against attempts "to detach Catholics from the ecclesiastical hierarchy, restricting relations between the two to the mere sphere of sacred ministry and proclaiming the believers' full autonomy in the civil sphere."[5]

Another concern about Kennedy was shared by certain members of the hierarchy and other conservative Catholics. Kennedy, whose presidency would be marked by a heightened East-West tension, was found to be wanting in anti-Communist fervor. This perceptual problem indicated the extreme conservatism of certain Catholics and was stated in "An Open Letter to American Catholics," drafted by James Buckley, who later became a senator: "There is a Catholic issue in the campaign, the Catholic opposition to Communism. . . . Kennedy has chosen to identify himself with that segment of American society which is either unwilling or unable to regard Communism as more than a childish bugaboo."

Spellman and conservative Catholics generally were worried that Communism as an issue was losing its impact. Eisenhower, for instance, had held a bilateral conference with the Soviets; at the time this was considered a major breakthrough in Washington-Moscow relations. Knowing the move would anger Spellman, Eisenhower had called the prelate to reassure him that such diplomacy in no way was a "surrender" on any issue and that the firm U.S. stand on

Berlin remained in effect.[6] Then, in 1959, Eisenhower had invited Nikita S. Khrushchev to the United States, despite objections by Spellman and other members of the hierarchy.

During the presidential campaign, Spellman disregarded such setbacks. He appeared publicly with Eisenhower and Nixon and spoke privately in support of the vice president. "In private the Cardinal was always very clear about where he stood," Herbert Brownell recalled.[7]

Spellman had known Nixon since his days as a prosecutor of Alger Hiss. The Cardinal's politics had always been close to those of the Republican, who always treated Spellman with an almost exaggerated deference. Also, the Cardinal's choice of candidates may have been shaped, at least to some degree, by resentment. Cushing was obviously the Democrat's favored prelate: the Boston archbishop had officiated at Jack's wedding, while Spellman had married Bobby and Teddy. Now the lantern-jawed Cushing was an active campaigner for Kennedy and a foe of Spellman.

Cushing was an unusual member of the hierarchy in that his political instincts weren't highly developed. A man of earthy good humor and straightforward manner, Cushing undertook his money-raising primarily among "the little people," as he called them. This knack had moved Cushing up the clerical ladder, and one of his prime supporters had been Spellman. As a bishop in Boston, Spellman had been impressed with Cushing's affable and effective fund-raising technique. He wrote to Rome on Cushing's behalf, first to have him named a bishop. Later he lobbied to have Cushing replace O'Connell when the old cardinal died in 1944. One reason Spellman promoted Cushing was that Cushing turned to him for advice. Cushing wasn't all that interested in power. He liked speaking, moving among people, and raising funds, but he had little interest in being an administrator. After being named archbishop of Boston, he continued deferring to Spellman, who began running the Boston archdiocese from New York. Cushing had inherited O'Connell's last secretary, a Monsignor John Wright, who kept the affairs of the archdiocese running smoothly; Spellman looked after the major issues, such as whom to promote and what political stands Cushing should take.

Like Cardinal Hayes and Arcessi, Cushing leaned on Spellman because he didn't know his way around Rome. The unpolished Boston archbishop always felt out of place at the Vatican. He hadn't attended the North American College, and he didn't speak Italian. A sympathetic monsignor said, "In Rome he was self-conscious and often wound up making a fool of himself. Like a socially ill-at-ease child, he became the clown. He spoke too loudly, slapped haughty little Italian ecclesiastics on the back, and told jokes that fell flat." Spellman, who knew the Vatican the way a chamberlain knows his court, had shielded Cushing on many occasions from Italian malice. When the two men later fell out, there was no one to deflect Spellman's blows from Cushing.

The split occurred when Cushing decided to take charge of his archdiocese in more than name only. One version has it that the move to independence was Cushing's own. By other accounts, the move was the idea of the very ambitious Bostonian, John Wright, the Cardinal's secretary (who later became a bishop in Pittsburgh). A brilliant, witty churchman, Wright resented the control Spellman exerted over Boston, yet he admired the Cardinal's ability to accumulate and wield power. Simultaneously, the sophisticated Wright was contemptuous of Spellman's anti-intellectualism, his Rotarian-style boosterism of America, and his love of the military.

When Cushing challenged Spellman, it was over the appointment of a bishop within the Boston archdiocese. After much bitterness the diocese in question, Springfield, was cut in two. Cushing made Wright a bishop for one area, and Spellman named Christopher Weldon, an ex-Navy chaplain and head of Catholic Charities, to the other half. As Cushing flexed the muscle that belonged to him, the sees of Boston and New York became the sites of bitter battles. Suddenly, Cushing found that his relations with the Vatican had cooled. After years of sending Rome favorable reports about Cushing, Spellman now sent the opposite. He couldn't fault the Boston archbishop for his fund-raising abilities, which remained as impressive as ever, so he sent information to the Pope that questioned Cushing's personal conduct. On one occasion a photograph appeared in the press that showed Cushing dancing with several old ladies. Spellman sent a copy of the newspaper to Pius, along with a cryptic note to the effect that Cushing's behavior was unseemly. The next time Cushing visited Rome, he was given a humiliating reprimand. On the pontiff's desk was the offending photo.[8]

When, in 1953, new cardinals were named, including the flinty McIntyre, Cushing had been passed over. Nothing went right for him in Rome. "I can't get anything out of this fellow," a Cushing aide remembers the bishop saying of the Pope. "He won't do anything for me." Spellman had the Pope's ear, as Cushing well knew. Later, during the Kennedy presidency, Cushing was especially delighted when it was he, not Spellman, who had access to the White House and Spellman who was in the shadows. And there was a new Pope, one who actually liked him.[9]

In the case of the 1960 presidential campaign, Cushing went out of his way to introduce Kennedy as "the next President of the United States." At one point Cushing tried to quash a whisper campaign that the candidate wasn't a practicing Catholic. The archbishop submitted to the Kennedy father and son a statement that he wanted to issue denying the rumor. They finally asked him to drop it. Kennedy wasn't much of a Catholic, and he didn't want the Church closely identified with his campaign. Cushing's closeness to the campaign resulted in other awkward moments. Once, for instance, he was on Joe Kennedy's yacht when the millionaire repeated to Cushing what he had said to Spellman: he couldn't believe the hierarchy had turned on his son after all he himself had done for the Church over the years.

"The bishops are against Jack," Kennedy said.

Recounting the story to one of his aides, Cushing said: "I didn't know what the hell to say." But he had had a moment of inspiration at the expense of other bishops. "That's the best news I've heard so far," Cushing had declared. "They're all born losers."

At one point during the campaign a Boston priest, a monsignor, worked on a magazine article about a Catholic presidency. Shortly after its publication he was at Spellman's for lunch when Jack Kennedy called to say how pleased he was with the article. When the monsignor returned to the table Spellman asked him what he had heard from "the *junior* senator from Massachusetts." Like many people, the priest was never sure whether he was being mocked by Spellman. The monsignor said something about the article; then he realized that Spellman was fishing for something about himself. Even though it was known in certain political circles that the Cardinal was in Nixon's camp, Spellman assumed that Kennedy had asked about him. He hadn't, but the monsignor diplomatically replied, "Oh yes, he sent you his very special regards." Spellman accepted the salutation as his due.[10]

Ignorant of the trouble Kennedy had with his Church, numerous Protestants raised their voices against the Democrat. The Reverend Norman Vincent Peale and some hundred fifty Protestants, for instance, organized a National Conference of Citizens for Religious Freedom. A pro-Nixon lobby, it was camouflaged as "an intelligent approach to the religious issue on a high philosophical level." Their message was blatant bigotry; they doubted that a Catholic President could separate his duties from his Church. Kennedy met this and similar challenges head-on. In a major speech before the American Society of Newspaper Editors, he argued that "there is only one legitimate question . . . would you, as President, be responsible in any way to ecclesiastic pressures or obligations of any kind that might in any fashion influence or interfere with your conduct or that office in the national interest? My answer was—and is—no. I am not a Catholic candidate for President."

After Kennedy's strong statement, *L'Osservatore Romano* editorialized that the Church "has the duty and the right" to tell Catholics how to vote. Vatican sources were reported to have said that the editorial, which many people at first thought was aimed at Communist candidates in Italy, applied to America as well, much to the disgust of the Democratic candidate. "Now I understand why Henry VIII set up his own Church," Kennedy remarked privately.[11]

Shortly before the election, several members of the hierarchy took a brazen step that embarrassed Kennedy, as it was meant to do. The incident occurred in Puerto Rico, which was considered part of Spellman's personal jurisdiction, so it was not only unlikely but probably impossible that the Cardinal wasn't aware of a major political action by his bishops. In late October, Archbishop James P. Davis of San Juan, Bishop Luis Aponte Martinez of Lares, and Bishop James E. McManus issued a pastoral letter forbidding Church members to vote for the Popular Democratic Party of Governor Luis Muñoz Marín. Thus, only two weeks before the presidential election, the bishops dramatically raised the age-old issue of conflicting Catholic obligations to Church and State. The ostensible reason for the ban was that the governor's platform supported birth control services for health reasons. The Popular Democratic Party was labeled by the hierarchy as "Godless, immoral, anti-Christian, and against the Ten Commandments." The whole affair smacked of one of Spellman's Machiavellian maneuvers. Reaction to the letter was immediate and caused as much of an uproar in the United States as in Puerto Rico.

Muñoz, who angrily stormed from Sunday mass when the statement was read, denounced the letter as "incredible medieval interference." In the United States the impact was more profound. New doubts were raised about Kennedy, and this seemed to have been the true intent of the action all along. "They said it couldn't happen in America, but it did," intoned the lead editorial in the *Baptist Standard*, the nation's largest Protestant weekly. "Puerto Rico is American soil." Other voices joined the outcry. "On November 8 I shall not mark my ballot for a Roman Catholic candidate for presidency," declared Methodist Bishop Glenn P. Phillips. He said the Catholic bishops' letter had doubly confirmed his stand. The letter fed Protestant anti-Catholic paranoia.

Spellman enjoyed the uproar. Kennedy had tried to disassociate himself from Catholicism, and the Cardinal believed the candidate was being taught a lesson that he would always be regarded as a Catholic no matter what his platform. Publicly, the Cardinal issued a mild statement saying that Puerto Rican voters wouldn't commit sin if they disregarded the bishops' letter. Though it was never proven, the likelihood that Spellman had a hand in the controversial letter was strong. He had been in Puerto Rico on October 12 for the consecration of Martinez, one of the signers. Two days later, he had installed Davis, another signer, as archbishop of San Juan. Spellman also met with the governor, a move in keeping with his history of acting publicly one way and privately another. Moreover, according to press accounts, he was with Davis in South Bend on October 23, only days after the letter was read; at Notre Dame, Davis defended his action.

After Kennedy had won the Democratic nomination, Spellman wrote him a note of congratulations:

Dear Jack,

Congratulations on your wonderful victory. I remained up until four fifteen this morning watching the proceedings and shall hear your acceptance speech tomorrow.

I hope you will arrange your speaking program so as to be with us at the Al Smith dinner at the Waldorf the evening of October 19. Vice President Nixon will also speak. I know how happy are your mother and father and brothers and sisters.

Devotedly and prayerfully,[12]

When Kennedy won the election, Spellman realized he had gambled and lost. Kennedy's was the first inauguration to which Spellman had not been invited since becoming an archbishop more than twenty years earlier. Spellman was bitter. In the place of honor was Cushing. The significance was obvious—Spellman's influence at the White House had disappeared overnight.

Though debated ad nauseam during the campaign, religion was not a decisive factor in the election. George Gallup contended that seventy-eight percent of all Catholics, who usually voted Democratic anyway, voted for Kennedy, but what was clear from the returns was that Kennedy was elected not by the Catholic vote but by a Protestant majority. The Protestant vote outnumbered the combined Catholic and Jewish vote and bespoke a religious tolerance in America that seemed surprising in light of the intolerance displayed by Spellman and Norman Vincent Peale, among other religious leaders. The election was also significant in showing that there was no longer any reason for the extreme defensiveness that was for so long a part of American Catholicism and a great source of Spellman's strength. It was difficult to throw the charge of bigotry in the face of a nation that had elected a Catholic President.

Spellman was unsettled by the election, recognizing, as Kennedy aide Dave Powers had suggested, that he was no longer the nation's most prominent Catholic. Before the inauguration Spellman challenged the new President. The Cardinal publicly demanded absolute financial equality in government grants to Catholic and public schools. "He never said a word about any of Eisenhower's bills for public schools only," the new President said, "and he didn't go that far in 1949 either."[13]

Spellman continued his onslaught, as though desperately trying to show that he hadn't lost his political power just because his candidate had lost an election. When Kennedy presented a massive federal-aid-to-education bill, the proposed legislation was limited to public schools "in accordance with the clear prohibition of the Constitution." The Cardinal and the National Catholic Welfare Conference, representing the full American hierarchy, furiously lobbied for the bill's defeat unless loans to nonpublic schools were added. The Catholic campaign was successful and the bill went down in flames.

By then Kennedy was sick of the hierarchy. He couldn't believe the bishops and cardinals didn't appreciate his awkward position as the first Catholic President. He was so sensitive on the Church issue that of all the messages of congratulations he received from world leaders, the one from Pope John XXIII was kept secret from the public. Likewise, the Vatican was asked not to publicize Kennedy's own innocuous reply. The President deeply resented the hierarchy's undermining him, and the Vatican felt his anger. Cicognani, now secretary of state, was repeatedly rebuffed when he tried to visit Kennedy. At one point he was informed by the White House that the U.S. government didn't officially recognize the Vatican and that Cicognani's presence would embarrass Kennedy. Eventually, Vagnozzi had someone intercede on Rome's behalf. Cicognani was allowed to make a "personal" visit, not an official one. The apostolic delegate and the Vatican secretary of state were actually told to present themselves at the back door. The visit was brief and photographers were banned.[14]

To add insult to injury, the President publicly received Paul Blanshard, the author of books critical of the Church. One of the topics they discussed was how much Spellman embarrassed the President, Blanshard later wrote.

CHAPTER TWELVE

The Obstructionist

SPELLMAN CAST A COLD EYE AT HIS CHURCH AND KNEW THAT certain change was inevitable. Even Pius XII had allowed small gusts of reform into the aged institution, though barely enough to set candles flickering. People could now meet their weekly mass duties on Saturday evening as well as Sunday, and Catholics no longer had to abstain from meat on Friday, an infraction once considered a serious sin. Pope John, however, wanted sweeping changes that would transform the Church.

The prelate rose from the head table at the 1962 Al Smith Memorial Dinner and bade good-night to the vast crowd, including Vice President Lyndon Johnson, Governor Rockefeller, and Mayor Wagner, the evening's featured speakers. Spellman explained that he had to leave early to fly to Rome for the opening of the Second Vatican Council. The Cardinal received a standing ovation as he left, many of his well-wishers mistakenly believing he would play a major role in the event.

Spellman wasn't eager to make the trip; it was more a defensive maneuver than anything else. As the ranking American Cardinal, his presence was required. Besides, he wanted to influence events as much as possible. Spellman considered the much-heralded council, the first since the infallibility of the Pope on moral teachings was proclaimed in 1870, to be yet another absurd exercise by a foolish pope. The gathering rebuked Spellman's world, and he wasn't alone in that view. When John had announced on January 6, 1959, that he would hold an ecumenical council, the response among cardinals generally was hardly enthusiastic. After all, what John proposed was not only startling to many of them but also frightening. The purpose of the council was the spiritual renewal of the Church and reconsideration of the position of the Church in the modern world.

Spellman was met at Ciampino Airport by Count Galeazzi, who over the years had become the most powerful layman at the Vatican and who, with his assistant Michele Sindona, watched over the Vatican bank and other massive financial holdings. The count's limousine took them to the Grand Hotel, the gracious residence where Spellman always stayed in Rome. Their conversation probably was about the Pope and his council, and like Spellman, the count wasn't enamored with either. Having been rewarded with prestige, riches, and power during their years of service to the Church, the men could not comprehend tampering with the institution in which they operated so skillfully. They especially couldn't understand such an attitude by a man who against long odds had been fortunate enough to become Pope.

John, though, worried about the creaky monolith that he now headed. He fretted that the vast, unwieldy, and unresponsive Church bureaucracy would collapse under the weight of useless tradition. The Pope expressed his view at the beginning of the council when he stood in the open window of his study to bless a multitude of ten thousand massed in St. Peter's Square. Among the gathering was a scattering of prelates who were delegates to the council, and to them the Pope's message was all too clear. "Slowly, slowly, we move from illness to convalescence," John said.

From the beginning Spellman was out of step with Vatican II, as the council was known. At age seventy-three, he wasn't concerned with theology or philosophy, nor would he ever be. "I *hire* theologians," he liked to say. The Cardinal viewed the council as another case of politics, where he had little to win and something to lose. Old as he was, he disliked change, and all this seventy-nine-year-old Pope wanted was change. Everything John did or said seemed to grate on Spellman.

Spellman had cause to feel aggrieved. One of the Pope's professed aims was reform of the liturgy in order to bring laymen into closer participation in Church services and to encourage diversity in languages and practices. Spellman enjoyed the centuries-old rituals and didn't want to see them altered. He did not want to share the role of priest with laymen. Even more disturbing to the Cardinal was the great emphasis the Pope placed on the pastoral duties of bishops, as distinct from administrative duties. Spellman always believed a churchman should spend time in a parish, but he viewed it as a duty necessary for better understanding the Church as an institution and for picking up practical experience. His attitude was much like that of a corporate chief executive who believed junior executives should perform the less glamorous jobs on the way to the top. Spellman took Pope John's attempt at de-emphasizing the role of money-managers as another sign of the Pope's foolishness. Where would the Church be, the Cardinal asked, without practical administrators like him? He was amused because he knew what a hold he retained on the Church just because of his role as a man who controlled purse strings.

Before leaving for Rome, Spellman had made a vow that his subordinates fully expected him to keep: "No change will get past the Statue of Liberty." America would remain free of the Pope's meddlesome nonsense. Spellman had reason to feel confident of his forecast. Pope John was ill with inoperable cancer and wasn't expected to live another year.

When the council finally convened, Spellman's expectations seemed to be borne out. The hierarchy swiftly broke down into two camps: progressives and conservatives. During the eight weeks of the opening session, there was much rhetoric and little action. Among the Americans, Spellman led the faction opposed to innovation; Cardinals Joseph E. Ritter of St. Louis and Albert Meyer of Chicago were the leading proponents of change.

Spellman made no effort to conceal his position. On October 21, for instance, the American bishops met at the North American College to set a strategy whereby they could meet regularly during the council sessions. There were proposals to establish committees that would correspond to the official Vatican II commissions, such as the one on liturgy which was scheduled to meet the next day. Spellman flatly opposed a number of candidates proposed for the committees, which he charged were being "stacked" with liberals. Eventually, an American bishop's committee on the liturgy was named but Spellman fought for a heavy conservative representation. It soon became obvious that Spellman was at odds with most of the American delegation, some of whom appeared to relish standing against him after years of bending to his will during the reign of Pope Pius XII.

Rome was overflowing with visitors during the session. Not just Catholics but people of all religions swarmed over the Vatican, in accordance with John's wishes. The Pope sought a spirit of ecumenism that was startling for the insular religion. John wanted to remove as many of the differences among Christian religions as possible. The press was out in force as well; even Paul Blanshard was there to cover the historic event. Although the Pope and the Cardinal didn't like one another, they were forced to rely on each other.

Spellman was still a powerful money machine and accomplished much for the Church. For instance, Spellman was in charge of planning for a Vatican Pavilion at the World's Fair to be held in New York in 1964–65, and he wanted as much press coverage as possible, including a *Life* magazine spread on Vatican art. For his publicity, Spellman also wanted to use illuminations of the art by one of the magazine's photographers, Dimitri Kessel. "Don Luce made a deal with Spellman for the pictures in exchange for an exclusive interview with the Pope," Robert Blair Kaiser, *Time*'s Rome correspondent at the time, recalled. Spellman arranged for an informal "accidental" meeting for Kaiser with Pope John at Castel Gandolfo.[1]

During the council session Spellman continued his self-assigned role as obstructionist. One of the major liturgical issues was whether the mass could be said in the vernacular, which Spellman adamantly opposed. "The Latin language, which is truly the Catholic language, is unchangeable," he declared, "is not vulgar, and has for many centuries been the guardian of the unity of the Western Church." Later, Spellman gave his view of the entire proceedings: he warned against a "zeal for novelties." Unlike the past, however, his words were challenged. Declared Cardinal Ritter of St. Louis: "The very nature of the liturgy and the Church strongly persuades and even demonstrates the need for reform." The Ritter forces prevailed, but the fight was long and hard.

At the conclusion of the first session on December 8, 1962, Pope John himself was disappointed with how little was accomplished. Confusion, more than anything else, reigned. A host of Church-related issues and the Church itself were beginning to be critically examined, and questions were raised to which there were no simple answers. Spellman, for the moment, was satisfied. The Church still belonged more to him than to Pope John. But unknown to Spellman, the Church would change during council sessions held over the next three years.

With Nikita Khrushchev as the Soviet Premier, John had reason to believe that a thaw in Vatican-Moscow relations was possible. One man he turned to was Norman Cousins, who, drawing on his credentials as a leader of the Dartmouth peace conference and a loud voice for disarmament, was to interview Khrushchev. Cousins had approached President Kennedy and offered his services as an intermediary; Kennedy asked him to try to determine Soviet intentions at the deadlocked Geneva Disarmament Talks. Next, Cousins offered similar assistance to the Pope, who, through intermediaries, accepted. When Cousins returned from Moscow to the Vatican, he gave John a list of Khrushchev statements that showed the Russian leader strongly wanted better relations with Rome. For instance, Moscow desired the Pope's mediation in moments of crisis; the world had recently trembled during the Cuban missile crisis. Moreover, Khrushchev said he wanted to open private lines of communication with the Vatican.[2]

Thus, change was sweeping through the Church. The Pope withdrew the Church from much of Italian politics.[3] In Latin America, churchmen began supporting movements opposed to the dictatorships that the Church had long supported. But for many Catholics, who were concerned with issues such as birth control, whether priests should marry, and a host of other issues that governed their lives, the change wasn't fast enough. Droves of Catholics, including priests and nuns, left the Church. But for others, the changes weren't wanted at all.

When he received word that Pope John XXIII had died on June 3, 1963, Cardinal Spellman wasn't surprised. For months he had known the Pope was seriously ill. Cancer had finally taken him, and John had seen no shining renewal of his religion in his final days. What had irritated Spellman up to the end was that John, although ill, had vigorously pursued his plans to change the Church and encouraged others to do so. Now, Spellman heaved a sigh of relief. There would be a new pope.

John had taken his toll. Spellman's Church was challenged from within as it had not been for centuries. The trappings of medieval grandeur and the endless rules and regulations binding people's lives were being stripped away. Spellman, in particular, chafed under the Church's liberal tilt in foreign policy.

As he prepared for John's funeral, Spellman was visited by a ranking C.I.A. officer.[4] The agency kept a wary eye on the Vatican and knew that the Cardinal and his conservative views had been unfashionable in Rome during John's reign. The agent sought some assurance that under the next pope the Vatican would get back on the right track—the one that Pacelli and Spellman had followed. The cooperation between the Church and the agency had been taken for granted during Pius's years; that made Pope John's turnaround so much more troublesome to the C.I.A. "Change in the Church," a C.I.A. report dated May 13, 1963, less than a month before John's death, noted that a number of Church officials, such as Spellman, were "disturbed about what was going on in the Church . . . and some fear he [the Pope] is politically naive and unduly influenced by the handful of 'liberal' clerics with whom he is in close contact."[5]

What was obvious was that Spellman and his old cronies—Count Galeazzi, Cardinal Pizzardo, and Mother Pascalina—were out of favor. John's inner circle had consisted of men Spellman disdained, such as Cicognani, Augustin Cardinal Bea, who headed the Secretariat for Promoting Christian Unity, and Igino Cardinale, the Vatican's chief of protocol. The agency report, for instance, lamented a "new approach toward Italian politics which is permissive rather than positive," because it marked a point when the Vatican stopped using every weapon at its disposal to oppose Communist candidates.[6]

The agent who visited Spellman was more troubled by the Church's shift in Latin America than anyplace else. Bishops had begun to speak out against some of the repressive Latin governments that the United States and Spellman had long supported. Conceding that the bishops had "genuine social grievances" in some cases, the agent nonetheless contended that the bishops, no matter how well-intentioned, were abetting Communism, even if that wasn't their intention.[7] Spellman was well aware of what was happening. He had reports about liberal priests and Pope John's bishops working in Central and South America.

The Cardinal himself had had a brush with John's liberalism. The Pope had once attempted to get Spellman to disassociate himself from the dictatorship of Nicaragua's Anastasio Somoza Debayle. John's problem was that he was too kind. Recognizing that Spellman's world had changed with the death of Pius, the Pope had tried to depend on Spellman where he thought he could. In 1959, John made Spellman his special delegate to a Eucharistic Congress, or church meeting to discuss regional problems, which was held in Guatemala. As usual, Spellman planned to visit a number of other countries en route. John asked the Cardinal to represent him but requested that Spellman, when in Nicaragua, refrain from having his picture taken with Somoza, who had just had a number of political prisoners executed. Spellman ignored the request. He had his picture taken with the dictator and agreed when Somoza asked him to permit his portrait to grace a Nicaraguan stamp. Spellman humbly said he didn't want just his picture on the stamp but Pope John's as well. Somoza issued two stamps, both bearing the likenesses of the Pope and Cardinal.[8]

The C.I.A. agent and Spellman both worried that John had robbed the Church of much of its political power. The agent wanted to know Spellman's thinking on the possibility of electing a pope who saw the world through the eyes of a Pius XII, rather than those of a John XXIII. Spellman wondered himself. The Cardinal was no longer the authority on Vatican undercurrents that he once was. Many of his pipelines were clogged, because John had been secretive and he hadn't trusted the kinds of men Spellman relied on. Moreover, Spellman's old high-handedness still grated on members of the curia, so even many conservatives within its ranks weren't willing to tell Spellman what they knew.

Thus Spellman was wary when he arrived in Rome. He had tentatively decided to support a movement behind Cardinal Siri. Spellman wasn't all that taken with the man whom he had known since his student days in Rome, but Siri's rabid anti-Communism was comparable to Spellman's own. Once at the Vatican, however, Spellman pragmatically changed candidates. The entire liberal Northern European contingent of cardinals opposed Siri, and when combined with other opponents, they had more than enough might to crush him. Therefore Spellman supported the man who was most likely to win, even though he was a man Spellman himself never would have chosen. The candidate was Montini, with whom Spellman had exchanged bitter words during the Mark Clark fiasco.

Montini, as Spellman knew, wasn't without his enemies. The Spanish cardinals, for instance, opposed him. Montini had incurred their wrath as well as Franco's a year earlier when, at the urging of left-wing students, he uncharacteristically fired off a letter to *Il Caudillo* imploring him not to execute an anarchist condemned to death. Franco was incensed; the anarchist hadn't been condemned to death, but to life in prison. Franco was further antagonized because he heard about Montini's blundering plea from the press before actually receiving the letter.[9]

When Spellman approached Montini the candidate was in a receptive mood. When the Cardinal emerged from a closed-door meeting with the candidate, they had reached some sort of agreement. Spellman joined the other American cardinals—Ritter, Cushing, Wright, and Meyer—who were already in Montini's camp. In Spellman, Montini knew he was actually getting two votes. McIntyre was bound to vote the way his mentor told him.

Thus, when the cardinals entered the conclave Montini was reasonably assured of victory. He was considered a progressive, but he wasn't expected to pursue change with the gusto of his predecessor. Moreover, he had Cicognani's support and that of many middle-of-the-roaders because he had agreed to keep Cicognani on as secretary of state rather than replace him with a liberal. Many conservatives and liberals felt they could abide Montini because he wasn't an extremist. Indeed, he often took so much time making up his mind that he did nothing.

As always, the conclave area was sealed off from the rest of the world. The marshal of the conclave and the colonel commandant of the Swiss Guards had scoured the premises for forbidden cameras, radios, bugs, and intruders. All telephones were disconnected. All windows over St. Peter's Square had been blacked out to prevent anyone from signaling to the outside. Outside, St. Peter's Square was mobbed. Television cameras were trained on the chimney atop the Sistine Chapel. The C.I.A. station in Rome was anxious to relay the news as well.

On June 21, just a day after the first ballots were cast, a puff of light-colored smoke arose from the chimney. There was a new pope. Roaring cheers burst from the crowd in the square. Montini had been elected. He chose the name Pope Paul VI. The mood inside the conclave was calm since few cardinals had expected the appearance of any last-minute dark horse.

Strangely, the puff of smoke hadn't been the first signal declaring that Montini had been elected. The news flashed to the C.I.A.'s headquarters in Langley, Virginia, from Rome before the press or anyone else had it. Immediately, it went to the White House. Just how the agency knew wasn't revealed. Later there was speculation in Rome that the C.I.A. had given one of the cardinals a tiny radio transmitter to conceal on his person.[10] The cardinal was almost certainly an American.

Cardinal Spellman's power base was washing away. Pope Paul didn't rely on Spellman for every twist and turn of foreign policy or recommendation as to whom to appoint to bishoprics around the nation. Indeed, an appointment was made to Buffalo, almost in Spellman's backyard, and he learned of it after the fact. Only at the White House had he gained in stature in recent years. After the assassination of John Kennedy, Lyndon Johnson turned to Spellman as so many other presidents had done. To much of the Catholic rank and file, to the wealthy, and even to many New York politicians, Spellman was still a man of great influence and importance. To those who knew him only slightly, he was still the humble man who had become archbishop in 1939. To those who knew him well, he was still a shrewd politician.

The applause was thunderous when Cardinal Spellman approached the microphone at the head table of the Waldorf-Astoria's Grand Ballroom. The four thousand guests, mostly clergy, wealthy Catholics, and Catholic politicians, stood almost in unison as their clapping and cheers filled the cavernous room. Some had tears in their eyes as they gazed on the Cardinal, who was almost lost behind a blanket of red roses. The dinner, the largest in the hotel's history, marked Spellman's seventy-fifth birthday.

The Cardinal had just been paid a glowing tribute by the Jesuit Robert Gannon, his old friend and the former president of Fordham, who had become Spellman's official biographer several years earlier. At the dinner the reason Spellman had chosen him for the biographer's task was obvious. Gannon portrayed his boss as the good shepherd of New York's two million Catholics, concluding that the Cardinal was "fearless, tireless, and shrewd as any Yankee in Whitman, but at the same time, he is humble, whimsical, sentimental, incredibly thoughtful, supremely loyal and, above all, a real priest."

That humbleness was the theme of a prayer Spellman had prepared for the occasion:

What return shall I make for all that I have received?
To my people, my care and my solicitude.

To my priests, justice and charity.

To the bishops, my brotherly affection.

To the Holy Father, Pope Paul, the love of a son and the undying fidelity of a Catholic Bishop.

And to God, for this grace to me unworthy, I bow my head and direct my prayer that his grace in me may not be in vain. The burden is heavy. Without God, my capacity is nothing. . . .

When he finished, women in the audience openly wept. Later, more than a thousand people who wished him "happy birthday" kissed his sapphire-and-diamond episcopal ring.

At the age of seventy-five, Spellman had accomplished a great deal. He had built thirty-seven churches, one hundred thirty schools, five hospitals, and scores of convents, old-age homes, and orphanages. As military vicar, he had made his imprint on the armed forces. He bore the major responsibility for the Church's largest charity, Catholic Relief Services, with its $176-million-a-year foreign aid program. For twenty-five years, he had had a strong hand in shaping the policies of his Church and his government.

Spellman was now moving against the tide. His tirades against Communism and his jingoism seemed increasingly out of place in a world that had been exposed to the benevolent Pope John. Moreover, social issues, including race and poverty, were becoming major concerns within his own nation, but they were topics about which the aged Cardinal was either silent or disdainful. When not angry Spellman was often philosophical about the erosion of the powerful conservative fortress he had erected. "I had it all," Monsignor Clark recalled his saying. "There won't be much left after I'm gone."

He was reminded of the decrease in his influence in a number of ways. Several months before his birthday Spellman had attacked a Broadway play, *The Deputy*, as "an outrageous desecration of the honor of a great and good man." The play, which Spellman, naturally, hadn't seen, was a critical look at Pope Pius XII's failure to speak out against the Holocaust. The very fact that the play had been written and produced in New York was vivid testimony to a world different from the one Spellman was accustomed to dominating. The Cardinal issued a statement contending that after Pacelli died, Spellman himself had received many messages from Jews who "felt deeply that they, as we, had lost a loving father." *The Deputy*, he declared, had been written to "drive a wedge between Christians and Jews."

But no longer was the entertainment industry cowed by the Cardinal. Herman Shumlin, the drama's producer, declared that Spellman's statement was a "calculated threat to really drive a wedge between Christians and Jews." The purpose of the play, Shumlin said, was to ask both "Christians and Jews to examine their conscience and their own responsibility." Further, he noted that Boston's Cardinal Cushing had stated, during a televised interview, "I don't think it would do any harm for any intelligent person to see the play." Cushing, when asked about Spellman's reaction, suggested that Spellman should see the play before condemning it.

Unlike his past campaigns, such as those against *The Miracle* and *Baby Doll*, which had made producers ill and state and city officials act like Spanish inquisitors, *The Deputy* sparked no massive rallies. No major Catholic organizations, such as the Holy Name Society or the Catholic War Veterans, took up the battle cry. A few pickets appeared, but most New Yorkers dismissed Spellman's rantings.

What may have been the Cardinal's last effective moral campaign ended when the comedian Lenny Bruce was sentenced, on December 21, 1964, in the longest, costliest, and most fiercely contested obscenity trial in the history of New York City. The Cardinal at times had been the object of Bruce satires. ("Spellman does *it* with the nuns.") After Spellman complained to city officials, Bruce was arrested routinely when he gave performances. But a direct cause and effect was never proved. "It was rumored that Spellman was behind the trial," Martin Garbus, Bruce's defense attorney, reminisced. "We wanted to believe desperately that Cardinal Spellman was behind the whole thing. Lenny firmly believed it and that raised it to the level of truth in many people's eyes."[11]

Spellman's heel-dragging on the issue of race was more obvious. The Catholic Church had done little to attract Negroes. The priesthood had few; there would be no black bishops in New York until after Spellman died. Racism wasn't unknown in the ranks of the hierarchy. Cardinal McIntyre, for example, never hid his prejudice and priests asked him in private not to make racial slurs.[12]

Spellman wasn't hostile to blacks, but they didn't have political power, nor could they help him in other ways. Thus, the Cardinal became angry when Bishop Maguire, as Spellman said, "wasted" $500 on a lifetime membership for Spellman in the National Association for the Advancement of Colored People. To make matters worse, Spellman found himself locked into attending an NAACP dinner. When he arrived at the banquet, the Cardinal was stunned and pleased to find that he was given a standing ovation that went on for many minutes. When he finally had a chance to speak, he humbly noted, "You know, I'm a lifetime member of the NAACP." Booming applause once again greeted him. After the dinner Spellman wondered about his show of popularity among blacks. He joked about it, but he couldn't understand its origin. It must have been simply a matter of his lofty office. More than anyone else, Spellman knew he had certainly done nothing to deserve it.[13]

In fact, Spellman, like his friend J. Edgar Hoover, was suspicious of the burgeoning black civil-rights movement, believing it probably was Communist-inspired. To the Cardinal, sit-ins and freedom marches smacked of subversion. He periodically met with Hoover, and they lamented what they perceived as the deteriorating state of the world. Spellman held similar discussions with F.B.I. contacts when cruising on Roy Cohn's yacht, *Wavemaker*, in Florida. One man who was frequently aboard when Spellman visited was Lou Nichols, a former F.B.I. agent who had been considered Hoover's unofficial public-relations man. Nichols had become a vice president at Lew Rosenstiel's Schenley Industries. Spellman loved the gossip that F.B.I. types related about the sexual practices of congressmen and other people of prominence. Much of the information apparently came directly from Hoover's files.

On one such occasion, an F.B.I. contact sought Spellman's assistance. The Cardinal was asked to make a public statement condemning the philandering of the Reverend Martin Luther King, Jr.[14] Spellman, much as he would have liked to do so, begged off. While Hoover was probably hoping against hope that the Cardinal would take on the task, the F.B.I. chief was amazed when Spellman was unable to prevent King from receiving a special honor. King had wanted an audience with the Pope. When Hoover learned of the request, he had asked Spellman to block the meeting. (Hoover apparently didn't know what animosity existed between Paul VI and Spellman.) After the audience Hoover couldn't be calmed. He wrote: "Astounding . . . I am amazed that the Pope gave an audience to such a ———." (Excised by the F.B.I.)[15]

By the mid-1960s, it had become obvious that Spellman as a churchman had to do something for the civil-rights movement. Churches of all denominations were supporting the cause with personnel and money. Moreover, priests and nuns from other archdioceses were getting involved. But when people looked to the Cardinal for inspiration, they were disappointed. Finally, a delegation of priests met with Spellman and bluntly told him that he must act. The Church in New York not only seemed coldly aloof but even appeared to be against a popular movement that was seen by many to have a base in a true religious spirit. Nuns from St. Louis, Chicago, and Detroit, where bishops were vocally in favor of civil rights, were heading to Selma, Alabama, for the most dramatic display of support for the movement to date. The priests made Spellman realize how awkward his archdiocese would look if it weren't represented. The Cardinal capitulated by providing funds to send a band of New York priests and nuns to the demonstration.

Several months later Apostolic Delegate Vagnozzi asked Spellman his views with regard to "priests, religious and Sisters participating in public demonstrations."[16] On June 29, 1965, Spellman responded: "My personal opinion is not in favor of these demonstrations." But he noted that he hadn't adopted a public position, adding that where religions had been involved, the reaction was one of approval by "organizations and communities in favor of civil rights."[17]

That Spellman relented on the Selma march didn't mean he was about to embrace other changes. He especially disliked the young priests around the nation whose social consciences increasingly rebuked his own brand of Catholicism. The Cardinal believed the needs of the aged, the sick, and the homeless were being met with money. But what he saw as practical, others viewed as mechanical. The Cardinal wasn't a proponent of better housing for the poor, civil-rights legislation, or increased job opportunities for the underprivileged. To date, Spellman's priests had taken his point of view for granted. With few exceptions, such as George Ford, Spellman's priests kept their heads down and performed their duties; the more ambitious among them came to the attention of the Powerhouse and were brought into administrative posts. Inevitably, however, the radical changes taking place within the United States—such preoccupations of the young as racism, poverty, and religious renewal—eventually found their way into the rigid, conservative New York archdiocese. The result was a fierce battle, which turned the Powerhouse into a fortress that seemed under steady attack.

One of the earliest radical priests in New York was Father David Kirk. A Southerner, he had converted to Catholicism at the University of Alabama, where he was always interested in social causes. As he described it, "What made me uneasy was the reactionary character of the Roman Catholic Church. In my part of Alabama, the Church was the Irish Catholicism associated with racial and political conservatism."[18]

Kirk found a Catholic church near his university that impressed him, but it wasn't of the Roman rite. He took instructions in the Melkite Church, one of several Eastern churches that hadn't broken with Rome but were responsible to their own patriarch, not the Pope in Rome. The pastor of the church struck Kirk as socially concerned, "unlike the materialistic Irish who ran the Church next door." He graduated from college in 1954 and spent the next several years teaching, working for the NAACP, getting involved in the civil-rights movement, and working for a master's degree. He wound up in New York, where he finished his master's degree at Columbia University and worked for Dorothy Day's *Catholic Worker*. Kirk spent a great deal of time considering becoming a priest, but he dismissed a traditional seminary as "being for children, not men." He finally went to Rome, where he entered Beda College, whose seminarians passed hours reading and doing social work. His exposure to Rome scandalized him. "The wealth of the Church! It seemed so wrong!"[19]

After his ordination in 1964, Kirk and another man he had met in the seminary, Lyle Young, returned to New York, where they taught school, worked with delinquent children, and saved money to open an ecumenical center that would serve the community and foster change. In the fall of 1966 they opened Emmaus House, which quickly became a center for radical Catholic activity. Informal masses were held; draft counseling was offered. Priests considering leaving their vocations stayed there while collecting their thoughts. Much of the activity of Emmaus House was rooted in Dorothy Day's Catholic Worker Movement. Like Day, Kirk looked askance at the Church's superstructure and the men such as Spellman who ruled over it. Indeed, a peek inside Emmaus House revealed a far different side of the Church than the one the Cardinal represented. Non-Catholics were frequent visitors; discussion groups about the Vietnam war, the role of missionaries in Latin America, or the level of help priests should give to guerrilla movements in Central America might be in progress. Mass was held to the accompaniment of guitars and singing. The walls were covered with pictures of Martin Luther King, Jr., Malcolm X, Gandhi, Thomas Merton, and other heroes of the Left. Vatican II had squeezed past the Statue of Liberty.

The Powerhouse was quick to respond. Kirk recalled that Spellman's emissary, Bishop Terence Cooke, had a formal list of grievances against him. Kirk was accused, among other things, of having Marxists at Emmaus House, of participating in peace demonstrations, and of being involved in liturgical experimentation. Later, Kirk said, the American Melkite bishop was pressured by Spellman into reassigning Kirk to a parish in Rochester, New York. Kirk talked his superior out of the move.[20] To Spellman's frustration, there was little he could do. The Melkite Church didn't come under his jurisdiction. Kirk continued his activities, fending off the forces of conservatism with one arm while trying to build a more human Church with the other.

Though disdainful of priests who worked with projects such as Emmaus House, Spellman was furious with two priests who symbolized a challenge not so much to his Church as to his Americanism. They were the brothers Daniel and Philip Berrigan, a Jesuit and a Josephite priest, respectively, who intuitively knew how to attract attention to themselves and their causes. Daniel Berrigan, the well-known poet, was close to Dorothy Day, and his poetry at times criticized the muffled social consciousness of the Church. Philip, a natural radical, raced into what he perceived as just causes. What grossly offended Spellman was the brothers' antiwar activism.

The Berrigans first became identified with the antiwar movement as a result of a petition, a "declaration of conscience," that condemned the round-the-clock bombing of North Vietnam that President Johnson had ordered in February 1965. The petition, signed by hundreds of people including Martin Luther King, Jr., Benjamin Spock, Linus Pauling, and Bayard Rustin, bore the signatures of only two prominent Catholics—the Berrigans. Soon, they were permanent fixtures at antiwar rallies, the first Catholic priests to participate in New York.

Spellman believed the brothers were duped into a Communist position. Furthermore, he was angered by their Jehovah-like pronouncements. Not only did the Berrigans contradict Spellman's jingoism, but they also used the same moral rhetoric as Spellman himself. "To wage war in modern times as it is being waged in Vietnam is forbidden," Daniel Berrigan declared at one rally. "In such a war, man stands outside the blessing of God. He stands, in fact, under his curse." Philip Berrigan went a step further and likened the war in Vietnam to racism in the United States, a position he adopted even before Martin Luther King, Jr., did. Initially, Catholics were reluctant to embrace the antiwar movement. Not just Spellman but many Catholics bent over backward to prove their Americanism, and in the process they became ardent patriots. They accepted the righteousness of their country, just as they accepted their Church. Thus, many Catholics were shocked and outraged when the Berrigans began condemning the government. The people of Newburgh, New York, where Philip Berrigan taught, became so alienated that he was transferred to Baltimore.

As the nation became polarized over the war, Spellman came to personify the hawks. Increasingly, he appeared with the President, military figures, and National Guard and ROTC units. And as Catholics filtered into the peace movement, the Cardinal increasingly blamed the Berrigans for much of the dissent he saw erupting around him. When David Miller, a twenty-two-year-old Catholic Worker who was close to the Berrigans, defied a law against destroying draft cards by burning his, Spellman blamed the Berrigans. The youth, he said, was "just a simple-minded fool."

The Powerhouse's unhappiness with Dan Berrigan was expressed through the Cardinal's secretaries, who routinely called the Jesuit "provincial" and let it be known that "the Cardinal isn't happy."[21] Such a warning wasn't taken lightly. Though officially autonomous, the Jesuits were in an awkward position in New York. The order had benefited greatly over the years from Spellman. Many individual Jesuits owed him for past favors. More significantly, he helped the order obtain a great deal of money. It was he who had mustered congressional forces behind a bill to pay for damaged religious property in the Philippines after World War II, for which the Jesuits had received millions of dollars. Also, he was constantly helping his alma mater, the Jesuit-run Fordham University.

Spellman finally moved to sterner action when tragedy occurred. A deranged young Catholic Worker, Roger LaPorte, dramatically protested U.S. involvement in the Vietnam war by dousing himself with gasoline and immolating himself on the steps of the United Nations. The act horrified the world. When Daniel Berrigan delivered the funeral sermon, he didn't condemn the youth's suicide, but ended his address on the note, "His death was offered so that others may live." Spellman was furious. He considered the tragedy a public embarrassment, and he believed Berrigan had acted irresponsibly. At the time of the youth's death on November 9, 1965, Spellman was in Rome for a session of the Vatican Council. He sent Bishop Maguire home, apparently with the mission of censuring Berrigan, who had become a symbol to Spellman of all that was wrong with both America and the Church since John XXIII had become Pope. The Cardinal saw his world disintegrating and his authority constantly challenged. Berrigan's prominence as a poet made him that much more formidable an enemy.[22]

In New York there was talk that Dan Berrigan would be thrown out of the priesthood. Instead, his superiors hastily dispatched him to Latin America. When he returned he was an even bigger thorn in Spellman's side as he stepped up his antiwar activities. In 1968 the Berrigans were part of a group arrested in Catonsville, Maryland, for invading a Selective Service System office, seizing draft records, and burning them. They became known as the Catonsville Nine. Philip left the priesthood; Daniel remained.

The Berrigans may have started out as an anomaly, but they soon became bellwethers of liberal Catholic thought. Within Spellman's Church, what had been unthinkable had become almost routine. Spellman, for example, was actually criticized in a student newspaper at Catholic Manhattan College, and the chancery and St. Patrick's became targets for antiwar protests. In December 1965 college students marched outside Spellman's residence, protesting what they termed the "muzzling" of certain priests active in the antiwar movement. The signs they carried told how much dissent now existed. One, for instance, stated: EXILE AND CONSTRAINT ARE TOOLS OF TOTALITARIANISM. A second proclaimed, END POWER POLITICS IN THE CHURCH. Inside his residence, Spellman berated the youths. He delighted in using the tunnel that connected his residence to St. Patrick's so that he could leave by means of the cathedral, thus outwitting the pickets who wanted to confront him.

Spellman knew that both he and all he symbolized were being rejected by a growing and vociferous segment of the Church. Instead of trying to accommodate his critics, the Cardinal became more obstinate. He was old and no longer saw a need to be flexible, at least not with Pope John's legions.

Rome trained its men well. Ranking churchmen, no matter what their personal feelings toward one another, publicly always tried to appear harmonious. Enmity must never be shown; feuds must never be obvious. They were viewed as family matters to be worked out behind the scenes, away from the prying eyes of others. Even the most independent of Church officials operated by the rules. The Cardinal knew it was a game that must be played so that the hierarchical structure of the Church remained fundamentally unchallenged. Thus, he and Pope John XXIII had always appeared publicly cordial to each other. The same was true for Spellman's relationship with Pope Paul VI, no matter how little he respected the former papal secretary Montini.

Cardinal Spellman stood on the apron of the runway at New York's Kennedy Airport on the clear, brisk morning of October 4, 1965. He was in the midst of a multitude of churchmen from around the nation who strained with excitement as the jet from Rome taxied to a halt. The roaring engines had barely died when Pope Paul VI, a hollow-eyed man in stark papal white, appeared in the aircraft's open doorway. The crowd cheered and pressed forward as the Pope raised his hand to bless the multitude. The first person he met was United Nations Secretary-General U Thant, but before greeting anyone else personally, the Pope wanted to address the massive crowd.

"Greetings to you, America," Paul said into a bank of microphones at the foot of the ramp he descended. "The first Pope to set foot upon your land blesses you with all his heart."

After his brief address the Pope was greeted individually by scores of public officials and churchmen. Their ranks included Secretary of State Dean Rusk, Governor Rockefeller, Mayor Wagner, and Senator Robert F. Kennedy. The Church's cardinals and bishops crushed around Paul, and in their midst the seventy-six-year-old Spellman shuffled forward. The Cardinal's arms were outstretched and his face was alit with a smile. "Welcome to America," Spellman yelled above the din that engulfed them. "God bless you," the Pope replied. They embraced for all the world to see.

The display of collegiality masked a deep bitterness. The Pope was in New York not to honor Spellman but to address the United Nations, where he intended to criticize indirectly Spellman's toughguy stance on Vietnam. The Pope's televised visit was an example of subtle Vatican diplomacy whereby a prelate could be humbled while unknowing millions witnessed a triumphant papal visit. Churchmen, however, knew that something was afoot. The Pope had arranged to stay only one day in New York, and this, considering the time and effort that went into the trip, was a sure sign that something was wrong.

Weeks earlier Spellman had correctly identified the snub when the Pope's advance men from Rome had visited the Powerhouse to make sure the visit went as smoothly as possible. The Cardinal had pressed for the Pope to stay longer, as his guest, but the men from Rome had been evasive. Finally, the Cardinal had grown angry.

"These crafty Italians," he muttered to Monsignor Patrick Ahern, one of his secretaries.[23]

Now, with Spellman at his side, the Pope entered a specially constructed open limousine to begin a twenty-five-mile procession through the streets of New York to St. Patrick's. Within minutes, however, the Pope and the Cardinal changed to a bubble-top limousine. A chilly wind whipped beneath the sunny skies, making the open car less than pleasant, but the reason for switching cars was due to F.B.I. reports that the Pope's life might be in danger. New York City police commissioner Vincent Broderick had conveyed a sense of urgency to the vast retinue of bishops and monsignors who had accompanied the Pope. Taking no chances, Broderick had eighteen thousand policemen lining the route the Pope would take.

The entourage wound through Harlem, where there had been a riot the year before, into the silk-stocking district of Manhattan's Upper East Side. The Pope and Spellman were in the second limousine. Broderick, who was in the third limousine, became angry when he saw the Pope's car suddenly slow down, as though about to stop in front of the Foundling Hospital. He had specifically warned Spellman that there must be no stops; the commissioner knew that even eighteen thousand policemen might not be able to stop a sniper's bullet. Spellman, however, had tried to deliver the Pope to the front door of his favorite charity. When he realized what was happening, Broderick angrily boomed over the police radio connecting the limousines, "Don't stop! Keep going! Don't stop!"[24]

The millions who thronged the parade route saw the Pope and the Cardinal amiably waving to one and all. But neither man had ever liked the other. What disturbed the Pope was Spellman's hawkishness on Vietnam while he was quietly trying to work for peace. After each of the Cardinal's outbursts, such as "less than victory is inconceivable," Paul found himself having to make counterbalancing statements about the necessity for peace. Pope Pius XII may have viewed Vietnam as another battleground between Communism and Christianity, but Paul saw the situation as a calamity that must be ended, and he had come to New York to deliver this message on American soil, Spellman's home ground.

Pope Paul never liked to confront problems directly, so Spellman believed that there was little chance such a man would embarrass him. Such an occurrence would have gone against the grain of Paul's personality and his Roman training. The two had had talks about Spellman's support of the U.S. war effort, but Paul's pleas to have Spellman temper his enthusiasm fell on deaf ears. The Vatican was much concerned about Spellman's holding too much power. The money he collected gave him enormous influence, and he still was the military vicar of the U.S. Armed Forces. There was growing sentiment in Rome that the Cardinal of New York should not also be the military vicar; the dual role vested too much authority in one man. Thus, the cautious Pope, who always wore wool trousers even in summer for fear of catching cold, had made this dramatic trip as a way of rebuking this disobedient cardinal and calling attention within the United States to the misguidedness of the war.

When the entourage arrived at St. Patrick's, the streets were filled with people who had been waiting as long as twelve hours to get a glimpse of the pontiff. The Pope moved up the cathedral's steps and down the main aisle, blessing people on either side. Spellman made the most of the occasion. The first Pope to visit the United States was in his cathedral and was constantly at his side: Spellman acted as though he had been given a special honor. Indeed, after Spellman welcomed Paul to the church, the Cardinal was pleased with the Pope's formal, courteous response: "We thank our beloved son, Cardinal Spellman, your esteemed archbishop, for his warm welcome. . . ."

The pews of St. Patrick's were filled with guests: government officials and their wives, members of the clergy, and many of Spellman's relatives. The Cardinal had personally overseen the details of the papal visit, ranging from what kinds of flowers should be on the altar to the guest list. He wanted the day as impressive as possible. He wasn't honoring Montini; he was honoring a pope, and Spellman was fully conscious of the impact of that office on the world at large.

Spellman arranged a lavish luncheon for the Pope and his party. Like a medieval monarch, the Cardinal surveyed the gathering in the vast walnut-paneled room at the chancery that served as a dining hall. The table was set with crystal, silver, and gold. Members of Spellman's family and his favorite priests and bishops mingled with the men from Rome. White-gloved waiters tended the table and the Pope himself sat on a hand-carved throne. When Spellman proposed a toast to the Pope the guests all rose. The Pope was polite, as always, but not warm. Spellman's relatives, who for years had basked in the glory of the Cardinal's closeness to Pope Pius XII and his power in Rome and America, were distanced from Paul.

The Pope himself appeared ill at ease, restlessly glancing around the room. When informed that President Johnson had arrived from Washington and awaited him at the Waldorf-Astoria, Paul almost seemed relieved when he said he must go. The meeting would be a historic one, the first between a Pope and a President in America. Moreover, there was the overshadowing issue of the war. Since Spellman had helped arrange the meeting he assumed he would act as the Pope's interpreter, a role he had undertaken more than thirty years earlier as an ambitious young priest. But Paul stopped him. The Pope had his own personal interpreter; Spellman wasn't needed. Moreover, the Pope made it clear that he didn't want Spellman present at the meeting. Cardinal Spellman was such a public supporter of Johnson's war policies that Pope Paul didn't want to confuse the public about where he and the Church stood.

The Pope didn't intend to challenge Johnson or to do anything that might be construed as such. Paul realized the difficulty of the President's position. Thus, when the Pope and the President met in suite 35-H of the Waldorf-Astoria, Paul was solicitous. He and Johnson later said they spoke in generalities about world peace and human welfare. But the President realized the Pope was against his military venture. Spellman's differences with the Pope became more obvious when the Pope moved over to the United Nations to address the General Assembly. The great hall was crowded with dignitaries from around the world. Of the one hundred seventeen countries then belonging to the organization, only the representatives of Albania boycotted the Pope's speech. The audience stirred when the Kennedys, including former First Lady Jacqueline Kennedy, arrived. A hush fell over the auditorium, however, when the Pope mounted the green marble rostrum. Though a fragile-looking man, Paul seemed to gain strength as he stood before them and intoned the message he had brought from Rome: "No more war, never again war!"

As the Pope gave his address he never mentioned Vietnam, but his purpose was clear. "Peace," he declared. "It is peace which must guide the destinies of peoples and all mankind."

Spellman sat amid the prominent audience, his benign smile in place. He viewed the Pope's position as another criticism of America, *his* nation. The men at the Vatican, he believed, were merely taking the United States to task again. Moreover, he believed that since the death of Pacelli the papacy had once again fallen into incapable hands.

After the speech their Roman training once again served the Pope and the Cardinal well. They continued to behave cordially toward one another. They posed for pictures, blessed throngs, and appeared to chat amiably; they were both diplomats. An overt sign of displeasure, they realized, would help neither man.

That evening the Pope continued his theme of peace when he addressed ninety thousand people who crowded Yankee Stadium. Eerily lit by thousands of candles held aloft, the stadium resounded with cheers. Paul's gold vestments rustled in the night wind as he ascended the steps to a platform containing an altar. The pontiff's voice echoed throughout the park: "First of all you must love peace. Second thought: You must serve the cause of peace. Serve it and not make use of it for aims other than the true aims of peace. Third thought: Peace must be based on moral and religious principles, which must make it sincere and stable."

The Pope's final refrain again seemed directed at Spellman. "Politics," he declared, "do not suffice to sustain a durable peace."

After the Pope's speech a mass was held. The rituals and pageantry of the service showed the impact of Vatican II on the Church in that much of the medieval splendor was muted. Cardinals, for instance, had given up their capa magna, a long scarlet cloak with a hood lined with fur, and their fifteen-foot scarlet silk robes.

When Paul finally descended from the platform and headed toward the limousine that would take him to the airport, Spellman followed him. The crowd applauded wildly. The Pope and the Cardinal departed, their limousine flanked by white-helmeted motorcycle police as they sped into the darkness. At the airport, Spellman and Pope Paul were under the gaze of hundreds of thousands of well-wishers and the glare of television cameras. The two embraced, Spellman bent and kissed the pontiff's ring, and the Cardinal remained long enough to watch the Pope's plane disappear into the sky. Paul's words of peace still seemed to ring in the night air.

The Pope soon realized that he had failed with Spellman. After he left New York, Paul was in the final stages of a delicate campaign to bring about a negotiated peace in Vietnam. Vatican communications offices had been reorganized to place greater emphasis on direct links with Vatican representatives in Southeast Asia. Rome beefed up its diplomatic missions in Asia, especially in countries that had direct contact with China and Hanoi. Archbishop Igino Cardinale, the apostolic delegate in London, was in touch with Vietnamese representatives in Europe. The apostolic delegate in Paris, Archbishop Paolo Bertoli, was working on the French to pressure both Hanoi and Saigon. The Vatican was even active in Eastern European capitals such as Budapest, where the so-called Red Bishop Endre Hamvas, who was appointed with the approval of the Communist regime, was trying to act as a mediator. Vatican representatives in Cambodia were reportedly in direct contact with the Vietcong. From all over the world, intelligence poured into the Vatican from diplomats, religious orders, missionaries, and Catholic laymen, and the Pope and Ho Chi Minh even exchanged direct messages.

But as the Pope's activities escalated, so did Spellman's. He became increasingly hawkish. Again, he returned to Vietnam to spend Christmas with the troops, just as he had done in previous wars. But this time his politics wasn't sanctioned by the Vatican. As he stepped off a military transport in Saigon, an American Army officer unwittingly noted a discouraging fact. "We hardly count it a war if you don't come," he told the Cardinal, and Spellman beamed his approval.

The Cardinal used his visit to propagandize the American war. In his mind, there was no question of the righteousness of the cause. When asked by a reporter in Saigon whether the U.S. presence was justified, Spellman responded with the kind of saber-rattling statement that now made many Catholics shudder and was bound to polarize Americans further. "My country, may it always be right," he replied. "Right or wrong, my country!" The concerns of his Church were now secondary in his hierarchy of values.

The response was largely one of dismay, and all the editorials by liberal Catholics and all the hand-wringing on the part of a growing number of priests were summarized in a letter to the editor of *The New York Times* on December 24, 1965. "It looks as if Cardinal Spellman is in Vietnam to bless the guns which the Pope is begging us to put down," wrote the Reverend William F. Powers, of Our Lady of Good Counsel Church. The priest touched what was a very raw nerve at the Vatican. Spellman's Americanism was out of control—the Cardinal had broken with the Pope. From a Vatican perspective, even Spellman's Christmas cards in 1965, the year the Pope negotiated a temporary truce, were an insult. The picture on the cards was of him standing before a fighter plane with two military officers.

CHAPTER THIRTEEN

The Powerhouse Falters

S PELLMAN'S CONTROVERSIAL POSITION HAD A CURIOUS EFFECT on his political power. On the local and state level, his influence began to wane. Wary of anyone contentious, New York politicians became shy about wanting to be seen with him; few were willing to support publicly his jingoistic remarks, even when they privately agreed with him. Not surprisingly, however, the Cardinal's influence on a national level increased dramatically. As his own war policies increasingly came under attack, President Johnson embraced Spellman. For a while, the Cardinal's moral authority helped Johnson fend off critics. Thus, the Cardinal's political career underwent yet another shift. While his moral pronouncements about such matters as movies and obscene literature fell on deaf ears within his own archdiocese, he became a prominent national figure once again. As in the 1940s and 1950s, Spellman was the face of the foe of the Red Menace, and he was the consecrator of an American military cause. Once again, he bustled in and out of the White House, a man with a mission.

When he became President, Johnson had looked around at traditional power bases and turned to Spellman. He had known, of course, of the antagonism between Spellman and Kennedy. But Johnson was just as likely to find a friend in a Kennedy foe and he wasn't about to carry on his predecessor's old feuds. Shortly after taking the reins of government, Johnson sent an intermediary to the Cardinal. The message was clear—the hard line about separation of Church and State was softened. Johnson swiftly proved that he had not spoken idly. On December 20, 1963, he signed into law the Higher Education Facilities Act, which provided $1.2 billion for college construction over a three-year period; some 842 Church-controlled colleges and universities—mostly Catholic—were among the beneficiaries. Months later, Johnson's Economic Opportunities Act of 1964 provided federal support for a variety of Church projects.

Johnson's motives weren't altruistic. He wanted Spellman's political support. Thus Spellman supported Johnson, not Barry Goldwater, for the presidency in 1964, even though the Cardinal was more attuned to Goldwater's conservatism. With Johnson, Spellman knew where he stood. He didn't like the President's liberal domestic policy, but Johnson had shown him that the Church would benefit from it. They were both practical men, and there was more than a tinge of the old Roosevelt-Spellman relationship about the way they understood one another. The President sought favors from the Cardinal, and Spellman expected favors in return. The bond with the President became the strongest that Spellman now had with any politician. The rest of his political alliances were collapsing.

Though neither man would have realized it when Johnson sent his emissary to Spellman in 1963, the area in which the President would most need the Cardinal was foreign affairs. In 1965, for instance, Johnson sought the churchman's help in the Dominican Republic. When leftists were involved in an uprising against one of the governments that came to power after Trujillo was assassinated four years earlier, Johnson had taken a Teddy Roosevelt "big stick" stand. Johnson sent U.S. Marines, ostensibly to restore order and safeguard American lives. In reality, the marines aided forces opposed to leftist supporters of Juan Bosch, whose own government fell in 1963.

The presence of the marines had sparked intense anti-Americanism in the Dominican Republic and a wave of criticism within the United States. While seeking a way to defuse the anti-Americanism, Johnson turned to Spellman, who had given the President his blessing for the invasion. The President wanted Spellman to dispatch priests to the Dominican Republic to beef up America's image, and he was willing to fund such a project generously. Pope Paul had apparently given the plan his imprimatur. Neither Spellman nor the Pope wanted to see the emergence of another Cuba.[1]

Cuba itself had been a lesson in frustration for Spellman, and he had vowed that another Castro wouldn't come to power. Before Castro was victorious, Spellman had tried to warn the U.S. government that the Cuban was a Communist, but State Department officials had ignored him. In the late 1950s many people at State had resented Spellman for backing McCarthy, who had sent tremors of terror throughout the entire department. "Spellman's information about Cuba was better than ours," Herbert Brownell would recall. "His intelligence was very, very good."[2]

(Whether Spellman actively tried to stop Castro isn't known. Nor is it known whether he played a role in the Bay of Pigs invasion of April 1961. Castro apparently believed he did. After the fiasco Castro criticized Spellman during radio broadcasts, referring to him as the "Cardinal of the Pentagon, the Central Intelligence Agency, and the North American monopolies." A week later, on May 5, 1961, priests in Cuba were accused of being "sources of hate" and "accomplices of Cardinal Spellman and Franco." Abruptly, Church schools were closed, many foreign priests were deported, and a handful were arrested for "warlike activities.")

Spellman aided Johnson in the Dominican Republic, even though he soon learned that the role the marines and the President played in the island's politics was different from what Johnson told the U.S. public. The information came to Spellman through Church channels. The Cardinal was contacted by the papal nuncio from Santo Domingo, Monsignor Clarizio, who begged Spellman to see for himself that the U.S. Marines weren't doing what the President said they were. Clarizio, however, had a credibility problem with Spellman. One of the post–Pope John liberal churchmen, Clarizio was identified with leftists and the pro-Bosch faction.

Spellman, of course, was too shrewd to investigate the issue personally. He dispatched a young intellectual, Father Robert Fox, the assistant director of Spanish missions in New York. Several weeks later, Fox returned from the Dominican Republic with a report that in essence substantiated what Clarizio had said, and criticized Johnson's methods and policies. The report never saw the light of day. Spellman shelved it and discounted Fox, whom he believed naive. Like Johnson, Spellman wanted to believe that Communists were behind the movement in the Dominican Republic, even when faced with evidence to the contrary.[3]

Thus, when Johnson raised the matter of sending priests to shine America's tarnished image, Spellman readily agreed and chose the Maryknoll order. As missionaries in any number of developing nations, the Maryknolls' presence wouldn't be considered odd. They could mingle with everyone from peasants to politicians. Besides, like most religious orders, the Maryknolls owed Spellman favors for helping them with fund-raising and recruiting programs.

Spellman approached John Considine, a politically active Maryknoll in Washington, and Maryknoll Bishop John Comber. As a result, a group of priests was assigned to the Dominican Republic. Their funding, $500,000 from the Agency for International Development, was for community projects and leadership training. When the priests arrived Clarizio wasn't happy. He knew that Fox's report had been dismissed. Now he saw what looked like another example of the kind of collusion between the Church and the U.S. government that had resulted in the overthrow of Arbenz in Guatemala in 1954. Clarizio did what he could to thwart the effort. "For about a month, the nuncio held us practically as his prisoners," said Frank O'Hara, one of the Maryknolls.[4] The priests were restricted to the nuncio's residence, while Clarizio fought his own political battles with enemies within the Church. One of his main antagonists was the Redemptorist superior in the nation, Bishop Riley, a conservative like Spellman. In the end, the nuncio had to let the Maryknolls go about their business.

Much of the order's work was innocuous—trying to establish community-development projects and identify youths who had leadership potential. The priests themselves wore white cassocks to emphasize the religious nature of their work, but they were often treated with suspicion. Not all their work was divorced from the U.S. government. For instance, they tried to find students who would accept pay to write favorable articles about the United States. The people were so embittered that the task proved impossible. "The anti-Americanism was so strong that we couldn't find a single student who would write anything positive," Renée Archambault, a member of the Maryknoll team, admitted.[5]

Most priests involved with the project eventually became disillusioned. They saw the Church as being on the wrong side of political as well as personal issues, such as the prohibition on priests' marrying. Most of them left the priesthood. Virtually all of them had started their careers as political conservatives and most wound up as liberals or radicals. One such priest was Miguel d'Escoto Brockman. Years later, Father d'Escoto became the foreign minister of Nicaragua under the revolutionary Sandinist government that overthrew Somoza.

The biggest support Spellman gave Johnson wasn't in Latin America but in Vietnam. Old as he was, Spellman's interest in military affairs remained as strong as ever, and his belief in an imperial America never flagged. He loved playing the role of a man who helped shape American foreign policy. He routinely had military leaders to lunch at the Powerhouse, and he visited the Pentagon and even attended strategy seminars given by army intelligence. According to military records, the last intelligence briefing Spellman attended was in March 1965, at the Carlisle, Pennsylvania, army barracks.

That Spellman continued his strong support of U.S. policy in Vietnam wasn't surprising in light of his history of involvement. More than simply his Americanism was at stake. The war effort was something Pope Pius XII had supported, and Pius, as far as Spellman was concerned, was the last Pope with a true understanding of power and the way it should be used.

For his part, Johnson exploited the Cardinal's jingoism. As the level of American troop commitment to the war escalated, the level of protest against the U.S. military presence in Vietnam increased. The President wanted his efforts blessed, and Spellman, more than any other churchman, was willing to proclaim Johnson's crusade a moral one. When Spellman returned from the front he immediately flew to Washington, where the President met with him at once and routinely asked the Cardinal's assessment of the war. While others wavered, Spellman was always certain that the President's actions were right. Thus, when Johnson asked both Spellman and Billy Graham at a luncheon what he should do next in Vietnam, Graham was uncomfortably silent. "Bomb them!" Spellman unhesitatingly ordered. "Just bomb them!"[6] And Johnson did.

As the war dragged on, Spellman had his picture taken not simply with generals and G.I.s but blessing bombers and machine guns. But what had been the symbols of a holy crusade during World War II appeared unseemly. As Spellman rushed in and out of the war zone, he was ridiculed by antiwar activists as "the Bob Hope of the clergy." His cathedral became a magnet for demonstrators. The war became known as "Spellman's War," which itself became a slogan on peace marchers' buttons.

While resenting his critics intensely, Spellman seemed to thrive on the criticism. At the age of seventy-seven, when most old men were ignored, he was at the heart of a great controversy, and he loved the attention. Nonetheless, the price he paid was steep. Increasingly, he was the object of ridicule and scorn, and the adverse publicity he received damaged him in far wider circles than those of antiwar activists and the Vatican. He began to lose his grip in New York, the heart of his political kingdom.

For decades Spellman moved through New York's political mainstream as a revered and feared entity. It wasn't unusual for the Cardinal, when he appeared at cocktail parties in people's homes, to sit in a parlor that was emptied of all but those Spellman wanted to see. People paid him court, sought favors from him, and, if they were men of prominence, usually spoke with Spellman of matters of common concern. One of the oddities about the Cardinal's political prowess was that it went largely untested. Politicians didn't know what would happen if they failed to woo him and seek his advice on candidates for office or political positions they should take. They had only to remember what had happened to John Kennedy's education bill or how Governor Lehman almost did not become Senator Lehman as a result of Spellman. "There were some who thought the Cardinal wielded a great deal of political power," asserted Carmine De Sapio, Tammany Hall boss in the 1950s and 1960s until he was imprisoned for extorting money from a company. As for the pragmatic De Sapio, he said he dealt with the Cardinal "as one of the forces in the city that one must take into account."[7]

Since the days of Mayor O'Dwyer, Cardinal Spellman was taken for granted as a powerful factor in city politics. O'Dwyer had hastily been appointed ambassador to Mexico in 1950, escaping city office before his house of cards fell on top of him. His administration at the time was under intense scrutiny by Senator Estes Kefauver's committee investigating organized crime. A number of racketeers on the city payroll, such as James F. ("Big Jim") Moran, an associate of Frank Costello, had used his job of issuing permits in the fire department to extort $500,000 a year from business owners.

When Vincent R. Impellitteri, an accident of fate who was city council president, became mayor, Spellman couldn't have asked for a more compliant personality. "Impy" had tumbled into the council presidency because the Democratic ticket had consisted of O'Dwyer (an Irishman) and Lazarus Joseph (a Jew), who was running for comptroller. The ethnic-conscious New Yorkers believed they needed an Italian to round out the ticket's appeal. An ardent Catholic, Impellitteri was in awe of Spellman and asked his blessing whenever the mayor met the Cardinal. During Impellitteri's forty months as mayor, the city got behind Spellman's campaign against *The Miracle*, and the Powerhouse's grip was believed to have been strengthened. Charlie Silver was appointed to the school board. Monsignors from the Powerhouse moved through the city's social-service and education offices, making their views known, and in time they seemed like permanent fixtures. "Monsignor Ahern was always in my office," Abe Beame would recall. "The Cardinal was always interested in everything that was going on, and his men were very good at presenting their case. Monsignor Ahern could have been a politician if he weren't a priest."[8]

The effectiveness of the Powerhouse was always difficult to quantify. Nothing was written down, but quite obviously the archdiocese prospered. The man most influential then wasn't Impellitteri but Robert Moses, whose massive building programs were changing the contours of the city. Moses needed Spellman's support for his projects, and Spellman needed Moses. The Church owned a great deal of property, and many Moses projects needed the relocation of archdiocesan holdings. "Sometimes he [Moses] and the Church swapped pieces of land as casually as if they were playing Monopoly," noted Robert A. Caro in his biography of Moses, *The Power Broker*.[9] As for the less than brilliant Impellitteri, he found Spellman "just great." The Cardinal sent him little notes on his speeches and gave him his public blessing. "The Cardinal was a wonderful man," according to Impellitteri. "He never asked me for a thing."[10]

One of the Cardinal's chief political conveyor belts was Thomas

J. Shanahan, from the O'Dwyer days, who was chairman of the Cardinal's Committee of the Laity from 1945 to 1960 and the Democratic Party's financial chairman for mayoral elections from 1945 to 1953. Shanahan loved money as much as Spellman did. A onetime bank cashier, he rose through the ranks to become vice president and treasurer of Federation Bank and Trust Company before he was thirty. He had shrewdly backed city contractors when they were in financial trouble and tremendously increased the assets of his bank. A fund-raiser for O'Dwyer, Shanahan collected the donations from the contractors with whom he did business at the bank. Soon contractors who had contributed generously received sizable construction contracts from the city, and the profits were deposited at Federation Bank and Trust. When O'Dwyer appointed Shanahan to the New York City Housing Authority, the banker became notorious. Anyone having anything to do with the building industry, including engineers, architects, landscapers, and insurers, had to bank at Federation and pay kickbacks to Shanahan. Spellman, however, was willing to overlook the man's failings because he was a highly effective fund-raiser for the Church. Moreover, he was an ardent anti-Communist whose face flushed crimson when he spoke of "the Reds." During his years as head of the Committee of the Laity, Shanahan raised millions of dollars for the Cardinal and he was routinely a communicant on Sunday.[11]

The cordial relationship between the Powerhouse and the mayor's office continued under Robert F. Wagner, Jr., who succeeded Impellitteri in 1954. Bob Wagner, as people who knew him liked to say, wanted to be remembered as the man who never had an unkind remark for anyone. The son of Senator Robert F. Wagner, Sr., a forceful, shrewd politician, Bob Wagner had come to political power because he was his father's son and was always around. He had run for mayor with De Sapio's blessing as a "Good Government" Democrat. Not a man to rock the boat, Wagner wasn't about to offend Spellman. He made John Connorton, Spellman's health services expert, a deputy mayor. Also during the Wagner administration, "Spelly's Jew," Charlie Silver, became head of the public school board and later an executive assistant to the mayor. One of the favors done for Spellman during the Wagner years—a favor from Robert Moses—was making a gift to Fordham University of the valuable land adjacent to the Lincoln Center project. The university wanted to relocate and enlarge its Manhattan campus, and when Spellman explained the problem to Moses, the school got what it wanted. Hundreds of people were removed from housing on six acres that were then turned over to Fordham. In turn, Spellman aided the city whenever he could. He helped avert transportation strikes, prodded contractors and unions to speed up stalled city building programs, and blessed the mayor's and Moses's projects.

Spellman's role in New York politics began deteriorating in the mid-1960s, and that was particularly noticeable during the 1965 mayoral election. John Vliet Lindsay, unlike past candidates, studiously avoided Spellman during the campaign. Lindsay wanted to break with the past, and, to a large measure, that meant breaking with Spellman. Thus, when Lindsay was inaugurated it was the first time in at least twenty years that Cardinal Spellman wasn't sitting at the candidate's right hand and offering his blessing.

Mayor Lindsay didn't want Spellman's hand involved in the selection of ranking city officials or judges. Over the years, Spellman's influence at City Hall had resulted in an informal patronage system that involved more than just department heads and school administrators. The Powerhouse had gotten jobs for low-level workers as well. Warren Moscow, a deputy mayor during the Wagner administration, remembered trying to get rid of a secretary who was generally incompetent. When Moscow tried to fire her, he found it was impossible. "Her brother was a monsignor at the Powerhouse. I received word from very important people that I couldn't get rid of her." Eventually, she was transferred.[12]

The new mayor disregarded Spellman when filling offices, and the Cardinal simmered. He knew that eventually Lindsay would have to turn to him for a favor. Sure enough, Lindsay called the Powerhouse one day asking to meet with Spellman. Despite his efforts to stay at arm's length from the Cardinal, the mayor found he needed the old prelate. Spellman was both curious and delighted to find the mayor humbling himself.

On the day of the Lindsay lunch, Spellman was well prepared. He lined up a half-dozen of his priests who dealt with city departments. "I don't know what he wants," Spellman told his men, "but he wants something."[13]

When the handsome mayor arrived, Spellman was quite cordial. During the lunch Lindsay kept the Cardinal in the dark about the purpose of his visit. Finally, Spellman encouraged the mayor to speak. "Is there anything I can do for you, Mr. Mayor?" the Cardinal asked.

Of course, there was. Lindsay's problem was most delicate. A Police Civilian Review Board had been proposed to look into the relationship between New York City police and the black community. Civil-rights leaders charged that the department engaged in police brutality and was generally insensitive to the city's Negroes. Something obviously had to be done. New York had been rocked by a devastating race riot in 1964 and black-white tension had enveloped the city in its wake. The review-board issue, however, was loaded. Police bristled at the idea, and Lindsay desperately sought ways to make it palatable to them. Thus he desired the Cardinal's imprimatur for the board's creation: he wanted Spellman to name a priest to the board. He reasoned that most cops were Irish and Catholic and respected their Church.

As Spellman knew, the issue was a political minefield. Floyd McKissick, the national director of the Congress of Racial Equality, declared that if the board were rejected, the decision would reflect "a climate of racism." But racial fears were already being fanned by board opponents. They had launched an advertising campaign that, in an age which automatically linked blacks to crime, was full of meaning. It depicted an attractive white girl alone at night, on an empty street and apparently in imminent danger of being raped.

As Lindsay realized, Spellman was philosophically opposed to the board's creation. The Cardinal believed it would hamstring the police as they went about their duty. Moreover, Spellman had dragged his heels on the whole racial issue. Lindsay hadn't come empty-handed and was willing to horse-trade. A Catholic hospital in the Bronx, St. Francis Hospital, was in deep financial trouble and was a source of embarrassment to Spellman. Six months earlier, hospital employees had picketed the Powerhouse, pleading with the Cardinal not to close the institution and thus turn his back on the poor who used it. Press accounts of nurses who were fired for supporting the strikers and of indigent women staging sit-ins had cast the Cardinal in a poor light.[14] Lindsay assured Spellman the city could help with the unfortunate hospital situation, possibly with increased public funding. All Spellman had to do was help with the prickly review board. In a much-publicized gesture, the Cardinal had sold his personal coin collection to raise money for the hospital, but if it were to remain open it needed more funding.

To Lindsay's amazement, Spellman turned down the hospital deal but offered his assistance anyway. "I'll be happy to help you," the Cardinal said. Spellman even suggested the name of an ideal candidate for the board—Monsignor Gregory Mooney, whose career had largely been in Harlem and who knew a great deal about the problems at stake.

Lindsay was overjoyed and thanked Spellman profusely. The priests who were present thought that Lindsay was so elated he would give the Cardinal whatever he wanted. "He looked like he'd give the Cardinal his wife," one recalled. What was apparent a few moments later was that Spellman was merely toying with the mayor. He stopped Lindsay in the midst of his gushing thanks. Before he could assign any of his priests to such a post, he said, he had to impose one condition. The suddenly suspicious mayor asked what that might be. Spellman said that a prominent Episcopalian bishop and an influential rabbi must also sit on the board with Mooney. "I want Bishop Donegan and Rabbi Hollander as co-chairmen," Spellman replied with a smile.

Lindsay knew he had been had. The mayor began spluttering and fuming, just as he had become effusive only moments earlier. He realized it was impossible to get either Donegan or Hollander to assume such controversial posts; neither religious figure was dumb enough to expose himself to the kind of controversy the board would encounter. "You didn't really want me to violate the ecumenical spirit of Vatican II," Spellman said humbly. This was the only occasion that the Cardinal found the Vatican Council of value. Lindsay angrily left.[15]

Though he won the round, Spellman lost the fight. No longer were the names of prospective candidates for city office marched around to the Powerhouse. The Cardinal's voice was no longer one that a mayor was accustomed to hearing. His counsel wasn't sought by deputy mayors, and his own monsignors and lay representatives no longer had the ease of access to city officials that they had long taken for granted.

Another sign of the enervation of the Cardinal's power came in 1966 when the New York State Assembly voted to reform the state's archaic divorce law. Grounds for divorce were expanded beyond adultery to include desertion, cruel and inhuman punishment, and imprisonment. The reaction at the Powerhouse to the passage of the reform legislation was one of shock and dismay. Neither Spellman nor his staff seemed able to determine what had happened—where the lines of defense had broken down. "Somehow the legislation just slipped by and nobody was quite sure how it happened," Monsignor George Kelly, head of the Cardinal's education department, reflected.[16]

What no one at the Powerhouse wanted to confront was that the Cardinal's once-awesome political muscle, which for years had blocked any previous divorce reform moves, had atrophied. Times had changed. State legislators, who once rubber-stamped Spellman's positions, now viewed the Church in a different light. Catholic voting patterns were fragmented in the city through presidential elections. Of greater importance, Catholics were no longer a unified force on controversial issues such as divorce and birth control.

Ironically, the man who had dramatically admonished Roman Catholics not to heed Spellman's Albany lobbyist Tobin was Joseph D. Hassett, a Jesuit, who was chairman of the philosophy department at Fordham. The fact that such a man challenged the Cardinal was a startling revelation to the assemblymen, who had always assumed Spellman controlled his priests with an iron hand. If the Cardinal couldn't keep his priests in line, it seemed that he couldn't keep voters in check. Indeed, Hassett directly confronted the issue of the Cardinal's political power when he presented his case. "Our bishops have the right and the duty to teach, in the name of the Church, concerning religious and moral practice," Hassett testified before the State Assembly. "Particular decisions, however, as to what laws would help most of the people of the state of New York are a proper concern of all Catholics as citizens."

For some reason, the Powerhouse had underestimated its opposition and hadn't rallied behind the cause the way it once would have. Lobbyist Tobin fought the measure, but the Cardinal himself hadn't gotten personally involved. The Albany bishop had gone through the motions of sandbagging the bill, but he too hadn't fought as hard as he could have. One reason was complacency; such battles had been easily won in the past. But a more important factor was the Cardinal, who was now seventy-seven years old and simply not as vigorous as he once had been. And the times themselves diminished Spellman's power: the national mood no longer matched his rigid reactionary stands. But the last people to recognize the shifting patterns were the men at the Powerhouse. Long used to the Cardinal's political influence being taken for granted, they didn't appreciate what was happening to their leader or their Church. To them, he was still a nearly omnipotent force. In New York, however, politicians began looking at Spellman not as a kingmaker but as an old political boss, albeit one who could still call in certain I.O.U.s.

With his recent political feats as well as his anti-Vatican Vietnam stand, there was much speculation in late 1966 that Spellman was about to be put out to pasture. The Pope had followed a recommendation that had emerged from Vatican II by asking for the voluntary resignation of sick and elderly bishops. The proposal had been made as a graceful way to rid the Church of many old conservative obstructionists. It seemed tailored for Spellman. Thus, when the Cardinal slowly mounted the steps of his pulpit on October 11, 1966, during the investiture of six new bishops, a ripple of excitement swept through the congregation of three thousand.

"On this occasion, I wish to make an announcement that affects me personally," Spellman said.

A hush fell over St. Patrick's. A few weeks earlier, on September 21, the Cardinal had complied with the Pope's request and had submitted his resignation. There was an edge of hopefulness in some of the younger priests who were present. The Spellman era, which stretched back almost thirty years in New York, appeared to be ending. But such hopes were premature.

"Just this morning, I received word from the Holy Father that he wishes me to continue for the present as the archbishop of New York and the military vicar," Spellman said. "I accept this decision of his Holiness as God's will for me. . . ."

Many people in the congregation, who had little knowledge of Church politics, were overjoyed; their Cardinal, though he said controversial things at times, always meant well, they believed. He was a man of God. Others, the liberals and the antiwar activists and the priests who were astute about Vatican politics, were shocked and dismayed. What, they wondered, was Pope Paul doing?

The Pope's action had contradicted his reasons for seeking the bishops' resignations. In Spellman's case, in particular, Pope Paul's allowing the Cardinal to remain in power was strange. There had been talk in Rome of a new archbishop of New York and of separating the military vicar role from the see. Now, the Pope had tossed away an opportunity to silence a man with whom he had had so much trouble. Once again, however, Montini was the victim of his own indecision. He accepted only one resignation among all of the old men in the Church hierarchy, that of a cardinal in poor health.

Soon enough, the Pope had reason to rue his mistake. In December 1966, Spellman was once again back in Vietnam where his public pronouncements were, if anything, a greater embarrassment than before. Old as he was, the Cardinal toured various outposts. Once again, he demonstrated his independence from Rome. In a lesson from the medieval Church, Spellman told the troops they were "holy crusaders" engaged in "Christ's war against the Vietcong and the people of North Vietnam." At the military base at Danang, he told three thousand soldiers gathered in an amphitheater that "less than total victory is inconceivable!" His words, picked up by war correspondents, flashed around the world, and the political repercussions were felt in Washington, Moscow, and the Vatican.

Several days later, on Christmas Day, Spellman said mass at a simple wooden table that faced thousands of soldiers. Security was tight, the eerie whir of helicopters filled the skies. A reinforced battalion of infantry patrolled the surrounding jungle, tanks rumbled around the perimeter. Instead of softening his tone because of the specialness of the occasion, Spellman declared the nobility of the American cause. "This war in Vietnam," he said, "is, I believe, a war for civilization!" He went on and on, defending the presence of the troops, telling the youths their calling was "the defense, protection, and salvation not only of our country, but, I believe, of civilization itself!"

The magnitude of Spellman's remarks couldn't be overestimated. He deliberately challenged the Vatican. The Cardinal was angry because the Pope had just made it clear that he would be happy to see a negotiated peace, not an American victory. No longer was the Catholic Church the Cold War Church that seized any opportunity to crush Communism. Spellman placed the Pope's peace mission in peril. Radio Moscow gloated that the Cardinal "openly contradicts the Pope's appeal for peace in Vietnam."

The reaction at the Vatican was shock. Not only had Spellman disregarded the Pope, but he even seemed to mock him. In a rare criticism of a prelate, L'Osservatore Romano alluded to the Cardinal by recalling that all Catholics had a duty to give loyalty to the Pope's peace initiatives. To Vatican observers, such a display of public anger was startling. Privately, Montini fumed. But once again he was unable to act. He didn't know how to treat the pugnacious Spellman.

On his return to the United States, the Cardinal refused to back down. He was unperturbed by the controversy. In Manila, on December 28, he was asked by reporters if his remarks were meant to rule out the possibility of a negotiated peace. "Total victory means peace," he declared.

At home, Spellman was generally castigated in the press. *The New York Times* editorialized on December 29: "It is a pity that he felt the need to speak at all in terms which momentarily forgot that of the three abiding Pauline virtues, the greatest is Charity." *Commonweal* printed an article about Spellman lamenting that his remarks did not "occasion any surprise in those who have followed the Cardinal's career." James O'Gara, *Commonweal*'s editor, noted: "We are, of course, embarrassed before the world that a Catholic bishop should take a posture that would seem exaggerated in an American legionnaire. . . ."

Letters besieged the chancery and priests were stopped on the street by Catholics demanding to know what Spellman was trying to do. The Cardinal wasn't without his supporters, of course, but they were hard-pressed to defend him. *New York World Journal Tribune* columnist Bob Considine remained a Spellman loyalist: "Judging from the tone of the attacks on the man, it looks like we'll have to put Cardinal Spellman on trial when he gets back from his annual visit to troops fighting in Vietnam. . . . He thinks that as long as we're in it and have spilled all that blood and money, we ought to make sure we win it."

One of the most striking results of the Cardinal's warmongering rhetoric was an abrupt shift in the way many people perceived him. They saw him as a mean-spirited man, not as an ecclesiastic who deserved automatic respect because of his lofty office. As much as any other man, Spellman shook Catholics' implicit respect for their hierarchy. To date, numerous Catholics had defended his public stances, ranging from his support of Franco to his vicious condemnation of Mrs. Roosevelt. But Vietnam changed that. For the first time, the anger that was found in the streets was brought into American churches. In large measure, Spellman was to blame.

On Sunday, January 22, 1967, antiwar demonstrators disrupted high mass at St. Patrick's. At a given signal, they moved into the center aisle and displayed signs and placards condemning the Cardinal. No wild-eyed youths, the demonstrators were conservative in appearance. The short-haired men wore suits and ties; the women, dresses. One of the posters they held aloft was a reproduction of a devastating caricature of Spellman that had been drawn by Edward Sorel. The illustration depicted Spellman's plump face staring balefully, an olive branch tucked in his mouth. His body was that of a cardinal (the bird) and clutched in his talons was a fluttering banner: "In religion alone lies the hope of lasting peace." He was riding a missile over St. Patrick's. Police, tipped off to the demonstration, hustled the men and women out of the cathedral into a waiting van.

Spellman was bitterly angry. The demonstration had invaded his cathedral sanctuary, and there had been no way to prevent it. For a man used to exercising power, his helplessness infuriated him. Far from reconsidering his position, he became more obstinate. Now, when the Cardinal visited campuses, churches, and various public affairs meetings, he was never sure when he would be the object of a demonstration. Like President Johnson, Spellman could safely visit few places other than military academies without encountering lines of relentless pickets with jeering faces. He became a harassed and harried figure.

"Draft Spellman!" and "Warmonger!" were cries that dogged his footsteps. Spellman's old nemesis Drew Pearson noted that the war in Vietnam had become known as "Spellman's War." Then the Cardinal suffered a severe setback on the war front. Fulton Sheen declared he was convinced that if President Johnson withdrew all U.S. troops he would show great moral leadership. Sheen's statement was like a battering ram against the doors of St. Patrick's. Members of the clergy, aware of the bitter Spellman-Sheen relationship, wondered whether the Sheen stance was more out of a desire to embarrass Spellman than true conviction. To date, Sheen had been one of the Church's most virulent anti-Communists.

At the Powerhouse, Spellman took little trouble to hide the way he felt about his critics. He sneered at the civil-rights and Vietnam stands of Martin Luther King, Jr., and Bobby Kennedy. Priests knew what he thought of Sheen. In what had become a pattern for a man who had changed little during his lifetime, the more he was criticized the less flexible Spellman became. Publicly he continued to leap to President Johnson's defense. When his old friend J. Edgar Hoover was criticized for foot-dragging on civil rights and other matters, Spellman rallied to his cause.

The Cardinal may well have been speaking about himself when he defended the F.B.I. director. Hoover, Spellman declared, was like a wounded old lion surrounded by jackals. "It now appears that the Red hounds are in full cry for the hide of F.B.I. director J. Edgar Hoover. . . . For the Reds have had their sights on Hoover for a long time. The very fact they and their liberal allies now feel secure enough to openly take him on is an ill omen indeed for the American people. . . . One supposes that it is too much to expect that the American people should for once rally to the support of one of their most distinguished public servants. . . . We need him as long as his health and age permit him to serve."

Gone were the days when he and Hoover gave national radio addresses, were reflexively honored wherever they went, and made public pronouncements that went unquestioned. They were now two old men guarding their flanks and trying to stay in power. Spellman, as always, never blamed himself for the turn of events. But for the first time, he lashed out at Americans generally, not simply at Communists and their sympathizers. Spellman's long pent-up disdain of the public burst into the open.

That the prelate gave vent to such feelings was understandable. He wasn't simply being criticized; the political ground beneath him was turning to quicksand. No longer could he count on an obedient monolithic Catholic constituency; his own priests challenged him. But like many of the men who worked for him at the Powerhouse and many old-line politicians, the Cardinal found it difficult to believe that his authority and political power had diminished to the degree they had. As for the war protestors, he still believed that they marched against the mainstream of America and were the product of a sensation-starved press. But he couldn't find the mainstream, and he became frantic.

Thus, in his seventy-eighth year, Spellman stoked the boilers at the Powerhouse for one last great political battle, in an arena where he had been least successful during his reign as archbishop of New York.

CHAPTER FOURTEEN

The Last Hurrah

SPELLMAN'S LACK OF SUCCESS IN GETTING GOVERNMENT AID for parochial schools always bothered him. When he was named archbishop in 1939 that had been one of his mandates from Pope Pius XII. The prelate had some victories, of course, most notably in concessions by President Johnson and Governor Rockefeller. Yet Spellman wanted to shape a law that included parochial schools in general education programs.

By the mid-1960s, the Cardinal's concern wasn't simply a matter of massaging his own ego. There were signs of trouble within the massive Catholic school system that he had erected. The amount of funding needed to maintain it increased at an alarming rate. The cost of everything from construction and utility bills to salaries spiraled dizzyingly. Priests and nuns, the traditional schoolteachers who had worked for little, were being replaced by lay teachers who demanded a living wage. In 1967, for the first time since World War II, no new elementary schools opened in the New York archdiocese. A more ominous sign of the problems confronting Spellman was that his high schools, in the same year, operated $1.8 million in the red.

Spellman focused his attention on a convention held in New York to streamline and modernize the state's constitution. One existing amendment—the so-called Blaine Amendment—the Cardinal wanted changed prohibited direct or indirect aid to religious schools. Old as he was, Spellman still juggled many balls. He was the hawk on Vietnam, the Boss in the archdiocese, and the political manipulator. In this latter role, he intruded in redesigning the New York State Constitution.

Spellman wanted something the Church hierarchy had long encouraged Catholics to proclaim as justly theirs. Known as the "child-benefit" theory, the argument held that any public funding of Catholic schools helped the child rather than the religion. To buttress the cause, Catholics pointed out that the nearly 800,000 children attending Catholic schools in the state would be an additional taxpayer burden if they attended public schools. Thus, Catholics contended they were the victims of double taxation, first for public schools, which they didn't use, and second for their own. Somehow, the fact that they chose to send their children to parochial schools became obscured. Also, the separation of Church and State was ignored.

When a constitutional convention opened in Albany on April 4, 1967, Spellman had reason to believe that New York State would finally place parochial schools on the same footing as public schools. It was he who gave the opening invocation and who later moved, smiling, through the sea of delegates. At his side, beaming at everyone, was Anthony J. Travia, the speaker of the State Assembly and president of the convention—and one of Spellman's conveyor belts.[1]

Spellman's optimism was based on more than having the convention's key politician in his pocket. The archdiocese had organized an extremely effective lobby. The man in charge of Spellman's fight was Monsignor George Kelly, who could turn on the charm of a Spencer Tracy–movie priest. Kelly was an example of how Spellman pragmatically redeemed priests. Kelly had been in the Cardinal's doghouse over the gravediggers' strike, but Spellman let Maguire rehabilitate him because Kelly was bright, ambitious, and useful.[2] Now, Kelly might become a bishop if he pulled off a state-charter revision, one that could benefit the Church with millions, eventually billions, of dollars.

Kelly's principal lobby was the Citizens for Educational Freedom, a nominally nonsectarian but overwhelmingly Catholic organization that had raised the issue of aid to parochial schools in a number of primary elections.[3] Initially, Kelly and his troops met a great deal of voter apathy, but gradually they made an impact. They bombarded parishioners with pamphlets as they left mass each Sunday, while priests sermonized about the importance of the cause. They organized meetings in parish halls across the state to discuss ways of pressuring politicians into changing the constitution. By the time of the constitutional convention, Kelly and the Citizens for Educational Freedom were confident of victory. "A majority of the 186 delegates chosen for the 1967 Constitutional Convention are pledged to work for the removal of the Amendment," the *Tablet* reported on November 10, 1966.

Convention delegates were charged with drafting a new charter that would serve as a sophisticated model for other states for generations to come in such important matters as legislative apportionment and relations between state and local governments. The overshadowing issue, as everyone knew, was whether the education amendment would be repealed, and all signs pointed go.

As politicians realized, the Powerhouse was able to galvanize tremendous support. The issue was one that brought Catholics together. They might be divided on Vietnam, abortion, birth control, divorce, and whether they wanted the mass in English or Latin, but there was near universal agreement among them on the justice of public aid to parochial schools. Prominent politicians saw the groundswell of support and jumped onto the bandwagon. Spellman had the backing of Governor Rockefeller; Senators Robert Kennedy and Jacob Javits; Earl Brydges, the Catholic majority leader of the State Senate; Frank O'Connor, the Catholic president of the New York city council, and others, including, of course, Travia, the president of the convention.

Though Rockefeller was reticent about making an outright public commitment to the cause, his support was taken for granted. Over the years, the governor had done a great deal for Spellman. He had supported and signed into law a tuition subsidy, in the form of a scholarship grant to students, that was a bonanza for Church schools. He had urged other forms of aid to schools that always included Church schools. The governor always told Spellman that he admired parochial schools.[4]

Organizations such as Americans United for Separation of Church and State were dismayed by Rockefeller's track record. "In one vital area, Nelson Rockefeller's leadership has been definitely narrow gauge and parochial," lamented Americans United's publication *Church and State* in October 1967. "He has exhibited for years a rather pathetic acquiescence to every demand posed by Cardinal Spellman, the Roman Catholic Archbishop of New York."

Rockefeller had reason to be grateful to Spellman. Their close relationship had started only in 1962, when Rockefeller divorced his wife of thirty years, embroiling him in a scandal that almost destroyed his public career. He was roundly condemned by Protestant religious figures, a major reason being that a divorce was then granted only on grounds of adultery in New York. In the midst of being vilified, Rockefeller was thankful when a prominent religious figure stepped forward and publicly embraced him, doing much to save the governor from disgrace. "Who should embrace him but Cardinal Spellman," Joseph Persico, a Rockefeller aide, related. Persico resented the

Cardinal's action because of the Church's harsh condemnation of divorced people. But Persico had watched Spellman's maneuverings for years, and he believed he knew what motivated the prelate. Spellman saw a chance to increase his power base and place a prominent man in his debt. "Spellman was a power sniffer, so he buttered up Nelson. Nelson got respectable again," in Persico's opinion.[5]

Thus, over the years, in return for his support of the Cardinal's education causes, the governor received Spellman's political blessing. When Rockefeller called on the Cardinal during the 1966 gubernatorial campaign to discuss matters of mutual concern, Spellman offered his unconditional support. "As Rockefeller left, the Cardinal pressed an envelope on him as a campaign contribution," a former Spellman aide remembered. "The governor was reluctant, but the Cardinal insisted. 'Take it! Take it!' the Cardinal kept saying."[6]

Monsignor Kelly's lobbying efforts were imaginative, expensive, and effective. The propaganda blitz included closed-circuit television programs that were shown to parishes across the state and consisted of statements by delegates pledged to repeal the amendment and by politicians trying to curry the Catholic vote. Senator Javits, who was seeking reelection, appeared several times.

Some of the publicity, however, was disturbing because it was not only overkill but deceptive. To stress the child-benefit argument, a series of highly emotional, full-page advertisements were run in newspapers across the state. They depicted children allegedly discriminated against because of the schools they attended. One ad showed a child with a speech defect, another with a reading problem, and still another who had been denied psychological counseling. The ads were misleading. Remedial services were available to children if schools paid for them, but at the time they generally weren't very good for public school children, either. The ads were no longer aired after the American Civil Liberties Union challenged them.

The Catholic lobbyists spent an estimated $2 million on the campaign.[7] The advertising and public-relations bills were enormous. Pamphlets and position papers raised ominous questions about the United States and the Soviet Union being the "only two major countries in the world that did not give some form of aid to children in non-public elementary and secondary schools," as though Communism had inspired the separation of Church and State in America. Packages of editorial information from the Citizens for Educational Freedom inundated newspaper, television, and radio editors.

There were also elements of intimidation in the lobbyists' arsenal of tactics. Elected state officials were asked where they stood on the amendment and were told that their answers would be publicized. Ninety percent of the politicians refused to participate, and many were offended by the implicit threat to chastise them if they didn't agree with the lobbyists. William Hadad, a reform Democrat in New

York City, and Percy Sutton, the Manhattan borough president, went so far as to call a news conference at which they charged that delegates to the constitutional convention had been threatened with political reprisals if they voted to retain the amendment.

Spellman's lobbyists had gone too far. They had had the field much to themselves, but now opposition to the repeal movement began forming. Soon, battle lines were drawn with the formation of the Committee for Public Education and Religious Liberty, or PEARL, which aimed to stop Spellman by insisting on the separation of Church and State. The co-chairmen were Hadad and Sutton. Soon PEARL had a surprisingly large and diverse backing, including the United Federation of Teachers, Americans for Democratic Action, the American Jewish Congress, the City Club of New York, and the New York State Council of Churches.

PEARL revved up its own counter-propaganda. The New York Civil Liberties Union issued a pamphlet, "Questions and Answers About Aid to Parochial Schools." Americans United printed a treatise, "New York's Constitutional Crisis," which the State Council of Churches distributed. Money was pumped into advertising, public relations, and lobbying efforts. By late May 1967, however, Sutton was worried that the counter-lobby had gotten off the ground too late. Thus, he wanted the public alerted to what was happening and urged that public hearings be held.

Spellman was conscious that an enormous amount of money was being gobbled up. Part of the advertising and public-relations efforts were the costs of sending priest-lobbyists to Albany. Tobin, the Church's chief lobbyist, raced about everywhere. Every time Kelly turned around, someone wanted money and he worried because his resources weren't limitless.

At one point Senator Robert Kennedy's aides approached Kelly and told him their boss was willing to make a television commercial favoring repeal of the amendment. At first Kelly was gratified, then he worried. The Kennedy forces needed $150,000 to make the TV spot. The monsignor finally amassed $100,000. His coffers were dangerously low; he was probably overcommitted. He approached Spellman to see if the Cardinal had any suggestions about where to find the money. Kelly hated to go to Spellman. He didn't want to look like a failure, but he was desperate. The Kennedy endorsement would give the campaign a big boost; it would also make him look good. But the Kennedy people wanted the money right away or the deal was off.

When Kelly explained the situation to Spellman, the prelate was annoyed. "I've managed to get a hundred thousand dollars together," Kelly admitted, "but I can't find the other fifty thousand."

The Cardinal looked at his subordinate coldly. "What's fifty thousand dollars when more than a million dollars has already gone on this thing?'' Spellman answered. His message was clear: Get the money. Kelly did.[8]

There were always rumors that Spellman used his influence to do questionable favors for friends and even people who weren't yet friends. Thus, in the midst of the campaign to quash the education amendment, Spellman came up with a potential money-making scheme. The Cardinal proposed to intervene in the case of Louis E. Wolfson, a corporate high roller who was in a serious jam with the Securities and Exchange Commission. Wolfson, chairman of Merritt-Chapman & Scott construction company, and one of the nation's most controversial corporate raiders, had been charged with stock manipulation in the sale of shares of Continental Enterprises Inc., a Jacksonville, Florida, theater-management company controlled by him, his family, and associates. According to the government, Wolfson hyped publicity about the stock to increase its price while he sold his own shares, at a profit of some $1.5 million, without bothering to register the transaction with the S.E.C.

The handsome, articulate Wolfson, who had built a business empire, would recall that in September 1967 he was approached by Dr. Samuel Belkin, president of Yeshiva University, who was acting as an intermediary for Cardinal Spellman. Belkin, who had gotten to know Spellman through Charlie Silver, had an unusual proposition. If Wolfson contributed heftily to Catholic Charities, "my legal problems would be over," Wolfson reported.[9] Their meeting in Wolfson's suite at the Plaza Hotel included a discussion of the businessman's initial contribution and then a bigger one "when the Cardinal produces," Wolfson said. Wolfson didn't recall that a price tag had been set, but an associate would put the figure at $1 million.[10]

Wolfson was startled. He had met Spellman once at a cocktail party for about a hundred people, and they had both attended a dinner afterward. When he thought about the offer Wolfson became furious. "I refused to buy any political influence or any other type of influence," he contended. "I spent in excess of two million [dollars] fighting this injustice."[11]

Wolfson was defended by the law firm of Arnold Fortas & Porter. Eventually, Federal Judge Edmund L. Palmieri, a friend of Spellman's, sentenced Wolfson to a year in prison and fined him $100,000. Two years later Abe Fortas resigned his Supreme Court seat when it was revealed that Fortas had received $20,000 from the Wolfson Family Foundation, ostensibly for advising the foundation on philanthropic affairs. Fortas returned the foundation money after Wolfson was indicted, saying he was too busy with Court affairs to devote time to the foundation. The question remained, however, whether Fortas's name or influence had been used on Wolfson's behalf.

Whatever the case, Wolfson swore that he had turned down Spellman's offer.[12]

Whether Spellman intended to divert whatever sums Wolfson might have given him to the campaign to change the New York State Constitution isn't known, but Spellman's need for money was great. The lobbying costs kept escalating. The Cardinal's cause received a boost on June 1 when the New York Court of Appeals, the state's highest court, decided that the state could lend textbooks to parochial-school students. The child-benefit theory was cited in reversing a 1938 appeals court ruling. Spellman lost no time. He immediately contended the new ruling should inspire the convention to repeal the amendment. The issue, Spellman declared, "is the gravest crisis in the history of the Catholic Church in America."

The fight over the amendment heated up. Kelly and his group contended the future of the parochial-school system was at stake. The Reverend Nicholas Cardell, Jr., minister of the First Unitarian Church of Albany and president of the Albany area Minister's Association, summarized the attitude of the opposition when he stated that "private and special interest groups are proposing that we sacrifice the long-run, general interest of the people of New York State."

As far as convention president Travia was concerned, there might as well have been no debate. Travia declared that "I feel that repeal of the . . . amendment was a foregone conclusion before the convention opened." The forces opposed to repeal believed he was probably right. The deck seemed to have been stacked against them from the outset. PEARL co-chairmen Sutton and Hadad charged that pressures brought on convention delegates had them "so badly frightened that there is a kind of gentleman's agreement not to discuss the question" because of "arm-twisting and political pressure."

On August 15 the delegates voted on the controversial issue and it seemed *pro forma*. By a majority of 132 to 49, they voted to replace the specific language of the amendment with looser language. The Spellman forces had won.

The Cardinal was pleased, but next he made a costly mistake. The vote on whether to repeal the disputed amendment would come before voters in November. Instead of shepherding the legislation through to its conclusion, Spellman stopped pressing when he believed he had won, and he unwisely allowed Travia to have his way on a critical matter. Travia wanted to wrap the education issue into a package of changes with regard to the entire constitution.[13] Spellman agreed. He gave Travia a great deal of credit for the overwhelming support of the repeal movement, and he believed the politician knew what he was doing. The education issue was lumped together with other controversial matters, including the assumption by the state of welfare and court costs and the elimination of voter referendums on new bond issues.

State Republicans were dismayed by the Cardinal's letting Travia shape the package. They were committed to challenging certain changes, including the elimination of new bond referendums. Rockefeller found himself in the awkward position of having to buck the Cardinal. At one point, he dispatched Lieutenant Governor Malcolm Wilson, the house Catholic and a man who was always in awe of Spellman, to the Powerhouse to try to change Spellman's mind. "It was Travia and Monsignor Kelly who talked the Cardinal into it," Wilson asserted.[14] Wilson's message was clear: Rockefeller would vote to repeal the education amendment only if it were a separate issue.

The Cardinal stubbornly stuck to Travia's insistence that the amendment had a better chance of getting through as part of a package deal. The argument wasn't without its merits. As the *New York Post* noted, the Church-State question would be the hottest issue before voters and the repeal motion was a "transparent attempt to purchase the support of a powerful church for the charter." Spellman determined that the voters were receptive to a new charter.[15]

Thus, when the convention ended on September 26, Spellman proclaimed the new charter "worthy of support by the people of New York State." The following evening, a huge crowd gathered at Madison Square Garden for a "Fairness to Children" rally. Several hundred buses brought people from as far away as Albany, Buffalo, Syracuse, Rochester, and Niagara Falls. Thousands more came by car, train, and subway. Bands played and balloons filled the air as prominent Catholics, such as Travia, Jim Farley, William Buckley, Jr., and Congressman Hugh Carey, told the gathering that a historic occasion was at hand. Catholic schools would get public funds. Suddenly, the houselights dimmed and a single spotlight shone on Spellman as he slowly climbed the steps to the dais. He was flanked by cadets from the Cardinal Farley Military Academy. At the sight of him, the multitude rose from their chairs and cheered and applauded. The Cardinal Spellman High School Band played a tribute to the school's namesak   At the microphone, the Cardinal dramatically glared at the aud._ nce. "And how are we going to vote?" he demanded.

"Yes!" the audience screamed. "Yes!"

Other speakers, including Fulton Sheen, Senator Eugene McCarthy, and George Meany, followed the Cardinal, but there was little doubt that the evening belonged to Spellman. The audience saw only a crusader for a worthy Catholic cause. And the ensuing campaign seemed to turn back the clock. A Catholic voter registration drive was launched to ensure passage of the new charter. The *Daily News* reported that "get out and register" sermons were ringing from pulpits. The *Tablet* conducted its own campaign; the September 21 issue even contained absentee ballots for servicemen. The Knights of Columbus rallied as in old times, urging communities to adopt the new constitution, "thereby eliminating from the law of the state a legal stricture that was born of religious hypocrisy and hatred."

The six weeks before the November 7 election marked one of the most bitter political campaigns in the state's history. While Spellman's forces harangued about religious hatred, opponents talked of an assault on the separation of Church and State. The Conservative Party of New York declared the new charter was "a prescription for fiscal disaster," and state budget director T. Norman Hurd said it would cost $23 billion over the next decade and raise taxes eighty percent.

Politicians became increasingly wary. Rockefeller waffled. He refused to campaign for the new charter, but said he was in favor of repealing the controversial education amendment. Like others, he tried to disassociate himself from what was swiftly becoming a mess. In the final days, only Catholic and Orthodox Jewish groups, such as the Union of Orthodox Jewish Congregations of America, promoted the new charter. Just about everyone else was opposed. On October 19 an Associated Press survey of New York daily newspapers showed practically all of them opposed to the new constitution.

Spellman was so identified with the issue that politicians steered clear of him as well. They reluctantly answered his phone calls and were evasive about their support. Suddenly, his stand on the constitution was as controversial as his stand on Vietnam.

In mid-October, Rockefeller tried to find a compromise. He discussed with Spellman the possibility of softening the Church's stand on the education amendment. If Spellman backed away, the governor indicated, he would have the amendment repealed through the legislative process. The governor bluntly told Spellman that he had to sidestep the issue and might even have to vote against the new charter. Rockefeller didn't want to be embarrassed, and he was dismayed when Spellman refused to budge.[16] The Cardinal still believed there were enough votes to push the new charter through. Moreover, he didn't want to be embarrassed by backing down on an issue on which he was the avowed leader.

Spellman's calculations were wrong, and he was publicly humiliated in a fashion that he never expected. Suddenly, regrets began arriving for the 1967 Al Smith dinner, which was always held in October. Neither President Johnson nor Vice President Humphrey could attend; neither wanted to be caught up in a Church-State battle. Various city, state, and congressional figures also found their calendars difficult to juggle that day and backed out of the dinner. Then, unbelievably, two men of great prominence, although already listed on the printed programs as speakers, announced that they would not be able to attend. They were Governor Rockefeller, who used the excuse of the annual governors' conference, and Mayor Lindsay, who didn't even bother to offer a gracious excuse. Lindsay took a vacation to the Virgin Islands.

Spellman's aides were mortified, and they began to realize to what degree the Cardinal had lost his influence in recent years. Spellman himself was bitter and he spoke of the missing as "bums who use you when they want to." During the dinner the Cardinal hid his feelings, but a pall had been cast over the evening. Many who attended were uncomfortable because they weren't sure how to act around the Cardinal. Afterward, William Buckley noted in his newspaper column that the failure of the lofty politicians to appear was "incredible." "If the Cardinal had been a few years younger, the Governor would have hired himself a Lear or something and come home for the evening," Buckley wrote. As for Lindsay, Buckley stated that in the past, "the Mayor of New York must be hospitalized to permit him to be absent from the dinner."

Lindsay apparently vividly remembered the incident with Spellman about the Police Civilian Review Board, and he went a step further to strike back at the Cardinal. On October 23, just after returning from vacation, he announced his opposition to the new charter. "Any constitutional provision which permits the diversion of public funds to private schools poses a serious threat to the already hard-pressed public school system," he declared. The mayor was denounced in the *Tablet* for "a dastardly act."

In the final week of the campaign, Spellman, reeling from his setbacks, desperately attempted to muster his forces. Some Democrats, state AFL-CIO officials, the Church hierarchy, Orthodox Jewish leaders, and the Catholic lobbies diligently pushed for a yes vote. Just two days before the referendum, Spellman issued a pastoral letter that was read in all his parishes. The proposed charter, he contended, "addresses itself to the fulfillment of our lives as citizens . . . the convention has produced a document worthy of support by the people of New York State."

On Tuesday, November 7, 1967, voters went to the polls. Spellman watched the results on television, although there was little doubt as to the constitution's fate. The voter turnout was unexpectedly large, as was the vote against the new charter. By a margin of nearly three to one, New Yorkers rejected the new constitution.

Spellman's power was broken, and the pieces were scattered about for all to see. The Cardinal sat slumped in his chair, not stirring, and his aides became worried. He hadn't been in the best of health of late, and it struck the men at the Powerhouse that more than Spellman's expectations for the constitution had been dashed. Something seemed to have broken in the Cardinal.[17]

CHAPTER FIFTEEN

The End of an Era

A WEEK AFTER HIS IGNOMINIOUS DEFEAT, SPELLMAN SUR-
reptitiously entered the Cleveland Clinic for a checkup,
registering as Father Conway, his mother's maiden name.
The Cardinal was supposed to be attending the National Conference
of Catholic Bishops in Washington.

For ten years, Spellman had suffered from hypertension and car-
diovascular problems. The most obvious sign of his ailments was
his painfully slow, shuffling walk. After the disaster with the state
constitution, he felt worse than ever, and Bishop Cooke, who tended
to the Cardinal's personal needs as well as to running the financial
side of the archdiocese for him, insisted that he get a complete physical examination. Cooke had many reasons for concern. Spellman
had long been depressed and drinking heavily. At times, the bishop
called up Judge Edward Chapman, an old classmate of Spellman's
from Fordham, and asked him to bring some of the old alumni around
to talk, reminisce, and sing. "The Cardinal's down in the dumps,"
Cooke would say. Also, he would have the Cardinal's secretaries,
Ahern and Vincent Broderick, sing to cheer up Spellman. When depressed, Spellman was sour and cynical. "I've had it all," he told
his secretaries. "After me there won't be anything."[1]

It was probably inevitable that Spellman would be recognized at
the Cleveland Clinic. His anonymity dissolved when Cleveland tel-

evision station WKYC received a tip that Cardinal Spellman was at the hospital. After being bombarded with inquiries from newsmen, hospital officials reluctantly admitted that the Cardinal was a patient, but they refused to give any details. Because of the institution's reputation for treating cancer victims, rumors quickly spread that Spellman had cancer.

The Cardinal was released in midweek and returned to New York. He knew that death was near. His medical problems, coupled with his seventy-eight years, didn't leave much cause for hope. Always realistic, Spellman accepted the inevitable. Now, he had only one last wish, and he tried to make it come true. That was selecting his successor.

The man most New York priests expected to succeed Spellman was Archbishop John Maguire, who had become chancellor several years after McIntyre had left the archdiocese to head the see of Los Angeles. (The train that carried McIntyre to the West Coast was cynically called "the Freedom Train" by New York priests who were glad to be rid of him.[2]) A rarity, Maguire had gotten ahead as much on talent as on politics. He wasn't so much a yes man as many on the chancery staff were. During the gravediggers' strike, he had registered a protest and wound up in Spellman's doghouse. The pragmatic Cardinal forgave him when he needed someone with strong managerial talents to run the archdiocese and found no one else of Maguire's caliber. What priests found refreshing about Maguire was his fairness. A big, inscrutable fellow, he was called "the Buddha" by the staff. After the humorless, vindictive McIntyre, the priests appreciated Maguire's wry touch. If a man objected to a solution that the chancellor proposed, he nonchalantly asked: "Do you want to take it up with the Cardinal?" The suggestion was so daunting that priests grabbed at Maguire's alternative.[3]

Like all men at the chancery, Maguire was at Spellman's beck and call. If there was an empty place at the Cardinal's dining table, Maguire received an urgent phone call from the residence. He had to drop what he was doing, rush across the street, pretend to be late, and apologize for his offense.[4] The job of chancellor, he found, wasn't as grand as it seemed from afar. Spellman expected him to be knowledgeable about every area of the archdiocese, from stocks and bonds to education. And Spellman publicly rebuked Maguire or sarcastically belittled him, as he did other department heads, if he didn't have an answer on the tip of his tongue. Such incidents were rare, however, because Maguire was good at his job. "God help you if you didn't know the answer to one of the Cardinal's questions," admitted Bishop Furlong, who spent eight years as Spellman's education minister.[5]

In the mid-1950s, Maguire had proven himself by his concern about the rapid influx of Spanish-speaking Catholics into New York. He believed the Church should help them. In many instances, the pastors of parishes affected by the Hispanic immigration were Irish Catholics who were intolerant and didn't like the newcomers, whom they found noisy and immoral. When Maguire first broached Spellman about the Puerto Rican population, he was brushed off. The chancellor persisted and, as when anything had to be done, he appealed to the Cardinal's pragmatic nature. Puerto Ricans, he said, were a problem. They drained financial resources from the Church and displaced traditional parishioners who had contributed to the archdiocese. They had to be brought into the mainstream in order to pay their own way.

Spellman listened as Maguire suggested having priests in largely Puerto Rican parishes take Spanish lessons, pay attention to the holy days of the newcomers, and give special attention to Spanish-speaking children in the schools. The appeal was the right approach. Not only had Maguire correctly posed a problem, but he also had a solution. Spellman hated for a problem to be left hanging. "Now what am *I* supposed to do?" he often asked.

The Cardinal's consciousness of the Spanish problem had been further heightened by the arrival of a strange young priest named Ivan Illich, a bundle of contradictions who gave Spellman a number of headaches over the years. A protégé of Bishop Griffiths, Illich was a dynamic, obsessed man who brought a burning intensity to whatever he did. With his sharp features and black hair and eyes, he looked like a raven. New York priests quickly broke into two camps: those who idolized Illich and those who loathed him. The former found him a brilliant spokesman for necessary change in the Church. The latter found him a manipulative man who trampled on others in order to call attention to himself.

In Rome, Illich had had a brilliant academic record and friends in high places. He brought to New York a passion for everything that interested him and a religious fervor that approached zealotry. He entered a church early in the morning and spent hours on his knees in a sort of trance. He made whirlwind visits to hospitals and prisons, and he seemed intent on convincing every young woman he met to enter the convent. His demands for frequent confessions and communion struck some priests as a self-proclamation that he was more spiritual than the rest of the clergy.

What prevented Illich from being dismissed as a mad eccentric was that he became involved with, or rather he seemed to take over, New York's Spanish community. Soon, Illich had job-placement centers and Sunday camps for Puerto Ricans. He worked with social workers and encouraged them to live among their Spanish clients. He organized Spanish festivals similar to those the people had left behind in Puerto Rico. Illich had done what Maguire wanted to do, on a much larger scale. In effect, Illich laid the groundwork for the kind of social activism that would mark the ministry of priests and nuns whom Spellman opposed in the 1960s. But, in 1956, Spellman had been so impressed with Illich's dynamism that he appointed him vice rector of the Catholic University in Puerto Rico, where Illich started a training program for young priests who were going to become missionaries in Latin America. At Maguire's suggestion, Spellman placed half of all seminary graduating classes in the Spanish program.[6]

It wasn't hard to find the reason for Spellman's concern about Spanish-speaking Catholics. Illich had cleverly sold the Cardinal on the necessity for such measures as a way of preventing the Latin underclass from embracing Communism. That buzzword, as always, had had the desired effect. Puerto Rico was a Latin crossroad. As he had shown in Guatemala, Spellman was ready to do anything to prevent Communism from gaining a toehold in the region. Illich eventually moved his operation to Cuernavaca, Mexico, where his controversial methods and his own radical theology made him many enemies in the Church. The Cardinal saw that the critics sniped at Illich because he was Spellman's man, and that he wouldn't tolerate. Spellman continued to fund and protect him, even though he loathed Illich's radicalism. (Within weeks of Spellman's death, Illich's enemies moved against him, shut down his operation, and eventually drummed him out of the priesthood. Thus, for Spellman, Illich had been a test of power.)

One man who rose to great heights at the chancery, and who besides Maguire was considered a possible successor to Spellman, was Monsignor Terence J. Cooke. A colorless young man, his background was the classic poor-boy-makes-good story. Born on March 1, 1921, Cooke was the son of an Irish immigrant who started life in America as a chauffeur and was employed by the actor John Barrymore, among others. Shortly after he was born, Cooke's parents moved to a pleasant section of the Bronx where Cooke proved to be a quiet, studious youth. He studied doggedly at the seminary and was ordained by Spellman in 1945. A brief stint in a parish was followed by graduate work in the social sciences at the University of Chicago, which he abandoned because of poor eyesight.

In 1949, Cooke was assigned to Catholic Charities, where he found his calling. Young Cooke loved the certainty of working with numbers as he traced the comings and goings of the fortunes of the organization. Then, in 1957, he became a secretary to Spellman, who was always on the lookout for young men with good heads for finance. Nicknamed "Cookie," the tall, bespectacled monsignor was similar to Spellman in a major respect. He did little but work. Even at the dinner table, he could be found mechanically spooning soup into his mouth while poring over a stack of corporate annual reports. Eager to please, Cooke always tried to have the facts and figures Spellman wanted, so much so that he reminded some priests of a cash register whose keys the Cardinal pushed.

An ambitious man, Cooke undertook the less pleasant tasks the Cardinal demanded, such as functioning as a stern dispenser of justice when a priest was believed to have erred. Thus, Cooke refused to renew Father Peter Jacobs's priestly faculties after Jacobs was accused of actively promoting the marriage of Catholics to non-Catholics. Cooke even had conservative priests spy on Jacobs and other priests who allegedly broke the rules. When Jacobs, who taught at Rice High School, a black Catholic high school in Harlem, began operating a restaurant, he was again suspended, in 1982. He was accused of running a bar, even though Cooke had been told it was a restaurant. The fact that any profits were earmarked for charity and scholarships and that there was a precedent for priests operating restaurants that served alcoholic beverages elsewhere in the United States as well as in Europe didn't change Cooke's attitude.[7] Jacobs, an exasperated chancery spokesman told a reporter for the *Baltimore Sun*, "is a pain in the ass."

When it came to Maguire and Cooke, Spellman never really saw a choice. While Maguire received the Cardinal's grudging respect, Cooke had his favor. Spellman disliked Maguire's disagreeing with him about certain policies. Maguire, for instance, didn't believe the Church should collaborate with the F.B.I. or the C.I.A., finding such collusion unseemly. When Daniel Berrigan was holed up at St. Gregory's Church in Manhattan, Maguire had objected when Spellman helped F.B.I. agents in their efforts to keep the Jesuit under surveillance.[8] (The spying had resulted in an embarrassing disclosure. Monsignor Harry Brown, St. Gregory's pastor, was secretly married, the F.B.I. men sheepishly told Spellman. Brown was sacked the same day.) Moreover, Cooke worked into the night, while Maguire liked to relax in the evening with a book.

Spellman told Rome that he wanted Cooke to succeed him, a recommendation that he knew wouldn't be greeted enthusiastically coming from him. Each day, Spellman checked his mail for confirmation from Rome that Cooke had been appointed. Each day he was disappointed. Just what Spellman, the man so out of favor with the Pope, used for leverage isn't known. He may simply have been motivated by the same brashness that drove him through his life. He may have thought he could bully the hesitant Pope Paul into accepting his choice. (Rome finally gave Cooke the job, apparently accepting the fact that he knew how to run the complex archdiocese.)

The Cardinal continued living much as before, but he struck people now as a man whose life seemed hollow despite all he had achieved. The last time *New York Post* publisher Schiff went to the Powerhouse, she was suddenly struck with pity for the man she had never liked. "He seemed so lonely," she recalled. On this occasion, he showed her through his residence and asked that she have a drink with him.[9]

In the final days of his life, the Cardinal attended dinners, speeches, and cocktail parties, although his attendance at such affairs had diminished in the past two years. On the night of December 1 he attended two functions at the Waldorf-Astoria, where he had spent so many gala evenings being feted by thousands of important people. On that evening he cited his continued support of American military forces in Vietnam and spoke pleasantly to the guests at both functions. He told a friend that he was considering a request from General Westmoreland to spend yet another Christmas in Vietnam, even though he had earlier said that he would not make the trip again.

On Saturday morning, December 2, Spellman was unable to get out of bed. His aides immediately called Dr. Fontana. "The Boss has had an attack," one of Spellman's secretaries told the doctor.

When Fontana arrived he realized the situation was extremely serious. He ordered an ambulance, and Spellman was carried out of his residence on a stretcher. The ambulance raced to St. Vincent's Hospital. "Now don't you worry about anything," Spellman told his doctor friend, and he squeezed the doctor's hand.[10]

Fontana knew he was about to lose his friend. Over the past decade and a half the doctor and the Cardinal had become very close, a friendship that rivaled only Bishop Cooke's. Fontana had gone on vacations with the prelate to wealthy Catholics' summer homes and Roy Cohn's yacht anchored at Key West. The doctor had reason to be grateful to the Cardinal. Several years earlier Spellman had asked, "What can I do for Doctor Fontana?" He had answered the question himself. The Cardinal had appointed his young friend director of St. Vincent's and Foundling hospitals.[11]

Shortly after being admitted to the hospital, seventy-eight-year-old Spellman died. An era in American Catholicism came to a close on December 2, 1967. The Spellman legacy of conservative politics, militarism, and pragmatism, however, was so strongly imprinted on the Church that it was to be felt for years to come. The American hierarchy was Spellmanized.

The flurry of activity surrounding the funeral arrangements consumed the attention of the men at the Powerhouse. There were squabbles about the kinds of altar flowers to be ordered and whether the prelate should be laid out wearing papal white or a cardinal's scarlet. Finally a compromise was reached: white vestments and a red skullcap. The evening after his death, Spellman's coffin was carried into the cathedral under the crossed swords of a dozen Knights of Columbus wearing white-plumed hats and navy uniforms. His body was placed in the center aisle in front of the main altar, on a black-draped catafalque surrounded by six towering candles.

St. Patrick's was bathed in the soft lights of hundreds of votive candles that had been lit by mourners. Thousands of people came to see the body of the man who had ruled the archdiocese of New York for nearly thirty years. Day and night, some three thousand mourners passed his casket each hour. Many of them hesitatingly reached out to touch the Cardinal's clasped hands or his skullcap. Thousands of them openly cried. Messages of condolence from around the world flooded the chancery.

In death, as in life, Spellman posed a political problem. At the White House the pros and cons of whether President Johnson should attend the funeral were debated. Tommy Corcoran, the old New Dealer, wrote a note to Johnson offering his services if the President wanted to attend and felt Corcoran could be helpful: "If it will help in the Catholic-Kennedy situation in New York where my relationship to the Cardinal is well known to the clergy and lay Catholics alike, I will be very happy to go along as part of the party. If you want me, I shall be in Washington today and New York tonight . . . although I am making no plans to go alone to the funeral. . . . I don't know what the Kennedy picture will be. They broke with the Cardinal."[12]

In New York, there was no question that politicians would attend. Their concern was striking the proper tone. Spellman had been a friend of some and an enemy of others. In light of his recent public snub of Spellman, Lindsay especially tried to strike a balance of noncommittal praise. The mayor finally said, "I am saddened by the death of Cardinal Spellman, who was a towering symbol of spiritual strength in our society."

On December 5 the whir of helicopters, like the sounds of a Vietnam battlefield, filled Central Park as President Johnson secretly landed. He had flown from Washington to the Floyd Bennett Naval Air Base in Brooklyn, where he had transferred to the helicopter. The President wanted to avoid danger and antiwar demonstrators. Thus, even to attend a cardinal's funeral, especially Cardinal Spellman's, Johnson had to be vigilant for his own safety. The President slipped into a black, bullet-proof limousine for the last leg of a journey through the open streets of New York. Police had arrested hundreds of demonstrators before Johnson's arrival. No one was taking any chances. Secret police combed crowds while uniformed police lined the presidential route. Suddenly, when the President's limousine glided into sight, hundreds of war protestors erupted in a chilling chant that had become the singsong refrain for the Johnson presidency: "Hey, hey, LBJ. How many kids have you killed today??"

As demonstrators chanted outside the cathedral, the eeriness of the occasion was rendered even more so by the barrenness of the funeral service itself. The mass was less than two hours long, or about half the length of the three-and-a-half-hour funeral for Spellman's predecessor, Cardinal Hayes. The powerful lament "Dies Irae," which dated to the thirteenth century, wasn't sung. Like so many changes in the Church that Spellman resented, the dirge had fallen victim to the new emphasis on joy and optimism at Catholic funerals. Ironically, traditional Protestant hymns, such as "For All the Saints," were sung and the entire service was in English, in keeping with the liturgical reforms resulting from Vatican II. Moreover, in another departure from tradition, invitations had been extended to Protestant, Jewish, and Orthodox leaders, many of whom sat next to the Catholic bishops at the foot of the altar. In the end, Spellman had lost.

The Cardinal's powerful past was reflected by the presence of the legions of churchmen, politicians, and military leaders who filled pew after pew as they came to pay their last respects to the man who had so much to do with them. Flags on government buildings and department stores in New York were at half mast, and the American Stock Exchange halted trading for a minute in honor of the unusual archbishop.

"Grant him mercy and peace everlasting," intoned the Pope's personal representative.

Spellman's body was buried in the Archbishop's Crypt directly beneath the high altar at St. Patrick's. At the conclusion of the service, the papal representative, "in the name of His Holiness," declared: "We have lost a spiritual leader, a father—and a dear friend. However, he will, I am sure, pray for us. May his devotion to our Church and to his fellow man continue to be a source of inspiration to us. May his brave, Christlike, priestly soul rest in peace."

When the ceremony ended, the priests, politicians, and military brass spilled out of the front doors of St. Patrick's and into the gusts of cold air and the eyes of the mourners and the demonstrators. As he pulled the collar of his overcoat higher around his neck, Father Joseph Fitzpatrick, a sociology professor at Fordham, turned to a friend and remarked, "That's the end of an era."

The thought was one that priests within the archdiocese all had. "Good!" his friend replied. The two priests walked away from Spellman's church.[13]

Chapter Notes

PROLOGUE

1. General Albert Wedemeyer to the author, Jan. 5, 1983.
2. I. F. Stone to the author, May 18, 1982.
3. William O. Douglas, *Go East Young Man: The Early Years*, p. 111.
4. Theodore Sorensen, former special counsel to President John Kennedy, to the author, Jan. 14, 1982.
5. Sorensen and David Powers, former aide to President Kennedy, to the author, March 15, 1982.
6. Powers to the author, March 15, 1982.

CHAPTER ONE

1. For the history of the Church, I drew upon many sources, including Geoffrey Barraclough, *The Medieval Papacy*; Paolo Brezzi, *The Papacy: Its Origins and Historical Evolution*; Wladimir d'Ormesson, *The Papacy*; Eric John, ed., *The Popes: A Concise Biographical History*; Peter Nichols, *The Politics of the Vatican*.
2. Spellman often told the story on himself. It was repeated by priests and reported by Robert I. Gannon, S.J., Spellman's official biographer in *The Cardinal Spellman Story*, p. 5.
3. Gannon, *The Cardinal Spellman Story*, p. 11.
4. Spellman told the story often on himself, including at testimonial dinners in his honor.
5. Spellman classmate to the author, Feb. 11, 1983.
6. Gannon, *The Cardinal Spellman Story*, pp. 19–20, and interviews with priests in New York and Boston.

7. Gannon, *The Cardinal Spellman Story*, pp. 25–26, plus interviews with priests in Boston, New York, Washington, and Rome.
8. *Ibid.*, p. 27.

CHAPTER TWO

1. For Church ethnic history, my sources included James Hennessey, S.J., *American Catholics: A History of the Roman Catholic Community in the United States*; Thomas McAvoy, *A History of the Catholic Church in the United States*.
2. A comprehensive background on the American Catholic Church and its relationship with the Vatican is found in Gerald P. Fogarty, *The Vatican and the American Hierarchy*.
3. *Ibid.*, p. 196.
4. Msgr. Harry O'Connor to the author, March 17, 1982.
5. A former secretary to Cardinal Spellman to the author.
6. Spellman told this story often on himself and it was reported by Gannon in *The Cardinal Spellman Story*, p. 35.
7. Memorandum to Spellman from Msgr. James O'Connell, in Boston archdiocesan archives.
8. Letter to Rev. R. J. Haberlin from Rev. D. J. Toomey, Aug. 14, 1918, in Boston archdiocesan archives.
9. Letter to Archbishop O'Connell from Spellman, Oct. 8, 1918, in Boston archdiocesan archives.
10. The plight of Msgr. O'Connell was an open secret in clerical circles. James O'Toole, archivist of the Boston archdiocese, told the author on March 16, 1982, that the $75,000 figure, while privately frequently quoted, has never been proven.
11. Letter in Boston archdiocesan archives.
12. Dorothy G. Wayman, *Cardinal O'Connell of Boston*, pp. 180–181. This sketchy account was supplemented by interviews with priests who were aware of the confrontation.
13. O'Connor to the author, March 17, 1982.
14. Spellman sent at least two such notes, one to Francis A. Burke, O'Connell's acting secretary, May 7, 1925, and one to Msgr. Richard J. Haberlin, Feb. 7, 1925, in Boston archdiocesan archives.
15. Gannon, *The Cardinal Spellman Story*, p. 42.
16. Interviews with priests in Boston, New York, and Washington.

CHAPTER THREE

1. Malachi Martin, *The Decline and Fall of the Roman Church*, p. 145.
2. Nino Lo Bello, *Vatican U.S.A.*, pp. 215–16.
3. Interviews with priests who monitored Spellman's career for years. Tales about his career climb are legion.
4. Gannon, *The Cardinal Spellman Story*, p. 53.
5. Spellman traced his relationship with the Bradys in his diary, including writing that they put him in their will for $100,000.
6. Gannon, *The Cardinal Spellman Story*, p. 63.
7. Earl Brennan to the author, Jan. 11, 1982.
8. Gannon, *The Cardinal Spellman Story*, pp. 62–63.
9. *Ibid.*, pp. 56–60. Other sources were Spellman's diary and interviews.
10. Martin, *Decline and Fall*, p. 261.

11. *Ibid.*, pp. 264–65; Malachi Martin, *Three Popes and the Cardinal*, pp. 5–7.
12. *Ibid.*, p. 6, plus interviews with priests in New York and Rome.
13. Accounts of Spellman's friendship with Pacelli were drawn from interviews with priests. His relationship with Mother Pascalina can be found in *La Popessa* by Paul Murphy.
14. Nino Lo Bello, *Vatican Empire*, pp. 26–30.
15. There are many accounts of the Church–State relationship in fascist Italy. Sources include D. A. Binchy, *Church and State in Fascist Italy*; F. L. Carsten, *The Rise of Fascism*; A. Cassel, *Fascist Italy*; S. W. Halperin, *Mussolini and Italian Fascism*; J. D. Holmes, *The Papacy in the Modern World*.
16. Spellman diary, May 31, 1931.
17. *Ibid.*
18. Priests and Edward "Ned" Spellman were the sources of the secret police story.
19. Gannon, *Cardinal Spellman Story*, p. 77.
20. Holmes, *Papacy in the Modern World*, p. 67.
21. *Ibid.*, pp. 69–70.
22. *Ibid.*, p. 74.
23. Spellman letter to O'Connell, May 10, 1931, in Boston archdiocesan archives.
24. *Ibid.*
25. Spellman diary, February (undated).
26. *Ibid.*, January (undated).
27. *Ibid.*, March (undated).
28. Brennan to the author, May 21, 1982.
29. Murphy, *La Popessa*, pp. 95–97.
30. Spellman diary, March 1, 2; April 25, 26, 28–30, 1932.
31. Gannon, *Cardinal Spellman Story*, p. 83.
32. Letter in Boston archdiocesan archives.

CHAPTER FOUR

1. Statement in Boston archdiocesan archives.
2. Cable, Oct. 6, 1932, in Boston archdiocesan archives.
3. Letter dated April 6, 1933, from Spellman to O'Connell, in Boston archdiocesan archives; Spellman diary entry, April 10, 1933.
4. Spellman diary, March 19, 20, and April 20, 21, 1933.
5. Thomas Corcoran to the author, Sept. 1, 1981.
6. Gannon, *Cardinal Spellman Story*, pp. 124–25.
7. O'Connor to the author, March 17, 1982.
8. Much of the Kennedy material is drawn from Richard J. Whalen, *The Founding Father: The Story of Joseph P. Kennedy,* and Michael R. Beschloss, *Kennedy and Roosevelt: The Uneasy Alliance.*
9. Material in the Boston archdiocesan archives.
10. Spellman diary, Aug. 5, 1934.
11. *Ibid.*, Aug. 5–6, 1934.
12. *Ibid.*, Aug. 10, 1934.
13. *Ibid.*, Sept. 2, 1934.
14. Enrico Galeazzi to the author, April 29, 1982.
15. Beschloss, *Kennedy and Roosevelt*, p. 116.
16. Spellman diary, Sept. 27, 1936.
17. Fogarty, *Vatican and the American Hierarchy*, p. 248.

18. Spellman diary, Dec. 22, 1936.
19. *Ibid.*, Dec. 26, 1936.
20. *Ibid.*, Dec. 15, 1936.
21. The note is in the Boston archdiocesan archives.
22. Spellman diary, Feb. 11, 1939.
23. Spellman diary. Entries were recorded in April, but are undated. (Spellman kept his diary erratically and didn't always record happenings on the date they occurred.)
24. *Ibid.*, March 16, 1939.
25. *Ibid.*, March 17, 1939.
26. *Ibid.*, June 29, 30, 1939.
27. O'Connor to the author, March 17, 1982.

CHAPTER FIVE

1. Interviews with New York priests.
2. George Barry Ford, *A Degree of Difference: Memoirs of George Barry Ford*, plus Ford's Oral History at Columbia University.
3. *Ibid.*
4. Bishop Philip J. Furlong to the author, Feb. 23, 1982.
5. Spellman letter to Apostolic Delegate Amleto Cicognani on his accomplishments as archbishop.
6. Msgr. Joseph Dunn to the author, March 11, 1982.
7. Bishop Patrick Ahern to the author, Nov. 23, 1981.
8. O'Connor to the author, March 17, 1982.
9. Based on interviews with Archbishop John Maguire on Feb. 25, 1982, and other priests. Also Gannon, *Cardinal Spellman Story*, pp. 249–50, and Spellman diary, July 19, 1939.
10. Jonah J. Goldstein, Columbia Oral History.
11. Murphy, *La Popessa*, p. 182.
12. Gannon, *Cardinal Spellman Story*, pp. 263–64.
13. *The Compass*, Nov. 2, 1950.
14. Victor Lasky, *Robert F. Kennedy: The Myth and the Man*, p. 63.
15. Arthur Schlesinger, Jr., *Robert Kennedy and His Times*, pp. 56–57.
16. Stephen Birmingham, *Real Lace: America's Irish Rich*, p. 91.
17. *Ibid.*, p. 92.
18. Francis Quillinan to the author, Oct. 1, 1982.
19. Father Albert Nevins to the author, May 24, 1982.
20. Herbert Brownell to the author, April 24, 1983.
21. Frederick Cuneo to the author, Sept. 23, 1982.
22. Letters to Spellman from La Guardia, March 19, 1945; June 10, 1940; June 7, 1940. Spellman to La Guardia, March 26, 1945.
23. Cuneo to the author, Sept. 23, 1982.
24. *New York Post*, Sept. 20, 1957, plus interviews with former Spellman aides.
25. From interviews with C. A. Tripp, a sex researcher affiliated with Dr. Alfred C. Kinsey of the Institute for Sex Research, March 12, 1982; Bruce Veller, president of the Mariposa Educational Foundation, August 3, 1984; David McWhirter, a psychiatrist and associate professor at the University of California at San Diego School of Medicine, August 2, 1984; Philip Nobile, a former seminarian who served as one of Spellman's altar boys, April 2, 1982; and many anonymous sources.
26. Gore Vidal in undated note to the author.

CHAPTER SIX

1. James Rowe to the author, April 12, 1982.
2. Joseph Alsop to the author, May 11, 1982.
3. Holmes, *Papacy in the Modern World*, p. 130.
4. Fogarty, *Vatican and the American Hierarchy*, pp. 261–62.
5. Roosevelt memo to Taylor, Feb. 13, 1940.
6. Harold L. Ickes, *The Secret Diary of Harold L. Ickes,* vol. III, p. 55.
7. *Ibid.,* p. 110.
8. *Ibid.,* p. 65.
9. Fogarty, *Vatican and the American Hierarchy*, p. 264.
10. John Patrick Monaghan told his labor priests about the Haas visit. Tommy Corcoran said, "That sounds right," when asked about the matter.
11. Holmes, *Papacy in the Modern World*, p. 160. The author stated that certain Franciscans participated in the slaughter.
12. Vatican memorandum to Spellman, March 13, 1942.
13. Roosevelt note to Spellman, March 14, 1942.
14. Memo to Roosevelt from Rep. John McCormack, Nov. 27, 1941.
15. Roosevelt to Donald M. Nelson, chairman of the War Production Board, Oct. 19, 1942.
16. Spruille Braden, Columbia Oral History.
17. *Ibid.*
18. *Ibid.*
19. Dispatch from American embassy in Madrid to Washington, Feb. 18, 1943.
20. *Ibid.*
21. *Ibid.*
22. Records of the National Security Agency, SRS 900, "Magic" Summaries No. 349, March 10, 1943.
23. *Ibid.*
24. James Hennessey, "An American Jesuit in Wartime Rome: The Diary of Vincent A. McCormick, S.J. (1942–1945)," *Mid-America.* vol. 56 (1974), p. 40.
25. At the time, there was speculation in the press that Spellman had a hand in Mussolini's downfall as well as negotiating an armistice for Italy.
26. Wedemeyer to the author, Jan. 5, 1983.
27. A report on the Spellman–de Gaulle meeting was recorded in Report No. 55953, Military Intelligence Division, April 16, 1943.
28. *Ibid.*
29. *Ibid.*
30. *Ibid.*
31. U.S. Legation in Baghdad report, May 21, 1943, State Department Archives 033.1166A/28 GSAW.
32. Spellman diary, Aug. 1, 1943; Gannon, *The Cardinal Spellman Story*, pp. 220–21.
33. Letter from Roosevelt to Pope Pius XII (undated).
34. Hennessey, "McCormick Diary," p. 48.
35. Letter from Pope Pius XII to Roosevelt, July 20, 1943.
36. Hennessey, "McCormick Diary," p. 51.
37. Spellman memorandum to the Vatican on the meeting.
38. *PM,* Oct. 21, 1943.

39. Spellman diary, July 28, 29; Aug. 3, 4, 1944.
40. Hennessey, "McCormick Diary," pp. 51–52.
41. Holmes, *Papacy in the Modern World*, pp. 135–36.
42. See Bertram Gordon, *Collaborationism in France During the Second World War;* Robert O. Paxton, *Vichy France: Old Guard and New Order 1940–1944.*
43. Spellman diary, Aug. 11, 1944; also interviews with churchmen in New York, Washington, and Rome.
44. Office of Strategic Services cable, Paris to Washington, Dec. 28, 1944.
45. Roland Flamini, *Pope, Premier, President: The Cold War Summit That Never Was*, p. 51, interview with Malachi Martin on March 30, 1982, plus interviews with priests who knew of the issue.
46. Spellman diary, Aug. 20, 21, 1944.
47. *Ibid.*, Sept. 28, 1944.
48. Federal Bureau of Investigation memorandum to J. Edgar Hoover.
49. O.S.S. report #56, Jan. 14, 1945.
50. Camille Cianfarra, *The Vatican and the War*, p. 297; O.S.S. files JOV 55.
51. O.S.S. files JOV 55.
52. George O. Flynn, *Roosevelt and Romanism: Catholics and American Diplomacy 1937-1945*, pp. 220–27, plus interviews with former Spellman aides.
53. O.S.S. document for accounting of Operational Funds for James Angleton, Sept. 10, 1945.
54. O.S.S. documents (undated).

CHAPTER SEVEN

1. F.B.I. report, NY 62-8845; also confidential F.B.I. memorandum June 25, 1946. Quotation is paraphrased from report.
2. Interviews with confidential sources from New York archdiocese. For international, Malachi Martin as well as New York priests provided information.
3. F.B.I. memos.
4. Geoffrey Perrett, *A Dream of Greatness: The American People 1945–1963*, p. 237.
5. *Izvestia*, Jan. 27, 1946.
6. Gannon, *The Cardinal Spellman Story*, p. 291.
7. Robert H. Jackson, Columbia Oral History.
8. *Time*, Feb. 22, 1960, for Stepinac; Donald F. Crosby, *God, Church and Flag: Senator Joseph R. McCarthy and the Catholic Church 1950-1957*, p. 11.
9. Crosby, *Ibid.*, p. 18.
10. Spellman to Truman, Jan. 15, 1946.
11. Truman to Spellman, Feb. 15, 1946.
12. Confidential State Department report, June 22, 1948: J. Graham Parsons, assistant to Myron Taylor (840.4 Vatican).
13. *Ibid.*
14. Confidential report to U.S. Secretary of State from Franklin C. Gowen, assistant to Myron Taylor, March 20, 1947.
15. Msgr. James H. Griffiths report to Spellman, Aug. 18, 1948.
16. Griffiths memo to Spellman, March 4, 1948.

17. Telegram to the U.S. State Department from J. Graham Parsons, Jan. 16, 1948 (865-00/1-2848A/VS).
18. Report from Parsons to State Department on *Vatican Pre-Election Activities*, March 2, 1948 (865-00/3-248).
19. *Ibid.*
20. Spellman memo to the Vatican on his meeting with Marshall (undated).
21. *Ibid.*
22. *Ibid.*
23. Josef Cardinal Mindszenty, *Mindszenty Memoirs*, p. 89.
24. American embassy documents from Budapest, Oct. 22 and 28, 1947: State Department letter (OSW 000.4 relics); Secret American embassy memo to Parsons (840.4 Hungary); War Department memos from Budapest, Feb. 1947 (387.6-2-10).
25. *Ibid.*
26. U.S. government report, "Some Areas of Psychiatric Interest," Sept. 5, 1952.

    (The name of the agency responsible for the document was deleted and the only identification is Psychological Strategy Board.) The report details the procedures of the brainwashing of Mindszenty, including the kinds of drugs administered and the length of time it took to break him. "The strategy that was employed here represents apparently the acme of training, fine judgment and experience on the hands of the skilled interrogators who were selected for this particular case," the report notes.

CHAPTER EIGHT

1. Father Robert Fox to the author, Dec. 23, 1981; plus other interviews.
2. Francis Quillinan to the author, Oct. 1, 1982.
3. Frank Adams to the author, May 6, 1982.
4. Warren Moscow, *The Last of the Big-Time Bosses: The Life and Times of Carmine De Sapio and the Decline and Fall of Tammany Hall*, p. 61.
5. Julius Edelstein to the author, Oct. 22, 1981.
6. Abraham Beame to the author, Oct. 26, 1981.
7. Moscow to the author, Sept. 30, 1981.
8. *Ibid.*
9. *Ibid.*
10. Peter J. Brennan, former president of the Building and Construction Trade Council, to the author, Oct. 17, 1981.
11. Msgr. E. Harold Smith to the author, Oct. 12, 1981; plus other interviews.
12. Hennessey, *American Catholics: A History of the Roman Catholic Community in the United States,* p. 56.
13. Edelstein to the author, Oct. 22, 1981.
14. Joseph P. Lash, *Eleanor: The Years Alone,* p. 161.
15. Moscow, *Last of the Big-Time Bosses*, p. 122.
16. Patrick Flynn, son of Ed Flynn, to the author, March 12, 1981; plus other sources.
17. Lash, *Eleanor: The Years Alone,* p. 163.
18. Joseph Alsop to the author, March 24, 1982.
19. Lash, *Eleanor: The Years Alone,* p. 163.

20. Moscow related to the author that he was told of the trip by Flynn.
21. Lehman Collection, Columbia University.
22. Lash, *Eleanor: The Years Alone,* p. 165.
23. *Ibid.*
24. Charles Silver to the author, Dec. 20, 1981.
25. Report dated May 19, 1952 (097.3 210.92).
26. Memorandum #5914 from Spellman to the Vatican on the meeting with Marshall.
27. O'Connor to the author, March 17, 1982.
28. Silver to the author, Dec. 20, 1981.
29. Letter from Ruth Tov, wife of Moshe Tov, to the author, March 24, 1983.
30. Letter from Spellman to Truman, April 29, 1949.
31. Report: "Israel's Open Disregard of Christian Claims in Palestine" (undated).
32. Associates of Charlie Silver.
33. Testimony of Charles Lipsky, April 25, 1951.
34. The dialogue is reconstructed from interviews with gravediggers Sam Cimaglia, Stephen Cimaglia, and Siggy Czak, Godfrey Schmidt, the archdiocesan attorney during the strike, and priests who were involved either as seminarians or in other roles.
35. Msgr. George Kelly to the author, Sept. 18, 1982.
36. James O'Gara, *Commonweal* editor, to the author, Nov. 11, 1981.
37. Carlos Baker, ed., *Ernest Hemingway: Selected Letters 1917–1961,* pp. 661–62.
38. Several New York chancery personnel to the author.
39. Godfrey Schmidt to the author, Jan. 14, 1983.
40. Msgr. Myles Burke to the author, Nov. 17, 1981.
41. Spellman to Matthew J. Connelly, secretary to Truman, March 25, 1949.
42. Connelly to Spellman letter, April 1, 1949.
43. Frank Getlein to the author, May 12, 1982.
44. Mrs. Otto Spaeth to the author, March 10, 1982.
45. Dr. Vincent J. Fontana to the author, Sept. 16, 1982.
46. *Ibid.*
47. Arnold Rogow, *James Forrestal: A Study of Personality, Politics and Policy,* p. 130.
48. Dorothy Schiff kept extensive memos on matters she considered important. The conversations are as she recorded them on Jan. 25, 1952.
49. Mrs. Schiff to the author, March 19, 1982.
50. Murray Kempton to the author, May 14, 1982.
51. The luncheon conversation is derived from Mrs. Schiff's notes dated Feb. 12, 1952; plus an interview.

CHAPTER NINE

1. Msgr. Eugene Clark to the author, Jan. 28, 1982; plus other chancery sources.
2. State Department memorandum regarding Vatican–U.S. relations (Declassified Documents Defense System Retrospective Collection 777-C).
3. Fogarty, *The Vatican and the American Hierarchy,* p. 323.
4. Spellman to James Byrnes letter, Jan. 6, 1951.

5. Dean Rusk to the author, May 12, 1982.
6. Giovanni Battista Montini letter to Spellman, March 12, 1953.
7. Father Robert A. Graham to the author, April 4, 1982.
8. Spellman to Montini, April 17, 1953.
9. *Ibid.*
10. Spellman letter to Count Enrico Galeazzi, May 27, 1953.
11. Frank Adams to the author, May 6, 1982.
12. F.B.I. memorandum, July 24, 1953.
13. Drew Pearson reported on March 14, 1950, that Walsh was the source of McCarthy's inspiration.
14. Fred J. Cook, *The Nightmare Decade: The Life and Times of Senator Joe McCarthy*, p. 259.
15. Father Fred McGuire to the author, Jan. 13, 1982.
16. A Spellman relative to the author, Feb. 18, 1982.
17. Geoffrey Perrett, *A Dream of Greatness*, p. 271.
18. Lately Thomas, *When Even Angels Wept: The Senator Joseph McCarthy Affair—A Story Without a Hero*, pp. 470–71.
19. Herbert Brownell to the author, Jan. 22, 1983.
20. J. Edgar Hoover note to Roy Cohn, Dec. 5, 1958.
21. Roy Cohn to the author, Feb. 16, 1982.
22. William F. Buckley, Jr., to the author, Aug. 2, 1982.
23. Cohn to the author, Feb. 16, 1982.
24. Stephen Schlesinger and Stephen Kinzer, *Bitter Fruit: The Untold Story of the American Coup in Guatemala,* p. 155.
25. Fogarty, *Vatican and American Hierarchy*, p. 336.
26. Foreign Service dispatch from Lima.
27. Foreign Service dispatch from La Paz.
28. Foreign Service dispatch from Asunción.
29. I am heavily indebted to *Bitter Fruit* for the Guatemala material, much of which doesn't appear elsewhere.
30. Flamini, *Pope, Premier, President*, p. 23. Victor Marchetti and John Marks in *The CIA and the Cult of Intelligence* said the C.I.A. involved Church employees in its activities in Asia, Africa, and Latin America.
31. Brownell to the author, Jan. 22, 1983.
32. Bernard Shanley to the author, Feb. 22, 1982. The following episode was recounted by Shanley and supplemented by interviews with chancery sources and Herbert Brownell.
33. Brownell to the author, Jan. 22, 1983.
34. Shanley to the author, Feb. 22, 1982.
35. McGuire to the author, Jan. 13, 1982.
36. Joseph Buttinger, *Vietnam: A Dragon Embattled*, pp. 486–87.
37. McGuire to the author, Jan. 13, 1982.
38. Malachi Martin to the author, March 30, 1982.
39. Ralph W. McGhee, *Deadly Deceits: My 25 Years in the C.I.A.*, p. 132.
40. Department of State document, Dec. 18, 1954.
41. *National Catholic Reporter*, Dec. 17, 1976; plus back issues.
42. Dorothy Schiff memo, June 20, 1965.

CHAPTER TEN

1. Murphy, *La Popessa*, p. 275; plus interviews.
2. *Ibid.*, pp. 276–79.
3. Interviews with priests in New York, Washington, and Rome.

4. The Rev. D. P. Noonan, *The Passion of Fulton Sheen*, p. 13.
5. McGuire to the author, Jan. 13, 1982.
6. Noonan and others to the author.
7. *Ibid.*
8. *Ibid.*
9. Barrett McGurn, *A Reporter Looks at the Vatican*, p. 26.
10. Malachi Martin, *The Decline and Fall of the Roman Church*, pp. 156–57.
11. Carlo Falconi, *The Popes in the Twentieth Century*, pp. 306–9.
12. *Ibid.*

CHAPTER ELEVEN

1. Msgr. Eugene Clark to the author, Jan. 28, 1982.
2. Powers and others to the author.
3. Paul Hofmann memo to Arthur Krock, March 9, 1960.
4. *Ibid.*
5. *Ibid.*
6. Dwight D. Eisenhower, *Waging Peace 1956–1961: The White House Years*, p. 432.
7. Brownell to the author, Jan. 22, 1983.
8. Interviews with priests in New York, Boston, and Washington.
9. *Ibid.*
10. A monsignor to the author, Jan. 18, 1982.
11. Laurence Fuchs, *John F. Kennedy and American Catholicism*, p. 175.
12. Spellman note to Kennedy, July 14, 1960.
13. Theodore Sorensen, *Kennedy*, p. 360.
14. Nino Lo Bello, *Vatican U.S.A.*, pp. 166–67.

CHAPTER TWELVE

1. Robert Blair Kaiser to the author, Sept. 22, 1982.
2. Flamini, *Pope, Premier, President*, pp. 64–65.
3. Peter Nichols, *Politics of the Vatican*, pp. 224–25.
4. Flamini, *Pope, Premier, President,* p. 161.
5. C.I.A. report, Staff Memorandum No. 27-63, May 13, 1963.
6. *Ibid.*
7. Flamini, *Pope, Premier, President*, p. 161.
8. Told by priests in New York. The stamp was issued by the Nicaraguan government in August 1959.
9. Flamini, *Pope, Premier, President*, pp. 169–70.
10. *Ibid.*, p. 174; plus interviews.
11. Martin Garbus to the author, Oct. 1, 1981.
12. Interviews with priests in New York and Washington.
13. Interviews with Archbishop John Maguire and other priests.
14. A Spellman relative to the author, Feb. 18, 1982.
15. Harris Wofford, *Of Kennedys and Kings: Making Sense of the Sixties,* p. 208.
16. Letter from Egidio Vagnozzi to Spellman (undated but given the file no. 381/35).
17. Letter from Spellman to Vagnozzi, June 29, 1965.
18. Father David Kirk to the author, Nov. 11, 1981.
19. Francine du Plessix Gray, *Divine Disobedience: Profiles in Catholic Radicalism*, p. 21.

20. Kirk to the author, Nov. 11, 1981.
21. Rev. Vincent O'Keefe, former president of Fordham, to the author, April 27, 1982.
22. du Plessix Gray, *Divine Disobedience*, pp. 101–2.
23. Bishop Patrick Ahern to the author, Nov. 23, 1981.
24. Vincent Broderick to the author, March 27, 1981.

CHAPTER THIRTEEN

1. Based on interviews with Father Robert Fox; former Maryknoll priests Frank O'Hara and Renée Archambault; a note from an aide to Father Miguel d'Escoto Brockman; and a former Maryknoll priest and a current Maryknoll priest, both of whom asked not to be identified.
2. Brownell to the author, Jan. 22, 1983.
3. Fox to the author, Dec. 16, 1981.
4. O'Hara to the author, June 12, 1983.
5. Archambault to the author, June 12, 1983.
6. Marshall Frady, *Billy Graham: A Parable of American Righteousness*, p. 429.
7. Carmine De Sapio to the author, Sept. 17, 1982.
8. Beame to the author, Oct. 26, 1981.
9. Robert Caro, *The Power Broker: Robert Moses and the Fall of New York*, p. 741.
10. Vincent R. Impellitteri to the author, Feb. 20, 1982.
11. Caro, *The Power Broker*, pp. 722–26.
12. Moscow to the author, Sept. 30, 1981.
13. Interviews with Msgr. George Kelly and anonymous source.
14. *Ibid.*
15. *Ibid.* (Lindsay declined twice to be interviewed.)
16. Kelly to the author, Sept. 18, 1982.

CHAPTER FOURTEEN

1. Julius Edelstein, Monsignor George Kelly, and others said Travia was viewed as one of Spellman's men.
2. Kelly to the author, Sept. 18, 1982.
3. Americans United for Separation of Church and State estimated the C.E.F. was 95 percent Roman Catholic.
4. Joseph Persico, Rockefeller aide, to the author, May 18, 1982.
5. *Ibid.*
6. New York priests to the author.
7. Kelly to the author, Sept. 18, 1982.
8. *Ibid.*
9. Wolfson in a letter to the author, Sept. 30, 1981.
10. *Ibid.*
11. *Ibid.*
12. *Ibid.*
13. Malcolm Wilson, former lieutenant governor, to the author, Sept. 30, 1981.
14. Wilson to the author.
15. Kelly to the author.
16. Wilson to the author.
17. Spellman aides to the author.

CHAPTER FIFTEEN

1. Bishop Ahern, Monsignor Clark, and others to the author.
2. Ford, *A Degree of Difference*, p. 158.
3. Chancery priests to the author.
4. Archbishop Maguire to the author.
5. Bishop Furlong to the author, Jan. 28, 1982.
6. Father Joseph Fitzpatrick to the author, Feb. 1, 1982.
7. Father Peter Jacobs to the author, Feb. 3, 1983.
8. Chancery priests to the author.
9. Mrs. Schiff to the author, March 19, 1982.
10. Dr. Fontana to the author, Sept. 16, 1982.
11. *Ibid.*
12. Corcoran note, undated (in Johnson Library).
13. Fitzpatrick to the author, Feb. 1, 1982.

Bibliography and Sources

Archives and Manuscript Collections

Freedom of Information Act, F.B.I. and State Department Documents

Collections

Boston Archdiocesan Archives
Columbia University Oral History
James A. Farley Papers, Library of Congress
Lyndon B. Johnson Library
John F. Kennedy Library
Herbert Lehman Papers, Columbia University
National Archives
New York Municipal Archives
Princeton Library (Mudd Library—Bernard Baruch Papers; Arthur Krock
    Papers)
Franklin D. Roosevelt Library
Harry S Truman Library
United Nations Archives
Diary of Cardinal Spellman
United Nations Special Committee on Palestine. Report to the General As-
    sembly 1947. Vols. I, II, IV

Magazines and Periodicals
(By Chronology)

O'Brien, David, "Toward an American Catholic Church," *Cross Currents*, vol. XXXI, no. 4 (Winter 1981–82).

Corry, J., "Cardinal Spellman and New York Politics," *Harper*, March 1968.

Adamo, S. J., "Unknown Spellman," *America*, Dec. 23, 1967.

Cameron, J. H., "Cardinal Spellman, Charles Davis," *Commonweal* 85:417–18 (Dec. 20, 1967).

"Cardinal Spellman Succumbs at Seventy Eight," *Christian Century*, Dec. 20, 1967.

"Requiem for a Cardinal," *Time*, Dec. 15, 1967.

Obituary, *Commonweal*, Dec. 15, 1967.

"Organization Man," *Newsweek*, Dec. 11, 1967.

"Master Builder," *Time*, Dec. 8, 1967.

O'Gara, J., "Catholic Super Patriots," *Commonweal*, May 12, 1967.

"Cardinal's Mistake," *Nation* 204:69 (Jan. 16, 1967).

"Cardinal, Pope and War," *Commonweal* 85:391–92 (Jan. 13, 1967).

"Cardinal Spellman's Holy War," *Christian Century* 84:36 (Jan. 11, 1967).

"Cardinal Under Fire: Spellman's Views Irk Reds," *U.S. News* 64:14 (Jan. 9, 1967).

"Fatima's 50th: The Day the Sun Danced," *Saturday Review* 50:70 (Jan. 7, 1967).

Leo, J., "News and Views," *Commonweal* 85:4 (Oct. 7, 1966).

"Spellman of New York: 50th Anniversary of Ordination," *Newsweek* 67:61–62 (May 30, 1966).

"New Yorkers Hail Their Cardinal," *America* 114:762 (May 28, 1966).

"Cardinal Spellman Calls for Censorship Group," *Publishers Weekly* 185:68 (June 22, 1964).

"Pastor-Executive," *Time* 83:54 (May 15, 1964).

"Cardinal Spellman's Twenty-Five Years," *America* 110:529 (April 18, 1964).

"Unlocking the Icebox: Christian Services in Antarctica," *Time* 83:41 (Jan. 3, 1964).

"Cardinal Spellman Reminisces," *Christian Century* 80:1531 (Dec. 4, 1963).

"U.S. and Vatican: An Untold Story; Excerpt Gannon," *U.S. News* 52:108–19 (Nov. 19, 1962).

"Cardinal Spellman Story. Excerpts. R. I. Gannon," *Look* 26:64–67 (March 13, 1962); 26:50–52 (Feb. 27, 1962); 26:58–62 (Feb. 13, 1962).

"Cardinal Says No," *Time* 79:46 (Feb. 16, 1962).

"Cardinal vs. Senator," *U.S. News* 51:20 (Sept. 4, 1961).

"Cardinal Spellman Tries Again," *Christian Century* 78:613 (May 17, 1961).

"Regrettable Revival: Discussion," *Christian Century* 78:275–76 (March 1, 1961); 78:131–32 (Feb. 1, 1961).

"Under Catholic Church Fire: Kennedy's School Plan. Statement January 17," *U.S. News* 50:54–55 (Jan. 30, 1961).

Murphy, C. J. V., "Cardinal," *Fortune* 61:150–54 (Feb. 1960).

"Cardinal's Moment," *Newsweek* 50:96 (Sept. 9, 1959).

"Cardinal's Birthday," *Time* 73:68 (May 11, 1959).

"Racism in Housing," *America* 100:590 (Feb. 21, 1959).

"Cardinal Spellman in Ceylon," *America* 98:684 (March 15, 1958).

"Cardinal's Jubilee," *America* 97:474 (Aug. 10, 1957).

"Annual Mr. Travel Award Presented to His Eminence," *Travel* 105:11–13 (March 1956).

"Korean Christmas," *Newsweek* 46:42 (Dec. 26, 1955).

"Cardinal's Christmas," *America* 94:346 (Dec. 24, 1955).

"Hobbies of the Famous," *Coronet* 39:10 (Nov. 1955).

"Pilgrims of the East," *Newsweek* 45:42 (Jan. 24, 1955).

"Alternatives to Coexistence," *Nation* 179:204 (Sept. 11, 1954).

"Communism Has a World Plan: Address, August 30, 1954," *Vital Speeches* 20:709–11 (Sept. 15, 1954); Excerpt, *Time* 64:27 (Sept. 13, 1954).

"Dien Bien Phu: A Reveille," *Vital Speeches* 20:567–9 (June 1, 1954).

"Fast-Traveling Cardinal, His Fast Growing Church," *Newsweek* 43:54–57 (May 24, 1954).

"Soldier's Pastor in Korea," *America* 90:340 (Jan. 16, 1954).

"America, Grateful Child of Mother Europe; Address, October 23, 1953," *Vital Speeches* 20:101–4 (Dec. 1, 1953); Excerpt, *U.S. News* 35:126–27 (Nov. 6, 1953); Excerpt, *Reader's Digest* 64:26–27 (Nov. 6, 1953).

"Cardinal Defends Good Name of the U.S.," *America* 90:141 (Nov. 7, 1953).

"Cardinal Spellman Talks to Europeans About McCarthyism," *U.S. News* 35:126–27 (Nov. 6, 1953).

Oberhardt, L., "Obie, The Modern Headhunter" (with editorial comment), *American Artist* 17:38; 71–73 (Sept. 1953).

Cogley, J., "Who Will Be the Next Pope?" *Collier's* 131:22–36 (March 14, 1953).

"Two Visits to Korea," *Time* 61:84 (Jan. 5, 1953).

"How Red China Tortures Protestant and Catholic Missionaries," *Collier's* 129:15–17 (May 10, 1952).

Portrait, *Publishers Weekly* 161:212 (Jan. 19, 1952).

Portrait, *Saturday Review of Literature* 34:17 (May 26, 1951).

"Loyalty," *Scholastic* 58:5 (Feb. 21, 1951).

"Foundling," *Good Housekeeping* 132:56–57; 60–61 (Feb. 1951).

"Author," *New Yorker* 26:26–27 (Dec. 16, 1950).

Portrait, *New York Times Magazine*, March 12, 1950, p. 32.

Portrait, *U.S. News* 28:24 (Feb. 10, 1950).

"Was Bishop Oxnam Right?" *Christian Century* 66:981–83 (Aug. 24, 1949).

"Clarifying and Fair: Cardinal Spellman and Federal Aid," *Commonweal* 50:452 (Aug. 19, 1949).

"Truce 1," *Time* 54:15 (Aug. 15, 1949).

Laughlin, N. B., "Christian Attitude," *Nation* 169:163–64 (Aug. 13, 1949).

"Mrs. Roosevelt Replies to the Cardinal," *Christian Century* 66:931 (Aug. 10, 1949).

"Echoes," *Time* 54:54–55 (Aug. 8, 1949).

Burnham, P., "Separation of Cardinal Spellman and Mrs. Roosevelt," *Commonweal* 50:404–5 (Aug. 5, 1949).

"Cardinal Spellman Overreaches: Barden Bill for Aid to Public Schools," *Christian Century* 66:907 (Aug. 3, 1949).

"Cardinal and the Lady," *Newsweek* 34:18 (Aug. 1, 1949).

"My Day in the Lion's Mouth," *Time* 54:11 (Aug. 1, 1949).

"Strike in the Graveyard," *Time* 53:63 (March 14, 1949).

"Rebellion to Tyrants: Excerpts from Sermon," *Time* 53:31 (Feb. 14, 1949).

"Waiting for the Sunrise" (poem), *Good Housekeeping* 127:15 (Oct. 1948).

"Hirohito and the Cardinal," *Newsweek* 31:41 (June 21, 1948).

"Mankind's Moment of Decision," *Vital Speeches* 14:389–91 (April 15, 1948).

"Cardinal Looks for Trouble," *Christian Century* 64:787–88 (June 25, 1947).
Biography, *Current Biography*, April 1947.
"Hunger: Terror of Peace," *Good Housekeeping* 123:41 (Sept. 1946).
"Communism Is Un-American," *American Magazine* 142:26–28 (June 1946).
"Resurrection" (poem), *Life* 20:27 (April 22, 1946).
Malloy, J. I. "Welcome Home," *Catholic World* 163:82–83 (April 1946).
"Rare Distinction," *Nation* 162–245 (March 2, 1946).
"America in Rome," *Time* 47:43–46 (Feb. 25, 1946).
Butterfield, R., "Cardinal Designate," *Life* 20:100–102 (Jan. 21, 1946); 20:
    87–88 (Jan. 28, 1946).
Woolf, S. J., "Spellman Points Out the Road to Peace," *New York Times
    Magazine*, Jan. 13, 1946, p. 8.
"Francis Cardinal Spellman," *Newsweek* 26:79 (Dec. 31, 1945).
"Our Sleeping Soldiers" (poem), *Good Housekeeping* 121:42 (Dec. 1945).
"American May Be Papal Secretary of State," *Christian Century* 62:747
    (June 27, 1945).
"This Peace Must Last," *Collier's* 116:29–30 (June 7, 1945).
"Liberated France," *Collier's* 115:24 (April 28, 1945).
"England and the Boys," *Collier's* 115:24 (March 24, 1945).
"Journey into France," *Collier's* 115:20 (Feb. 17, 1945).
"Report from Italy," *Collier's* 115:11 (Jan. 20, 1945).
"Prayer for Children," *Collier's* 114:18–19 (Dec. 30, 1944).
Malloy, J. I., "Archbishop Spellman Overseas,"*Catholic World* 159:562
    (Sept. 1944).
"Red Hats for the U.S.?" *Time* 44:47 (Aug. 7, 1944).
"Spiritually We Are Semitics," *Time* 44:82 (June 3, 1944).
"Risen Soldier," *Collier's* 113:11 (April 15, 1944).
"Bigotry Is Un-American," *American Magazine* 137:20–21 (April 1944).
"Meaning of Christmas," *Reader's Digest* 43:72 (Dec. 1943).
"Action This Day," *Collier's* 112:21 (Nov. 20, 1943); 112:24 (Nov. 13, 1943);
    112:18 (Nov. 6, 1943); 112:21 (Oct. 30, 1943); 112:12 (Oct. 23, 1943); 112:11
    (Oct. 16, 1943).
"Deal With Franco?" *Christian Century* 60:1255–257 (Nov. 3, 1943).
"Some Spaniards on Archbishop Spellman Call Sources of Information into
    Question," *New Republic* 109:605 (Nov. 1, 1943).
"Globetrotting Prelate," *Scholastic* 43:11 (Oct. 25, 1943).
"Spellman on Spain," *New Republic* 109:557 (Oct. 25, 1943).
Kirchwey, F., "Absolution from Franco: Archbishop Spellman's Support
    of Franco's Regime," *Nation* 157:459–61 (Oct. 23, 1943).
"Archbishop's Travels," *Life* 15:71–72 (Sept. 20, 1943).
Malloy, J. I., "Return," *Catholic World* 157:654–55 (Sept. 1943).
"Odyssey for the Millennium," *Time* 41:34 (June 7, 1943).
"Archbishop's Progress," *Newsweek* 21:82 (April 19, 1943).
"Spellman's Itinerary Raises Questions," *Christian Century* 60:412 (April
    7, 1943).
Malloy, J. I., "Archbishop Spellman Visits Vatican," *Catholic World* 157:93
    (April 1943).
"Archbishop's Mission," *Scholastic* 42:12 (March 8, 1943).
"Flight to Rome," *Time* 41:31 (Feb. 22, 1943).

Books

Allen, Roger Van, ed., *The Commonweal and American Catholicism* (Phil-
    adelphia: Fortress Press, 1974).

Alsop, Joseph Stuart, *The Reporter's Trade* (New York: Reynal, 1958).

Ambrose, Stephen E., *Ike's Spies: Eisenhower and the Espionage Establishment* (New York: Doubleday, 1981).

Baker, Carlos, ed., *Ernest Hemingway: Selected Letters 1917–1961* (New York: Charles Scribner's Sons, 1981).

Barraclough, Geoffrey, *The Medieval Papacy* (London: Historical Association, 1950).

Belfrage, Cedric, *The American Inquisition 1945–1960* (New York: Bobbs-Merrill, 1974).

Beschloss, Michael R., *Kennedy and Roosevelt: The Uneasy Alliance* (New York: Norton, 1980).

Binchy, D. A., *Church and State in Fascist Italy* (London: Oxford University Press, 1941).

Birmingham, Stephen, *Real Lace: America's Irish Rich* (New York: Harper & Row, 1973).

Blanshard, Paul, *American Freedom and Catholic Power* (Boston: Beacon Press, 1949).

———, *Communism, Democracy and Catholic Power* (Boston: Beacon Press, 1951).

———, *Personal and Controversial: An Autobiography* (Boston: Beacon Press, 1973).

Blum, John Morton, ed., *The Diary of Henry Wallace 1942–1946* (Boston: Houghton Mifflin, 1973).

Brezzi, Paolo, *The Papacy: Its Origins and Historical Evolution*, translated by Harry J. Yannone (Westminster: Newman Press, 1958).

Brown, Anthony Cave, *Bodyguard of Lies* (New York: Harper & Row, 1975).

———, *Wild Bill Donovan: The Last Hero* (New York: Times Books, 1982).

Budenz, Louis, *The Bolshevik Invasion of the West* (Linden, N.J.: The Bookmailer, Inc., 1969).

Buttinger, Joseph A., *Vietnam: A Dragon Embattled* (New York: Praeger, 1967).

Caro, Robert A., *The Power Broker: Robert Moses and the Fall of New York* (New York: Vintage Books, 1975).

Carocci, Giampiero, *Italian Fascism* (New York: Penguin Books, 1972).

Carsten, F. L., *The Rise of Fascism* (London: Batsford, 1967).

Cassel, A., *Fascist Italy* (New York: Crowell, 1968).

Cianfarra, Camille, *The Vatican and the Kremlin* (New York: Dutton, 1950).

———, *The Vatican and the War* (New York: Dutton, 1944).

Cogley, John, *Catholic America* (New York: Doubleday, 1974).

Cohen, Aharon, *Israel and the Arab World* (New York: Funk & Wagnalls, 1970).

Cohn, Roy, *McCarthy* (New York: Lancer Books, 1978).

Cook, Fred J., *The Nightmare Decade: The Life and Times of Senator Joe McCarthy* (New York: Random House, 1971).

Corson, William, *The Armies of Ignorance* (New York: Dial, 1977).

Crosby, Donald F., S.J., *God, Church and Flag: Senator Joseph R. McCarthy and the Catholic Church 1950–1957* (University of North Carolina Press, 1978).

Cutler, John Henry, *Cardinal Cushing of Boston* (New York: Hawthorn, 1970).

Dohen, Dorothy, *Nationalism and American Catholicism* (New York: Sheed & Ward, 1967).

d'Ormesson, Wladimir, *The Papacy* (New York: Hawthorn, 1959).

Douglas, William O., *Go East Young Man* (New York: Random House, 1974).

du Plessix Gray, Francine, *Divine Disobedience: Profiles in Catholic Radicalism* (New York: Vintage Books, 1969).

Eisenhower, Dwight, *Waging Peace 1956–1961: The White House Years* (New York: Doubleday, 1965).

Ellis, John Tracy, *American Catholicism* (University of Chicago Press, 1969).

Falconi, Carlo, *The Popes in the Twentieth Century* (London: Weidenfeld & Nicholson, 1967).

Farley, Jim, *The Jim Farley Story* (New York: McGraw-Hill, 1948).

Flamini, Roland, *Pope, Premier, President: The Cold War Summit That Never Was* (New York: Macmillan, 1980).

Flynn, George Q., *Roosevelt and Romanism: Catholics and American Diplomacy 1937–1945* (Westport, Ct.: Greenwood Press, 1976).

Fogarty, Gerald P., *The Vatican and the American Hierarchy From 1870–1965* (Stuttgart: Anton Hiersemann, 1982).

Ford, George Barry, *A Degree of Difference: Memoirs of George Barry Ford* (New York: Farrar, Straus & Giroux, 1969).

Frady, Marshall, *Billy Graham: A Parable of American Righteousness* (Boston: Little, Brown, 1979).

Friedländer, Saul, *Pius XII and the Third Reich: A Documentation* (New York: Knopf, 1966).

Fuchs, Lawrence, *John F. Kennedy and American Catholicism* (New York: Meredith Press, 1967).

Gannon, Robert I., S.J., *The Cardinal Spellman Story* (New York: Doubleday, 1962).

Gollin, James, *Worldly Goods: The Wealth and Power of the American Catholic Church, The Vatican and the Men Who Control the Money* (New York: Random House, 1971).

Gordon, Bertram, *Collaboration in France During the Second World War* (Ithaca, N.Y.: Cornell University Press, 1980).

Graham, Robert A., S.J., *Vatican Diplomacy: A Study of Church and State on the International Plan* (Princeton, N.J.: Princeton University Press, 1959).

Halperin, S. W., *Mussolini and Italian Fascism* (Princeton, N.J.: Princeton University Press, 1964).

Hamma, Ellen J., *The Struggle for Indochina* (Stanford, Calif.: Stanford University Press, 1966).

Hassett, William, *Off the Record* (New Brunswick, N.J.: Rutgers University Press, 1958).

Hatch, Alden, *Ambassador: Extraordinary Clare Boothe Luce* (New York: Holt, 1955).

Hennessey, James, S.J., *American Catholics: A History of the Roman Catholic Community in the United States* (New York: Oxford University Press, 1981).

Holmes, J. Derek, *The Papacy in the Modern World* (New York: Crossroad, 1981).

Ickes, Harold L., *The Secret Diary of Harold L. Ickes, vol. III* (New York: Simon & Schuster, 1954).

John, Eric, ed., *The Popes: A Concise Biographical History.* (London: Burns & Oates, 1954).

Johnson, Lady Bird, *A White House Diary* (New York: Holt, Rinehart & Winston, 1970).

Johnson, Paul, *Pope John XXIII* (Boston: Little, Brown, 1974).

Kalb, Martin and Elie Abel, *Roots of Involvement* (New York: Norton, 1971).

Keesings Research Report, *South Vietnam: A Political History* (New York: Charles Scribner's Sons, 1970).

Kennan, George F., *Memoirs 1950–1963* (Boston: Little, Brown, 1972).

Kennedy, Paul P., *The Middle Beat: A Correspondent's View of Honduras, Guatemala and El Salvador* (New York: Teachers College Press, 1971).

Larson, Martin A. and C. Stanley Lowell, *The Religion Empire: The Growth and Danger of Tax-Exempt Property in the U.S.* (New York: Robert B. Luce Co., 1976).

Lash, Joseph, *Eleanor and Franklin: The Story of Their Relationship Based on Eleanor Roosevelt's Private Papers* (New York: Norton, 1971).

_____ , *Eleanor Roosevelt: A Friend's Memoir* (Garden City, N.Y.: Doubleday, 1964).

_____ , *Eleanor: The Years Alone* (New York: Norton, 1972).

_____ , *Roosevelt and Churchill 1939–1941: The Partnership That Saved the West* (New York: Norton, 1976).

Lasky, Victor, *J.F.K.: The Man and the Myth* (New York: Arlington House, 1966).

_____ , *Robert F. Kennedy, The Myth and the Man* (New York: Trident, 1968).

Leckie, Robert, *America and Catholics* (New York: Doubleday, 1970).

Lernoux, Penny, *Cry of the People: The Struggle for Human Rights in Latin America—The Catholic Church in Conflict with U.S. Policy* (New York: Penguin, 1980).

Linden, Eugene, *The Alms Race* (New York: Random House, 1976).

Lo Bello, Nino, *Vatican U.S.A.* (New York: Trident, 1973).

_____ , *Vatican Empire* (New York: Simon & Schuster, 1970).

Lukacs, John, *A History of the Cold War* (New York: Anchor, 1962).

Macdonald, Dwight, *Politics Past* (New York: Viking, 1957).

Mac Eoin, Gary, *What Happened at Rome* (New York: Holt, Rinehart & Winston, 1966).

Marchetti, Victor and John D. Marks, *The C.I.A. and the Cult of Intelligence* (New York: Dell, 1975).

Marcus, Sheldon, *Father Coughlin: The Tumultuous Life of the Priest of the Little Flower* (Boston: Little, Brown, 1973).

Martin, Malachi, *The Decline and Fall of the Roman Church* (New York: Putnam, 1981).

_____ , *Three Popes and the Cardinal: The Church of Pius, John, and Paul with Human History* (New York: Farrar, Straus & Giroux, 1972).

McAvoy, Thomas, *A History of the Catholic Church in the United States* (South Bend, Ind.: Notre Dame, 1969).

McGhee, Ralph W., *Deadly Deceits: My 25 Years in the C.I.A.* (New York: Sheridan Square Publications, 1983).

McGurn, Barrett, *A Reporter Looks at the Vatican* (New York: Coward McCann, 1962).

McLellan, David S., *The Cold War in Transition* (New York: Macmillan, 1966).

Mindszenty, Josef Cardinal, *Mindszenty Memoirs* (New York: Macmillan, 1974).

Morgan, Thomas B., *A Reporter Looks at the Papal Court* (New York: Putnam, 1937).

————, *The Listening Post* (New York: Putnam, 1944).

Moscow, Warren, *The Last of the Big-Time Bosses: The Life and Times of Carmine De Sapio and the Decline and Fall of Tammany Hall* (New York: Stein & Day, 1971).

————, *Politics in the Empire State* (New York: Knopf, 1948).

Mosley, Leonard, *Dulles: A Biography of Eleanor, Allen and John Foster Dulles and Their Family Network* (New York: Dial, 1978).

Murphy, Paul I., *La Popessa* (New York: Warner Books, 1983).

Neuvecelle, Jean, *The Vatican: Its Organization, Customs and Way of Life* (New York: Criterion Books, 1955).

Neville, Robert, *The World of the Vatican* (New York: Harper & Row, 1962).

Nichols, Peter, *The Politics of the Vatican* (New York: Praeger, 1968).

Noonan, D. P., the Rev., *The Passion of Fulton Sheen* (New York: Dodd, Mead, 1972).

O'Brien, David J., *The Renewal of American Catholicism* (New York: Oxford University Press, 1972).

O'Connor, John, *The People Versus Rome: Radical Split in the American Church* (New York: Random House, 1969).

Parmett, Herbert S., *Eisenhower and the American Crusades* (New York: Macmillan, 1972).

————, *Jack: The Struggles of John F. Kennedy* (New York: Dial, 1980).

Paxton, Robert O., *Vichy France: Old Guard and New Order 1940–1944* (New York: Columbia University Press, 1972).

Pearson, Drew, *Drew Pearson Diaries 1949–1959* (New York: Holt, Rinehart & Winston, 1974).

Perrett, Geoffrey, *A Dream of Greatness: The American People 1945–1963* (New York: Coward, McCann & Geoghegan, 1979).

Phillips, Cabell, *The Truman Presidency: The History of a Triumphant Succession* (New York: Macmillan, 1966).

Pichon, Charles, *Vatican and Its Role in World Affairs*, translated by Jean Masrohi (Westport, Ct.: Greenwood Press, 1950).

Prouty, L. Fletcher, *The Secret Team: The CIA and Its Allies in Control of the U.S. and the World* (Englewood, N.J.: Prentice Hall, 1973).

Purdy, W. A., *The Church on the Move: The Characters and Policies of Pius XII and John XXIII* (New York: John Day, 1965).

Raskin, Marcus G. and Bernard B. Fall, eds., *The Viet-Nam Reader* (New York: Random House, 1965).

Rhodes, Anthony, *The Vatican in the Age of Dictators* (New York: Holt, Rinehart & Winston, 1973).

Ridley, Francis A., *The Papacy and Racism: The Crisis of the Twentieth Century* (New York: AMS Press, 1973).

Roemer, Theodore, *The Catholic Church in the United States* (St. Louis: B. Herder, 1950).

Rogow, Arnold, *James Forrestal: A Study of Personality, Politics and Policy* (New York: Macmillan, 1963).

Rynne, Xavier, *Letters from Vatican City* (New York: Farrar, Straus, 1963).

Schlesinger, Arthur M., *Robert Kennedy and His Times*, vol. I (Boston: Houghton Mifflin, 1978).

Schlesinger, Stephen and Stephen Kinzer, *Bitter Fruit: The Untold Story of the American Coup in Guatemala* (New York: Doubleday, 1982).

Sherwood, Robert E., *Roosevelt & Hopkins: An Intimate History* (New York: Haysert Brothers, 1948).

Shodegg, Stephen, *Clare Boothe Luce: A Biography* (New York: Simon & Schuster, 1970).

Smith, Dennis Mack, *Mussolini* (New York: Knopf, 1980).

Sorensen, Theodore, *Kennedy* (New York: Harper & Row, 1965).

Steibel, Warren, *Cardinal Spellman: The Man* (New York: Appleton Century, 1966).

Stroup, Herbert, *Church and State in Competition* (New York: Seabury, 1967).

Teeling, William, *Pius XI and World Affairs* (London: I. Dickson, 1937).

Thomas, Dana L., *Lords of the Land* (New York: Putnam, 1939).

Thomas, Lately, *When Even Angels Wept: The Senator Joseph McCarthy Affair—A Story Without a Hero* (New York: Morrow, 1973).

Wakin, Edward and Father Joseph Scheuer, *The De-Romanization of the American Catholic Church* (New York: Macmillan, 1966).

Wayman, Dorothy G., *Cardinal O'Connell of Boston* (New York: Farrar, Straus & Young, 1955).

Whalen, Richard J., *The Founding Father: The Story of Joseph P. Kennedy* (New York: New American Library, 1964).

Wofford, Harris, *Of Kennedys and Kings: Making Sense of the Sixties* (New York: Farrar, Straus & Giroux, 1980).

Yzermans, Vincent, *American Participation in the Second Vatican Council* (New York: Sheed & Ward, 1967).

Ziegler, Edward, *The Vested Interests* (New York: Macmillan, 1964).

Index

Ford, Father George Barry, 88–90, 190, 229, 248, 285
Fordham University, 3, 11–12, 14, 15, 70, 99, 190, 287, 301, 304, 320, 327
Ford, Henry, II, 251
Forever Amber, 200
Fortas, Abe, 315
Fox, Father Robert, 297, 298
France, 130, 139–40
Franco, Francisco, 112, 125–26, 136, 152, 176, 183, 220, 280, 297
Frankfurter, Justice Felix, 202
Frederick I, Emperor, 6
Frederick II, Emperor, 6
Free French, 130, 139
Friendly Sons of St. Patrick's, 155, 156, 157
Fugazy, William, 224
Furlong, Bishop Philip, 90, 321

Galeazzi, Count Enrico, 40, 42, 59, 64, 65, 68, 72, 74, 75, 134, 149, 160–61, 212, 215, 216, 255, 275, 278
Gallagher, Archbishop Michael, 67
Gallup, George, 272
Gannon, Father Robert, 281
Garbo, Greta, 108
Garbus, Martin, 283
Garcias, Cardinal, 259
Gasparri, Pietro Cardinal, 27, 30, 35, 37–38, 44, 45, 48, 54, 73, 87
Gemelli, Agostino, 49
Geneva Disarmament Talks, 277
George, Henry, 20
George V, King, 46
Gerard, Mrs. Lillian, 197
Germany, 40–41, 49, 59, 65
    World War II and, 114, 123, 128, 134–35, 138, 140
Getlein, Frank, 198
Gibbons, James Cardinal, 19, 27
Giraud, Henri, 130
Glennon, John Cardinal, 150
Going My Way, 200
Goldstein, Jonah J., 98
Goldwater, Barry, 296
Gotham Ball, 102
Gowen, Franklin C., 158
Graham, Billy, 299
Graham, Bob, 38
Graham, Father Robert A., 213, 216
Grand Street Boys, 106
Gravediggers strike, 187–95, 212, 321
    Communist allegations and, 191–95
Gray, David, 131
Greece, 160

Greene, Graham, 244
Gregory I, Pope, 6
Gregory VII, Pope, 6, 35
Griffiths, Bishop James H., 124, 140, 158, 159, 187, 213, 241, 322
    death of, 249–50
Gross, Benjamin, 166–67
Guatemala, 231–36, 323

Haas, Monsignor Francis J., 118–19
Haberlin, Monsignor R. J., 25, 30
Hadad, William, 313–14, 316
Haffey, John, 131
Haile Selassie, 132
Hamvas, Bishop Endre, 293
Hapsburg, Otto von, 164, 168
Harada, Ken, 127
Harlan, Justice John M., 237
Harnett, Monsignor, 242, 243
Harrington, Donald, 198
Hartington, Billy, 101
Hassett, Bill, 181
Hassett, Father Joseph D., 304
Hayes, Patrick Cardinal, 50, 77–78, 79, 86, 87, 94, 95, 96, 175, 206
    death of, 72, 76, 327
    politics and, 103
    Spellman and, 65, 68, 70, 268
Hearn, Edward L., 35, 36, 39–40, 42
Hearst, William Randolph, 204, 220, 224, 226
Hemingway, Ernest, 191
Henry II, King, 6
Henry VIII, King, 271
Higher Education Facilities Act, 296
Hilton, Conrad, 229
Hinsley, Arthur Cardinal, 129
Hiss, Alger, 162, 207, 220, 268
Hitler, Adolf, 40, 73, 86, 112, 114, 129, 151, 221, 226
Ho Chi Minh, 240, 242, 293
Hofmann, Paul, 267
Hoguet, Mrs. Robert L., 103
Hollander, Rabbi, 303–304
Holmes, John Hayes, 198
Holy Name Society, 196, 218, 223, 249, 283
Homosexuality, 91, 109
Hoover, J. Edgar, 146, 147, 148, 166, 224
    civil-rights movement and, 283–84, 308
House Un-American Activities Committee, 162
Hughes, Archbishop John, 103
Hull, Cordell, 114, 133
Humphrey, Hubert, 318